Introduction to Film

Also by Nick Lacey

Image and Representation★
Narrative and Genre★
Media Institutions and Audiences★
Blade Runner
Se7en

★ also published by Palgrave Macmillan

Introduction to Film

Nick Lacey

First published 2005 by
PALGRAVE MACMILLAN
Houndmills, Basingstoke, Hampshire RG21 6XS and
175 Fifth Avenue, New York, N.Y. 10010
Companies and representatives throughout the world

PALGRAVE MACMILLAN is the global academic imprint of the Palgrave
Macmillan division of St. Martin's Press, LLC and of Palgrave Macmillan Ltd.
Macmillan® is a registered trademark in the United States, United Kingdom
and other countries. Palgrave is a registered trademark in the European
Union and other countries.

ISBN-13: 978–14039–1626–6 hardback
ISBN-10:   1–4039–1626–8 hardback
ISBN-13: 978–14039–1627–3 paperback
ISBN-10:   1–4039–1627–6 paperback

This book is printed on paper suitable for recycling and made from fully
managed and sustained forest sources.

A catalogue record for this book is available from the British Library.

A catalog record for this book is available from the Library of Congress.

10 9 8 7 6 5 4 3 2 1
14 13 12 11 10 09 08 07 06 05

Printed and bound in China

For

Charlotte, Richard and Victor

who introduced me to the study of film

Contents

 # Figures

Film Stills

# Tables

Acknowledgements

Thanks to Jenny Grahame of *Media Magazine* for permission to reprint 'The Publicity Circus – For Consumers Only' from the English and Media Centre's excellent *Media Magazine*.

Thanks to Wing-Leung Fai, Ewa Morris and Roy; not forgetting Kirsten (for watching with me).

Making sense of films can only be done through dialogue so thanks to colleagues and students for their thoughts, many of which I've nicked.

Every effort has been made to trace all the copyright-holders, but if any have been inadvertently overlooked the publisher will be pleased to make the necessary arrangement at the first opportunity.

Nick Lacey

Preface

The intention of this book is to offer an introduction to film studies that will appeal both to the film buff and the academic enthusiast. It is therefore necessary that this text 'covers the ground' by offering the reader a summary of approaches to the subject. However there is always a tension between using categories, essential for summary as they enable groups of similar films to be put together, and the differences between the films that the categories ignore. For example, many summative approaches to European cinema focus on art films and so reduce:

> a vast and diverse European production to what is ... only one section of the market [and it] reinforce[s] American-centrism: if a variety of diverse practices ... are reduced to an 'alternative', then Hollywood is reinforced as for ever 'the norm'.
>
> (Vincendeau, 1998: 441a)

It is impossible in an introductory text to do other than reflect this tendency, but readers should be aware that film studies is a subject in constant flux. History is constantly being rewritten in the light of research and altering perspectives. In order to mitigate the 'shallowness' of an introductory text, Chapters 2 and 5 offer both further viewing and reading for those who wish to pursue a particular topic in more detail. Chapter 4, on theory, suggests further reading and it is always sensible for the student to go back to the original material rather than rely upon glosses, such as those provided by this book.

A major and related problem is access to films. The market-driven ethos of capitalist economies ensures that popular films are always available for distribution, either on celluloid or video. However, the extra expense incurred by subtitling, and the inevitable diminution in attractiveness to the market because of the language barrier, means that, on the whole, only 'canonised' or fashionable foreign language films are readily available. The situation is worse for 'pre-sound' films, where availability decreases to a point where many of the films are non-existent. It does appear, however, that the massive popularity of DVD will lead to many 'lost' treasures becoming available.

This book uses contemporary cinema, as dominated by Hollywood, as its starting point for a journey that will move in space (across different nations throughout the world) and in time (drawing upon the 'classics' and contemporary cinema). Throughout the book there are boxes that are meant to complement the main body of text. Some of these focus on one film and it is assumed that the reader has seen the film. These boxes can, however, be skipped as they are intended to illustrate points raised in the main narrative.

I have not necessarily used films that most people will be familiar with; however I have always used films that are well worth seeing. Inevitably the choice of film will reflect my own experience of film watching, and although I have tried to be as 'catholic' as possible there is no escaping, I'm afraid, my ingrained western perspective. However I hope I haven't been too Eurocentric.

A list of key films, from throughout history, can be accessed on my website (www.nicklacey.org.uk, follow the key films link). The key films pages also give an indication of their availability on DVD in the UK and will be updated. In addition, the publishers will host a companion site (www.palgrave.com/culturalmedia/lacey/) in support of the book where extra material will be regularly made available.

Nick Lacey
October 2004

# Introduction

Although the medium of film is now in its second full century, it was only during the last third of the twentieth century that film studies established itself in the academy. The first degree in the subject was not available in Britain until Warwick University's Film/Literature course appeared in 1979. However, this has been long enough to establish a canon of criticism, traced from early theorists such as Balazs and Kracauer to Truffaut's 'politique des auteurs', through *Movie*, Andrew Sarris, May '68, *Screen* and the plethora of theories that have vied for attention in the postmodern era.

Outside of the academy, movie watching, if not movie going, has never been so popular. In the 1990s, dedicated satellite/cable channels joined the 1970s entrant, video, in complementing cinema and free-to-air transmissions of films. DVD has heralded a new revolution in film ownership, with good quality sound and a good quality picture that is usually in more or less the correct aspect ratio. And since the advent of the multiplex, audiences for the 'real thing' have been growing steadily. The multiplex, an American invention, hints at Hollywood's hegemony, and there is a sense that many film fans' understanding of cinema history begins with *Star Wars* (1977) rather than Louis Lumiére or his forebears, and World Cinema might as well be from Mars, as subtitles are definitely out. And if it's black and white then it's 'boring'!

Film studies, at post-16 and undergraduate level, along with media studies, is the most obvious way each generation becomes inculcated into academic film culture. However there is a tension in this: most students prefer recent films and so are often hesitant about watching black and white (and foreign language) films. While film studies can offer a greater appreciation of contemporary cinema, if it only focused on the 'now', the roots of modern cinema would be obliterated and access to past treasures denied. This book attempts an assiduous mix of past and present.

Despite the rise of television and the Internet during the latter half of the twentieth century, film still remains the most potent medium. Both television (not forgetting radio) and the Internet are media that are channels for extremely diverse texts and/or information. Films, however, are discrete texts and so a single film can have a worldwide impact. Unlike any other medium, films can communicate to vast swathes of the world, even if it is via television or the Internet.

In addition, it is virtually the only medium, though there is competition from music, which can communicate across cultures. Many people probably learn far more about the developing world through films such as *City of God* (*Cidade de Deus*, Brazil, 2002), than any other medium, so for example a European's understanding of how rapidly China is changing is most likely to be derived from the films of the fifth and sixth generations of directors (see 5.12).

Chapter 1 begins at the point of pleasure, the film itself. While we implicitly learn the language of film from the moment we start watching television as young children, our understanding often remains unconscious even into adulthood. By breaking down the constituents of film language into its components, we can see how meaning is created and what seems 'natural' are, in fact, conventions developed in specific social contexts. The chapter concludes with a consideration of the role of stars in creating a film's meaning.

Chapter 2 also focuses on how a film creates meaning, this time through its use of genre and narrative. These are sets of expectations we bring to every film, which aid easy understanding. In addition, genres articulate particular ideas, rooted in their time, and so we can see how society's views change through how a genre develops (such as the shift in the Western from characterizing native North Americans as savages to portraying them as victims of genocide). It is arguable that narrative is a universal structure which at once elaborates meaning and contains ideological messages.

Much to many critics' chagrin, films are commodities produced by an industry. While the first two chapters treat them as artefacts, Chapter 3 attempts to show how the way a film is produced directly affects the aesthetics of the movie. The focus here is on Hollywood, financially the biggest film industry in the world and the one that has the greatest reach.

While it is likely that the first three chapters will appeal to the film buff and student alike, Chapter 4 looks at films solely through an academic perspective. Although some aspects of film theory, such as the *auteur* approach, have infiltrated mainstream discourse, much theory since the late 1960s has spoken only to the academic, and as a result the language and concepts used are complex. The chapter attempts to guide the curious, and the student, through the entangled difficulties without inducing (too many) headaches.

Chapter 5 offers a potted history of film. It is impossible to fully appreciate any art form without knowing something of its social background. Indeed, much of the reluctance to watch old or foreign films is caused by ignorance of their social context. Five appendices offer 'thumbnail' sketches of nations 'neglected' in the rest of the book.

Chapter 6 considers how film can represent a large group of people (with a focus on African–Americans) and a nation state. While we must avoid the pitfalls of assuming that one can 'read off' society from film, there is no doubt that the ways in which a society understands others, and itself, can be articulated in film. For a national cinema we shall consider Britain as a case study.

Finally, the technological basis of film is examined in Chapter 7. All media are limited by their technology and all meaning is expressed through technology. Film was the first new medium of the technological age and the mechanics of filmmaking have never stopped developing. The chapter will briefly consider some of the aesthetic implications of the use of technology.

After reading the book, film fans should find their appreciation of film heightened, which will increase the manifold pleasures already offered by the medium.

Note on film titles

The English versions of films' titles are used throughout, with the original given at the film's first mention, unless (as for *Amores Perros*) the film is better known by its original title, when the English version is given in parenthesis. The main country of origin, as well as the year of release, is included next to films unless they were produced in the United States, when the year alone is given, or when the country is obvious from the context – such as the sections on British cinema. The reader may notice a degree of tension in the book between my desire to sidestep the *auteurist*'s insistence that the director is the author of a film and the fact that there is no doubt that some directors have an immense influence on their movies. So occasionally I may 'lapse' into *auteurist* speak such as 'Alfred Hitchcock's *Psycho* (1960)'; however, most of the time the directors of films are only mentioned if they are germane to the issue being discussed or to indicate a historically important figure, such as D. W. Griffith.

1 — Film Language

1.1 Introduction

Implicit to this book is the belief that it is valid to analyse and inter-
pret films. Analysis is the 'objective' reading based upon what we
observe in a film; the interpretation is the ideas we bring to how we
(choose to) read the film. So while two people may agree on what
happens in a film (the analysis) they may also have diametrically
opposed interpretations.

The purpose of this chapter is to investigate how meaning is created
in film and so give the student the tools for analysis. However, it
should not be forgotten that interpretation is never far from analysis
(and indeed informs analysis in the sense that what we see in a film
can be structured by personal experience). The chapter will focus on
conventional cinema because it is necessary to understand the 'rules'
(even if these only became the rules because of Hollywood's
economic dominance). The examples will be drawn mainly from
contemporary films as the reader is more likely to be familiar with
them.

1.2 Introduction to *mise en scène*

Mise en scène is the starting point for analysis of 'film as film' (the title of
a 'classic' introduction to film analysis, Perkins 1993) as distinct from film
in its social context. First used by critics in *Cahiers du Cinema* in the
1950s, *mise en scène* analysis focuses on what can be seen *in the picture.*
What can be seen (unless we are dealing with computer generated
imagery) must exist before it can be filmed and this is the pro-filmic
event. Usually this event will consist of actors performing in a setting
and the point of view from which audiences see this is wholly determined by the position of the camera. The film's director usually decides
where the camera is positioned.

For some writers this pro-filmic event defines *mise en scène*. For
example, in the first edition of the classic text *Film Art* (1979), David
Bordwell and Kristin Thompson state that *mise en scène* consists of
setting, lighting, costume and figure expression and movement (that is

character's behaviour and movement in the scene); they consider camera placement (framing) in a separate chapter. Bruce Kawin's definition (1992), however, also includes:

> choice of filmstock (black-and-white or color, fine-grain or grainy)... aspect ratio (the proportion of the screen) ... framing (how much of the set or cast will be shown at a time) ... camera placement and movement, and ... sound environment.
>
> (Kawin, 1992: 98)

Kawin is unusual in including sound, but he has a point as there seems little point in divorcing sound produced in the narrative world from what is producing it. This is a question of definition and it matters little, when analysing film, whether you consider camera positioning as part of *mise en scène* or not, as long as you do consider *all* the elements. I prefer Kawin's inclusion of camera placement because the position can transform the way audiences see the pro-filmic event and will include diegetic (that is 'from the narrative world': see below) sound in the following list, as most films we see are not silent.

Although camera movement also changes the way we see the pro-filmic space, it does draw attention to itself and so awareness is split between what is 'in the picture' and how the camera is transforming what we see. For our purposes *mise en scène* refers to the still image, with diegetic sound, and movement will be considered separately, as will filmstock, which can alter the look of the scene even though it is exterior to it.

Mise en scène consists of:

➤ production design: sets, props and costumes
➤ colour (present in both production design and lighting)
➤ lighting
➤ actors' performance (including casting and make-up) and movement (blocking)
➤ diegetic sound (that is, sound that emanates from the scene and is not extraneous to it, such as the music that is not being played within the scene or a voice-over)
➤ framing including position; depth of field; aspect ratio; height and angle (but not movement).

As we shall see, *mise en scène* is designed, in mainstream cinema, to both create the narrative space and help progress the narrative.

1.3 Production design: sets, props and costumes

For our purposes we are not going to distinguish between a set and setting. A set refers to a studio-built space; however, many films are shot on location. This location may be the actual place it is intended to represent or may be standing in for the narrative's location; for example, although *Three Kings* (1999) was set in Iraq it was filmed in Arizona, USA.

1.3.1 Settings and props

The most controlled pro-filmic events are created in a studio where everything is fabricated, as against the use of location settings that do exist independently of the film being made. The production designer, in consultation with the cinematographer and director, will be responsible for the look of the film, which includes the sets, props and costumes. While verisimilitude ('it looks real') is often a guiding feature of production design, choices are not simply made on the basis of an accurate portrayal of the world described by the narrative.

Polish art director Allan Starski described how he created a convincing Security Service office, in Wajda's *Man of Marble* (*Czlowiek z Marmuru*, Poland, 1977), where a character is interrogated with his friend waiting outside for him:

> I designed the room classically: apart from the officer's desk, a cupboard for documents, a little table and a chair, there were some typical props. Just before we started shooting, [director Andrzej] Wajda asked that the whole room be emptied! All that was left was a completely bare desk and the officer's chair. Now, when the friend looks into the room his gaze is met by complete emptiness. His friend's disappearance becomes absurd, shocking.
>
> (Starski, 1994: 72)

For Wajda the symbolic effect of having a room empty, emphasising the man's disappearance, was far more important than having it look exactly like a Security Service office. It should all be noted that very few of us know what the inside of a Security Service office looks like in actuality. However, we do know how such places are conventionally represented in film. In fact, in order to be convincing it is more important that a setting looks like how it is conventionally represented, which might not be like the place in actuality.

1.3.2 Costume

For some people clothes are functional: they serve to protect us from the elements and/or aid whatever activity you're doing. For others, clothes are a crucial part of identity; they speak to others about self either through *haute couture* or subculturally, such as a Goth's predilection for black. In film, clothes are always costumes (even if it is a documentary) in that they necessarily take on significance in speaking about the character. For example, Nathan Algren's (Tom Cruise's) development, in *The Last Samurai* (USA–New Zealand–Japan, 2003), from a disillusioned ex-soldier to one who embraces the samurai code is evident in his change of costume.

In *The Look of the Con* (*Ocean's Eleven* DVD extra) designer Jeffrey Kumland described how he costumed *Ocean's Eleven's* (2001) central characters. For example, Rusty's (Brad Pitt's) clothing was shiny and reflective offering a sheen which complemented the 'quick, fast and sharp' character. Most interesting, he describes how he clothed the villain Terry Benedict (Andy Garcia). He had to be cool in order to attract Tess (Julia Roberts) but it had to be a contrasting cool to that of Danny Ocean (George Clooney). He did this by giving Garcia's costume an Asian look; the cut of his tuxedo was 'western in fit, built like a kimono'. Tess's clothing, too, reflects this style, emphasizing the fact she is 'beholden to Benedict'.

Costumes can be iconographic, and the cowboy outfit is indelibly associated with the Western as is the combat uniform with war movies; the latter will vary depending upon the era in which the film is set.

1.3.3 Colour

Colour is similarly used as an expressive device. In Martin Scorsese's *Gangs of New York* (USA–Germany–Italy–UK–Netherlands, 2002) the ethnic warfare between the Irish immigrants and the 'native' Americans (who ironically were also immigrants) is counterpointed against the upper classes that rule New York:

> [Production designer Dante] Ferretti used color – and its absence – to make essential distinctions about the class conflicts at the heart of Scorsese's film. 'There are many levels of society – the politicians and upper classes, the middle class and the lower class – and we used color only for the upper class,' he explains. 'Their world is [depicted in] red, ochre and yellow, all blended together

Gangs of New York (2002) deals with the ethnic warfare between the Irish immigrants and the 'native' Americans led by Bill the Butcher (Daniel Day Lewis)

in a very vulgar way. They dress very colorfully but in very bad taste. The upper classes in *The Age of Innocence* were more elegant, whereas these people are more *nouveau riche*. The colors are a little stronger, and everything is a bit overdressed. But for the poor, life is very monochromatic, like tintypes. I did not use any color in their world except for some in their costumes – no color, no hope.'

(Magid, 2003)

Colour is obviously present in the setting, props and costumes. In addition, the colour seen will be greatly affected by the type of lighting used – see below. Until the 1960s most films were made in black and white. However, as Kawin points out:

Although black-and-white may be thought of as the 'absence' of color, it is actually a complete palette or repertoire of shades. It is a system with its own terms... its limits make its art possible.

(Kawin, 1992: 179)

So light and shade is important in the *mise en scène* of 'black and white' films. During the silent era, prints were usually tinted. This may have been to indicate particular times of day or moods such as blue for night or red for love scenes. (See Box 1.1.)

1.4 Lighting

The cinematographer, or director of photography, has a crucial influence on the *look* of a film. Usually working in conjunction with the director, he or she will be responsible not only for the lighting but also the type of lens, exposure level and filmstock used. As might be expected, lighting a film requires much more than pointing a camera and switching it on, for example:

> [Martin] Scorsese gave Ballhaus a book of Rembrandt paintings during prep to illustrate the dark, warm look he desired for *Gangs of New York*.
>
> (Bosley, 2003)

The standard tripartite lighting system consists of a *key* light, supervised by the key grip, placed at a high angle of sufficient brightness to produce clear shadows. The key light, for example, is crucial in the look of *film noir*, which dispenses with the *fill* light so shadow can be used to create a claustrophobic *mise en scène*. However, mainstream films usually want to show the setting clearly and so the shadows are, at least, toned down by the *fill* light. Whilst *noir* utilises low-key lighting (a high degree of contrast between light and dark) musicals, for example, are usually lit in a high key and so everything is seen clearly. Finally the *back* light is used to differentiate characters from the background by shining from behind the person. Similarly, glamour photography uses back lighting to create a halo effect (by shining through the edges of hair).

In *Chopper* (Australia, 2000) the lighting is used expressionistically, that is, its primary function is not to look real but convey atmosphere. For example, Chopper's (Eric Bana's) mate's flat is bathed in a lurid green signifying what an unpleasant home it is; similarly, when Chopper shoots Sammy the Turk, the scene is suffused in red, an appropriate colour for violence.

Filters are sometimes used to change the colour of the scene. For example in *28 Days Later* (UK–USA, 2002), Jim and Selena's journey to Deptford has a yellow hue appropriate to the apocalyptic scenario.

Box 1.1 Production design in *The Sixth Sense* (USA, 1999)

(DVD Ch. 12, 58 min 18 sec)

Lynn asks Cole whether he has taken grandma's bumblebee pendant

Cole's mother (Toni Collette) asks whether he (Cole: Haley Joel Osment) has taken Grandma's bumblebee pendant, which he denies. The characters are sitting opposite one another at a small table eating their meal.

The setting is a kitchen clearly signified by the fridge, which dominates the centre-left background. On the right-hand side of the frame, again in the background, there is a cupboard and counter.

The most obvious props in the scene are the chairs, the table and its contents: food, plates and cutlery. A fridge magnet holds a picture drawn by Cole in place and he is wearing gloves.

Cole is costumed in pyjamas whilst his mother is wearing a checked fleece (she is cold, the heating appears to have broken), two large rings and earrings.

The colour in the sequence is muted, with pale yellow predominant in the walls and Cole's pyjamas.

The above simply describes what is in the scene. In semiotic terms (see Lacey, 1998), it has considered the scene at the level of denotation. As such it is not very interesting; analysis must go a step further and deal with connotations, which is what we associate with signs, or elements, in the scene. So in this case we must consider connotations of the kitchen – signified by the setting and props – and what the costume tells us about the characters.

As noted above, this scene occurs 58 minutes into the movie and so inevitably gains meaning from what has gone before. Of course, the only part of a film that can offer meaning in isolation is the opening sequence; however even this will be coloured by our expectations created by (among other things) marketing, genre and stars. In addition, once a film has been viewed, the opening sequence may well take on added meaning. For example, the opening shot of *The Sixth Sense* is the first time we see an important motif that runs throughout the film. Shot one fades in on a close-up of a light bulb: the first thing we see is the red element (before it brightens to orange) of the bulb. Red is a significant colour, as we shall see below. ·

The fact the pair are eating in the kitchen suggests they are not well off. The table they're eating off is collapsible and is being used as a space saver, again hinting at their lack of money. The picture on the fridge, along with Cole wearing the gloves, emphasize that he is only a young boy, having to deal with frightening events. His youth is also emphasized by his wearing pyjamas at mealtime. The ostentatious jewellery on the mother connotes her working-class status as they are in 'bad taste'. (It should be noted that I am decoding a conventional sign and not suggesting that the working classes lack taste.) The pallid colour of the scene gives the setting an · unattractive pall, once again emphasizing the less than luxurious home.

NB It should be noted that the degree of significance of a *mise en scène* varies greatly from film to film; and, indeed, within a film (see Box 1.5).

1.5 Performance

When interviewed about their latest film, actors normally say how much fun they had and how it was hard work and everyone was wonderful to work with. They will talk about how challenging the role was for them and how they are really pleased with the film. The primary function of this interview is to market the film (see 3.18). When interviewed about their craft they usually fail to say anything about technique. In this Ian Richardson is typical:

> Don't ask me how I achieved it. It's like asking me, almost, how I make love. I can't tell you because I don't want to tell you and if I did tell you I might spoil it for myself ...
>
> (Zucker, 1999: 158)

The glamorous mystique that surrounds the profession is probably to do with the insecurity felt by its members. Apart from during the Golden Age of the studio system when they were contracted, actors are usually freelance artists who are – more or less – only as good as their last performance. The importance of youth and good looks means that their career may already be in decline by the time they have 'made it' (if, indeed, they ever do).

Acting during the 'silent' era of cinema now looks histrionic, consisting, it seems, of rolling eyes and twiddling moustaches. This style of acting derived from theatrical melodrama, which itself developed out of necessity when the Puritans banned theatrical dialogue in 1642. Performing without dialogue circumvented the ban, and to make up for the absence of speech, music was emphasized (the 'melos' of melodrama) and actors exaggerated expression and gesture.

Although dialogue had long been allowed, melodrama (see Box 2.5) was very popular during the nineteenth century and so it was almost inevitable that this style of acting should transfer to cinema, especially because, once again, the actors would have to be mute.

The 'over-the-top' histrionics of melodramatic acting works against the grain of realist films because:

> Realism emphasises the ordinary, not the extraordinary, rejecting unbelievable plots and implausible characters ... one-dimensional heroes and villains of melodrama, whose personalities were often signified by physical attributes, with more complex, multi-dimensional and psychologised characters created by the ... realists.
>
> (Hallam and Marshment, 2000: 20)

This more subtle form of acting, the 'verisimilar code', was present in 'silent' cinema, particularly in D. W. Griffith's films made after 1921 (Pearson, 1992: 50). Clearly the use of the close-up facilitates an actor's ability to use subtle gestures to convey a character's thoughts and feelings.

Theatre acting also had a great influence upon cinema during the 1950s when Lee Strasberg adapted Stanislavsky's Moscow-based System as the Method, although the two systems are often erroneously thought to be the same:

> Stanislavsky's System express(es) the belief that the actor creates the performance, the actor is 'auteur'. Strasberg, in contrast, shifts responsibility for the interpretive shaping of performance to the director...
>
> (Carnicke, 1999: 78)

In the Method, actors are required to create an 'inner life' which exists beyond the confines of the script. Similarly, it is not sufficient for an actor simply to perform a script, he or she must behave 'naturally'. One consequence of this is the Method actor's mumble, most (in)famously performed by Marlon Brando. Method acting often seems mannered to modern audiences, though this is not to deny the power of performances such as James Dean's in *Rebel Without a Cause* (1955).

When analysing performance we can focus on:

➤ gesture
➤ tone of voice, accent and type of language used
➤ body posture and movement (blocking)
➤ make-up and hair.

All these elements, except for the type of language used (for example, sophisticated vocabulary might indicate a highly educated individual just as a vernacular might suggest a 'down to earth', less intellectual, type), are examples of non-verbal communication (see Lacey, 1998: 11–13; Box 1.2).

Box 1.2 Performance: Toni Collette in *The Sixth Sense* (USA, 1999) and analysis: blocking in *Minority Report* (USA, 2002)

Performance: Toni Collette in The Sixth Sense (DVD Ch. 17, 127 min 52 sec)

In the climactic scene of *The Sixth Sense*, when Cole (Haley Joel Osment) 'communicates' with his mother about the ghosts he sees, Toni Collette, who plays Lynne, has to demonstrate a variety of emotions including motherly concern, anger and grief mingled with happiness.

When Cole tells his mother about how Grandma sneaked into the back to watch her dance recital Lynne knows, for the first time, that he is telling the truth about ghosts. He tells her that Grandma's answer to the question asked by Lynne is 'every day', and asks what was the question. Lynne is virtually overcome with grief at this moment as she realizes that her mother is proud of her and so has no 'business left unfinished' at her death. Grief manifests itself because she misses her mother; however she is also happy because she has learned of her mother's pride.

Throughout the film the character speaks with a distinct accent, which usually signifies a working-class background. A 'received pronunciation' accent is used to signify 'posh'; working-class accents tend to be broader and can also signify a particular place. The relatively heavy use of make-up (Lynne wears bright lipstick), and obvious jewellery (her rings) is meant to be indicative of a 'less refined' taste, which is also intended to characterize working-class individuals.

In order to answer Cole's question she needs to compose herself. Her hands are in front of her face (as if hiding her grief from the world and so denying vulnerability) and she tries to 'swallow' her tears (part of the physical reaction caused by crying is a lump in the throat). This is emphasized by the way she uses her hands to prod just beneath her throat; as if pushing the tears away. She is suppressing sobs, and her expression changes to one of a person trying to explain something that might be embarrassing (that is, asking the dead a question). This expression is emphasized by the way she nods her head to one side.

Having managed to gain a degree of composure, she can then look directly at Cole to tell him her question: 'Do I make her proud?' This line is not delivered directly; she hesitates and says 'her' twice (and breathily) demonstrating the degree of emotion that she still feels for her mother. This is capped by a brief look up as if exchanging a glance with her dead mum.

Although there is a degree of detail in the above paragraph, it does not come close to conveying the nuances of Collette's performance. Writing about performance is like writing about music; words can only diminish what is being described.

Analysis: blocking in Minority Report (DVD Ch. 4, 21 min 11 sec)

The scene begins with a close-up on a ball (on which the victim and perpetrator of the pre-crime are inscribed). The camera dollies back and we see John Anderton's (Tom Cruise's) three assistants standing either side of Danny Witwer (Colin Farrell) in the middle of a discussion. As Witwer says, 'Let's not kid ourselves on this, Jeff, we are arresting individuals who have broken no law.' He moves to the left of the frame (the camera pans with him, emphasizing his dominance in the scene) between two of the characters, and this places him outside the group of three assistants. They also move, so all three are facing him. Their positions emphasize conflict: Witwer is an outsider disrupting the team.

Anderton enters the scene and takes over the argument with Witwer. Farrell and Cruise walk toward one another, emphasizing their adversarial status. When Jeff answers one of Witwer's questions Anderton sits down, placing him with his assistants, leaving Witwer alone on the frame's left. In sitting down Anderton has allowed Witwer to dominate the space above him: he needs to look up while Witwer looks down on him. This is appropriate as Witwer wins the battle for authority; he moves to stand next to Anderton when he says he has a warrant to certify his authority.

However, at the end of the scene Witwer crouches down to *beneath* Anderton's level to say 'You are now operating under my supervision.' This subordinate position may hint at Witwer's status as an *apparent* villain.

1.6 Sound (and music)

There are, broadly, two types of sound: diegetic and non–diegetic. Within diegetic sound, which emanates from the narrative world, we can consider:

➤ dialogue
➤ sound effects
➤ ambient (background) sound.

While film is obviously primarily a visual medium, it is wrong to assume that the soundtrack merely reinforces what we see. Sound's role is much more important, as it not only adds an aural dimension to the scene, it also, through the mix, emphasizes what is important, and through the music, helps to cue audience response.

Sound on film is not naturalistic; that is, it does not necessarily sound the same as we would hear it if we were in the camera's position. What the audience hears is determined by the needs of the narrative. For example, in the second scene from *The Others* analysed in Box 1.3, there is little chance that a person standing in the camera's position would hear the movement of thread on Grace's sewing. (See Box 1.3.)

Box 1.3 Sound in *The Others* (Spain-USA, 2002)

Sound is a vital component, in this ghost story, in the spooking of the audience. What follows is analysis of two scenes from *The Others*.

DVD Ch. 9

The *mise en scène* of most of the film is shrouded in dark, which makes the soundtrack an even more important carrier of information. Forty

---

minutes into the film Grace (Nicole Kidman) is sitting sobbing quietly when she hears piano music (a Chopin waltz) coming from what she thinks is an empty room. As Grace rushes, shotgun in hand, to investigate who is playing the music, her jerky (terrified) breathing is to the fore, with the swirling and echoing waltz in the background. As she opens the door, the piano playing stops, allowing us to hear the very quiet creaking of wood, and the non-diegetic music – conventionally, for a horror film, discordant – begins. Having found the room empty, Grace locks the keyboard and looks around; the non-diegetic music reaches a climax, signifying something is about to happen. Grace whirls around, to see nothing, and the music stops.

The use of music to suggest something is about to happen is a generic convention of horror. The discordant sound helps set the audience's nerves on edge. However, aficionados will know the shock often comes when audiences are not expecting it, and so is not cued by the music; and this is what immediately follows.

Grace leaves but the door closes itself. Assuming it's a problem with the hinges, she tests how it is 'sitting'. Suddenly it slams (very loud on the soundtrack) shut in her face, knocking her over. The non-diegetic music 'shrieks' loudly in accompaniment to Grace's screams of 'Mrs Mills!' A diminuendo from a gong accompanies the scene's end, an exotic sound that, as it reduces in volume, signifies calm has returned.

In a different scene, when Grace hears running on the floor above her, the sound originates far offscreen, to the right, but is approaching, creating a very alarming effect – as the audience does not know the steps originate above her. Whatever it is, it could be it will be entering screen right in the next second.

DVD Ch. 7, 29 min 45 sec

Grace has asked Mrs Mills (Fionnula Flanagan) to tell another servant, Lydia, not to make so much noise cleaning upstairs. Mills leaves, closing the door and we hear her footsteps clearly recede on the wooden floor. Grace's daughter can be heard reading the Bible in another room; her voice reverberates in the large rooms as ambient sound.

The camera pans left, from the door, and when Grace comes into the frame, the sound of her sewing appears in the mix. This delicate sound helps set up the contrast with the loud steps and rolling noise that is suddenly heard. Grace moves her head in disapproval, and we assume it is Lydia making too much noise again upstairs. Grace's exasperation is emphasized by a sharp exhalation of breath.

The noise upstairs returns, and when Grace looks up an edit takes the camera to an overhead shot – Grace is almost looking directly into the camera. The camera 'tracks' with Grace's gaze as she follows the sound of the footsteps across the ceiling. This brings the chandelier into shot, which adds to the sound mix with its tinkling caused by the vibrating floorboards. So far, within a few seconds, we have moved from a very quiet activity (sewing) to very loud noise. A crescendo, consisting of running feet and a rattling chandelier, is 'topped' by an enormous metallic thud that is likely to make the audience jump as much as it did Grace.

There is little ambient (background) sound in this extract, but dialogue is present, as are the sound effects, primarily the sewing, footsteps and rattling chandelier. Most, if not all, of these effects will be added to the soundtrack by the Foley artist (see 7.6), as it would be impossible to record the sound of Grace sewing without catching all the other quiet sounds. Similarly, once the camera is overhead the sounds from above the ceiling have to be added, because the ceiling is no longer there; the camera is.

Rick Altman shows how the sound of a debate on the floor of the US Senate, in *Union Pacific* (1939), maintains a sound level commensurate with an audience being in a medium close-up (see 1.8) position throughout:

> The image changes scale repeatedly, however, matching the dramatic effect of the words uttered. The constant-level sound track thus serves to anchor a pasted-up, discontinuous image sequence which remains obedient to narrative concerns.
>
> (Altman, 1992a: 56)

So regardless whether the character speaking is in close-up or long shot, the sound level is the same. This, of course, would not be the case if we were present at the proceedings. This uniformity of soundtrack makes it possible to cut in mid-phrase rather than being limited to the pauses between dialogue.

Sound is also used as a 'bridge' between scenes, so a change of locale may be heralded by the sounds from the new location before the actual edit.

As cinema is obviously primarily a visual medium (only very unusual films such as Derek Jarman's *Blue*, UK, 1993, de-emphasise vision), sound is often forgotten as it usually 'naturally' accompanies the visuals or seems merely to be offering a musical accompaniment. However, try watching a sequence without sound; it is like having a shower with a coat on.

Dialogue on the soundtrack is usually carefully mixed to make it very clear, if a film wishes to signify itself as realist, then speech may be obscured (as it can be in 'real life'). Sound can either be recorded at the same time as the scene was filmed or added later (*post-dubbed*).

Sound effects are anything significant that is not spoken and have a clear source within the world represented. This includes the opening and shutting of doors, characters moving around the scene and so on; an offscreen knock at a door would also be considered as a sound effect. These sounds can be post-dubbed. For example, the sound of fistfights is usually added later to emphasize the violence.

Ambient sound is the background noise, usually used to signify location. 'Spot effects' of traffic will probably accompany city scenes, or birds will cheep in the countryside.

The most potent non-diegetic sound is *music*. Music can be used in a variety of ways, such as cueing suspense and signifying the emotion being evoked. Music is not always non-diegetic: for example in *Bird* (1988), a biopic of jazz saxophonist Charlie Parker, the performance of music onscreen must be considered a 'sound effect'.

Music has been an important component of cinema since its early days. Even 'silent cinema' is a misnomer, as live music (and occasionally recorded music on early gramophone technology) accompanied the images. This had two main functions: it helped drown the noise of the projector, and helped audiences understand the images; the music would cue the emotional tone of scenes:

> The classical score features a high degree of synchronization between music and narrative action, and thus commonly relies on such devices as ostinati, 'stingers', and mickey-mousing. (An ostinato is a repeated melodic or rhythmic figure to propel scenes which lack dynamic visual action; a stinger is a musical sforzando to emphasize dramatically an action or a character's sudden strong emotion; mickey-mousing is the musical 'imitation', through pitch and/or rhythm, of visual action.)
>
> (Gorbman, 1998: 45a)

It is interesting that audiences, who would otherwise never do so, are happy to listen to 'classical-style' music in films. Indeed, horror films are often accompanied by music that has a minority following even within 'classical' music. The atonal dissonances that assist in raising tension have their roots in Schoenberg's 12-tone system; he tutored Hollywood composers during the 1940s (Davis, 1998: 52).

The classical score (in a Romantic, that is nineteenth-century, idiom), featuring the symphony orchestra, remains ubiquitous even despite the growth of compilation soundtracks which consist of already existing pop/rock music. Pop music is used to generate publicity for a film; each time the song is performed, or the accompanying pop video broadcast, the movie is promoted. However, the choice of music also usually comments on the narrative. For example the music chosen for both *Philadelphia* (1993) and *Forrest Gump* (1994) comes 'loaded with a cultural over determination that belies any notion of a song's "innocent" use' (Romney and Wootton, 1995: 5). In the case of *Philadelphia*, the use of liberal, post-Woodstock artistes emphasizes the progressive tone of the film, which sympathetically focuses on an AIDS victim (Tom Hanks).

While music, whether orchestral or a compilation, usually remains secondary to the film itself, the 'blaxploitation' pics of the early 1970s are welded to the scores composed by the likes of Curtis Mayfield. See Box 1.4.

In summary Jeff Smith, quoting composer Aaron Copland, suggests that music has five uses:

1. It conveys a convincing atmosphere of time and place.
2. It underlines the unspoken feelings or psychological states of characters.
3. It serves as a kind of neutral background fill to the action.
4. It gives a sense of continuity to the editing.
5. It accentuates the theatrical build-up of a scene and rounds it off with a feeling of finality.

(Smith, 1998: 6)

Films without any accompanying music are rare. Even *The Birds* (1963), which is without a score, credits composer Bernard Herrmann as a 'sound consultant' for the electronic noises made by the birds. Herrmann was one of the greatest of film composers. His scores range from the gothic pastiche of *Citizen Kane* (1941), through the neurotic *On Dangerous Ground* (1952) to the jazz-inflected *Taxi Driver* (1976). Herrmann was also responsible for persuading his regular collaborator, Alfred Hitchcock, to have music accompanying Marion Crane's (Janet Leigh's) slaughter in *Psycho* (1960).

Box 1.4 Music in *The Sixth Sense* (USA, 1999) and
Vanilla Sky (USA, 2000)

*Analysis: **music in The Sixth Sense** (DVD Ch. 10, 48 min 12 sec)*

Music is often used to cue significance: when Cole (Haley Joel Osment) announces that he wants to tell Crowe (Bruce Willis) his secret, a quiet sustained note is heard played by violins. When he confesses that he 'sees dead people', a horn's sustained note appears 'above' the violins. When he nods, assenting to Crowe's question as to whether he sees these people while he is awake, discordant notes are heard on the violins. While the dynamics are mostly *piano* (quiet) in the mix, they do vary slightly. After the discord, more conventional orchestral music, including woodwind, is heard until it is interrupted by the discordant insect-like, spooky violin sound when Cole says he sees them 'all the time'.

The music is in three stages:

➤ emphasizing something significant is about to be said
➤ using spooky, generically horror, sounds to create a visceral reaction in the audience
➤ to assuage the potential for terror with conventional music.

In such a static scene, the music 'prods' an audience's attention so they do not miss anything of significance. It also signifies the genre, but suggests that this is not the sort of horror that offers visceral thrills; it is a ghost story, so 'chills' rather than 'revulsion' is the desired audience response.

It is rare now for a film to be released without an accompanying soundtrack album. While these can be of the music written for the film, the most popular ones are compilations of pop songs, old and new. Although it should be noted that the use of pop music was not new, *The Blackboard Jungle* (1955) used Bill Haley's 'Rock Around the Clock' to great effect.

The choice of song in compilation soundtracks can be arbitrary; it may simply be upbeat and so suit the mood of the scene. However, it is unsurprising that ex-*Rolling Stone* journalist Cameron Crowe should take particular care with the music in his films. In *Vanilla Sky*, when David Aames (Tom Cruise) leaves Sofia (Penelope Cruz) and makes his fateful choice to join Julie Gianni (Cameron Diaz), Jeff Buckley is singing 'Last Goodbye'. Bob Dylan's 'Fourth Time Around' coincides with the love scene after Aames has taken his mask off and appears to be cured –

the lyrics suggest that the situation is 'lies' and their relationship will not last. Radiohead's 'Everything in its Right Place' ironically accompanies the dream sequence in Times Square.

Although it is not on the soundtrack album, John Coltrane is heard, and seen as a hologram, playing 'My Favourite Things' at Aames' birthday party. The music's title suggesting that Aames has everything he wants, while simultaneously appropriating jazz culture to suggest he thinks he is sophisticated.

1.7 Framing: position; depth of field; aspect ratio; height and angle (but not movement)

1.7.1 Framing position

Thus far in this chapter we have focused on what is 'in the picture'. However the camera position has a crucial influence on what we can see. Although technologically it appears that film's antecedent is 'still photography', aesthetically there can be little doubt that theatre had a much greater influence. Andre Bazin suggests that a cinema audience watch film as if they are sitting in the orchestral pit in front of the screen (Bazin, 1967a).

This is not an entirely accurate simile, as conventionally the camera is placed at eye level, and theatrical orchestras are usually below the level of the stage. The camera in fact usually places audiences hovering in the air, just in front of the stage, so we get the best view. From this position we can see everything clearly, from the expression on a character's face to the position of the characters in the setting.

The informing aesthetic for the framing of a still shot is derived from Renaissance painting: the Quattrocento system, inherited by cinema via photography. This system places spectators in the position of the central perspective so they can see everything from the best possible, static, position (see Heath, 1981: 19–76). However, film cannot simply organize its space in such a fashion because it usually contains movement so:

> the centring of the frame is based on action.... The continual relocation and realisation of a compositional centre accords with the centre of interest as defined by the narrative. In this way, 'the seen' is converted into 'a scene', space becomes place, and the spectator is situated by a constant renewal of perspective.
>
> (Lapsley and Westlake, 1988: 139)

changes this.

The narrative is the 'superordinate' determinant of conventional film form, as it determines where the camera is placed, how and where it moves, and how shots are put together (see 1.10).

The most noticeable element is the position of the camera in relation to the frame's contents, which can range from an extreme close-up, such as the eye in the opening of *Blade Runner* (1982), to an extreme long shot, which might be used to show landscape or the universe (*Dark City*, 1997). Roughly the shots are defined as follows:

- Extreme close-up – for example, part of a face.
- Close-up – face.
- Medium close-up – head and shoulders.
- Medium shot – most of a body.
- Medium long shot – the whole body.
- Long shot – two or three people's whole bodies.
- Extreme long shot – landscape.

These are only approximate guidelines, and it should be noted that Bazin's theatrical simile also breaks down with the extreme framings. Technology can also determine the type of framing used. For example, during the early years of 'sound' cinema the microphones could be only used with close-ups, so action had to be shown in medium shot. If a long shot were used, the jump to a close-up for the dialogue would have been jarring.

However we are not particularly interested in what sort of framing is used; that is mere description. We must analyse the aesthetic effect of framing. For example, close-ups are often used to emphasize a character's response to an event. There would have been little point in M. Night Shyamalan filming the conversation in *The Sixth Sense* (see Box 1.2.) from outside the car. We would not be able to see clearly the nuances of Collette's performance, and the private moment between mother and son would have been depersonalized. In addition, the camera position emphasizes 'frontality': that is, the tendency for characters to face the camera even if this is not the obvious position to take in a scene. For example, in a crucial and relatively long conversation about Islam in *Malcolm X* (1992), between the eponymous protagonist (Denzel Washington) and Baines in a prison exercise yard, they are standing next to one another (but not facing each other) and are therefore 'front on' to the camera. The narrative provides a motive for this by having them watch a baseball game.

1.7.2 Depth of field

It is of course possible to have a frame that offers both a close-up and a long shot of different elements in the frame. This requires deep-focus

23

photography, which allows both foreground and background to be in focus at the same time. Usually only the fore to mid-ground is in focus, as these are the areas the director wants audiences to concentrate on. A shallow depth of field would offer, say, a total of three metres in focus (one and a half metres either side of focus point). For deep-focus cinematography a wide-angle lens is required, as well as an increase in light and/or light sensitive filmstock (see 7.5).

For example, in *Minority Report* (2002), when Anderton's wife realizes that Lamar Burgess might not be the venerable old man she supposes, he stands very close in a threatening manner. The pair are in long shot; in the background Burgess's secretary appears to tell him his press conference is starting. The tension created by the threat is relieved by the secretary's appearance – Burgess will not do anything while there is a witness. However, because she is some way from this scene's principal characters the secretary is not likely to notice the threat inherent in Lamar's position: from her position he could be behaving in a paternal manner. So although the threat is reduced it is not eradicated, because no other character knows about it.

Depth of field can be altered within a shot. For example in *Solaris* (2002) the dream-like nature of the space station is emphasized by point-of-view shots from Kelvin (George Clooney) as he wakes up. These shots gradually come into focus – in other words the depth of field is altered – dramatizing Kelvin's return to consciousness. When out of focus, people appear indistinct, ghost-like, and therefore enigmatic, in keeping with the film's theme about the relationship between reality and memory.

1.7.3 Composition and aspect ratio

'Composition' refers to the placement of objects in the frame. As indicated in Chapter 1.6, blocking refers to the movement of characters within the frame, and their positioning relative to one another is important. However, equally important are their positions in relation to the frame itself. It is the frame that allows the *mise en scène* to be composed.

Conventional composition utilizes the 'rule of thirds', which breaks the frame, either vertically or horizontally, into – surprise! – three. So a shot of the sea would place the horizon either two-thirds or one-third of the way up the screen.

In the scene discussed from *Minority Report*, in Box 1.2, it is not simply Witwer's crouching that places Anderton in the position of authority above him. Tom Cruise's character is shot in a medium close-up that shows his shoulders but cuts off the top of his head. The fact that he 'breaks through' the frame above him emphasizes his position above Witwer, who is looking up at him.

Minority Report is presented in an aspect ratio of 1:2.35, where compositions tend to be horizontally constructed (although a good quarter of the right-hand side of the frame in this scene can be redundant, since it is outside the 'safe action zone' – see 7.4). The Academy ratio (1:1.35 – also see 7.4), on the other hand, is exceptionally flexible in that it allows both horizontal and vertical composition to be used.

Sergio Leone used the full width of the 'scope ratio in his 'Spaghetti Westerns'. In the opening scene of *A Fistful of Dollars* (*Per un Pugno di Dollari*, West Germany-Spain-Italy, 1964) a 'bad guy' beats up a Mexican. Framed in close-up he turns to look at the 'man with no name' (Clint Eastwood), who is in the background watching events from a waterhole. The 'bad guy's' sombrero fills the top of the frame from the left to (almost) the right edge. Eastwood is positioned just beyond the tip of the hat, a diminutive figure; however, a piano phrase on the soundtrack heard at this moment suggests the character's significance, although the *mise en scène* puts him in an 'inferior' position.

Akira Kurosawa used the Academy frame in *Seven Samurai* (*Shichinin no Samurai*, Japan, 1954), which readily allows vertical compositions. When the Samurai Kambei (Takashi Shimura) holds out a bowl of rice, it dominates the foreground (it is in deep focus); in the background the peasants look on, amazed that their 'better', in class terms, should offer them food. All the action is in the centre; hence it is a vertical composition. In order to get the same position in a widescreen composition there would have been a lot of redundant space either side of the characters (Joan Mellen suggests the shot emphasizes 'Kamei's moral elegance': 2002: 41).

Similarly, at Heihachi's funeral a low-angle shot looks up at the funeral mound surrounded by the surviving Samurai. The peasants, heads bowed on their knees, are below the mound, and spears point upwards in the right of the frame. The focus of the *mise en scène* is on the mound, a small heap of earth in the middle and top third of the frame, created by vertical composition.

1.7.4 Camera height and angle

Conventionally the camera is at adult head height so a scene can be filmed straight on. The *Minority Report* shot referred to in Box 1.2 is filmed from Witwer's level after he has crouched down. Therefore the shot of him standing before he crouches, alone in the frame, is looking up and is therefore a low-angle shot. This angle emphasizes his superiority over

Anderton – as he has the authority to do what he likes – and so it is something of a surprise when he crouches down. The camera tilts down with him, bringing Anderton into the shot in a position where he can look down on Witwer. As suggested in 1.6, this might be hinting that Witwer is not as threatening to our hero as he appears.

If a low-angle shot is often used to convey power, the opposite is true: high-angle shots look down and suggest subservience. In the second scene of *The Others* the camera is from a low angle when shooting Grace as she questions the servants, who are filmed from a high angle, emphasizing their relative positions of power.

We should not fall into the trap of assuming that, for example, low-angle shots always represent subservience. The meaning of *mise en scène* is determined by context, and is not an inflexible grammar of film. For example, in the opening scene of *The Red Squirrel* (*La Ardilla Roja*, Spain, 1993), writer/director Julio Medem shows Jota looking down on a beach from a promenade; we see him at his level and from a low-angle shot from the beach. The function of these shots is to show how far it is from the prom to the beach, as this is the distance Lisa/Sofie is about to fly through.

Occasionally the camera is canted. In *Enemy of the State* (1998), when Robert Dean (Will Smith) is confronted by his wife with his apparent involvement with an 'old flame', the cant emphasizes the disruption to his domestic life.

This section has covered the basic elements of *mise en scène* analysis. There are three distinct types of *mise en scène*; these are covered in Box 1.5.

Box 1.5 Types of *mise en scène*

Adrian Martin (1992) suggested there are three types of *mise en scène*: classical, expressionist and mannerist. Elsaesser and Buckland summarize the types as follows:

> In classical *mise en scène* the film style is unobtrusive, for it is motivated by the film's themes and dramatic developments...
>
> In expressionist *mise en scène* ... there is a broad fit between style and theme.
>
> In mannerist *mise en scène*, style is autonomous, for it is not linked to function but draws attention to itself.
>
> (Elsaesser and Buckland, 2002: 89)

Their description of 'expressionist' style needs elaborating. While 'classical' is totally at the service of the narrative, the 'expressionist' style seeks to add to the *mise en scène* through, for example, an unusual camera angle or high key lighting casting deep shadows. Like the 'mannerist' style, 'expressionist' *mise en scène* will draw attention to itself, but do so with a narrative purpose. *Films noir* were distinguished by, among other things, their use of unusual camera positions, such as the 'choker' shot (low-angle, 'cutting' the head off at the chin), which would emphasize a character's grotesqueness (see Place and Peterson, 1985).

Movie magazine, in Britain, was one of the first exponents of 'classical' criticism. It showed intolerance of directors who would place the camera in a position unmotivated by the narrative. For example, in William Wyler's *The Loudest Whisper* (aka *The Children's Hour*, 1961), when a young girl, in the back of a car, is just about to accuse a teacher of being homosexual:

> We are shown a schoolgirl telling her strait-laced grandmother a scandalous lie about the relationship between two of her teachers. However, we do not hear the accusation because at the moment the child begins to speak Wyler cuts in a shot from the front seat of the car in which they are travelling. The glass panel behind the chauffeur prevents our hearing the rest of the conversation... When Wyler changes our viewpoint he quite clearly does so at his own convenience and at our expense. The camera changes position only in order to explain the silence... The change of angle covers the silence, but gives us no new or interesting information which would justify the change itself.
>
> (Perkins, 1972: 125)

For Perkins this is a cheat, as there is no narrative motivation for the camera's position being alongside the chauffeur, and the purpose of classical *mise en scène* is to produce an organic whole. Perkins contrasts Wyler's scene with a sequence in Alfred Hitchcock's *Rope* (1948), where the camera position – which also prevents audiences getting vital information – is carefully set up and so is not arbitrary. John Gibbs ably sums up the purpose of classical *mise en scène* : 'The point is that everything is pulling in the same direction: the decisions are integrated in the service of the drama' (Gibbs, 2002: 41).

While 'expressionist' *mise en scène* will be motivated by 'the drama', it will also draw attention to itself as a rhetorical device. For example, when Jeffrey Wigand (Russell Crowe) leaves his place of work for the final time early in *The Insider* (1999), the camera is placed virtually on his shoulder. This both places the audience sympathetically with Wigand and, through the unbalanced *mise en scène*, emphasizes the trauma that Wigand is experiencing as he leaves to become a whistle-blower against the tobacco industry. Unusually for a documentary, *Wisconsin Death Trip* (UK-USA, 1999) is virtually wholly shot in an 'expressionist' style. Film documentaries usually eschew a style that draws attention to itself as they want to appear to be a 'window on the world'. This is in keeping with the bizarre events the film narrates.

'Mannerist' *mise en scène* is exemplified by post-classical Hollywood (see 3.16), and offers style for its own sake. For example, both the opening sequences of the two *Charlie's Angels* films (2000 and 2003) are shot with extremely long takes (outdone in length by *Snake Eyes*, 1998). However, these are simply virtuoso pieces of camerawork and add nothing to the drama of the scenes.

The 'classical' *mise en scène*, in particular, exemplifies the bourgeois ideal of 'transparent' form. However, a number of filmmakers, particularly during the 1960s, rejected the classical notion of film form and sought to subvert its conventions for political purposes. For example, Jean-Luc Godard uses the 'flat' *mise en scène* and long take to draw attention to the image so:

> The viewer is not drawn into the image, nor does he (sic) make choices within it; he stands outside the image and judges it as a whole.
>
> (Henderson, 1976: 425)

This is a Brechtian alienation device that seeks to divorce spectators from the film, so that they think about what they are experiencing rather than just consuming it. Henderson cites Godard's films from the mid to late 1960s as exemplifying this technique, including *Weekend* (France-Italy, 1967) and *La Chinoise* (*The Chinese*, France-Italy, 1967).

1.8 Camera movement

Camera movement in itself, just like shot composition, is not interesting. We must consider what the movement intends to convey in the context of the scene. However, we do need to identify types of movement:

- ➤ handheld (including steadicam)
- ➤ pan (including swish pan)
- ➤ dolly
- ➤ tracking
- ➤ crane
- ➤ aerial (or helicopter)
- ➤ tilt
- ➤ zoom/telephoto.

Handheld shots are usually signified through a shaky movement as the camera operator walks. The degree of shakiness can vary from the exceptionally smooth to the lateral 'to and fro' movement at the climax of *Alien* (UK, 1979), when Ripley (Sigourney Weaver) tries to evade the eponymous monster. These latter shots are also subjective, as they are directly from Ripley's point of view.

Handheld shots offer greater flexibility of movement as they can go wherever a camera can be carried, so changes of direction or meandering through a crowd are easier to do with handheld than with any other type of movement. Documentaries often use handheld to demonstrate a lack of artifice, as it helps signify that the camera is observing what is going on.

Although *steadicam* is handheld, it avoids any jerky movement by using weights to move the camera's centre of gravity to outside the camera, where it is easier to manipulate. Steadicams combine the smooth movement of a dolly shot with the freedom of handheld. One early distinctive use of the steadicam was in Stanley Kubrick's *The Shining* (UK, 1980), where the fluid movement contributed to the sense of a haunted place, as audiences 'moved' with appropriately unnatural smoothness throughout the hotel.

Handheld pans are useful, in both documentaries and films that are 'realist', as the movement suggests the camera is following the action, as against a highly choreographed film when the camera 'knows' where the action is going. Lukas Moodyson used this technique in his first two features (*Show Me Love – Fucking Åmål*, Sweden, 1998, and *Together – Tillsammans*, Sweden-Denmark-Italy, 2000). Characters can move out of, or partially out of, the frame before the pan 'catches' up with them.

Pans offer a panorama: that is the camera pivots on a spot. Pans can be up to 360 degrees in length. This technique is distinctively (and puzzlingly) used in Michelangelo Antonioni's *The Passenger* (*Professione: Reporter*, France-Italy-USA-Spain, 1975) where a pan starts with a live protagonist (Jack Nicholson) on a bed; when it reaches the end of the shot he is dead. Pans can move in either direction but are unlikely to change direction, unless character movement motivates this.

A pan following a character movement is likely to start after the character has moved, as the movement within the frame distracts attention away from the movement of the frame. It is also likely to begin, and end, with well-composed images.

Dolly shots move forward or backwards in a smooth motion; they usually pass objects to emphasize the movement and give a sense of depth to a scene. They are similar to tracking shots; indeed dolly shots that move parallel to the action appear to be tracking shots in which, unsurprisingly, cameras move on tracks, allowing a very smooth movement in straight lines. They tend to be used to shoot parallel to the action, so the tracks cannot be seen. (Director Max Ophuls was a master of the tracking shot – see, for example, *Letter from an Unknown Woman*, 1948.)

A *crane* allows movement up or down, which is usually accompanied by either a backward or forward movement. These can be particularly spectacular shots as they allow for an often exciting and smooth movement through space. One of Hitchcock's trademark shots was an extreme and high-angle long shot that cranes in to a close-up (see *Young and Innocent*, UK, 1937, and *Notorious*, 1946).

Martin Scorsese used a crane shot in *Gangs of New York* (2002) to show Irish immigrants arriving in New York and immediately being conscripted and put onto a troop ship. The crane allowed this to be shown in one elaborate movement, hence emphasizing how the Irish men became soldiers the moment they arrived in America. The 'punchline' to this shot was a coffin being offloaded from the troop ship, in the foreground of the shot, suggesting that the end of the men's journey would be death.

The use of the *zoom* was in vogue in the late 1960s and 1970s; however contemporary filmmakers are far more likely to move the camera when reframing a scene. Zooms are still used, though: for example in *Die Hard with a Vengeance* (1995), when Zeus (Samuel L. Jackson) first sees John McClane (Bruce Willis) wearing a sandwich board with a racist statement, a zoom is used to signify his shock at what he sees.

The Graduate (1967) details the eponymous character's sexual liaison with a woman twice his age. His girlfriend Elaine rejects Ben, the graduate, when she realizes he had been having sex with her mother, Mrs Robinson (Anne Bancroft). Mrs Robinson is framed in close-up which then 'zooms back' to reveal Ben in the foreground as she says 'Goodbye Benjamin'. The zoom emphasizes their separation.

Zooms can allow characters who are walking to be kept in a medium long shot framing without the camera moving; it simply pans and zooms in as they 'approach' and zooms out as they walk away. They also allow a rapid change in framing from a close-up to a long shot without the distraction of having the camera hurtle through space.

Camera movements are often combined to emphasize important points in the narrative: for example in *The Sixth Sense* (DVD Ch. 10, 45 min 40 sec) when Crowe (Bruce Willis) tries to comfort Cole (Haley Joel Osment) after the boy is traumatized at the party. Crowe sits at the foot of the boy's bed and tells, ineptly, a bedtime story. When Cole advises him to add some twists to the story, Crowe uses the opportunity to move closer, and moves the chair to the head of the bed. The camera movement starts with a pan right from Cole's point of view, and this is followed by a dolly shot that moves toward Cole, from Crowe's viewpoint, finishing with the boy in a medium close-up. Then the two can be framed together, in a new shot from behind Cole (relative to Crowe's position). It is important that they can be seen in the same frame, as their relationship is getting closer and the dolly has emphasized this growing closeness.

1.9 Editing

The first film to be exhibited, the Lumière brothers' *Workers Leaving the Lumière Factory* (France, 1895), was approximately a minute-long take of workers leaving through factory gates. According to Barry Salt (1992), the first film to consist of more than one scene was *Come Along, Do!* (UK, 1898). So it was three years before cinemagoers, and filmmakers, had to deal with the meaning of an edit.

While editing refers to the join between shots, it also concerns the content of the two shots and how this content relates each to the other. Initially, we shall consider the types of edits used, then we look at how shots are combined to create Hollywood's continuity editing. Finally, this section will look at how montage is used, both in Hollywood and in alternative systems of film form.

1.9.1 Types of edit

There are five main types of edit that join shots:

➤ Cut – an immediate change (no temporal break between shots).
➤ Dissolve (also called a lap dissolve) – a gradual transition between shots that can vary in speed from being very quick, and barely noticeable, to slow. (The latter is often used to signify time has passed.)

➤ Wipe – the following shot is drawn, like a curtain, over the first shot (the events shown are happening at the same time). This is rarely used in contemporary cinema (although Kevin Smith does so in *Dogma*, 1999, maybe to suggest a 'comic book' way of organizing a narrative).

➤ Fade out/in – fades to, or from, black (a definite ending/beginning of a scene – time usually elapses between the scenes).

➤ Iris – common in silent film, now used as pastiche, where the image is either revealed or obscured from or to a small circle of the frame.

While these do have conventional meanings, the context is extremely important. The actual edit itself is far less important than how it is organized. Scenes will usually have a 'master shot', a long shot that shows all of the setting; this shot may be shown in the film or simply used to aid editing.

There are several conventional ways of organizing edits:

➤ Eyeline match – a character looks/cut/we see what they are looking at.

➤ Frame cutting – a character moves out of frame right/cut/they enter frame left.

➤ Match on action – where a character's gesture starts in one shot and is completed in the next; the edit cuts nothing out of the gesture.

➤ Shot/reverse-shot – for conversations (see below).

➤ Cross-cutting (parallel editing) – often used for chases: we see the pursuer and then the pursued in turn.

➤ Montage – a collection of shots that shows discrete stages in an event that takes a relatively large amount of time, such as a journey or the building of a house. (There is also Eisenstein's distinct use of montage – see 5.4.)

The eyeline match is obviously used for point-of-view shots. However, it should be noted that the camera is rarely exactly in the position of the character whose point of view we are taking. For example, if character A looks at character B (who is returning A's gaze), B will look slightly to one side of the camera. Only if B *looks* into the camera are we strictly in A's position, and the shot can be dubbed 'subjective' (as in the whole of *Russian Ark*, *Russkij Kovcheg*, Russia-Germany, 2002). Characters who look directly into the camera are, in effect, looking directly at the audience. This draws attention to the medium of film, which the conventional displacement of the camera in point-of-view shots avoids. The system that strives to appear invisible is continuity editing – see below.

Cross-cutting is a commonly used device. It allows concurrent events to be shown one after the other. This is a rare example, in conventional cinema, where temporal continuity is sacrificed for narrative drama.

1.9.2 Continuity editing

The edit is a potentially disrupting device, as it changes the audience's perspective. However continuity editing was developed with the purpose of preventing disruption, and audiences rarely notice editing. Ask any non-film student to watch a minute of film, then ask her or him how many different shots there were. You are likely to find that the victim of your exercise grossly underestimates the number of edits. This is because the continuity system creates a smooth transition between shots. It is only in rapidly edited sequences, such as in action scenes, that audiences notice the editing (although they'll still struggle to come up with an accurate number). However, it is not the edits themselves that 'appear invisible': the crucial point is the camera's position in relation to its previous and next position. This depends on the 180 degree rule.

Conventionally a scene will start with an establishing shot. This can be an extreme long shot that signifies the setting, and/or a long shot where characters can be seen in relation to their environment. Particularly in the case of the latter, an imaginary 180 degree (to the spectator) line is drawn through the scene. If another camera set-up is required, it must always stay on the spectator's side of that line.

For example shot 1 in Figure 1.1 establishes the 'axis of action' between the characters. If the camera crosses the line, as in shot 4, it would appear that the characters had swapped places.

Like all rules, the 180-degree can be broken. For example, during the prologue of *The Mummy* (1999), Meela Nais/Anck Su Namun walks left to right toward Imhotep. When she passes through the curtains, a cut crosses the line, so she appears to be moving right to left. However, the match of action, moving through the curtains, is strong enough to disguise the discontinuity. In *In the Mood for Love* (*Fa yeung nin wa*, Hong Kong-France-Thailand, 2001) Wong Kar-Wai constantly breaks continuity during dialogue between the protagonists at a cafe. However, their medium two-shot framing precludes confusion; and we expect unconventionalities in arthouse film.

The position of this 'axis of action' will inform all other camera positions. The most obvious pattern is shot/reverse-shot for conversations – see shots 2 and 3 in Figure 1.1. The second shot is the 'reverse' (the mirror image using a plane at 90 degrees to the 'axis of action') of the first.

Figure 1.1

1. Establishing shot – characters can be seen clearly in the context of their setting. The 180-degree line is established as the 'axis of action' running through the characters and the table

2. Over-the-shoulder shot – stays on this side of the 'axis of action'; both characters remain on the side of the frame they occupied in the establishing shot

3. A shot/reverse-shot pattern is established. This shot is, approximately, at the same angle to the 'axis of action' as shot 2, but taken from the other side

4. If this shot followed the previous three (or shot 1) audiences might be confused as it appears the characters have swapped places. (The fact that the background has changed gives us a clue that the camera has switched position but as audiences tend to focus on the subject of the shot they would probably not have noticed this.)

5 (above). If the establishing shot had shown a third character then cutting to shot 6 (right), while still unconventional, is far less likely to disorientate audiences.

There are other variants such as 'subjective camera angles', which are placed directly on the axis of action and facing the characters (see 4.6 for an explanation of how this pattern, arguably, 'stitches' the spectator into the film). Alternatively the shot/reverse-shot pattern can be shot from inside a triangle (formed by the point of the establishing shot and the two people), and so only one person is seen in shot; Figure 1.1 shows shots 2 and 3 from outside the triangle.

Bordwell and Thompson (1979) suggested that there are four dimensions to editing: spatial, rhythmic, graphical and temporal.

1.9.3 Spatial

The spatial dimension is the way in which narrative space is created. We have seen how the 180 degree rule is crucial in creating a coherent space for the narrative to flow. As noted in the section on shot/reverse-shot sequence, continuity editing creates space through organizing the 'looks' of the characters and the audience. The most important element of this looking is to orientate the spectator (the individual member of the audience) in his or her position in front of the stage; this type of 'smooth' cutting is known as match editing.

However, not all editing seeks a seamless flow of images. For example, in *The Birds* (1963), when Lydia (Jessica Tandy) visits a local farmer, to find he has had his eyes pecked out by birds, we see the man slumped, and two rapid cuts take us progressively closer to a close-up of his bloody eye sockets. Instead of a camera movement taking us from a long shot to a close-up, the intervening movement – except for the moment he's in medium shot – is taken out. This is a jump cut. Jump cuts can also be caused by an altered camera position in relation to the subject. This new position must not be less than 30 degrees from the previous position, otherwise audiences are not likely to notice the 'jump'. Jump cutting characterised *Breathless* (*A Bout de Souffle*, France, 1959) where director Jean-Luc Godard:

> flaunts [the film's] spatial and temporal discontinuity from the very first frames. Virtually every other cut in the film is unmatched.
>
> (Opren, 2003: 61)

What must have appeared audacious in the early 1960s barely registers with contemporary audiences. This does not mean, however, that continuity editing is neglected now; we are much more used to jump cuts and so notice them far less than audiences of 40 years ago.

1.9.4 Rhythm

The rhythm of editing refers to the shot lengths of a sequence. This may be regular, with each shot approximately the same length, or the rhythm might alter, such as in the build-up to action (which is often characterized by increasingly rapid editing: that is, a gradual reduction in average shot length – ASL).

Barry Salt's (1992) exhaustive analysis of ASLs showed that by the mid-1910s the ASL had already reduced from the length of the whole film at cinema's birth, about 60 seconds, to 7.5 seconds in D. W. Griffith's *Broken Blossoms* (1919). Salt shows there was a wide variation of ASL, but it did get longer with the coming of sound (see 3.5) in the late 1920s. This was because it was easier to edit sound film with longer takes. However, the introduction of 'code numbering' (also known as rubber numbering – numbers printed on film; this is the timecode on digital video) facilitated faster cutting rates, and therefore a lower ASL, from 1932.

By the 1970s the ASL had reduced to 6 seconds, suggesting an inexorable move to more rapid cutting; however Salt's research indicated that it had lengthened again by the 1980s. The rise of the action film in the 1990s has reintroduced the trend toward more rapid cutting. For example in *The Matrix* (1999) the 'lobby scene' lasts for 111 seconds and has 87 shots (1.7 seconds ASL). However, even within this rapid rhythm the sequence is paced, and so the build-up (when Trinity and Neo enter) lasts 21 seconds and has four shots (5.3 seconds ASL) while the battle sequence has 73 shots in 104 seconds (1.4 seconds ASL). For a more detailed analysis of this, see Lacey and Stafford (2003).

David Bordwell usefully summarized the varying ASLs of the sound era:

> Hollywood films of the 1930s–1950s typically contained between 300 and 700 shots, giving them an average shot length of 8 to 11 seconds. In the 1960s, this norms (sic) starts to change: Most films drop to between 6–8 seconds, and some down to 3–5. In the 1970s, the average accelerates more, with 5–8 seconds being the norm. By now films typically have 1000 shots. The 1980s see some narrowing: many films are averaging 5–7 seconds per shot, and several drop to 3–4 seconds ASL, including music–video movies like STREETS OF FIRE and TOP GUN ... After 1993 or so, many films have 2–3 seconds ASL, such as ARMAGEDDON and SOUTH PARK.
>
> (Bordwell, 2003)

One of the consequences of the hyper-cutting of many contemporary films:

> has been accompanied by a simultaneous simplification of composition by cinematographers seeking to keep shots easily legible.
>
> (Thompson, 1999: 19)

It is possible that audiences have been more readily able to accept extremely short shots since the advent of MTV. Salt suggested that the film with the fastest ASL in the 1990s was *End of Days* (1999) 'with 3,875 shots in 112.5 minutes, an average shot length of 1.74 seconds' (Salt, 2004: 72).

We would expect action sequences to be rapidly edited, so audiences can simultaneously follow all the action and be overwhelmed by what's happening. Much slower rhythms – or long takes – have their own aesthetic effect. For example, *And Your Mother Too* (*Y Tu Mamá Tambien*, Mexico, 2001) – a teen pic and road movie hybrid – is characterized by long handheld shots. On their first night on the road the 'lads' stop at an inn where they learn about Ana's background (DVD Ch. 7, 33 min 20 sec). The scene lasts 165 seconds, all in one take. While long takes often have a documentary feel, giving the impression nothing of the pro filmic event has been cut out, here the camera's constant movement (either following the action or still with unsteady handheld) draws attention to itself in a way that documentaries normally would not. At the scene's end the camera follows a woman into the kitchen where a family work (and play). The woman is not an important character, and so this movement is unmotivated by the narrative and draws attention to what is normally hidden from a film's view.

1.9.5 Graphical

Another variable is the strength of the cut; the graphical dimension. This deals with 'spatiotemporal displacement from one shot to the next' (Buckland, 2003: 85). An extreme long shot can be followed by an extreme close-up; for example the opening shot of *The Last Picture Show* (1971) is a slow pan across the street of a run-down town. This is followed by a very short close-up of Sonny Crawford (Timothy Bottoms) pulling out the choke (a device for increasing the flow of petrol that was situated on the dashboard) of his car. The switch in framing from extreme long shot to close-up, along with the abrupt change in the length (time) of the shot, 'wakes' the audience after the 'soporific' pan. This however is unusual, as continuity editing eschews big differences between shot scales.

The graphical relationship between shots can also serve to link images and make smooth transitions. For example, in *Sex and Lucía* (*Lucía y el Sexo*, France–Spain, 2001), after Lorenzo and Elena have 'wild sex' in the sea, the scene ends with a shot of a full moon. This then dissolves onto the white circle of a pregnancy test. The link between a woman's sexual cycle and the moon is thus shown graphically.

1.9.6 Temporal

Editing does not just organize space, it is important in conveying time too: the temporal dimension. *Timecode* (2000) is unusual in that the 90-plus minutes of running time exactly covers the amount of time depicted on the screen. Most films show more time on screen than is experienced in the cinema. This time can range from hours (*Do the Right Thing*, 1989) to eons (*2001: A Space Odyssey*, UK–USA, 1968). The dissolve is often used to signify the passing of time. For example a character's journey may be shown by him or her getting into a car and then, after a dissolve, arriving at a destination; the intervening journey (which would involve space and time) 'disappears' in a narrative ellipsis.

Editing is essentially a potentially disrupting device. While films can be made with one shot (*Russian Ark*, 2002) or edited to look as if they have been filmed in one take (*Rope*), these are rare examples. The norm is hundreds of edits, and therefore potential disruptions, throughout the film. Western cinema uses continuity editing to smooth, and make invisible, these disruptions. The soundtrack is also important in creating this continuity:

> The image displaces us incessantly, offering us diverse angles on objects located at radically different distance ... we flit about at our own peril, constantly risking dizziness ... however the sound track holds out its hand, offering continuity of scale as an effective stabilizer.
>
> (Altman, 1992a: 62)

It is probably best to view the 'rules' of continuity editing outlined above as a template that can be used to analyse films. While many films follow the 'rules' slavishly, many play with the conventions for aesthetic effect. For example, Thelma Schoonmaker's editing in Martin Scorsese's *Raging Bull* (1980) leads:

> Certain dialogue sequences [do] depart from the norm; some temporal ellipses verge on discontinuity, barely noticeable jump

cuts propel the action forward ... establishing shots follow, rather than precede, close-ups, and so on.

(Opren, 2003: 45)

We might excuse the bending of the rules in *Raging Bull* as an example of 'art movie' self-consciousness. However, Opren also demonstrates how editing could work 'against' the narrative in 'classical Hollywood'. For example the opening scene of *The Searchers* (1956) uses editing to emphasize the arrival of the star (rather than the character), John Wayne, and in *To Have and Have Not* (1944) the editing creates anticipation for the appearance of Lauren Bacall's character by letting the audience hear her before she is seen.

1.9.7 Montage

Continuity editing is concerned with the creation of a coherent narrative space; montage, on the other hand, dispenses with continuity in favour of conveying narrative information, such as a journey, concisely. For example, the opening of *The Perfect Storm* (2000) sets the scene of a fishing community by showing a series of shots including:

➤ a boat arriving the harbour
➤ fish being unloaded from boats
➤ workshops and men repairing nets
➤ the town hall
➤ lists of the dead on the hall's walls
➤ a low shot of a statue of a seaman.

This collection of shots tells us of the main occupation of the town and its long history, which includes much loss of life to the sea. It suggests that the fishermen display heroism in their occupation. The sequence is not concerned with giving the audience a clear sense of space; we do not know where either the workshop or the town hall is in relation to the harbour.

Montage also formed the basis of theories of Soviet cinema (see 5.4), which was in a different form from that practised by mainstream cinema. Soviet cinema of the 1920s was avant-garde as it attempted to subvert the intentions of bourgeois Hollywood films, which try to suggest that the world is a coherent place that can be understood with reference to individual actions.

Avant-garde cinema (see 5.3) could parade its subversive characteristics through non-continuity editing. For example in the surrealist *Un Chien Andalou* (*An Andalucian Dog*, France, 1928) a character appears to walk out of a city first-floor flat directly onto a beach, and the director (Luis Bunuel) uses a dissolve within a scene. However this use of a dissolve is not, in itself, sufficient to disturb an audience's perception; it is also used in *The Brotherhood of the Wolf* (*Le Pacte des Loups*, France, 2001) as an ellipsis showing characters first in the distance and then closer, the dissolve signifying the time passed travelling between the two points.

1.10 Film stars as texts

Richard Dyer (1979) suggests that we can study stars in three ways:

- ➤ economically
- ➤ through audience reception
- ➤ as a text in themselves.

The first two points are investigated in Sections 3.17 and 4.10 respectively. Here we shall consider stars in terms of the meanings they can generate in films.

It was noted by film theorist Bela Balazs, writing in the 1920s and 1930s, that movies as a medium could give stars god-like qualities with the use of the close-up:

> When we see the fact of things, we do what the ancients did in creating gods in man's (sic) image and breathing a human soul into them.
>
> (Balazs, 1979: 290)

However, despite the potential for deity, stars manage to remain ordinary people. They are portrayed as being 'just like us' while in possession of immense wealth and, usually, exceptional looks. Whilst all stars are actors, not all actors are stars.

Actors become stars once they gain a following, and usually have a body of work behind them in which they have played similar types of character. The similarity of character is important, as it this persona with which audiences identify. It is difficult for actors who have a chameleon-like ability to change themselves with their roles to become stars, although Meryl Streep gained this status during the 1980s, possibly more through critical appraisal than through a traditional fan base.

Although films are the primary text through which personas are circulated (see Box 1.6), other secondary texts are also crucial in the dissemination of the persona. These include promotional material, such as interviews, film reviews, fan material (widely available on the Internet) and, for the last 30 years or so, academic analysis. This variety of texts about stars, and the importance of fans in the construction of star images, mean:

> Knowledge of stars is ... differently dispersed across society. Moviegoers ... bring many different social and cultural competencies to their understanding of a star's identity, so that the image will be interpreted in many different ways. The meaning of a star's image... is produced in the moment of interaction between moviegoers and star texts.
>
> (McDonald, 2000: 7)

One of the crucial aspects of a star's quality is his or her 'charisma'. While many people can be described as charismatic, a star's charisma must be visible (indeed may only be visible) to the camera. In addition, this charisma may be rooted in a particular time and place. (It is hard to imagine Valentino's version of masculine sexuality having much appeal to contemporary audiences but he was extremely popular in the 1920s.) However it may be possible that a star's charisma can transcend (as far as we can tell having only had 100 years of cinema history) the context of its production.

For example, Marilyn Monroe was a very popular star in the 1950s, embodying the male fantasy of female sexuality extant during that decade. That embodiment is very different to today's conventional representation of female sexuality. However she remains a household name over 40 years after her death. Dyer describes Monroe as:

> encapsulating the 'flux of ideas about morality and sexuality that characterised the fifties.... Monroe's combination of sexuality and innocence is part of that flux but one can also say her 'charisma' is the apparent condensation of all that flux...
>
> (Dyer, 1979: 36)

Monroe's charisma has allowed her popularity to continue beyond the 1950s. A star's embodiment of ideas may explain his or her appeal, and it is interesting to speculate why a muscle-bound machismo became popular in the mid-1980s (Arnold Schwarzenegger and Sylvester Stallone), only to be replaced in the 1990s with more feminine action heroes, such as Keanu Reeves (*Speed*, 1994) and Leonardo DiCaprio (*Titanic*, 1997). By the early twenty-first century the 'he-man' appeared to be back in fashion, with Vin Diesel and 'the Rock' (aka Dwayne Johnson).

Box 1.6 Star personas: Cruise and Diaz in
Vanilla Sky (2001)

Tom Cruise has been a big star since *Top Gun* (1986), which was his eighth film. However it is possible to see the Cruise persona in *Risky Business* (1983) – his second lead role – where he plays a middle-class teenager looking to 'get laid'. Like Julia Roberts, Cruise's smile is an important visual trait, as is his character's tendency to 'explode' into anger after sarcastically making a point.

Cameron Diaz also came to notice in her debut *The Mask* (1994), a special effects vehicle for Jim Carrey. However afterwards she eschewed straight Hollywood fare by spending much of the rest of the decade working in the independent sector. As she stated in a *Premiere* magazine interview:

> I was a kid who'd just turned 21… I'd played this bombshell girl with, like, the boobs, the makeup, the hair – and I didn't know *anything*.
>
> (Bardin, 2002)

The 'blonde bombshell', with a hint of 'bimbo', has formed part of her persona since. She played up this part of her persona in the *Premiere* interview by claiming she did not understand what 'oeuvre' meant. (It's irrelevant whether Diaz understood the word or not: her professed ignorance contributes to her persona.) However, she knew enough to learn her craft in low-profile movies.

Another interview describes Diaz as 'alluring and frequently giggly' (Fischer, 2001). In the *Charlie's Angels* films (2000 and 2003) she enacts this not exactly dumb but certainly gauche blonde with postmodern ironic delight: she tells her postman, when dressed only in T-shirt and knickers, that he can put anything into her slot. Another joke in the first film was she could not get a boyfriend.

The line between being represented as a 'dumb sex symbol' and an emancipated woman in control of her sexuality is thin. For example, three women complained to *Sight and Sound* about the magazine's gratuitous use of a publicity still showing a bikini-clad Diaz and Demi Moore. Their point was that in the magazine, divorced from the context of the film, the picture was simply 'eye candy' for a heterosexual male audience. However in the context of the sequel *Charlie's Angels: Full Throttle* they concluded that:

> Diaz in particular is almost shouting to the audience: 'What you're looking at is MY body, but you're doing it because I have decided you may, and I will decide when you may not!'
>
> (Kartas, Fielding and Moylan, 2003: 72)

There are few (and they are racial) more reprehensible stereotypes than the dumb blonde, but it is clear that however ditzy Diaz's character is (as in *My Best Friend's Wedding*, 1997, and *There's Something About Mary*, 1998), she is able to convey that she is in control of how she is being represented. This was emphasized by her performance in *Being John Malkovich* (1999), where she was unrecognizably dowdy. Clearly Diaz does not suffer the vanity of many stars who dread to look, in public, anything other than their glamorous best.

Vanilla Sky is a fascinating remake of *Open Your Eyes* (*Abre Los Ojos*, Spain, 1997). Where in the Spanish original the playboy character was a restaurateur, Cruise's David Aames is a lifestyle magazine publisher, which situates him within mainstream pop culture, only a hair's breadth away from movies. Cameron Crowe's adaptation of Alejandro Amenábar's original grafts on numerous popular culture references, suggesting they are an important part of our identity. (See also Box 1.4.)

The film is very much built around Cruise, although it's less a star vehicle than a deconstruction of stardom. Diaz plays Aames' lover, Julia Gianni, who he treats as a 'fuck buddy'. Diaz's appears to be a 'typically' frivolous blonde, but is shown to be homicidally unstable given her shallow treatment by Aames. The film draws upon Diaz's persona but subverts it with a psychotic twist of character, suggesting that if men treat women simply as sex objects they deserve the 'psycho' treatment.

The film's deconstruction of stardom, and its attendant celebrity, focuses on Cruise, whose nightmare, at the film's beginning, shows him plucking a grey hair from his head. A line later in the film he states, 'Isn't that what being young is about – believing you're going to live forever?' Ageing is a particularly difficult process for stars (satirized in *Death Becomes Her*, 1992), as their younger selves are forever in the public, and their, eye.

In typically postmodern fashion, *Vanilla Sky* references aspects of Cruise's persona that have circulated for many years in secondary texts: his sexuality (he sued someone who stated he was gay) and his sensitivity about his short stature (Nicole Kidman, upon her divorce from Cruise, said she looked forward to wearing high heels again). In *Vanilla Sky* he tells the male technician who appears to be trying to 'pick him up' that 'I'm straight, okay?' in a friendly fashion, and is shown after his arrest being photographed in front of a height measure, which reveals he is five foot eight inches tall. By blatantly dealing with these issues Cruise, through his proxy Aames, is stating his sexuality and refuting accusations that he cares about his height.

After Aames' disfigurement he wears a mask, a symbol of the film's investigation into identity, and in particular the identity of celebrities. The word 'persona' derives from masks that Ancient Greek actors wore.

Stars' personas are identifiable across a body of films, as well as through secondary texts such as interviews. This persona consists of their look and the type of character they portray. Clint Eastwood, Arnold Schwarzenegger and Sylvester Stallone tended to play men of few words and violent actions. Julia Roberts' characters are often skittish with a 'girl next door' quality, despite her dazzling smile and undoubted beauty. Contradiction (girls next door are not normally beautiful) is characteristic of star personas: for example Marilyn Monroe's innocent sexuality and Humphrey Bogart's tough-guy vulnerability (especially in *In a Lonely Place*, 1950).

A star's persona is a mask insofar that it may have little to do with the actual individual. The 'sex goddess' of the 1940s, Rita Hayworth, complained that men always went to bed with Rita Hayworth but woke up with her (that is, an ordinary person). Stars are to an extent trapped by their persona once they have established it, as audiences expect to see a typical performance. Many stars' attempts to broaden their range has led them toward box office failure, such as Jim Carrey in *The Majestic* (2001) and Will Smith in *The Legend of Bagger Vance* (2000). Both went back to their familiar personas to regenerate their box office worth.

This chapter has attempted to explain the basics of film language. It should be clear that there are no 'hard and set' rules. Film language evolves, and it is always open to interpretation depending upon the context in which the devices are used.

2 Film Genre and Narrative

2.1 Introduction

The critical concept of genre has had a much longer existence than that of narrative, as we can trace its inception to Aristotle's distinction between tragedy and comedy. It was also used later in literary criticism to distinguish between lyric and epic poetry. However film studies, in a democratic gesture of great significance, used genre to address *popular* culture. Eschewing the bourgeois notion of 'high art', from the late 1960s onwards film studies has operated on the premise that all films are worthy of study. This position is often misrepresented as suggesting that *all* films are of equal *value*. Just as the *auteur* theory (see 4.3) had rescued Hollywood's 'artisans' for art, genre theory was used to categorize those films that were made by directors not considered *auteurs,* and as a way of investigating critically maligned films, such as the 'women's picture'.

Although not all narratives are generic, all genre films do have narrative, which suggests that narrative is a more fundamental concept. However, we shall start this chapter with a consideration of genre, as it is a concept that 'ordinary' cinemagoers use, while their understanding of narrative is likely to be more implicit.

2.2 Defining genre

All those who consume films understand genre (although they may not use the term). Film producers use the concept in both the production (knowing what to include and the audience to target) and marketing (selling via posters, trailers and so on) of texts; Tom Ryall (1975) characterized genre as a negotiation between producers, film and audiences.

Genre is a product of the interaction between institutions (media producers and critics), audience and the text. It is a classification that allows both repetition and difference. Audiences usually simultaneously want something familiar (the genre's repeated 'formula') and a small degree of novelty (the difference). Both producers and audiences must share the knowledge of the genre's characteristics. This shared

Figure 2.1

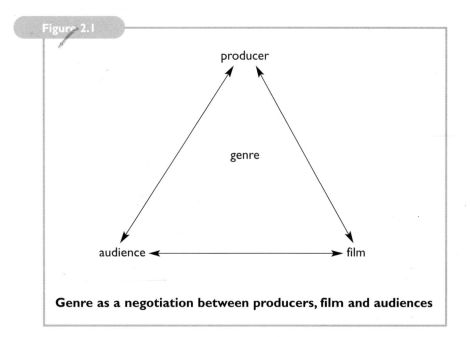

Genre as a negotiation between producers, film and audiences

knowledge, however, is not set in stone. Different people will have divergent understandings of genre. In addition, genres are often combined as hyphenates or hybrids (see 2.6.3). Genre is a very fluid concept.

Genres offer a set of expectations that create a clear idea, for audiences, about what is possible in the film's diegesis (narrative world). The rules of the genre define the limits of that genre's verisimilitude:

> Regimes of verisimilitude vary from genre to genre. Bursting into song is appropriate, therefore probable – therefore believable – in a musical, but not in a war film or a thriller. Killing one's lover is possible in a gangster film, a thriller, or even a romantic drama, but unlikely in romantic comedy.

> (Neale, 2000: 32)

This is why the most futuristic of landscapes can appear 'realistic' to audiences if it conforms to what one would expect in the context of science fiction. Spoofs often break the rules of a genre's verisimilitude in order to poke fun at its source material; for example the killer asks for another chance to hide when discovered in *Scary Movie* (2000).

In the most straightforward definition, the 'rules', or formula, of genre are its repertoire of elements.

2.3 The repertoire of elements

A number of genres can be categorized by their 'repertoire of elements': iconography (significant objects or sounds), narratives, settings and characters. A producer will draw upon the elements and try to combine them in a way that offers a fresh spin on the elements.

2.3.1 Iconography

The term 'iconography' derives from art history, where it only referred to visual signs. However, sounds are also often associated with a genre, such as the machine gun in gangster movies, so it is appropriate to extend the concept to include aural signs.

Science fiction's (SF) iconography is heavily rooted in the genre, so for example the appearance of any futuristic setting means the text *is* SF. Spaceships are iconographic of SF; however, as they have existed outside media texts since 1957, they can also appear in many different types of film such as the 'true-life story' *Apollo 13* (1995) – see Box 2.1.

The context in which an object, or sound, is used is crucial in defining its meaning. For example, a crucifix is readily associated with the church as a symbol of Christ's resurrection, and is not simply an example of horror iconography. In the context of a horror film this sign takes on an added meaning: obviously it is still associated with Christ but it is also seen as a weapon against evil. Similarly, a sharp knife in a horror context is likely to be used to eviscerate somebody; in a romantic comedy the only thing it is likely to cut is food.

Not all genres have a clear set of iconographic signs: biopics, for example, usually strain to create a period authenticity through an array of visual sights and sounds (usually musical). Thus the signs deployed by such a film will depend wholly upon the central character and the time in which it is set. However they do have recognizable narratives:

> The biopics the old studios used to churn out were necessarily episodic, but they adhered to a near formula. The intrepid writer, composer, scientist or whoever endures a period of bitter struggle, then makes the startling breakthrough that certifies his or her genius.
>
> (Matthews, 2001: 39d)

Box 2.1 Science fiction (SF)

Identifying science fiction (SF) is a relatively straightforward process. However, it is very difficult to produce an actual definition that clearly delineates what is, and what is not, SF:

> At first glance, it might appear to invite self-evident definition, as detective fiction is fiction about detectives and the art of solving crimes. Yet this is not the case, as is proved by the innumerable attempts that have been made to define it.
>
> (Parrinder, 1980: 1)

SF is often about science, and the narrative premise may be based on the invention of a technological device (such as the S.Q.U.I.D. in *Strange Days*, 1995). However science can also be insignificant (as in *The Astronaut's Wife*, 1999). In addition there are two broad types of SF texts: those that deal with what it means to be human (hard SF) and those that, while deploying the repertoire of elements, do not address this question (soft SF). *Dark City* (1997), for example, suggests that memory is crucial to our understanding of ourselves as human beings; *Independence Day* (1996), on the other hand, is an action movie with no philosophical leanings – unlike *The Matrix* (1999). In a key scene in the latter film, when the main agent (Hugo Weaving) is interrogating Morpheus (Laurence Fishburn), 'he' states that humankind is a virus because we constantly destroy what we inhabit (also see Lacey, 2000a). This equation of human beings with a disease suggests a rather bleak view on humanity. The film also spawned a number of books on its engagement with philosophy (for example, Irwin, 2002).

Many SF films have dealt with the question of what it means to be human through the doppelganger. In *Screamers* (Canada-USA-Japan, 1995) the protagonist (Peter Weller) tries to work out who is human and what is a simulacrum (that is, merely looks human). He notes wryly at the climax, where two non-human 'Jessicas' fight one another, that the screamers have quickly learned the human trait of destroying one another. *Screamers* is based upon a Philip K. Dick short story, 'Second Version', and he is one of the most influential SF writers. The best-known adaptations of his stories are *Blade Runner* (1982, director's cut 1991), *Total Recall* (1990), *Minority Report* (2002) and *Paycheck* (2003).

Other films that use the doppelganger to investigate what it is that makes us human include *Invasion of the Body Snatchers* (1956, remade

1978 and – as *Body Snatchers* – in 1993) and *The Thing from Another World* (1951, remade as *The Thing*, 1982).

There are other ways of investigating definitions of humanity. For example, 'what if ...' scenarios place human characters in situations that are different from the contemporary world. In *Gattaca* (1998), babies are genetically typed at birth, and those who are less than perfect are condemned to menial jobs, while the rest form part of the elite. The protagonist, Vincent Freeman (Ethan Hawke), has to overcome his genetic inferiority in order to fulfil his dream of being an astronaut. In doing so, the film suggests, human beings are not constrained by their genetic make-up, only by their spirit. Genetic mutation and eugenics was a theme taken up by *X-Men* (2000).

As a genre, SF often articulates humanity's relationship with technology, usually in a cautionary fashion. The premise of such narratives relies upon a technological device that does not yet exist; from this its possible influence on society is extrapolated. This can make SF look as if it is a literature of prediction (consider *The Truman Show*, 1998, and the recent explosion of TV reality shows), but this is to miss the point. Hard SF is always about now; it holds a mirror up to contemporary society to 'make strange' the familiar.

SF has been an important genre in Hollywood during the last few decades, as it has been an ideal form through which to demonstrate state-of-the-art special effects. While many of the films have been simply vehicles for a 'roller-coaster' ride – such as the *Star Wars* series – many have offered visual thrills and intellectual stimulation.

It is, interestingly, a specifically western genre:

> Science fiction is a very particular expression of just one tradition – Western civilisation. It does not exist in India, China (leaving out the special case of Hong Kong), Indonesia or Egypt – countries with flourishing and extensive film industries.
>
> (Sardar, 2002a: 2)

(Note: an extremely rare Chinese SF film, *All Tomorrow's Parties*, was released in 2003.) This cultural specificity, Sardar suggests, is due to the genre's Other being Islam:

> This *War of the Worlds* may be an imagined future, but it directly connects with the most familiar trope of the Western past. It is the Battle of Tours (Poitiers) all over again. It is the armies of Charles

Martel turning the tide, its is (*sic*) Charlemagne and his paladins at Ronscesvalles mustering for the first time a common sense of European identity, gathering the armies of Western Christendom to confront the Muslim hordes.

(Sardar, 2002a: 6)

The Other stands in opposition to the norm, and so defines the conventional through representing everything that the normal is not. Aliens often represent the Other, and Barbara Creed (1993) has suggested that they are often feminine in conception, and so reinforce patriarchy as the norm.

SF will probably remain a genre misunderstood by most viewers (to the (smug) satisfaction of aficionados), but enjoyed for the spectacle engendered in film; yet it will still be the most fascinating genre of the twenty-first century.

Further viewing
AI: Artificial Intelligence (2001)
Alien series (1979, 1986, 1992, 1997)
Cube (Canada, 1997)
Cypher (2002)
eXistenZ (Canada-UK-France, 1999)
Frequency (2000)
La Jetée (*The Jetty*, France, 1962)
Open Your Eyes (*Abre Los Ojos*, Spain-France-Italy, 1997)
Solaris (*Solyaris*, USSR, 1972; USA, 2002)
Stalker (USSR, 1979)
The Terminator (1984)
Twelve Monkeys (1995)
Vanilla Sky (2001)

Further reading
King, G. and Krzywinska, T. (2000) *Science Fiction Cinema: From Outerspace to Cyberspace,* London: Wallflower.
Kuhn, A. (ed.) (1990) *Alien Zone: Cultural Theory and Contemporary Science Fiction Cinema,* London and New York: Verso.
Kuhn, A. (ed.) (1999) *Alien Zone II: The Spaces of Science Fiction Cinema,* London and New York: Verso.
Lacey, N. (1999) *Blade Runner,* London: York Press.
Rushing, J. H. and Frentz, T. S. (1995) *Projecting the Shadow: The Cyborg Hero in American Film,* Chicago and London: University of Chicago Press.

Sardar, S. and Cubbitt, S. (eds) (2002) *Aliens R Us: The Other in Science Fiction Cinema,* London and Sterling: Pluto Press.

Sobchack, V. (2001, 2nd edn.) *Screening Space: The American Science Fiction Film,* New Brunswick and London: Rutgers University Press.

2.3.2 Narrative

'Narrative' is the way in which the other three of the repertoire of elements are combined, giving both a context to the signs deployed and a framework for audiences to use to make sense of events. By definition, genre films are conventional, and so usually deploy the structure described by Todorov (see 2.9). Genres can, in part, be defined by what the narrative disruption is. For example, if the problem is conflict within a family, we are probably watching a melodrama; a drugs baron trying to take over an area is likely to be in a gangster (or 'gangsta') film.

Some genres offer a limited number of very specific narratives. For example the Western has seven: Union Pacific/Pony Express fighting the elements to build a business; homesteader versus cattlemen; dedicated lawmen; ranch empire built and then destroyed by second generation; outlaw as good guy; revenge; cavalry versus Indians (see Lacey 2000: 139–41).

Of course, because of the fluid nature of genre, narratives can belong in more than one genre. For example, a murderer on the loose can be resolved by several genres including cop, detective, thriller and horror. Most genres offer a narrative of reassurance: for example, the murderers are usually captured and punished.

2.3.3 Setting

Setting is probably the loosest of the 'repertoire of elements'. For some genres, particularly the Western, which is usually set in the period 1865–90 on the American frontier, the setting can be very specific in terms of time and place. Other genres (such as romance and thrillers) can operate in virtually any setting.

SF's setting is particularly varied, as it ranges from the present through to a distant future. SF films can also be set in the past, although this is relatively rare; for example, the opening scenes of *2001: A Space Odyssey* (UK–USA, 1968).

2.3.4 Characters

Genres often have particular villains and heroes associated with them, for example the 'bitches' and 'geeks' in teen pictures. Some characters are so tightly associated with a genre that they attain the status of generic types; for example, the police captain who attempts to keep a rein on the protagonists, who will break the rules to attain justice, in cop movies. While we may know the characters associated with teen pics in reality, the general public do not know whether police captains do behave in the way they are commonly portrayed in films: hence they are a generic type.

Characters can be a defining factor of a genre, so the presence of an alien guarantees SF – and can you imagine a horror film without a monster? Even *The Sixth Sense* (1999), in which a monster was never seen, had this 'character' – it was humans' fear of death (the Other of life). Generic characters have their origins in the characters of medieval morality plays (such as Everyman and Perseverance) and melodrama's stock characters (such as 'noble' hero and 'long-suffering' heroine).

Genres can also be defined by the emotion they try to invoke in the audience. Romance may try to elicit tears; horror, fear; thrillers, thrills; comedy, laughter. However, more importantly, genres are often associated with particular themes: for example the wilderness versus civilisation opposition in Westerns, and the human:non–human opposition in SF – see 2.6.8.

Genres with clear repertoires of elements were among the first to be investigated by critics; for example Colin MacArthur's gangster book, *Underworld USA* (1972) and Robert Warshow (2000) on the Western. These elements are important to an understanding of how genres evolve.

2.4 Generic evolution

It is genre's use of a repertoire of elements that has led many to consider genre texts to be formulaic, intent on appealing only to the 'lowest common denominator' taste of the mass audience. Genre texts are often contrasted unfavourably with 'high art', aimed at an elite intellectual audience. Genres are, in this view, characterized as being simplistic entertainment (see 4.11).

This is a fundamental misconception on two levels. First, it ignores the fact that virtually all texts use a set of conventions (not necessarily genre) and so can be considered formulaic; for example, Mozart wrote a lot of music in sonata form. Second, while genre texts inevitably draw upon conventions (which can be characterized as a formula), they do not necessarily simply reproduce them. Genre texts are not only characterized by being the *same* as others in the 'family', they are also *different*; if they were not, audiences would soon get bored. As Steve Neale expresses it:

> the repertoire of generic conventions available at any one point in time is always in play rather than simply being re-played.
>
> (Neale, 2000: 219)

This 'play' occurs in two ways: the choice *and* combination of elements. Each new expression of a genre is likely to be different in some way from previous examples. For example *Psycho* (1960) introduced a particularly visceral form of horror in the shower slaying of Marion Crane (Janet Leigh), and in Norman Bates (Anthony Perkins), a monster who appeared to be a normal human being. The influence *Psycho* had on subsequent horror films was based on the *generic* change that the film wrought. It is difficult, maybe impossible, to understand the fundamental shift that particular film had on audience expectation of horror over 40 years after the event.

This 'same but different' appeal manifests itself in Hollywood's obsession with sequels. The trailer's use of 'Arnie's' dialogue, in *Terminator 3: Rise of the Machines* (USA-Germany-UK, 2003), 'She'll be back,' promises more of the pleasures of the first two films but with a difference: the villain is 'female'.

Similarly *Alien* (UK, 1979), which draws upon both horror and SF, was immensely influential in its conception of the alien life form. So effective was H. R. Giger's creation that over 20 years later, in *Pitch Black* (USA–Australia, 2000), it was still being referenced. In the same way, *Blade Runner's* (1982) evocation of the city in the future has been a touchstone of a number of dystopias including *Strange Days* (1995).

Despite the exceptions to the rule that constantly occur, the repertoire of elements remains a useful starting point for the categorization of many genres. This categorization process is mostly descriptive, allowing the genre to create a context in which meaning is made.

Genres must continually evolve to stay fresh. If a particular genre suddenly becomes popular, it is likely that a relatively large number of texts in that genre will be made, and the genre might evolve relatively quickly. This often leads to the creation of a cycle – see 2.6.1. Genres do not simply evolve through the development of the repertoire of elements: it is possible for genres to be created by critics, as in the case of *film noir*.

Box 2.2 Romantic comedy

Comedy is an interesting genre in terms of definition because though everyone can recognize the fact that such films are designed to make you laugh, attaching a clearly defined repertoire of elements to the genre is not a straightforward, or particularly useful, process. There are also many different types of comedy, such as spoofs, slapstick or farce, and comedy can be added to any genre to create a hybrid (see 2.6.3), such as an action comedy. In addition, there are a number of subgenres like screwball comedy and romantic comedy. Romantic comedy is also a hybrid in its mix of romance and comedy. It has further cross-fertilized for financial reasons:

> Where 'straight' romantic comedy is known for its appeal to women, the cross-genre film can attract a broader audience base.
> (Krutnik, 2002: 134)

Hence the action adventure genre (it is not a hyphenate but a distinct genre) is mixed with romantic comedy to appeal to both men and women (see *Jewel of the Nile*, 1985, and *Six Days Seven Nights*, 1998).

Romantic comedy does not have a clear repertoire of elements, though it does have a generic narrative its characters, setting and iconography are much less focused. Traditionally the narrative aim of romance is to get the principal protagonists married. Often the male half does not realize this is a state he wishes for, but he is always convinced at the end. The romantic comedy has undergone a revival in recent years, and it has been argued that this genre serves to reinforce the ideology of heterosexual romance. Its reappearance:

> followed a period in the 1970s and 1980s during which significant challenges had been mounted to that ideology, and during which romantic comedy itself seemed either to have taken the form of Woody Allen-like 'nervous romances'... or disappeared altogether.
> (Neale, 2000: 70)

It could be that such 'nervous romances' are now aimed at a younger age group than romantic comedies. Such teen pictures as *American Pie 1 and 2* (1999 and 2001) and *10 Things I Hate About You* (1999) focus on the adolescent trauma associated with teenage sex and love.

In *Runaway Bride* (1999) the central narrative conceit, that Maggie Carpenter (Julia Roberts) runs from the altar in fear of marriage, emphasizes the importance of marriage to the genre, as the resolution will undoubtedly be the cleaving of herself to Ike Graham (Richard Gere). Unlike screwball comedy, which is usually an extreme version of the genre (see, for instance, *Bringing Up Baby*, 1938, *I Was a Male War Bride*, 1949, and *There's Something About Mary*, 1998), gender roles are rarely questioned in romantic comedy. Even in screwball comedies, however, marriage usually brings together the warring parties.

Obviously there needs to be an impediment to marriage: in *Runaway Bride* Julia Roberts' aversion to the institution is matched by Richard Gere's misogyny and cynicism. In *Notting Hill* (USA-UK, 1999) the primary conflict is between Anna Scott's (Roberts again) status as a Hollywood star contrasted with William Thacker's (Hugh Grant) lowly bookseller. The film also sets up an opposition between England and America, with the former representing culture (Thacker suggests Scott might appear in a film based on a book by Henry James, a very European American novelist, rather than a science fiction film) and financial failure. America, on the other hand, represents fame, shallowness and pecuniary success.

Clearly narrative is important to the romantic comedy; can you imagine a film of the genre that did not end up with the couple together? The path to the 'marriage' will differ but the romantic comedy will end in marriage (or heterosexual 'coupledom'). Thus the institution of marriage, under attack from many couples not bothering with it in reality, is reaffirmed as an important part of bourgeois society. *Pretty Woman* (1990) – the film that made Roberts a star – also articulates the importance of consumerism to bourgeois ideology:

> 'Pretty Woman becomes 'pretty' when she learns to shop. The free market is, thus, 'fixed' through compulsory heterosexuality and commodity consumption.
>
> (Radner, 1993: 60)

Radner also points out how the film shifted the importance of female chastity, evident in the traditional romance, to another type of 'morality':

> For although Vivian is not chaste, she does have 'moral values,' a firm sense of decency and fairness towards others. This is what Edward, a corporate raider, lacks and what he needs Vivian to teach him: Edward is a rake in the 18th-Century sense, but one who rapes companies instead of women.
>
> (Radner, 1993: 62)

Through Vivian's (Julia Roberts) influence, Edward (Richard Gere) takes on a paternal role toward his workers, and the film concludes with him (apparently) proposing marriage to Vivian the prostitute.

Runaway Bride was made as a follow-up (not a sequel as the characters are different) to *Pretty Woman*, and the films share not only the principal cast members but also Hector Elizondo (the hotel manager in the earlier film) and director Garry Marshall.

Kissing Jessica Stein (2001), an independent film distributed by Fox Searchlight (20th Century Fox's 'indie' division), offered a different perspective, as the protagonist experiments with being a lesbian. While the narrative problem remains getting the partners together, the difficulty is caused by Jessica's fear of her family and friends' reactions to her sexuality. Refreshingly the film does not conclude with the acceptance of Jessica (Jennifer Westfeldt) and Helen (Heather Jurgenson) as a couple, but offers a coda where they split up.

Further viewing
40 Days and 40 Nights (USA-UK-France, 2002)
Clueless (1995)
Groundhog Day (1993)
Muriel's Wedding (Australia, 1994)
Sleepless in Seattle (1993)
Tin Cup (1996)
When Harry Met Sally (1989)

Further reading
Krutnik, F. (2002) 'Conforming passions? contemporary romantic comedy', in S. Neale (ed.), *Genre and Contemporary Hollywood*, London: British Film Institute.
Radner, H. (1993) 'Pretty is as pretty does: free enterprise and the marriage plot', in J. Collins, H. Radner and A. P. Collins (eds), *Film Theory Goes to the Movies*, New York and London: Routledge.

2.5 Approaches to genre

Genres are 'ideal types': that is, they are an abstract idea, and no one film ever fully uses all of the elements of a genre. The only types of films that come close to using everything of a genre's repertoire of elements are spoofs. The abstract nature of genre leads us to a tricky philosophical problem, a variant of the chicken–egg question, 'Which came first, the genre or the texts that make up the genre?'

> To take a genre such as a western, analyze it, and list its principal characteristics is to beg the question that we must first isolate the body of films that are western. But they can only be isolated on the basis of the 'principal characteristics', which can only be discovered from the films themselves after they have been isolated. That is, we are caught in a circle that first requires that the films be isolated, for which purposes a criterion is necessary, but the criterion is, in turn, meant to emerge from the empirically established common characteristics of the films.
>
> (Tudor, 1995: 5)

How do we know we are watching a teen pic? Answer: because we've seen teen pics before and recognize the genre's repertoire of elements. However, how did we know that these elements belonged to teen pics in the first place?

> Todorov offered a means of addressing this tension in his proposition that whereas the historical genre is amorphous and continually growing, splitting or shrinking, the theoretical genre is provisional and subject to adjustment with every new addition to the generic corpus.
>
> (Gledhill, 2000a: 223)

The 'historical genre' refers to the films themselves (the laid egg) whereas the 'theoretical genre' is the abstraction of the genre by academics (the chicken). Most people experience genres as an audience and are not bothered about chickens or eggs. They are socialized to recognise genres and, if they are fans, learn a genre's evolution. Academics, on the other hand, are constantly redefining their understanding of films from the past as well as observing contemporary generic changes.

While we do not have to worry too much about what came first, we must bear in mind that our understanding of the history of a genre is, like genre itself, always in 'play', and depends on our way of categorizing texts. Each new genre film potentially contributes to the evolution of that genre, and can lead us to reconsider our understanding of the genre both now and historically. In addition, as genre is a multi-media concept, genres can have histories in other media. The Western, for instance, drew upon pulp fiction, Wild West shows and paintings.

Despite the difficulty in defining genres, it is obvious that genre is a potent concept because both audiences and institutions use genre to define texts, and producers use genre to generate and articulate meaning.

2.6 Twelve uses of genre

Arthur Asa Berger (1992: 54–5) suggests ways in which genre could be used to analyse films.

2.6.1 A historical study of the evolution of a genre

By comparing texts of the same genre from different periods, it can become clear how society's understanding of particular issues has changed. For example, consider the way in which the Native American Indian evolved from being the narrative villain to the narrative princess. A history of the Hollywood Western has to consider the films of John Ford, who made an unprecedented number of classics of the genre, from *The Iron Horse* (1924) to *The Man Who Shot Liberty Valance* (1962). The portrayal of the Native American Indians in his films evolved from representing them as savage (for example, *Stagecoach*, 1939) to victims of white expansionism in *Cheyenne Autumn* (1964).

The classic gangster film cycle of the 1930s grew out of the high profile of actual gangsters at the time, particularly in Chicago during the Prohibition. The topical nature of the films encouraged a 'realist' approach to their making (something that Warner Bros became famous for) as well as helping to market them. It has been argued that after the Depression the genre mutated into *film noir,* where a more cynical worldview replaced the 'heroic rise and near tragic fall … structure' (Gledhill, 1985: 87b).

2.6.2 Relation of a film to a genre

As noted in 2.4, genres, while essentially formulaic, thrive on difference. Hence if we have a clear idea of what a particular genre consists of, this can be contrasted with how the generic conventions are used by individual texts. Such differences may simply be in the mix of ingredients, such as a film star appearing in a genre not associated with her or him (for example Jim Carrey appearing in a melodrama). Similarly hybrids can be used to reinvigorate genres, such as the *Halloween*'s (1978) mix of slasher movie and teen pic. Arguably *The Texas Chain Saw Massacre*

(1974) introduced this hybrid; however it did not have the cultural impact of the later film, as it was not a big box office success, and so inevitably had less influence on the genre. Similarly *Wes Craven's New Nightmare's* (1994) postmodern playfulness predated *Scream* (1996).

Another way in which texts can use genre to make a point is by playing against expectation. Hence the appearance of a motorcar in Sam Peckinpah's Western *The Wild Bunch* (1968) shocks audience into realizing the film is set in the twentieth century; the same director's *Ride the High Country* (aka *Guns in the Afternoon*, 1962) features a horse racing a camel.

By the 1990s the 'operatic' (in this sense of flamboyant use of camera) style of director Francis Coppola's *The Godfather* series was reflected in *Goodfellas* (1990) and *Casino* (USA-France, 1995) – both directed by Martin Scorsese – as well as *Carlito's Way* (1993). In this context *Donnie Brasco* (1997) can be seen as a throwback to 1930s realism, albeit using a different set of 'realist' conventions.

2.6.3 How genres relate to one another – the creation of hybrids

One of the ways in which genres renew themselves is by combining with other genres. As noted above, this can create a hybrid, such as 'action comedy', where the genres do not actually merge to form something distinctive. Genuine hybrids create something new, such as teen horror and cyberpunk.

The 'teen horror' movie mixed the 'slasher' (a horror subgenre) with the 'youth pic'. The horror element dramatizes the trauma, both physical and mental, that many teenagers seem to experience in the western world in their transition to adulthood. The 'gross–out' viscera associated with teen horror may be connected to the anxieties associated with the bodily changes of puberty. The teen pic's 'rites of passage' narrative becomes a life or death issue.

Teen horror can be seen to be particularly conservative in its agenda. For example in *Halloween* the virginal Laurie Strode (Jamie Lee Curtis) survives, while those females who 'sleep around' are 'punished'. This narrative reinforces the virgin:whore dichotomy that informs conservative representations of female sexuality. In *The Craft* (1996) the teenage witches swagger with sexual power, only to ultimately find that witchcraft has its price, and they 'go back' to being as they were. In a wonderful reversal, *Cherry Falls* (2000) offers a serial killer who attacks virgins; so a mass orgy is organized to protect the 'innocent'. Despite the 'progressive' representation of sex, the film falls back on the tired trope – also offered by *Psycho* – that the mother (that is, femininity) is to blame.

During the 1980s, horror movies targeted the young cinemagoer, and video watcher, with flimsy plots that were an excuse to hang on as many jaw dropping, gross-out special effects that could be crammed into the film. In this sense the real stars were the make-up artists and special effects supervisors, such as Tom Savini of *Friday the 13th* (1980).

The variations on the slasher genre became increasingly unconvincing, and the cycle came to a conclusion in the early 1990s. *Nightmare on Elm Street* (1984) had been directed by Wes Craven, and it was his intervention that reinvented the slasher genre in the 1990s. Both scripted and directed by Craven, *Wes Craven's New Nightmare* thrust the postmodern aesthetic, which had often lurked in horror's shadows, into the spotlight (see Box 2.3).

Box 2.3 The 'slasher' subgenre

The slasher film (exemplified by John Carpenter's *Halloween*, 1978) has been defined as including:

> the killer ... the psychotic product of a sick family, but still recognizably human; the victim is a beautiful, sexually active woman; the location is not-home, at a Terrible Place; the weapon is something other than a gun; the attack is registered from the victim's point of view and comes with shocking suddenness.
>
> (Clover, 1993: 23–4)

In genre there are always exceptions to the rules (*Halloween* is set in a 'homely' suburbia and the first victim is seen from the point of view of the psycho, Michael). That is both a tribute to the concept's fluidity and a warning against being dogmatic in describing genre. We can see that the repertoire of elements is evident in Clover's definition. All of these elements can appear in non-slasher horror films: it is their particular *combination* that makes them part of the slasher subgenre. Slashers are also often teen horror movies, a combination of horror and the youth picture.

Andrew Tudor suggests that horror movies made post-1960 offer a paradigm shift from those produced earlier. He cites two films from 1960, *Psycho* and *Peeping Tom*, as the progenitors of what he terms 'paranoid' horror, in contrast to 'secure horror'. It was not until *The Texas Chain Saw Massacre* (1974) that the generic 'challenge' of these films were taken up and so in the 1970s onwards the horror films presume:

---

a world in which the monstrous threat is increasingly beyond control and order is therefore unlikely to be restored at narrative end. Experts can no longer provide credible protection, the threat from the unknown pervades the everyday world, and there always remains potential for escalating disorder.

(Tudor, 2002: 108)

Hence monsters such as *Halloween's* Michael cannot be stopped, and there is never any reason offered for his psychosis. Not all slasher films, however, necessarily feature teenagers; see Dario Argento's work.

As suggested by the 'shocking suddenness' in Clover's definition, the key to slasher films is their success in setting up suspense, then delivering extreme violence: the slashing suggests multiple wounds requiring time and physical force to effect. This explicit violence on characters has led academics to investigate the voyeurism associated with the sub-genre: why do we take pleasure at watching extreme violence?

The slasher movies often have a female protagonist, who Carol Clover called the 'Final Girl': the only survivor who despatches the monster. While on the face of it these offer a strong character with whom women can identify, Clover suggests that these apparently feminist heroes are merely reproducing the values of patriarchy:

If the slasher film is 'on the face of it' a genre with at least a strong female presence, it is in these figurative readings a thoroughly male exercise, one that finally has very little to do with femaleness and very much to do with phallocentrism.

(Clover, 1992: 53)

Clover argues that the women only survive by acting like a male, and so patriarchy is in fact reaffirmed. Indeed, the very randomness of the attacks in the subgenre is also indicative of its conservative agenda:

The world thus appears irrational, a jungle governed by no logic or law. It is only in such a context that the conservative view that the world cannot be redeemed makes sense. What is irrational cannot be dealt with rationally; instead, it should be controlled or repressed.

(Ryan and Kellner, 1988: 192)

Maybe this is why most (all?) teen horror films form part of the slasher subgenre; is the monster a projection of teen's fear of taking responsibilities in the irrational adult world? Whereas in reality the world can be understood in terms of, for example, the class struggle or the capitalist exploitation of the environment, conservative ideology would prefer these explanations to be denied, hence the portrayal of the world as an irrational place.

Further viewing

Carrie (1976)
The Evil Dead (1982)
Jeepers Creepers (Germany-USA, 2001)
Scream (1996)
Tenebrae (*Sotto gli Occhi dell' Assassino*, Italy, 1982)

Further reading

Grant, B. K. (ed.) (1996) *The Dread of Difference: Gender and the Horror Film,* Austin: University of Texas Press.
Rockoff, A. (2002) *Going to Pieces: The Rise and Fall of the Slasher Film 1978-1986,* Jefferson: McFarlane and Company.
Wells, P. (2000) *The Horror Genre: From Beelzebub to Blair Witch,* London: Wallflower Press.

2.6.4 How genres in different media influence one another

As noted above, many genres predate cinema and so obviously influenced how the genre was articulated in film. In addition, genres that seem to belong to one medium can have an influence on film. For example, television's 'MTV music video' genre has had an immense effect on films all over the world, from the 'high concept' (see 3.11) of *Flashdance* (1983) to Bollywood. The glossy visuals (themselves derived from advertising), and the rapid rhythm of the editing dictated by the music's beat and bravura camera positions might have reached its apotheosis with *Moulin Rouge* (2001, USA–Australia).

The influence of MTV is often cited as an example of trivialization of 'cinema art'. However, in *Run Lola Run* (*Lola Rennt*, Germany, 1998) writer/director Tom Tykwer uses the form of music video to meld together the genres of action, teen pic, thriller and melodrama.

Cinema has also influenced television: the 'kitchen sink' drama of early 1960s British cinema appeared in series such as *The Likely Lads* (1965–6) and *cinema verité* (see Box 4.1) became 'reality TV'.

In *Run Lola Run* (Germany, 1998) writer/director Tom Tykwer uses the form of music video to meld together the genres of action, teen pic, thriller and melodrama

If we are studying a particular genre then we should consider all manifestations of the form in the media; it would be daft studying horror without reading books of the genre. Even though our focus is on film we should be aware that the medium does not exist in isolation.

2.6.5 Comparison of the same genres in different countries

While Westerns are a particularly North American genre, Sergio Leone's 'Spaghetti' Westerns had a profound influence on the form in the 1960s (for example, *A Fistful of Dollars*, (*Per un Pugno di Dollari*, West Germany-Spain-Italy, 1964)); he also offered his distinctive 'epic' take on the gangster movie with *Once Upon a Time in America* (*C'era una volta in America*, USA-Italy, 1984).

The gangster genre thrives in Far Eastern cinema particularly in the work of John Woo (for example, *Hard Boiled*, (*Lashou Shenten*, Hong Kong, 1992)) and Takeshi Kitano's arthouse movies (such as *Violent Cop*, (*Sono Otoko, Kyobo ni Tsuku*, Japan, 1989)). Woo's films, in particular, have heavily influenced Hollywood action films. The elaborate pieces of violence – watch the opening scene of *Hard Boiled* – have altered audience expectations about the representation of violence in film.

These generic influences can be recycled, such as Hollywood's appropriation of the generic tropes (defining ideas) of Hong Kong gangster movies:

> Directors show close-ups, made famous by the likes of John Woo and Ringo Lam, of speeding bullets, and stunt actors imitate the physical martial arts moves of Jackie Chan and Jet Li.
>
> (Stokes and Hoover, 1999: 35)

Possibly more than anyone else, Quentin Tarantino has popularized the use of Hong Kong cinema. His *Reservoir Dogs* (1991), which was based, loosely, on *City on Fire* (*Longhu Fengyun*, Hong Kong, 1987), and *Kill Bill Volume 1* (2003) is a martial art tribute. Tarantino's influence, in turn, can be seen on the British gangster film (a generally sorry affair), such as *Lock, Stock and Two Smoking Barrels* (1998), and his narrative playfulness, as well as a blood-soaked car, can be seen in the Mexican *Amores Perros* (*Love's A Bitch,* 2000) (this film's central section is also influenced by Spanish director Luis Bunuel who worked extensively in Mexico during the 1950s).

2.6.6 Distinctive characteristics of characters in different genres

If a cowboy is present then you're watching a Western; an alien is SF and so on. However, we can also consider how the same character can change, for example the detective is very different in 'whodunnits' (the respectable Hercule Poirot in various Agatha Christie adaptations) from the 'hard boiled bastard' of *film noir* (Mike Hammer in *Kiss Me Deadly*, 1956, and Nick Curran in *Basic Instinct*, 1992). The radically different protagonists on offer are indicative of the worldview of these genres: the cosy conservatism, which reinforces feudal notions of social class, where the division between good and evil is usually clear, versus the nihilistic world where good and evil are inextricably intertwined.

Occasionally generic characters will appear outside 'their' genre and take the resonance of their filmic origins with them. So the mute (Native American) Indian, in the satirical *One Flew Over the Cuckoo's Nest* (1975), carries the Western connotations of the 'pre-civilized' American west (see 2.6.7) as a counterpoint to the 'civilizing' influence of the mental asylum.

2.6.7 Analysis of what genres reflect about society

We need to take care with any suggestion that media texts 'reflect' society. This approach is better thought of in terms of how particular genres articulate ideological issues:

> Hollywood genre films ... tended to promote the American dream and dominant American myths and ideologies. The Hollywood genres taught that money and success were important values; that heterosexual romance, marriage, and family were the proper social forms; that the state, police and legal system were legitimate sources of power and authority; that violence was justified to destroy any threats to the system; and that American values and institutions were basically sound, benevolent, and beneficial to society as a whole.
>
> (Kellner, 1998: 358b–9a)

Although Kellner writes in the past tense, his view is still applicable. The action film, Hollywood's summer box-office staple, in particular, tends to articulate a conservative view of society (see Box 2.4). Despite this there is room in genre films for subversive comment. For instance, in the Western *The Searchers* (1956) the protagonist Ethan Edwards (John Wayne) is portrayed as a racist who has no place in civilised society, and the 'business' of the mafia was equated with the business of capitalism in *The Godfather* (1971). *The Matrix* (1999) suggested contemporary society was a dystopia.

The way the representation of the enemy in war films has changed is indicative of developments in how society views history. For example, we can contrast the representation of the North Vietnamese in Hollywood war films: in *The Green Berets* (1968) they are sneaky degenerates; in *The Deer Hunter* (1978) they are cruel psychopaths; in *We Were Soldiers* (USA-Germany, 2002) they are worthy opponents. Before we conclude that Hollywood is becoming able to empathize with the enemy we should consider *Black Hawk Down* (2001), where the opposition are reminiscent of the zombies in *Night of the Living Dead* (1968): it does not matter how many are killed, they keep on coming.

Box 2.4 Hollywood action films

The action film has been prevalent since the rise of narrative cinema; for example *The Birth of a Nation* (1915) offers action sequences in its portrayal of the Civil War. 'Action' can be thought of as a 'super genre' in the way it can appear in many different genres; while the Western and the war movie are almost certain to have action in them, science fiction can be action-based (*Star Wars*, 1977 or *Independence Day*, 1996) or be virtually devoid of action (*Gattaca*, 1997 and *The Truman Show*, 1998). Yvonne Tasker suggests that 'in action cinema visual display is elevated to a defining feature of the genre.' (Tasker, 1993: 6) And this visual spectacle is usually generated by special effects. This has led some to argue that narrative is subordinate to the special effects:

> As in the most monumental ceilings of the Baroque, we confront in the special effect as such – the effect as it appears in films like ... *Armageddon* (Michael Bay, 1998) or *Volcano* (Mike Jackson, 1997), not in the service of narrative but as the purpose for which the narrative exists – not the representation but its obverse: the sublime.
>
> (Cubitt, 1999: 127)

However, as a number of other writers have suggested (see King, 2002), this has been overstated and narrative remains important to action cinema. Indeed, Elsaesser and Buckland (Ch. 2, 2002) offer an exhaustive narrative analysis of the seminal action film *Die Hard* (1988), and demonstrate how the film worked to confirm masculinity and American economic power in the face of the women's movement and the rise of Japanese business.

Much of the work on action cinema focuses on the representation of gender; although it is not always men who save the world: for example, Ripley of the *Alien* franchise (1979–97) and Lara Croft of the *Tomb Raider* films (2001 and 2003). On the other hand, Rikke Schubart identifies how action cinema of the 1980s was characterized by the *passion* of its protagonists (for example: the eponymous *Rambo* and Riggs, played by Mel Gibson, in the *Lethal Weapon* series); while in the 1990s *acceleration* was the key:

> The [acceleration] strategy requires more victims, faster speed, harder steel. The clue is not motivation, but movement.
>
> (Schubart, 2001: 199)

This movement is narrative-based, as the protagonist moves from one conflict to the next: the roller-coaster ride that can characterize action cinema. The fairground metaphor takes us back to the early days of cinema when it was a sideshow attraction. Indeed, Tom Gunning showed that most films before 1906 could be dubbed as forming a 'cinema of attractions' that was concerned to show audiences 'a series of views' (Gunning, 1990: 57). These attractions may have been typical of the circus, magicians' tricks, or of a more salacious kind, as in *The Bride Retires* (1902, France). Gunning suggests that Méliès' special effects movies are best seen as using narratives as a device on which to hang special effects.

Maybe the 'cinema of attractions' is still with us; maybe audiences flocked to *The Day After Tomorrow* (2004) simply to see New York flooded and then frozen. Undoubtedly large-format film, such as IMAX, is based on offering a 'cinema of attractions' (see Box 2.6), and has been trying to get a foothold in mainstream narrative cinema with its adaptation of 'normal format' films for the big screen (such as *The Lion King*, 1994) and custom-made narratives such as *Ghosts of the Abyss* (2003).

Further reading

Arroyo, J. (ed.) (1999) *Action/Spectacle Cinema: A Sight and Sound Reader*, London: British Film Institute.

Inness, S. A. (2004) *Action Chicks: New Images of Tough Women in Popular Culture*, Basingstoke: Palgrave Macmillan.

2.6.8 Impact of mythic and folkloristic content on texts and genres

Some critics have suggested that the formulaic nature of genres reflects archetypal structures in the human consciousness (based on Jungian psychology). John Cawelti (1976), for instance, stated that all genres are based on five moral fantasies: Adventure; Romance; Mystery; Melodrama; Alien Beings or States. He argues that differences between genres are often superficial, so the Western and the spy story are both adventures (as is much science fiction).

Structuralists (see 4.4) suggest that all meaning derives from difference; for example, we cannot understand light unless we know what darkness is, love without hate, male without female and so on. The fundamental (and arguably mythical) oppositions that structure our way of seeing the world are binary oppositions.

The Western articulates a relatively limited number of discourses usually centred on definitions of 'civilisation versus wilderness'.

Jim Kitses has provided a touchstone list of these oppositions:

The wilderness	Civilization
The individual	*The community*
Freedom	Restriction
Honour	Institutions
Self-knowledge	Illusion
Integrity	Compromise
Self-interest	Social responsibility
Solipsism	Democracy
Nature	*Culture*
Purity	Corruption
Experience	Knowledge
Empiricism	Legalism
Pragmatism	Idealism
Brutalization	Refinement
Savagery	Humanity
The West	*The East*
America	Europe
The frontier	America
Equality	Class
Agrarianism	Industrialism
Tradition	Change
The past	The future

(Kitses, 2004: 12)

The complex nature of the way these oppositions are articulated is evident in the moral ambiguity of the lists. For example, the first four dichotomies in the Individual versus Community list suggest individualism is best. However, the last two qualify that view. This ambiguity runs throughout: while purity seems to be better than corruption, savagery is unlikely to 'beat' humanity. Kitses' oppositions express the conflicts that the Western tries to resolve, although the list does lack 'ethnic or racial terms which underpin most aspects of frontier (or western) methodology' (Neale, 2000: 135).

It is notable how each of the oppositions embodies contradiction: the wilderness's 'equality' and self-interest' and civilization's 'corruption' and 'idealism' which 'demonstrates both the flexibility of the structure and the ideological tension which it embodies' (Gledhill, 1985: 68a). Kitses' antinomies emphasize the mythic power of the Western as it is, classically, set on the frontier (between 1865–90), a place that was neither wilderness nor civilized. Hence the conflict between the 'natural' past and the 'civilized' future could be dramatized.

The gangster film can be seen to be an 'urban Western' where the battle between the 'wilderness' and 'civilization' is transformed into the conflict between the gangsters and the forces of 'law and order':

> The classical Hollywood gangster films inculcated the message that 'crime does not pay' and showed the police and legal system able to contain crime and deal with criminals. But gangster films also explored cultural conflicts and contradictions central to American capitalism. Gangsters are, in fact, prototypical capitalists who will do anything to make a buck … [the films] explore the tensions within American life between making money and morality, between self-interest and legality, and between private and public interests.
>
> (Kellner, 1998: 357b)

The gangster film has often been caught up in issues of censorship due to the, often extreme, violence portrayed – from the grapefruit in Jean Harlow's face in *The Public Enemy* (1932) to the chainsaw in a bathroom (*Scarface*, 1983) and the various beatings in *Goodfellas* (1990).

2.6.9 Rise in popularity and decline in popularity of genres (genre cycles)

If genres become popular, a large number of texts are likely to be made. David Pirie (1996) pointed out how genre cycles are similar to financial cycles, as both are contra-cyclical. For example, when *Scream* broke through the $100 million barrier at the North American box office, it was the first successful teen horror movie for many years. So a new cycle was born and, at the time of writing, is still running its course.

There are various reasons that a genre suddenly becomes popular. It could be that technological developments, which fuelled the action movies in the 1990s, help reinvigorate a genre's conventions. It is possible that less obvious reasons contribute to a genre's popularity; for example, the series of films 'inspired' by *Fatal Attraction* (1987) may have been expressing the crisis in the bourgeois nuclear family as divorce rates increased and more people had children outside of marriage. (It could also have been a response to AIDS.)

The end of the twentieth century featured a relatively large number of texts that offered 'paranoid' versions of reality, including *The X Files* (television and a USA-Canada 1998 film), *The Spanish Prisoner* (1997) and *The Matrix* (1999). Did this paranoia hook into a *fin de siècle* zeitgeist, most obviously present in the over-hyped Millennium Bug? The answer is obviously that we do not know, and assuming that texts reflect reality is an approach fraught with reductionism.

The development of a cycle is not simply determined by the vagaries of the box office. The major studios may decide that a particular genre has reached saturation point and so stop making such films. This is an attempt to pre-empt a cycle's decline:

> Neither the end of the cycle nor the ensuing long-term decline in horror production [in the 1980s] were due to any observable decline in the popularity of horror films among audiences in America, or to any identifiable change in the basic nature of the films themselves.
>
> (Neale, 2000: 229)

There is usually a hiatus between the 'contra-cyclical' hit and the films that attempt to ride the genre's 'gravy train', because of the long lead-time required to produce and exhibit films. For example the success of *Saving Private Ryan* (1998) launched a war movie cycle in which only *Black Hawk Down* (2001) broke the $100 million 'barrier' in North America. It included a number of high-profile flops such as *Hart's War* – $19 million – and *Windtalkers* (both 2002) – $41 million. However, once these big-budget films are in production, they cannot be stopped even if it has become clear that the genre is not actually particularly popular.

2.6.10 Differences in genres in different media

Different media have particular ways of making meaning, and so different aspects of genres are likely to be emphasized depending upon the medium. Film, for instance, tends to have a much more compressed narrative than novels, hence film adaptations of novels tend to cut much of the plot. On the other hand, film's use of sound and image can convey an immense amount of information very quickly. Characters do not need to be described, for example: they can be seen.

There are also differences between audio-visual media, as Neale points out in relation to the gangster genre:

> most of the telefilms and miniseries, unlike most of the films made for initial theatrical release, have tended to emphasise the familial aspects of *The Godfather* and the Mafia mystique, to become a form of soap opera with concomitant appeal to women and with a concomitant prominence or focus on female characters.
>
> (Neale, 2002a: 35)

Soap opera is a broadcast form designed to hook audiences into a serial format and therefore facilitate audience (who, on a commercial station, are sold to advertisers) viewing. It is easier, because of the regulations, to show extreme imagery in cinema than on television, and the sound and image in cinema is also of a better quality. Films usually cost more than television programmes and so can boast higher production values. However, recent serials such as *Buffy the Vampire Slayer* (1997–2003) have been characterized by cinematic lighting and camera movement.

2.6.11 What uses and gratifications do different genres provide for audiences

This point refers to the 'uses and gratifications' model of audience (see 4.11) interaction with films. It suggests audiences use the media for entertainment, information, social interaction and personal identity. Documentaries are likely to be watched for information; horror offers entertainment and, to the aficionados described in Chapter 4, social interaction through fanzines.

Film is seen primarily as an entertainment medium. However, documentaries are released in cinemas, and arthouse films usually attempt to offer more than 'just' entertainment.

2.6.12 How do technical matters involving production and aesthetics impact on different genres

The classic gangster film cycle coincided with the emergence of sound on film, and this encouraged the 'realist' aesthetic. The Western thrived, in part, when filmmakers moved from New York to Los Angeles, because of the readily available locations. Inevitably the musical could not appear until sound on film was possible. The handheld cameras and synchronous sound of 'direct cinema' (realist documentary) could not exist before the late 1950s with the development of lightweight equipment.

Although not a technical matter, Richard Maltby showed how censorship could form a genre's aesthetics:

> The conventions determined ... that a character could not normally shoot another character in a two-shot [so] a shooting could be represented by either half of the action, ... whereas if the whole action was contained in a single shot, a censor's deletion might remove or obscure a key plot point.
>
> (Maltby, 2001: 121)

Digital filming and editing has made it possible to make films much more quickly. It is unlikely that the extraordinary opening battle in *Gangs of New York* would have been cut the way it is before the advent of digital editing.

Further viewing – the Western

Dead Man (USA–Germany–Japan, 1995)
Duel in the Sun (1946)
Forty Guns (1957)
My Darling Clementine (1946)
Open Range (2003)
She Wore a Yellow Ribbon (1949)
Unforgiven (1992)
Wagonmaster (1950)

Further reading – the Western

Buscombe, E. (ed.) (1993) *The BFI Companion to the Western,* London: Deutsch.
Henderson, B. (1985) 'The Searchers: An American dilemma' in B. Nichols (ed.), *Movies and Methods Vol. 2,* University of California Press.
Kitses, J (2004) *Horizons West: Directing the Western from John Ford to Clint Eastwood,* new edition, London: British film institute.
Wright, W. (1975) *Sixguns and Society,* University of California Press.

Further viewing – the gangster movie

A Better Tomorrow (*Yingxiong Bense,* Hong Kong, 1986)
Dead or Alive (*Hanzaisha,* Japan, 1999)
Gangster No. 1 (UK–Germany–Ireland, 2000)
Get Carter (UK, 1971)
Miller's Crossing (1990)
The Roaring Twenties (1939)
Le Samourai (France, 1967)

Further reading – the gangster movie

Christine Gledhill (1985) 'The gangster/crime film', in Pam Cook (ed.) *The Cinema Book,* London: British Film Institute.
McArthur, C. (1972) *Underworld USA,* London: Secker and Warburg/ British Film Institute.

Robert Warshow (1970) 'The gangster as tragic hero', in *The Immediate Experience*, Atheneum Books.

One of the most important genres not mentioned in the above is melodrama – see Box 2.5.

Box 2.5 Melodrama

Melodrama is one of fundamental genres of cinema. Popular in the theatre of the nineteenth century, just before cinema was 'invented', and originally designed for performance without dialogue, melodrama was an ideal vehicle for communicating to audiences in 'silent' cinema.

Melodrama is best characterized by excess: events are represented in an 'over-the-top' fashion. This is evident in the performing styles of actors (especially those in silent cinema where non-verbal expression was the only way a performer could 'speak'), the narratives (use of coincidences and plot contrivance, as in the novels of Thomas Hardy) and in expressionist *mise en scène* (see Box 1.5) where narrative points are over-determined by the placement of the camera in relation to the frame's contents. This can be seen best in films directed by Max Ophuls, Vincente Minnelli, Nicholas Ray and Douglas Sirk.

Melodrama is not concerned with creating three-dimensional characters – 'round' in E.M. Forster's (2000) terms – but with using recognizable types: 'the patient, suffering heroines; the upright, but often somewhat ineffectual heroes; the unscrupulous, scheming villains, usually with sexual designs on the virginal heroines; the saintly mother-figures; the stern "Victorian" father-figures' (Walker, 1982: 3–4). These are examples of generic types; they are characters that we associate explicitly with Victorian melodrama or, more likely as these texts are still occasionally screened, 'silent' films.

Melodrama is characterized by the following:

➤ identification of moral polarities of good and evil within the narrative
➤ comparable to tragedy except the characters are generally of lower social status and confront clearly identified antagonists
➤ the use of music for dramatic emphasis
➤ clear-cut solutions to conflict
➤ excess and exaggeration

➤ use of character types
➤ coincidence as a narrative device
➤ celebration of overt emotionalism
➤ use of emblems as visual signs.

Melodrama has many subgenres including soap opera; the 'Gothic romance' (*Great Expectations*, 1946 and 1997); the 'social problem' picture (*Dangerous Minds*, 1995); the family melodrama (*American Beauty*, 1999); the 'woman's' picture (*The End of the Affair*, USA-UK, 1999); the comedy (*East is East*, UK, 1999); the teen pic (*Rebel Without a Cause*, 1955).

Melodrama deals with crises within bourgeois institutions, usually that of the family. Social problem pictures focus on the breakdown of other institutions such as education and legal apparatuses. The resolution of melodrama usually seeks to recoup the disruption into the traditional social structures. Hence texts that deal with marriage problems rarely question the value of the institution of marriage, but focus on individuals' problems within that institution.

While melodrama is in many ways the antithesis of action, as it focuses on the home and relationships as against adventure and physical action, the two do have their similarities (as noted in 3.15, *Variety* calls action films melodramas) in their emphasis on excess.

Further viewing
All About My Mother (Todo Sobre Mi Madre, Spain, 1999)
Festen (Celebration, Denmark, 1998)
Erin Brockovich (2000)
Eve's Bayou (1997)
Legends of the Fall (1994)
Monster's Ball (USA-Canada, 2001)
Wings of the Dove (UK-USA, 1996)

Further reading
Byars, J. (1991) *All That Hollywood Allows: Re-Reading Gender in 1950s Melodrama,* Routledge.
Doane, M. A. (1987) *The Desire to Desire,* Macmillan Press.
Gledhill, C. (ed.) (1987) *Home is Where the Heart Is: Studies in Melodrama and the Woman's Film,* London: British Film Institute.
Harwood, S. (1997) *Family Fictions: Representations of the Family in 1980s Hollywood Cinema,* Macmillan Press.

2.7 Genre and audiences

Audiences use genre in three ways:

➤ to choose the text they wish to consume
➤ to help them understand (and enjoy) that text
➤ to talk about texts.

The prime reason audiences choose to watch films is for entertainment, and genre is a crucial factor in this as it assists in making films easier to choose and understand.

Film producers (who are also members of the audience when consuming texts they have not produced) are obviously aware of the conventions of genres they themselves produce. They try to encode these conventions into the text they are making (probably with some variation). The role of critics (including reviewers, interviewers and feature writers) is important as they help to anchor a text's genre(s), often by recycling material from the producers' press packs.

For example in *Empire* magazine's 2001 summer preview (issue number 144, June) the opening sentences of the thumbnail sketches of the first five films included the following genres:

Pearl Harbor – 'romantic drama'
Shrek – 'fable'
Series 7: The Contenders – 'satire'
Tomb Raider – 'female action hero'
Swordfish – 'slick thriller'.

It is noticeable that genre is used in a flexible manner: *Swordfish*'s genre is further characterized by the adjective 'slick', and I imagine very few multiplex-goers would describe going to see a 'fable', although the use of the term 'satire' is a possibility. In addition, the distinctive aspect of *Tomb Raider* is 'female'. This flexibility suits producers as it means the film is likely to have a wider appeal to audiences, rather than offering a narrow one-genre definition that will 'turn off' those to whom that genre does not appeal. This practice is not new, as Rick Altman demonstrated with the 1936 film *Sons O' Guns* the poster of which offered a:

> mirthful martial musical romantic comic dramatic poetic discourse.
> (Altman, 1999: 63)

One of the main pleasures audiences get from genre texts is recognizing generic elements; *The Simpsons* and spoofs, such as the *Scary Movie* series (2000–3), offer much of their pleasure through such intertextual references. Indeed the title of the latter is a genre, just as the *Scream* series used the aural iconography of horror films (see Box 3.2). Similarly, when a genre text breaks or bends the rules, this also can be a source of enjoyment. Genres can also be the focus of subcultural groups – see Box 4.11.

As noted in 2.5, genre is a concept that stands on uncertain ground. Jacques Derrida (see 4.10) suggests that all texts are generic in some way, and Steve Neale has pointed out that while there is much useful criticism done on well-known genres:

> Studies are needed of unrecognised genres like racetrack pics, of semi-recognized genres like drama, of cross-generic cycles and production trends like overland bus and prestige films, and of hybrid and combinations of all kinds.

> (Neale, 2000: 254)

There is much work still to be done.

2.8 Introduction to narrative

We are all familiar with stories, and it is this familiarity that narrative theory attempts to undermine, so as to allow us to be conscious of how films are structured. Much of what follows ranges from the straightforward – Todorov's idea of narrative disruptions – to the complex: the psychoanalytical and cognitive approaches.

Although Vladimir Propp published his seminal *Morphology of the Folktale* in 1928 it did not influence Western European thought until it was translated from Russian in the 1960s. By then Propp's structural approach found favour with the intellectual currents of the time. European and American intellectuals realised that the Russian Formalist School, which coalesced around the time of the Soviet 1917 Revolution, had made great strides in the theoretical analysis of literature. The advantage of the structural approach is that their theories could be applied to different media, including film.

In addition, the growth of film studies in academia during the 1960s, along with the politicization of cultural theories post-May '68 (see 5.10), meant the time was ripe for the development of theories of narrative based on film's formal characteristics.

It certainly was not preordained that film should be a narrative medium – photography is not – but there is no doubt that the vast majority of film now is narrative in form (also see Box 2.6). Narrative structure gives films a recognizable form, and the only films that are 'haphazard' in structure are those that intend to break narrative rules (or those that are ineptly made). Audiences expect a coherent narrative from mainstream films, and these regularly feature a three-act structure: (1) the setting and characters are established; (2) a struggle ensues between the protagonist and antagonist; (3) the final confrontation, usually ending in victory of the hero. These take approximately 25 per cent, 50 per cent and 25 per cent respectively of the running time.

Kristin Thompson (1999) has suggested that contemporary Hollywood is characterized by a four-act structure, which includes the initial set-up, a complicating action, the development, and the climax.

Thompson suggests that each of these four acts usually take about the same amount of time, and calls the junction between them a narrative 'turning point'. However the links between these acts, and the events that occur within them, must be logically constructed, as narrative is a cause–effect chain. For example, in *Eternal Sunshine of the Spotless Mind* (2004), Joel's (Jim Carrey) realization that Clementine (Kate Winslet) has erased him from her memory is a turning point, because he decides upon a particular action that leads the narrative in a 'different direction'; he stops trying to 'get her back' and has her removed from his memory. The acts are linked because it is logical that he should behave in this way once he has understood what Clementine has done.

Regardless of the number of acts, all conventional films are characterized by the same narrative structure described in the work of Tzvetan Todorov and Vladimir Propp.

2.9 Todorov and Propp

Todorov suggested that conventional narratives all have the same relatively simple structure:

> An 'ideal' narrative begins with a stable situation which is disturbed by some power of force. There results a state of disequilibrium; by the action of a force directed in the opposite direction, the equilibrium is re-established; the second equilibrium is similar to the first, but the two are never identical.
>
> (Todorov, 1977: 111)

For example, the crime in a detective story creates the disequilibrium. The forces of law and order try to restore the equilibrium by capturing the villain. They invariably succeed, although the status quo can never be totally restored, as the villain loses her or his freedom, and if the crime was murder, the corpse is unlikely to have been resurrected. A narrative in which the villain is apprehended straight away is not likely to grip audiences; on the other hand, if the perpetrator of the crime is never revealed the audience are likely to feel cheated.

Box 2.6 Early cinema and narrative

It is tempting to see the French pioneers of cinema, the Lumière brothers and Georges Méliès, as epitomizing two tendencies of cinema: realism and fantasy. Whilst the Lumière brothers filmed 'everyday' scenes such as *Leaving the Lumière Factory* (*La Sortie des Usines Lumière*, France, 1895), Méliès focused on fantastic special effects as in *Tunnelling the Channel* (*Tunnel sous La Manche ou Le Cauchemar Franco-Anglais*, France, 1907).

For the Lumière brothers, narrative was not important, although *The Waterer Watered* (*L'Arroseur Arrosé*, France, 1895) – featuring a man hosing his garden and being tricked by a boy – is considered to be the first filmed narrative. The Lumières' films were structured by the 50 ft length of film, so *Barque sortant du port* (France, 1895), showing a boat going out to sea, simply ends when the film runs out (Salt, *Early Cinema* video). Clearly the prime attraction of the Lumières' films, and their ilk, was their novelty value. This value was ephemeral, and it was necessary for films to offer more than 'everyday' scenes. The Lumières branched out with the 'travelogue', such as *Leaving Jerusalem by Railway* (France, 1896), and the 'topicals', reconstructions of newsworthy events, were also popular.

Film also had to 'evolve' formally to maintain popularity, and Georges Méliès found success with 'trick' films that used special effects such as in *Tunnelling the Channel* (1907). This 20-minute film consists of nine scenes (the longest of which is 206 seconds) joined by either dissolves or cuts. The camera remains static throughout, and all the scenes are in long shot. Although Méliès' special effects were sophisticated, his failure to develop film language further meant his films became repetitious, especially when compared with developments elsewhere. For example, the British pioneer R. W. Paul is credited with the first use of continuity editing, where one shot leads to another, in *Come Along, Do!* (1898) (Salt, 1992: 36b).

Edwin S. Porter, working in America, starting developing film's narrative form by using editing in a more sophisticated way, including an early version of 'cross-cutting' in *The Great Train Robbery* (1903). In this film, scenes at the telegraph office, the train robbery and a village dance are all shown using parallel editing (see 1.9).

The 'chase' film was important in the development of narrative cinema as it necessitated a narrative problem – the reason for the chase – and resolution, catching the fleeing individual(s). Similarly it encouraged the development of continuity editing:

> the disruption of the cut is naturalized by a continuity within the story. Specifically, this continuity is the actual movement of a character(s) that bridges the cuts. The end of one shot is signalled by characters leaving the frame, while the next shot is inaugurated by their reappearance. The disruption of the cut is... smoothed over by the continuity of the character's movement and the brief ellipsis of his action between shots is minimized rather than emphasized.
>
> (Gunning, 1990a: 91)

Gunning cites 1904 as the year the 'chase film' became established, and gives the example of *The Maniac Chase* and *Personal* from the American-based Biograph studio. It was at Biograph that D. W. Griffith was able to develop many aspects of film language familiar today. Although Griffith did not 'invent' these devices, such as the close-up, he did use them so effectively that they became entrenched in conventional film form almost immediately.

Gunning also suggested that Griffith established his reputation at a time when, in order to expand their market, filmmakers specifically addressed the middle-class audience. This led to an increase in censorship, administered by the newly formed Motion Picture Patents Company (MPPC) in 1908, to guarantee 'respectability', and higher production values:

> Attracting a middle-class audience entailed more than lighting the theatre and brightening the content of the films. The narrative structure of the films would have to be brought more in line with the traditions of bourgeois representation.
>
> (Gunning, 1990b: 339)

(It should be noted that it is debatable whether films were ever only attractive to mainly working-class audiences.) Griffith's morality was in tune with the bourgeoisie of the day, and so the racism in *The Birth of a Nation* (1915) was acceptable to many. The opening of *Broken Blossoms* (1919) has a title card that suggests there will be a moral lesson for us all in the tale, and so implies it is more than mere entertainment. Cinema, then, in the West at least, was consolidated as a bourgeois form with an emphasis on adaptations of plays and novels. Both theatre, and melodrama in particular, and novels are consummate narrative-based bourgeois creations (see Gledhill, 1987 and Watt, 2000). Before 1908:

> the primary sources for films seem to have been vaudeville and burlesque sketches, fairly-tales, comic strips and popular songs. These forms stressed spectacular effects of physical action, rather than psychological motivation.
>
> (Gunning, 1990b: 339–40)

It is interesting to note that pre-1908 cinema is not unlike some descriptions of contemporary Hollywood's 'high concept' movies (see 3.11).

Bordwell, Staiger and Thompson (1985) suggest that the 'classical' Hollywood style was formulated by 1917. However even by the time of *The General* (1926), a film considered to be quintessential 'classical' Hollywood cinema, there are occasionally 'lapses' in its use of editing. For example, when the protagonist's (Buster Keaton) 'girl' (Marion Mack) looks at him for a response when her brother enlists to fight in the Civil War, the 'eyeline match' shot is 'straight on' and not at the 45 degree angle it should be, given her position.

Tom Gunning offers an alternative view to that of the French pioneers of cinema, the Lumière brothers and Méliès, by suggesting that their respective 'realist' tendency and focus of spectacle can be united:

> ... in a conception that sees cinema less as a way of telling stories than as a way of presenting a series of views to an audience, fascinating because of their illusory power... and exoticism.
>
> (Gunning, 1990: 57)

Gunning dubs this a 'cinema of attractions' (see also Box 2.4), an exhibitionist cinema that included gazing directly at the camera that ruptured the 'invisible' fourth wall. While some commentators have suggested this looking into the camera, similar to a performer on stage directly addressing their audience, is symptomatic of 'primitive' cinema, Gunning believes that far from being primitive, it is a relatively sophisticated device used to hold audiences' attention, and it reinforced early cinema's link to fairground sideshows, with which it was competing for audiences.

It was not until the cinema became a primarily narrative medium, between 1907 and 1913, that the direct look at the camera became taboo; although Oliver Hardy continued to use it to great effect into the 1930s. Even Porter's *The Great Train Robbery*, an important film in the development of narrative cinema, included a last shot where a cowboy directly 'shoots' the audience, and so mixed narrative cinema with the 'sideshow stunt'.

In *28 Days Later* (Netherlands-UK-USA, 2002) Todorov's structure can be applied quite straightforwardly:

1. A state of equilibrium at the outset – 'everyday life'.
2. A disruption of the equilibrium by some action – release of virus.
3. A recognition that there has been a disruption – Jim (Cillian Murphy) wakes from a coma to find Britain has been 'wiped out'.
4. An attempt to repair the disruption – an attempt to get back to 'everyday life', although this will not be the same as life before the virus.
5. A reinstatement of the equilibrium – the survivors are found by a military aircraft.

Although this pattern is usually adhered to, there are exceptions. Applying 'Todorov' to *Minority Report* (2002) gives us the following pattern:

1. A state of equilibrium at the outset – in the future Precrime is used to capture people before they commit murder.
2. A disruption of the equilibrium by some action – Anderton (Tom Cruise) is found to commit a murder in the future.
3. A recognition that there has been a disruption – same as 2.
4. An attempt to repair the disruption – Anderton tries to prove he's been 'set up' (this is the narrative goal).
5. A reinstatement of the equilibrium – Anderton uncovers Lamar Burgess's (Max von Sydow's) plot, but Precrime is shut down.

Clearly the equilibrium here is not restored; the film is suggesting that it is wrong to go to any lengths in order to prevent crime. This is a topical issue in the twenty-first century, when greater surveillance of individuals is becoming the norm. However, the narrative of the film is not quite so straightforward. Witwer's (Colin Farrell's) attempt to close

Precrime can also be seen to be the narrative disruption. The fact that he is posthumously successful in this suggests that the narrative 'villain' (see Propp below) is successful, an extremely rare occurrence.

Narrative disruption can also be characterized as a 'lack'. For instance, in *American Pie 2* (2001) there is no equilibrium, as such, to be restored. What drives the narrative is the protagonists' lack of sex, a lack that is filled at the narrative's end. If the characters had been having sex and the opportunity for intercourse (as in *40 Days, 40 Nights*, USA-UK-France, 2002) was suddenly taken away from them, then the sudden lack would have been the disruption. The film deals with the (male?) teenager's perennial problem of getting the opportunity in the first place. In order to distinguish the film from the first *American Pie* (1999), the characters must have a goal that is separate from the problem of 'getting laid', and this is to have the 'party to remember for the rest of your life'.

Propp's contribution, based upon his analysis of fairy tales, offers a 31-stage structure that, essentially, adds more detail to Todorov's structure. Propp proposed that narratives have functions, usually enacted by characters, which motivate the cause–effect chain. For example, the villain causes the disruption of the equilibrium whilst the hero resolves it, often saving the (usually female) 'princess' in the process. Propp describes narrative as a linear cause–effect structure where the order of the 31 functions never varies, although all need not be included. In isolating the role of seven narrative functions Propp suggested that narratives were about the resolution of conflict, primarily between good and evil. Propp also emphasized the conventional movement toward heterosexual union (in fairy tales this is consummated in marriage).

So in *Spider-Man* (2002):

Heroes	Spider-Man/ Peter Parker	resolves disruption
Villains	Green Goblin/ Norman Osborn	creates disruption
Helpers	none	
Princesses	MJ	needs saving from villain
Donors	genetically modified spider	gives hero powers
Dispatchers of heroes	Uncle Ben	tells hero what to do
False heroes	none	

Interestingly *Spider-Man* does not have one disruption, caused by the Green Goblin, but two. The initial equilibrium is the ordinary life of Peter Parker (Tobey Maguire), who has the everyday 'teen' problems of being picked on by 'jocks' and not being able to compete with the rich kids to win the affections of his dream girl; generically the film is drawing upon the teen pic. This equilibrium is disrupted by the genetically modified spider, which gives Parker *heroic* powers that enable him to win his girl.

The second, and main, disruption (generically linked to the 'super hero-action' movie) is the appearance of the *villain*, the Green Goblin (Willem Dafoe), who uses MJ, the *princess* (Kirsten Dunst), as bait to get Spider-Man. Uncle Ben's advice about 'doing the right thing' guides Parker in his behaviour; he is, in effect, *dispatched* by Ben (Cliff Robertson) to do 'good'. As is usual, the hero overcomes the villain but, in an interesting twist, Parker realizes that as a superhero he cannot have a normal life and so rejects the princess he has won (which becomes the 'secondary' narrative problem in *Spider-Man 2*, 2004). This gives the conclusion, in a graveyard, a bleak twist at odds with most blockbuster films.

It is unusual for mainstream films to have two major disruptions, but this is explained – in this context – by the necessity to set up how Spider-Man gained his super powers. Throughout a narrative the hero will come across a number of obstacles he needs to overcome to ultimately triumph. Propp's 31 functions itemize these (see Lacey, 2000: 47) – they broadly correspond to Todorov's five points – and other writers have applied them to film (Christopher Vogler's influential *The Writer's Journey: Mythic Structure for Writers* (1998) clearly has its roots in Propp's work).

From a Proppian perspective, narratives are a conflict between two forces (the hero and villain), often conceived of as good versus evil. It is possible to read a film's ideological values from the principles the film's protagonist and antagonist have and from their behaviour. In *Spider-Man* doing good is defined as helping others, while the Green Goblin is a created by a rapacious capitalist. However definitions of good and bad change, so in the traditional Westerns the heroes were often involved in killing Native American Indians. At the time that was not seen to be a problem; however now the ideological consensus suggests that this was wrong. Modern Western heroes are more likely to be defending than killing Indians (See Box 2.7).

2.10 Story and Plot

Viktor Shklovsky, like Propp a Russian formalist, split narrative structure into *fabula* (story) and *syuzhet* (plot). Todorov's five-point structure equates to the 'story'; the plot may reorder these elements for aesthetic purposes.

For example, in murder mysteries the killing, which occurs near, or at, the start of the narrative, is the disruption. However the plot will probably not reveal the motivation for the killing, or the identity of the killer, until the end. The plot withholds a crucial part of the story. In addition the plot can reorder the chronology of the story through, for example, the use of flashbacks. *Memento's* (2000) 'plot' begins just before the 'story' ends.

Unusually *Memento*'s (2000) 'plot' *begins* just before the 'story' ends

The differences between 'story' and 'plot' can be summarized as shown in Figure 2.2.

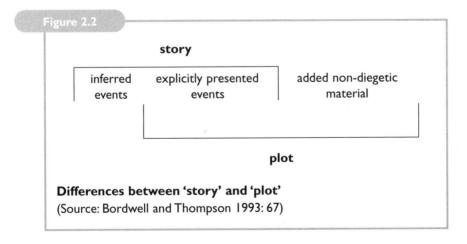

Figure 2.2		
story		
inferred events	explicitly presented events	added non-diegetic material
	plot	

Differences between 'story' and 'plot'
(Source: Bordwell and Thompson 1993: 67)

The 'story' is all the information, both shown and implied, in chronological order. Implied information can be both banal and crucial to the plot. For example a plot may indicate a character's journey by showing his or her departure and arrival. The middle part of the journey not shown by the plot is part of the 'story'. This is a narrative ellipsis, and a crucial creator of narrative economy. Implied information can also be given by dialogue, and this might be a crucial narrative point about, for example, a character's childhood (it can only be considered to be part of the 'plot' if it is shown in flashback).

The 'added non-diegetic material' refers to titles and voice-overs; these are not part of the story as they are external to it, but they are obviously aesthetic devices, hence they form part of the plot.

Box 2.7 Propp and *28 Days Later*

In *28 Days Later* (directed by Danny Boyle) the narrative disruption is caused by the virus (narrative 'villains' do not have to be people), which wipes out most of the population of Britain. One way of overcoming this disruption might have been to find a cure. However scriptwriter Alex Garland does not opt for that route. Once infected, humans become incurable zombies whose only desire is to infect others. If the virus is not to be cured, and the narrative is to be conventionally resolved, something else must take on the 'villain' function; this is Major Henry West, the commanding officer of a small group of troops.

Initially, it seems, he and his troops will save Jim (Cillian Murphy), Selena and Hannah (so he may therefore be seen as a 'false hero'). However, when it becomes clear that he intends to use Selena and Hannah as sexual outlets for his men, he becomes a problem that 'hero' Jim has to overcome.

Selena – particularly – and Hannah (Megan Burns) are Jim's 'helpers' and, when captured by West, 'princesses'. Initially, however, Jim was the 'princess' saved by Selena. This demonstrates a point Propp made, that the functions can move between characters.

'Heroes' are invariably male, and that remains the case in *28 Days Later*. However Selena is also a point of identification through her ability to *act*, rather than simply passively *respond*. In addition, Selena is played by a black actress (Naomi Harris), which points up the fact that strong black characters are even a rarer sight (in British cinema) than strong females. This play upon gender roles is further emphasized with Jim expressing the typically 'female' traits of caring (for Frank and Hannah) rather than 'survival at all costs', which Selena initially represents.

It should be emphasized that Propp was describing *function* and not character traits. So Major West, who is portrayed by Christopher Eccleston with some depth, is not simply villainous: he found that one of his men – who are mostly raw recruits – was about to commit suicide, so he promised 'women'. This saved the man's life, and women are necessary for procreation, which is the only reason for the survivors to live. For him the prostitution of the women is a necessary evil. Many of the heroes of *films noir* of the 1950s were not exactly paragons of morality; see for example *The Big Heat* (1953).

While Jim is the hero, and acts heroically in saving the women from being treated like unpaid prostitutes, he becomes very like (emphasized in performance and *mise en scène*) the zombies they have been fleeing. That he becomes a monster is emphasized by the way he gouges the eyes out of his last victim. Selena looks on apparently appalled, but then kisses Jim voraciously, signifying the animal strength of the survival (and sexual) instinct. In Freudian terms, the gouging of eyes is a symbolic castration, and so the sexual contest, between Jim and soldiers, for Selena is made explicit.

Not all narrative ellipses are about economy. As noted above, in mysteries essential information, such as the identity of the murderer, will be withheld from the 'plot' until the end. So in 'plot' terms *Minority Report* (2002) begins with Anderton preventing a murder; however Burgess' killing of Anne Lively (and the abduction of Anderton's son) happened before the plot began. They only become part of the 'plot' when shown through flashbacks. Clearly, if the film had started with showing Burgess committing his crime, an element of mystery would have been missing from the film. This mystery, and the questions 'who killed Lively and who abducted the boy?' are narrative 'enigmas' (see below) which keep audiences watching the film.

'Plot', then, is the aesthetic organization of the 'story' (which is structured as a cause–effect chain). The film's creator(s) choose(s) what elements to show and the order in which they appear. The opening of *Psycho* (1960) suggests that the camera could enter any one of the building's windows. However the narrative 'demands' that we find out what's going on in the bedroom inhabited by Marion (Janet Leigh) and Sam (John Gavin). There would be little point in entering a room inhabited by people who do not, in this film's case, meet Norman Bates (Anthony Perkins).

What we have considered so far deals with narrative structure, which is exterior to the content. Roland Barthes offered a 'micro' perspective by showing how narrative operated 'internally'.

2.11 Roland Barthes' narrative codes

Roland Barthes (1990, originally published in 1973) showed not only how five narrative codes combine to hook an audience into the narrative, but also how audiences bring their own understanding to the film. He helped establish the idea that consuming narratives is not simply a passive activity, and audiences are engaged in *creating* meaning through the reading of codes.

Realism is the dominant aesthetic in western society, and is based on the idea that an art form is mimicking reality by offering a window on the world. Barthes' insight was to show that realism in narratives was based upon the interaction of five codes: the enigma; action; semic; symbolic; cultural.

Enigma (hermeneutic) code: the function of this code is to engage audiences by offering a puzzle and then delaying the answer to the enigma. This delay does not necessarily take us to the end of a film (which it usually does in a murder mystery). For example the opening scene of Hitchcock's *Notorious* (1946) features Devlin (Cary Grant) sitting with his back to the camera and Alicia's (Ingrid Bergman's) gaze is constantly drawn to him. This sets up the enigma of who the character is (although audiences at the time were likely to recognize Grant) and what he is doing at the party. This is soon answered.

Occasionally, enigmas are not answered: when the 'Mystery man' in *Lost Highway* (1997) tells Fred (Bill Pullman) to his face, 'I'm at your home, phone me,' Fred complies to find that the man is in two places at once. This impossibility is never explained.

Enigma codes appear in five different ways. The 'snare' offers information that misleads audiences (for example through suggesting Witwer, in *Minority Report*, was a 'bad guy'). The 'equivocation' both snares and offers the truth (the suggestion, in *Signs* (2002) that the crop circles may have been created by aliens). The 'partial answer' stimulates the desire for the full answer (in *Psycho* the sheriff confirms that Norman's mother has been buried, leading to the question 'who is living in the house?'). The 'suspended answer' appears about to 'reveal all' but then the narrative turns another way (used as 'cliffhangers' in parallel editing, so in *The Day After Tomorrow* (2004) Jack Hall's (Dennis Quaid's) attempts to reach his son are cross-cut with Sam's (Jake Gyllenhaal's) fight for survival). 'Jamming' occurs in non-conventional films that refuse to 'explain all' (such as in the films of David Lynch).

Action (proairetic) code: this refers to an event that has a series of logical consequences. So a cowboy drawing a gun is an action code suggesting the probability of violence. The code is intended to help the audience comprehend where the narrative is going and, as a consequence, be motivated to continue watching the film. The other three codes are not about narrative flow but narrative detail.

Semic code: this refers to the connotations suggested by characters, objects and settings (see 1.3), which are all likely to work for the narrative. If we see cowboys with six-guns, we are confident that we are going to see a Western narrative. However, this is not always straightforwardly the case, as in *Tears of the Black Tiger* (*Far Talai Jone*, Thailand, 2000). Similarly, a shot of the Eiffel tower immediately tells us the narrative space is in France.

Symbolic code: as already noted, narratives are often about conflict between opposing forces. These forces often represent binary oppositions, and so the narrative function of the 'hero' conventionally embodies 'the good' while the 'villain' is 'bad'. In genres these oppositions can be definitive, such as the monster in horror films. By working out what they represent we can often find the ideological basis of a film. For example in *The Lord of the Rings* trilogy (New Zealand-USA, 2001–3) the symbolic code places Sauron in opposition to the hobbits. Sauron is represented through fascist imagery, while the communal aspects of the hobbits' lives are emphasized. The code can appear in many guises within one narrative, for example, the immortal:mortal opposition also articulated in the films. (Also see Box 2.8.)

Cultural (referential) code: this refers to the knowledge that audiences bring to a film. Spoofs, in particular, require audiences to know the films that are being referenced. For example, watching *Scary Movie* (2000) without knowledge of the *Scream* (1996–2000) trilogy was probably an (even more) empty experience. Genres too require audiences to possess cultural knowledge, although of course at some point audiences have to learn a genre's repertoire of elements (see 2.3). Similarly it is useful to have an understanding of Greek myths and the political climate of the 1990s Balkans to make sense of *Ulysses' Gaze* (*To Vlemma Tou Odyssea*, 1995, Greece-France-Italy) – see Appendix: 5.2.

Barthes emphasizes how meaning is created and is not a given 'natural'. Our understanding of semic codes, for instance, depends upon our cultural knowledge. As noted in the analysis of the production design in a scene from *The Sixth Sense* in Box 1.1, we gain meaning from understanding the connotations possessed by objects in the scene: for example, the meaning of a 'kitchen'. This cultural knowledge, what Bourdieu (1984) calls 'cultural competences', is not usually an issue in reading films, as most audiences tend to consume movies from cultures with which they are familiar. However, when reading other cultures, about which audiences have little or no knowledge, confusion is likely. For example:

> In *Xala*, the pestle is used as a metaphor to reinforce the impact of the collusion of African and Western cultures.... African customs demand that one must respect one's mother-in-law.
>
> (Ukadike, 1998: 574a)

However western feminist readings of the film (produced in Senegal, 1975) understood the pestle to represent a phallic symbol, leading to a complete misreading of the film's intentions. Similarly an understanding of the Japanese tradition of ghost stories aids comprehension of the *Ring* (*Ringu*) trilogy (1998–2000), as it is traditional in Japan that ghosts are female, and often they 'return from the dead' as a consequence of their fathers' actions. Similarly, the *obake yahsiki* (haunted house) is evoked in *Ringu 2* (Japan, 1999).

Cultural knowledge extends to understanding the way in which films make meaning. For example, the degree of a spectator's knowledge about a genre is crucial to his or her reading. Much of the misunderstanding of horror films is caused by the inability to read the filmic codes used because of a lack of cultural knowledge. For example, *The Evil Dead* (1981) was banned for many years in Britain, as the censors could not understand the ironic intent of the film.

Barthes used codes to contrast 'readerly' and 'writerly' texts. 'Readerly' films are easy to follow, as the codes are easy to understand and audiences can consume the film (relatively) passively. On the other hand, 'writerly' films require the audience to be active in the creation of meaning; here the coding is more complex. Mainstream films are usually 'readerly', whilst arthouse are 'writerly'. In arthouse films, for example, the enigmas may never be resolved (as in *Last Year in Marienbad* (*L'Année Dernière à Marienbad*), France-Italy, 1961).

Barthes' codes are useful in highlighting the particular purpose of a film's constituent parts. Other narrative theorists have taken a macro view.

2.12 Other approaches

A Freudian approach (see 4.6) to narrative emphasizes the Oedipal trajectory of conventional structures. Freud used the myth of Oedipus to explain the psychic processes necessary for a boy to become a man. This requires the boy to move his sexual fixation from his mother toward a mother substitute so he can become like his father. Raymond Bellour (2002) shows how Hitchcock's *North By Northwest* (1959) tightly fits this pattern, through Roger Thornhill (Cary Grant) being forced to 'stand up' to his mother, encountering an apparently 'loose' woman (aptly named Eve) who turns out to be 'good', saving her and then consummating their relationship (shown in the final shot of a train entering a tunnel):

> The hero proves his worthiness to take up his place as a man, by accomplishing a series of directed tests: a process which will often culminate, in self-contained narratives, with his integration into the cultural order through marriage... it provides the most familiar structure for such male-orientated Hollywood genres as the Western and the adventure film.
>
> (Krutnik, 1991: 87–8)

This trajectory is not necessarily triumphant. For example, in *Kiss Me Deadly* (1955), the hero's pathological greed for 'the great whatsit?', which he gets at the end, apparently leads to the destruction of the world.

The fact that Eve (Eva Marie Saint) in *North By Northwest* at first appears to be bad (a 'gangster's moll'), before being redeemed as a 'normal woman in need of a good man', emphasizes the role of gender definition inherent in the structure of Oedipal narratives. The movement toward heterosexual 'coupledom', with the woman in the subordinate position, allows transgression to be portrayed only to be 'earthed' in convention:

> The therapeutic function of mainstream Hollywood cinema would be to give play to fantasies of deviancy, disruption, and otherness, before channelling them in such a way as to affirm a single final goal: the establishment and maintenance of a nuclear family, under conditions of bourgeois ideology, capitalism, and patriarchy.
>
> (Elsaesser and Buckland, 2002: 223)

So difference is dramatized in order to be rejected in favour of conformity. For many the notion of the Oedipal complex is absurd ('how could I desire my mum!? Yuk!'). However Freudians dismiss this as symptomatic of how we deal with transgressive thoughts. Films rarely 'act out' this narrative explicitly (although Elsaesser and Buckland's analysis of *Back to the Future* (1985) shows how it can lie just beneath the surface) and require a 'symptomatic' reading (see 4.5) to unearth the trajectory.

For Freud the *fort-da* game, when a baby throws a rattle out of its cot for a responsible adult to return, is one of the first instances when a child realizes that he or she can have control over their environment. It is also:

> perhaps the shortest story we can imagine: an object is lost, and then recovered. But even the most complex narratives can be read as variants on this model …
>
> (Eagleton, 1983: 185)

For the child the lack is soon restored (or he/she bawls his or her eyes out if it is not). The psychoanalytical view suggests that the narrative 'problem' represents our lack of wholeness (as a subject), which the narrative resolution restores. However:

> The text provides substitutes for the missing object, but can never finally portray the moment of wholeness and completion. It must end as the lovers embrace, or the Nazis are conquered, but cannot show what comes afterwards, for any such material will always be a disappointment. It will always reawaken a sense of lack.
>
> (Jancovich, 1995: 140)

This sense of wholeness (Jacques Lacan's version of psychoanalysis suggests human beings 'lack' experience from the 'mirror phase' onwards: see 4.6) can only be a temporary phenomenon, and indeed ceases as soon as we leave the movie theatre or finish watching a film at home.

Contrary to the psychoanalytical approach, Bordwell (1985) outlined a cognitive way of understanding narrative. They used the discourse of cognitive psychology to try to understand how we both comprehend and recall narratives. Cognitive psychology studies how the mind makes sense of the world, and suggests that schemata serve a crucial function:

> A schema is an arrangement of knowledge *already possessed* by a perceiver that is used to predict and classify new sensory data.… A schema assigns probabilities to events and to parts of events.
>
> (Branigan, 1992: 13)

So once we have learned the schema of conventional narrative, as outlined in a basic form by Todorov, we have a framework with which to view a film. Genre is also a schema, as is the expectation that a star will play an important character. However schemata that we use in everyday life will also come into play, so any partial representation of information will be rendered complete by our expectation: if we can only see three sides of a cube, we 'add' the unseen sides in order to comprehend the object. It is in this way that audiences complete the story from the plot – see 2.10.

Film language acts in a similar fashion. For example we know that any close-up is likely to signify narrative importance. Thus in *Requiem for a Dream* (2001), the close-up of the wound in Harry's (Jared Leto's) arm tells us that this will become an important point later.

The use of schemata explains how we recall narrative:

> [we] tend to *remember* a story in terms of *categories of information stated as propositions, interpretations, and summaries* rather than remembering the way the story is actually presented or its surface features.
> (Brannigan, 1992: 15, emphasis in original)

So, for example, while we rarely recall exactly what characters say, or every action they make, we can offer summaries that are usually intelligible. Schemata can change through interaction with the environment, although the basic narrative structure has barely changed for thousands of years. Raymond Bellour (2002) has suggested that narrative, like genre, can be conceived of as being the 'same and different'.

2.13 Postmodern narratives

Postmodern narratives are characterized by their playfulness, self-referentiality, and, often, vacuity. Postmodernism, however, can go further than this and suggest that post-capitalist society (where the economy is driven by consumerism rather than manufacturing) has reduced everything to surfaces, including human beings. Our sense of ourselves, it is argued, is often derived from the media (for example, 'lifestyle' magazines), and our understanding of the world is (virtually) wholly constructed by the media (for example, news and documentaries).

One of the more radical stances of postmodernism suggests that we are posthuman. While the bourgeois conception of personality suggests that we consist of a coherent whole, although we may struggle to 'find our self', the postmodern human is a slippery concoction that denies the possibility of truly 'knowing ourselves'. For example the split and parallel identities of the characters in *Sex and Lucía* (Spain-France, 2001) offer a 'schizophrenic' representation of human beings (see Box 2.8), and *Suzhou River* (China-Germany, 2000) also splits its characters and offers a social critique of the (new) Chinese slacker generation.

Although postmodern films can be meaningful, in Hollywood the postmodern aesthetic is most likely to be apparent in the surface gloss of 'high concept' narratives. The typical summer action movies tend to use the narrative as a vehicle on which to hang special effects and pithy, self-referential one-liners. The argument that postmodern Hollywood has dispensed with narrative, however, is over-stated (although director Simon West did say that this was his ambition in *Lara Croft: Tomb Raider*, USA-UK-Germany-Japan, 2001), although *Moulin Rouge* (USA-Australia, 2001) came pretty close to doing so.

One of the symptoms of postmodernism is its lack of historical perspective, so Geoffrey Chaucer, in *A Knight's Tale* (2001), can be played by Paul Bettany as a 'warm up' comedian. That said, historical context was also absent in Shakespeare's time, so he could happily include clocks in *Julius Caesar*: the word 'anachronism' did not exist until 30 years after his death. It is not just Hollywood that exploits the attractions of postmodernism. In *Fulltime Killer* (*Chuen jik sat sau*, 2001, Hong Kong) postmodern playfulness is highlighted through explicit, and implicit, references to action cinema and having the end 'rewritten' by the disgraced investigating cop.

Pastiche is another aspect of the postmodern aesthetic. The 'TV reality show' formed the basis of the film *Series 7: The Contenders* (2000). The film's perfect mimicking of the formal characteristics of 'reality shows' – down to the pseudo-profound insights of the contestants speaking about their experiences after the event – marks it as a pastiche, as it lacks the exaggeration required of parody. Hopefully the content (as the show required contenders to kill each other) will remain an exaggeration. It is left to the audience to decide whether the film is satirizing reality shows or simply trying to make money by being funny; either way, audiences stayed away from the film's box office.

Blade Runner (1982) is often cited as an exemplary postmodern text in its mix of *film noir* and science fiction (so inspiring the creation of cyberpunk, which Frederic Jameson has called the 'supreme literary expression of if not postmodernism, then of late capitalism itself' (1991: 419)). The film's narrative space is filled with a range of architectural designs including the Mayan temples of the Tyrell Corporation and the Gothic grandeur of the Bradbury apartments. By mixing different eras into a future the original meanings of these architectural styles is lost. This recycling, appropriating signs and practices in such a way that their original meaning is lost, is called *bricolage*. *Bricolage* is characteristic of postmodernism as it is ahistorical in nature.

Box 2.8 Postmodern narratives – *Sex and Lucía* (Spain-France, 2001) and *Blue Velvet* (USA, 1987)

Postmodern films, amongst a plethora of other things, highlight their own existence as a medium, not with the modernist (or Brechtian) purpose of alienating audiences from the text, but in order to suggest that nothing can have definitive meaning. However, postmodernism can also be used to suggest uncomfortable 'truths' about contemporary (western) society.

The opening titles of *Sex and Lucía* (in Spanish the title, *Lucía y El Sexo*, draws attention to the character before libido), appears as if they are being typed – using traditional typewriter font – on a word processor, and a central character is a novelist, so the fabricated nature of the film is immediately emphasized.

In mainstream cinema we expect the narrative world presented to be logical in its own terms. The cause and effect chain of narrative is crucial in creating a convincing canvas on which events are acted out. In *Sex and Lucía* (directed by Julio Medem) it soon becomes clear (?!) that the events we are seeing are a dramatization of Lorenzo's novel. However, it is also possible that Lorenzo (Tristan Ulloa) is writing a novel based on his experiences, which we are being shown in flashback. In addition, of course, we are aware that we are watching a fictional film peopled by characters played by actors. Some critics have suggested that the film is a profound statement about the human condition, while others have decided it is simply an example of postmodern frippery:

> Medem may have disrobed most of the cast, leaving their bodies exposed, but the plot remains as guarded as a virgin with a chastity belt. That's why *Sex and Lucía* is so alluring.
> (Marta Barber, 2002)

Or:

> 'Sex and Lucía' is a beautifully made piece of unwatchable drivel.
> (Waldron-Mantgani, 2003)

Those who are unconvinced by the contrivance of the narrative can at least enjoy the craftsmanship of the filmmaking and the performances of the cast. In addition, pleasure can be gained from the film's use of Barthes' symbolic code:

➤ The moon (the daughter is called Luna), representing female sexuality, is graphically matched (via editing) with a light (Lucía) and a pregnancy test.

➤ The phallic lighthouse is juxtaposed with a hole into which both Lucía (Paz Vega) and Carlos/Antonio (Daniel Friere) fall (Lorenzo starts the film by telling Lucía he's 'in a hole'). This hole is also at the end of Lorenzo's story, where it takes us back to the middle of the narrative.

➤ Lucía's orgasm is followed by Elena giving birth.

The postmodern aesthetic is also present in the film's form, as Medem explains:

> the movie was shot using CineAlta Hi-Definition 24p. It was incredible. This was the third movie in the world using this format. Since Lucía was escaping from a tragedy, she escapes that beautiful island that she steps on. And suddenly those characters have the right to do with that island whatever they want; for example, with the light. Also, when I went to the island with the camera, I forced the light. This overexposed light that almost blinds you, it's like the characters erasing themselves and starting from zero, so they can start again. That's the idea I had when I was shooting with my small camera when I first went to the island...
>
> Every story, in a sense, is a search. You're searching for the reason for that story to exist. There's always a destiny.
>
> (www.indiewire.com/people/int_Medem_Julio_020711.html, accessed October 2003)

Although the film claims, at its conclusion, that stories can change halfway through, this obviously is not the case with film. The elusiveness of the film's narrative virtually requires a second viewing, but it may remain an enigma, or a chimera according to taste, even after close study.

Blue Velvet is also an elusive film. However it offers itself much more readily to traditional decoding. Director David Lynch, in the opening sequence, plunges us into small-town America. However, the too blue sky and the overly white picket fence suggests a hyper-reality; in other words, the excessiveness of the imagery draws attention to itself, and so we are conscious that we are looking at the representation of a representation. This is emphasized at the film's conclusion where a palpably mechanical robin, representing love, sings to the protagonists.

Lynch's small town is surreal. The picket fence is followed by a slow-motion fireman waving, with a dog sitting on the travelling fire engine's running board, and is shown to conceal an underworld (symbolized by bugs) where Frank (Dennis Hopper) and Dorothy (Isabella Rossellini), a long way from Oz, become 'nice boy next door' Jeffrey's (Kyle McLachlan's) surrogate parents.

Another postmodern symptom is the confusion about when the film is set:

> the locations and characters are from the 1950's, the stylistics are from the 1940's, the themes are from the 1980's.
>
> (Pearson, 1997)

As if in a supermarket (or maybe hypermarket) Lynch selects signs from cinema and appropriates them for his own purposes:

> The ideas of small town innocence borrow heavily from Hitchcock's *Shadow of a Doubt*, the opening heart-attack sequence refers to the Lumière brothers' *L'Arroseur Arrose* (1896). The Badalamenti score seems derivative of the music in *Experiment in Terror* (Blake Edwards 1962), a film set in a suburb called 'Twin Peaks' (Twin Peaks also featured heavy 'borrowing', with specific references to Preminger's *Laura* (1944), Hitchcock's *Vertigo* (1958) and Robert Wise's *Born To Kill* (1947)).
>
> (Pearson, 1997)

Pearson argues that the appropriation of the genre is pastiche rather than parody, as it simply lifts the imagery without subverting it. However, the innocence of the Lumière brothers' film is surely derided, as the gardener (Jeffrey's father) suffers a stroke; and the darkness that comes to town in the shape of Uncle Charlie (Joseph Cotton), in Hitchcock's *Shadow of a Doubt* (1943), is not quite as perverse as Frank.

There are many other aspects to postmodernism, for example its denial of meta-narratives such as religion. Postmodern films stretch from the banality of the most formulaic of Hollywood movies to the complexity evident in David Cronenberg and David Lynch.

Both genre and narrative are concepts used by all film watchers, the former explicitly, the latter implicitly. Because they are basic building blocks of meaning it is crucial that we study them. However we must be careful never to lapse into description ('that's part of the repertoire of elements; he's the narrative hero'), we must always strive to unearth what they represent. This may lead us simply to other texts (as in genre or postmodern playfulness) or enable us to understand the 'deep structures' of narratives that hold our, and millions of other people's, attention.

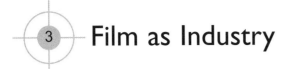

3 Film as Industry

3.1 Introduction

Films are very expensive to make. This fact is enough to mean that film is primarily a commercial venture; there are not many 'vanity' projects issued on celluloid (Mel Gibson's *The Passion of the Christ*, 2004, is one very successful example). The biggest industry in the word in terms of films produced is India. However in terms of money and global reach Hollywood reigns supreme. Hence this chapter will focus on the history of Hollywood as a business.

It should be noted that this is not without its problems:

> Asian countries, taken together, produce over half of the yearly world production. Burma, Pakistan, South Korea, Thailand, the Philippines, Indonesia, and even Bangladesh produce over 50 features films a year.
>
> (Stam, 2000: 21)

The reason very few films from the above countries feature in this book is due to the fact they are rarely distributed in Britain. This is partly because of the stranglehold American companies have upon distribution; I have never, for example, seen a film from Bangladesh.

3.2 The beginning of cinema

People watch films in the hope of gaining emotional and/or intellectual satisfaction; in other words they are watched as works of art. However, because most films exist to make money, the business is about entertainment. However art and entertainment are not mutually exclusive.

The first cinema screening was in Paris December 1895. The Lumière brothers showed what were, in effect, home movies. Georges Méliès established the fiction film as an audience favourite (Alice Guy-Blaché made the first fiction film in 1896) and, unlike the Lumières, who focused on 'everyday life', his films were special effect extravaganzas featuring, for example, *Le Voyage dans la Lune* (1902) – see also Box 2.6.

Cinema was established as a sideshow novelty and it probably was not until the more affluent middle classes got interested, by the mid-1900s, that purpose-built cinemas – Nickleodeons – were created. The formation of film exchanges also helped the industry expand:

> Exhibitors could change their programmes more frequently, even daily; if they could pay bigger fees than their rivals they could get new products and advertise 'first-run; pictures...'
>
> (Shipman, 1982: 36b)

In an attempt to corner the profits being generated by the nascent industry, several companies formed the Motion Picture Patents Company, which had, by the end of the decade, taken over virtually all of the most important film exchanges. Thus a cartel was formed (a group of companies acting together to create, in effect, a monopoly). Companies outside the cartel, which was based in New York, sought a new space to make films, and took the mythic American route west to the 'land of opportunity'. California offered a climate, landscape, cheap land and workers, which enabled Hollywood to become a place synonymous with commercial cinema. Hollywood became, within a few years, an institution with particular ways of producing, distributing and exhibiting movies.

Despite a dip in fortunes in 1918 (caused at least in part by the Spanish 'flu epidemic) Hollywood began its world dominance over most of the film-exhibiting nations soon after the First World War. Before the war, many European nations (including Britain, Sweden and Italy) had thriving industries. However, it is doubtful whether the war fatally wounded these national cinemas, for Hollywood was poised to dominate regardless of the socio-political events in the 'Old World'. The war years, however, did eradicate foreign competition in North America and after the war:

> while film-makers in France, Germany, and Sweden were discovering new artistic dimensions – the film's potentialities for exploring psychology and atmosphere, for lyricism and for new sensory and visual experiences – the American cinema had settled in its ways of being primarily a story-telling medium.
>
> (Robinson, 1968: 56)

3.3 Hollywood – the formation of the major studios

North America cinema benefited in its early years, as it does now, from having a massive indigenous market. In addition, a large number of immigrants who were flowing into the country, helping establish its economic supremacy, did not understand English, so 'silent' cinema was ideally placed to entertain this audience. If your local market is large, and demand is good, then it is relatively easy to make a profit. Any revenue gained after 'black ink' has registered (after distribution costs have been accounted for) is additional profit. Producers can therefore price their film very competitively (cheaply) when distributing it abroad, as they are no longer trying to recoup their initial investment.

In addition, having a large market means that more money can be spent on film, and so it has 'high production values'. This in itself forms part of Hollywood film's appeal. Producers can also afford the most expensive stars (see 3.17) and so on. By the 1920s Hollywood had evolved into the institution that is still recognizable:

> In 1912 Carl Laemmle had established Universal.... In 1914 Adoph Zukor had united his production company, Famous Players, with Jesse Lasky; and formed Paramount Pictures.... William Fox merged his Box Office Attractions into the Fox Film Company.... In 1915 Richard Rowland and a group of partners who included Louis B. Mayer inaugurated Metro Pictures. Sam Goldfish.... [formed] the Goldwyn Company.
>
> (Robinson, 1968: 26–7)

One thing that most of the men, the 'movie moguls', who formed Hollywood had in common is that they were European immigrants. The importance of immigrants to Hollywood's success cannot be over-stated. During the 1930s, when a lot of Germans and Jews, in particular, were fleeing the Nazis, there was a massive creative input into American cinema. This has continued in contemporary Hollywood, with the directors Wolfgang Petersen, Ridley and Tony Scott, John Woo and Lasse Hallstrom, among others, all having box office success.

The men who ran the studios were businessmen; the value of a film, for them, was measured by the box office revenue and not aesthetic value. They ran studios as factories, with strict division of labour and a clear managerial hierarchy. This emphasis on 'film as commodity' was intensified by Wall Street's early investment in the industry. The Wall Street:

> bureaucrats and accountants, eager to overcome the unpredictable and intractable elements in the creation of films, began to codify certain principles of commercial production that still prevail in the industry: the attempt to exploit proven success with formula

Table 3.1

Majors (the 'big five') 1920s	2004
Loew's/Metro-Goldwyn-Mayer	merged with United Artists in 1981 bought by Sony in 2004
Paramount	part of Viacom
RKO	went bust after being asset-stripped by Howard Hughes in the 1950s
Fox (became Twentieth Century-Fox in the 1930s)	part of News Corporation
Warner Bros.	part of Time Warner
Mini-majors (the 'little three')	
Universal	NBC bought controlling interest in 2003
Columbia	part of Sony Corporation
United Artists	became part of MGM in 1981, bought by Sony in 2004
Poverty Row	
Monogram	
Republic	
Tiffany	

The Hollywood studios 1920s and 2004

pictures and cycles of any particular genre which temporarily sells, at the expanse of other and perhaps unorthodox products; the quest for predictable sales values – star names, best-selling success titles, costly and showy production values – which in fact have little to do with art.

(Robinson, 1968: 30)

The majors were dominant because they were 'vertically integrated', that is they could produce, distribute and exhibit films. Although the mini-majors did not own any cinemas, they did have access to the majors' first-run theatres. Despite appearances of competition,

Hollywood's eight studios did not compete with each other and intimidated new entrants to the industry, so the film business was an oligopoly.

Because films were distributed initially to first-run theatres, the fact that the major studios owned four-fifths of these meant they could maximize their exhibition revenue. Overall they owned only about one-sixth of all cinemas.

First-run theatres charged a premium, but the studios also exercised control over exhibition in the theatres they did not own. The system of block booking meant that independent cinemas could not pick which movies they wanted to show; they had to take the selection on offer. For every potential hit in a selection there would be several duds. In addition, there was usually a 30 day 'clearance' between runs, so after the first run a film would be unavailable for a month before it started its second run and so on. This encouraged audiences to see the film when it was initially released, so they would pay more, usually in a studio-owned cinema. (A similar practice is employed with the release of DVDs now.)

Because exhibition of Hollywood products was guaranteed, the production line approach to filmmaking was possible. Stars, directors, script writers – indeed all personnel – were under contract, they were paid a fixed weekly amount regardless of whether they were working or not, and they were worked hard:

➤ One of the biggest box office stars of the early 1930s, Marie Dressler, appeared in over half a dozen films in 1930.
➤ John Ford directed five films in 1928.
➤ Scriptwriter Dudley Nichols was involved in eight productions in 1935.

(Source: Internet movie database, www.imdb.co.uk.)

Contrast this with contemporary Hollywood: Tom Cruise appeared in nine films during the *whole* of the 1990s; Steven Spielberg directed six films and William Goldman had nine writing credits during the decade. It is obviously a lot harder to *learn* the movie-making craft now than it was during the Golden Age.

Basing itself on Henry Ford's revolutionary production line techniques, Hollywood styled itself a dream factory with a production line that churned out films like cars:

MGM [produced] one feature film per week, a quota enabled by its standardized genres, enormous physical plant, strict definition of roles, and a star system whose performers remained as alienated from their tasks as any factory worker.

(Ray, 1998: 67–8)

The dominance of the oligopoly also made it very difficult for foreign distributors to get their films exhibited in America. This contrasts strongly with the easy access American films had, and continue to have, to most overseas markets.

3.4 Hollywood and censorship

To audiences brought up on Hollywood movies made since the 1970s, it appears that there was no sex in films made before that decade. While it is true that the representation of sex before the 1960s often owed a debt to Sigmund Freud (for example the cut to a – phallic – lighthouse in *Casablanca*, 1942), there is little doubt that many in the audiences of the time would have been adept at reading the subtext. On the other hand, contemporary audiences do not notice the subtle representations of sex as we are used to seeing explicit imagery.

While European cinema was more likely to feature nudity – see the Czechoslovakian *Extase* (1932) – Hollywood had prevented itself from using explicitly titillating images to appeal to the audience by creating the Hays Office. Hollywood was aware that its 'hicks in the sticks' audience did not like controversial material:

> New York exhibitor Arthur L. Mayer observed that [*Crime without Passion*, 1934]'s appeal was 'consciously directed to metropolitan audiences eager for the unconventional, the subtle and the artistic'. The patrons of small-town theatres, on the other hand, were 'more appreciative of human, conventional stories and of conservative technique in their presentation'.
>
> (Maltby, 1999: 27)

The self-regulatory Hays Office was set up to stave off outside interference engendered by a number of scandals engulfing Hollywood in the early 1920s. Most prominent was the alleged involvement – he was acquitted by the courts – of 'Fatty' Arbuckle in the death of actress Virginia Rappe. Led by William Randolph Hurst's 'yellow press' (the 'gutter press' of the time), Arbuckle was smeared with rape allegations which ended his career.

Cecil B. DeMille must have used all his contacts to get this scene, from *The Sign of the Cross* (1932), past the censors

All scripts had to be submitted to the Hays Office, whose 'Purity Code' insisted upon the 'law of compensating values'. In other words, it was necessary that any immoral (sexual or criminal) behaviour be punished at the end of the narrative. Hence the gangster films had to climax with the protagonist being 'killed off'.

When the Depression hit in the 1930s, producers began pushing at the boundaries of what the Hays Office would allow in an attempt to stimulate audience attendance. However, the Catholic League of Decency, and other conservative groups, pressurized the MPPDA (the Motion Picture Producers and Distributors of America) to put 'teeth' into self-regulation. Hence the Production Code was introduced in 1934, overseen by Joseph Breen. He ensured that films would offend (virtually) no one for the next two decades. The Code was also to act as a bar upon innovation, as conservatives, by their nature, do not like anything new.

Some of the Code's strictures are still evident in Hollywood now. For example, sexual relations between different races should not be shown; *Angel Heart* (1987) was subject to vilification because of the explicit sex scene between the (black) Lisa Bonet and (white) Mickey Rourke. However 2001's *crazy/beautiful* – including a sex scene with WASP Kirsten Dunst and Hispanic Jay Hernandez – seemed to have passed without controversy, as did the scene in the same year's *O*.

The influence of the code can also be seen in the way film was edited:

> The representation of what would now be called violence was in practice fairly precisely codified by the conventions of state and municipal censorship during the 1920s... for example... a character could not normally shoot another character in a two-shot; the image of the gun being fired had to be separated from the representation of its impact by a cut.
>
> (Maltby, 2001: 121)

The aesthetic implications of self-censorship did not bother Hollywood, they simply saw it as a way of avoiding outside interference in their pursuit of profit. In 1952 the Supreme Court declared films were 'a significant medium for communication of ideas' and were there-fore protected by constitutional freedom of speech. This meant, in effect, that states could no longer ban films, and this ruling started the process by which Hollywood films could engage with 'adult' themes. In 1953 *The Moon is Blue* started the ball rolling by using the words 'virgin' and 'mistress' in its script. During the 1960s films such as *The Pawnbroker* (1965), with female nudity, and 'foul-mouthed' *Who's Afraid of Virginia Woolf?* (1966) pushed the boundaries of self-regulation, culminating in the Oscar winning X-rated *Midnight Cowboy* (1969). However the 20th Century Fox-produced *Beyond the Valley of the Dolls* (1970), made by cult director Russ Meyer, was deemed to have overstepped the bounds of decency, and Hollywood has eschewed X-rated (now NC-17 rated) movies ever since; partly because many publications will not carry adverts for these films and Blockbuster video stores will not stock them.

3.5 Hollywood – the coming of sound

One of the abiding myths of Hollywood is that, as a business, it is badly run (that is, it's not really a business because 'there's no business like show business') and has persistently tried to ignore technological advances. By this account, Hollywood resisted the arrival of sound, radio and television. However, as Janet Wasko (1994) shows, the major studios were involved in experiments with early radio and television, and after a hesitant start, embraced sound film as a way to bolster profitability.

'Silent' cinema had never really been silent. Even the smallest theatres – fifth-run cinemas in the 'sticks' – would have, at least, piano accompaniment. The term 'theatre' was not simply a relic of cinema's similarity to stage shows, live performances were included:

> by the mid-1920s formulae had been established for live show presentations.... The picture palace show, of about two- to two-and-a-half hours, opened with music from the house orchestra. Then came the live presentation of usually twenty minutes, followed by a series of shorts, almost always including a set of newsreels. Next came the climax of the show, the feature film.
>
> (Gomery, 1992: 217)

Such an extravagant programme was limited to the larger theatres, usually in metropolitan areas. The coming of sound was initially motivated by the desire to replace the live vaudeville acts with one or two-reel versions of those acts and so make the show cheaper. Hence what is generally regarded as the first 'talkie', *The Jazz Singer* (1927), was made after Warner Bros. had run out of vaudeville acts.

Originally this film was to be conventionally made (that is, 'silent'), until the lead, and big vaudeville star of the time, Al Jolson, sang. It was simply a way of incorporating Jolson's act into a feature. In the event Jolson improvised a conversation with his 'mother' and also addressed a nightclub audience with the prescient line, 'You ain't heard nothing yet.' The movie was a box office sensation.

Warner Bros.'s talkie follow–up, *The Singing Fool* (1928), was an even bigger hit. The financial success of 'talkies' helped establish Warner Bros. as one of the five majors:

> The company's assets rose from $5 million in 1925 to a staggering $230 million in 1930.
>
> (Eyles, 1979: 17c)

Despite this, the arrival of sound – with its requirement for intensive capital investment – was badly timed, because it coincided with the stock market crash of 1929, which led to a severe recession during the 1930s.

3.6 Hollywood decline: the Paramount decrees and the baby boom

A vertically integrated Hollywood allowed the major studios to extract maximum profit at every stage of the cinematic process: production, distribution and exhibition. Having weathered the Depression the industry was booming when around 90 million people went to the movies every week in 1946. Hollywood was riding the crest of a wave. However, as the metaphor suggests, a crash was soon to follow. A simple version of history might suggest that the arrival of television was to blame for the precipitous decline in Hollywood's fortunes from the late 1940s; the real picture was more complex.

In 1938 the Department of Justice's Antitrust Division filed a suit (the Paramount decrees) against Hollywood which, it had decided, was acting in an anti-competitive fashion (the block bookings and 'clearances' mentioned in 3.3). It took nearly 10 years for the suit to yield fruit. Block booking was made illegal in 1946, and from 1948 the major studios started selling off their cinema chains; this took a decade to complete (Conant, 1976). This meant Hollywood could no longer guarantee all its films would be exhibited, and the studios lost revenue from cinemas, as well as their real estate value. This created some opportunities for independent producers – see below.

However audiences did not decline because the majors no longer owned the biggest cinemas. Demographic changes meant that the most frequent cinemagoers – that is, college-educated under-30s – were busy raising children and moving out to the suburbs, which lacked cinemas. The boom in baby making was not simply a result of the end of the Second World War: demand had been bottled up even earlier when the Depression had financially inhibited child rearing.

Although people did not have more income to spend straight after the war, their considerable savings (as there had been few 'luxury' goods to buy during the war) were spent on 'nesting'. The expansion of the suburbs, away from city-centre cinemas, exacerbated the problem: no one wanted to build cinemas as attendance was in decline; attendance was in decline because many people did not have a local cinema.

Television, which did not gain significant penetration until 1952, merely twisted the knife. Home-centred entertainment was ideal for parents struggling to bring up little 'brats'.

Without guaranteed exhibition, and the loss of cinema profits, plus declining audiences, the major studios had to reduce the number of films they made. This meant a reduction in the number of contracts. Stars would no longer work necessarily to a studio's dictates: they could be hired picture by picture. This led to the growth of independent producers and production companies, sometimes run by stars themselves.

Independent producers were not new; the 'Poverty Row' studios were independent, as was David O. Selznick, producer of the massive hit *Gone With the Wind* (1939). The two biggest films of 1946 were both 'indies': *The Best Years of Our Lives* (Sam Goldwyn) and *Duel in the Sun* (Selznick).

Their independent status was, however, qualified:

> few independents actually [were] free to decide the film's content and its method of production ... the majority of so-called independents, even since 1950, have had to go to a national distributor for at least part of their equity funds.
>
> (Conant, 1976: 353)

Ironically, the reduction in the majors' control over distribution and exhibition made it even harder for the independent sector:

> having fought hard to dismantle the vertically integrated power for the majors, the independents now made an about-turn, in an attempt to reinstate the stable industrial model upon which they had previously... depended upon for their livelihoods.
>
> (Allen, 2003: 29)

From the 1950s onward Hollywood experienced a slow decline, and eventually the majors were subsumed into larger conglomerates. By the 1950s the studios realized that television was not simply competition for audience, but also a way of making money from their old films. In addition they got involved in making 'films' for television. This did not, however, prevent the continued financial decline of Hollywood. It is worth noting that the studios reacted with similar hostility to the arrival of the videocassette in the 1970s, seeing the medium as competition rather than an additional source of revenue.

3.7 New Hollywood? The early 1970s

By 1970 annual attendance in North American cinemas had dipped below 20 million per week, the lowest figure since the birth of Hollywood, and the major studios had little idea how to arrest the decline. The studios had also indulged in over-production, using the mud-at-the-wall principle that if they produced a large number of big-budget films some of them would be massive hits, like *The Sound of Music* (1965) (Maltby, 1998). Out of this economic slump came 'New Hollywood' cinema or 'renaissance Hollywood'.

Bonnie and Clyde (1967) broke the mould of Hollywood product. The script (by David Newman and Robert Benton) was a conscious attempt to mimic the French *nouvelle vague* (New Wave) of the early 1960s (see 5.7), and was offered to both Jean-Luc Godard and François Truffaut. They declined, and it was not until Warren Beatty got attached to the script that Warner Bros. decided to finance the film. Indeed Beatty did not simply star in the movie, he also produced it, and was instrumental in getting the film re-released after its disastrous first run.

Bonnie and Clyde was unconventional in a number of ways. It was not simply because the central characters were anti-heroes, outlaws, as Warner Bros.'s gangster movies had celebrated villains in the 1930s; Clyde's bisexuality (played by pin-up Beatty) was groundbreaking, and the film's narrative focuses as much on the domestic squabbles of the Barrow gang as it does on the robberies and shootouts familiar in the genre. In addition, the 'heroes' meet their demise in an incredibly violent hail of bullets at once intensified, and aestheticized, by the use of slow motion.

The film was also heavily influenced formally by the New Wave, including the liberal use of jump cuts. The critics' reception of the film was as varied and violent as the stresses tearing at contemporary American society, which was embroiled in the Vietnam War as well as the civil and women's rights movements. *Bonnie and Clyde* was a belated box office hit appealing to the burgeoning counter culture. In the same year *The Graduate*, featuring Dustin Hoffman as a youth rebelling against middle-class materialism, grossed over $100 million in North America to make it one of the top five films of the decade.

Two years later the counter-culture movie of the decade, *Easy Rider*, hit the screens. *Easy Rider* was a cheaply made road movie featuring a drug deal, 'free' sex and a (psychedelic) 'trip'. It was released by Columbia pictures, which reaped a relatively large profit on its invest-ment. This was a departure for a major studio, most of which had not noticed that the youth of the late 1960s were very different from their parents. As a result of the film's success a new generation of filmmakers were able to get studio backing for their films, emphasizing how the 'old order' of the moguls, who had built the business, was coming to an end. This led to what many regard as a golden age of Hollywood, where the talent called the shots over the executives:

> By the end of 1970, the full impact of *Easy Rider* and the New Hollywood was evident in a whole range of releases: *Catch-22, The*

Boys in the Band, The Strawberry Statement, M*A*S*H, Woodstock, Medium Cool, Ice, The Great White Hope, Performance, Little Big Man, Tell Them Willie Boy Is Here, The Landlord, Getting Straight and *The Revolutionary.*

(Hill, 1996: 58)

However, the commercial prerogative remained unchanged. Hollywood produced these films because they thought they would make money. In addition, these movies – the ones that are 'remembered' and regularly broadcast or available on video – represent only a very small percentage of films released in that year. Most of the product was as predictable and banal as it is now or as it was before *Easy Rider*. In each year there are only ever a few exceptional movies that stand 'the test of time'.

The fact that the 'Hollywood renaissance' lasted into the 1970s was probably due, in large part, to the massive financial success of *The Godfather* (1972). The director, then known as Francis Ford Coppola, followed this up with the decidedly arty *The Conversation* (1974). The so-called movie brats, including – among others – Coppola, George Lucas, Martin Scorsese and Peter Bogdanovich, made flesh the auteur theory (see 4.3) and, apparently, would go on making personal, and therefore arty, movies. Unfortunately the box office shouted 'No!'.

3.8 Package Hollywood

By the 1970s the 'package' dominated Hollywood production. While this was not a new way of making and financing films, it has become the most important way of organizing production. The package consists of a script (or property) and the chief personnel (star(s) and director). Stars become attached to a property, and the bigger they are, the more likely it is that the package will attract finance. However, 'windows of opportunity' mean that the package is in constant flux, as stars and directors lose their availability as they sign up for other films. This creates 'development hell'. For example *The Mummy* (1999) was stuck in development for nearly a decade. In the late 1980s Clive Barker originally conceived of the film as an R-rated 'terror ride'. Soon after, Joe Dante got involved and the property became a contemporary horror adventure, with a central female protagonist and a sympathetic monster. However the studio, Universal, would not agree a budget over $15 million.

Another version of the film was stalled when two new executives, who had been put off horror movies by the losses accrued by *Mary Shelley's Frankenstein* (UK–USA–Japan, 1994) and *Mary Reilly* (1996), arrived from Tristar. Stephen Sommers then pitched the property as an action-adventure film without an R-rating. With the emphasis on period action, à la *Indiana Jones*, lashings of special effects and humour, the studio accepted the pitch (Fleming, 1999).

The film's success spawned a straight sequel, the imaginatively titled *The Mummy Returns* (2001), and a spin-off, *The Scorpion King* (2002).

The package system facilitated the rise of independents. In the 1980s Cannon, Orion, Castle Rock and Carolco indulged in competing with the majors in budget terms. Carolco made the most expensive film ever (at the time) in producing *Terminator 2: Judgment Day* (USA-France, 1991). Because the film was a remake, featuring one of the hottest stars of the early 1990s (Arnold Schwarzenegger), with the original's director, James Cameron, Carolco was able to raise around $100 million. Its sequel, *Terminator 3: Rise of the Machines* (USA-Germany-UK, 2003), also became the most expensive independently produced picture ($175 million) – produced by C2 Pictures with Intermedia and Hal Lieberman.

You may have noticed that recent Hollywood films are more likely to be co-productions with other countries. Deregulated global financial markets have made it easier to raise money from abroad, and help the studios spread their risk. Some of these deals came unstuck at the turn of the century as a number of companies, such as the German KirchMedia, over-extended themselves and went bust.

Despite the success of *T2*, Carolco went bankrupt and Castle Rock became part of Time Warner. Carolco's demise was hastened by the box office bomb *Cutthroat Island* (France-Italy-Germany, 1995); while the major studios can withstand expensive flops, the independent sector is more vulnerable if one costly movie fails.

The 1980s saw the rise of the agent (satirised in *Ivansxtc*, USA-UK, 2000) who, in representing their clients, realized they were in a position to put the 'package' together themselves. Foremost amongst them was Michael Ovitz of CAA.

Once a producer gets the 'green light' – funding for the film – s/he will hire production facilities. These are likely to be provided by the major studio that is putting up most or all of the finance. Producers may be independent and have deals with studios that get 'first refusal' on the properties they have to offer. For example, Art Linson's deal with 20th Century Fox meant that once he got approval for Mitch Glazer's screenplay of Charles Dickens' *Great Expectations* (1998) he could get a cast and director signed up:

> I had sent the script to several directors preapproved [by Fox]. This does not mean they were obligated to make the movie with these

directors.... After about a month, I received a call from Alfonso [Cuaron's] agent ...

(Linson, 2002: 100)

After studio approval of the director, the stars need to be cast:

> We had just received word from Gwyneth Paltrow's agent she wanted to do the movie.... Most savvy insiders knew that she was a 'comer'... [she] was perfect casting.
>
> (Linson, 2002: 99)

The executive's response? 'She has no chin' (ibid.). Paltrow did star in the movie opposite Ethan Hawke who, despite being an excellent actor, was well down the studio's list of desired leads. Robert (Bob) De Niro negotiated a cameo role that would be shot in just seven days:

> This means shooting the role of the convict consecutively, then interspersing those scenes through the film during the editing. The advantage to Bob would be that he could get all of his work done in a short time and still make the same amount of money. Maybe, he would have time to fit in another movie while this one was still shooting.
>
> (Linson, 2002: 105–6)

This would not endear him to the line producer whose job it is to make sure the movie stays on schedule. One way of reducing costs, for example, is to film all the scenes required at one location at the same time. De Niro's insistence made this impossible, as the crew would have to go to all 'his' locations in a seven-day period.

Books such as Art Linson's *What Just Happened?* (2002) and Peter Biskind's *Easy Riders, Raging Bulls* (1998) make it clear that it is a minor miracle that films ever get made.

3.9 Hollywood: conglomeration to media corporation

By the 1970s all the major studios were part of conglomerates (see Table 3.2).

Columbia Pictures aside, which looked liked a modern synergistic corporation (see below), the major film studios were merely one business among many. More importantly, many of the businesses under the corporate umbrella had little, or nothing, to do with one another.

Table 3.2

Columbia Pictures	Columbia Pictures Industries Including: Arista Records; EUE Screen Gems (commercials); Fred Levinson and Assoc.; Video Services; and a number of radio stations.
Paramount Pictures	Gulf + Western Inc. Including: Bostonian Shoes; New Jersey Zinc Co.; Simon & Schuster; Famous Music Corp.; Roosevelt Raceway; Collyer Insulated Wire and over 300 other companies.
Universal Films	MCA Inc. Including: MCA Records; Yosemite Park and Curry Company; MCA Merchandising; New Times Magazine; Mid-Continent Computer Services; Spencer Gifts.
United Artists	Transamerica Inc. Including: Hollywood Home Theatre; United Artists Television; Transamerica Life Insurance; Budget Rent-a-Car.
Twentieth Century-Fox	Twentieth Century-Fox Film Corporation Including: International Theatres Division; Keith Cole Photography; Aspen Skiing Corp; Coca-Cola Bottling Midwest.
Warner Bros.	Warner Communications Inc. Including: Independent News Co.; Warner Bros. Records; Knickerbocker Toy Co.; Warner Fragrances; Cosmos Soccer.

Majors in the mid-1970s (Source: Monaco, 1979: 36–7)

Contemporary Hollywood studios are now part of *media* corporations with no (or few) extraneous businesses.

Lew Wasserman, who started as an agent in the 1930s and ended up running Universal in the 1970s, initiated this process. He helped Hollywood divest itself of its movie-focused past for a media–orientated future. Among his innovations were:

1. The production of independent radio and television programmes.
2. Recognizing the importance of owning the rights to a film library (which could be sold over and over again).
3. Pioneering made-for-television films.
4. Set the trend for the summer blockbuster film.

(Gomery, 1998: 48–9)

Steven J. Ross took Wasserman's innovations a step further by building a fully integrated media corporation at Warner's. He was responsible for:

1. The pioneering of cable television (Home Box Office).
2. Recognizing that costs could be covered by selling films and TV shows to itself (that is, both films and TV shows produced by Warners could be shown on HBO).
3. Realizing the cross-subsidization would allow for constant innovation by using revenue from profitable businesses to invest in new projects.
4. Reciprocity in dealing with other companies. 'For example, the Paramount studio had to tender its top movies to Time Warner HBO because if Paramount did not, Time Warner's cable franchises would not book Paramount's Sci-Fi channel'

(Gomery, 1998: 53).

Steven J. Ross 'downsized' Warner Communications into:

a horizontally integrated company engaged in three areas of entertainment; (1) production and distribution of film and television
programming; (2) recorded music; and (3) publishing.

(Balio, 1998: 62)

This horizontal integration heralded the arrival of synergy which, as we shall see, marked a shift in business practices. The key element in Wasserman's and Ross's innovations was the recognition that Hollywood was no longer merely in the cinema business, it was in the media business. Cinema attendance had declined so precipitously that it appeared there was no future in simply making movies for theatrical distribution. By embracing the technological advances of cable TV and videocassettes, as well as the opportunity to cross-promote products in other media, the major studios have put themselves at the forefront of popular culture in the twenty-first century.

3.10 The importance of *Jaws*

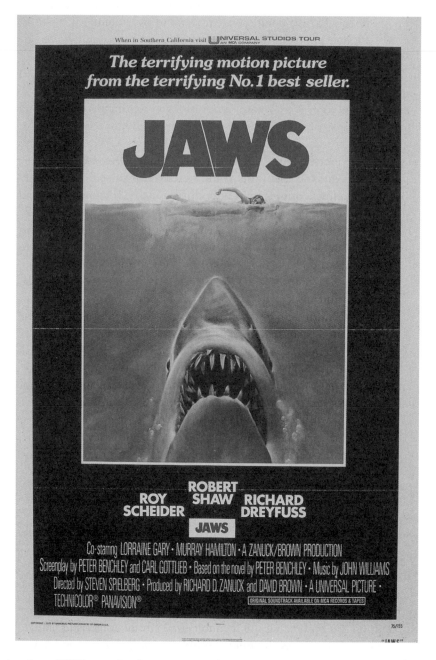

Jaws (1975) was the first summer blockbuster and heralded the dominance of high concept cinema in Hollywood

Jaws (1975) broke the Hollywood mould by showing how successful saturation distribution could be, when it stayed at the top of the box office charts all summer. Justin Wyatt (1994) points out that this technique was first used in 1973 with *Billy Jack*. Originally released in 1971, *Billy Jack* did little business, but its re-release two years later used a new pattern of distribution. Films at the time usually opened first in the big cities before rolling out across the nation. If you lived in the 'sticks' it was several weeks before you could get to see new movies. This was the 'platform' release. *Billy Jack* re-opened widely in South California backed by a massive advertising campaign. Different TV advertisements covered all the possible angles, showing the film could appeal to a broad audience. Its first weekend gross was over $1 million, and this success was then mirrored in all territories.

Jaws took this technique nationwide and opened simultaneously in North America in 409 theatres. It was backed by saturation television advertising and posted a $7 million opening weekend. Eventually it grossed $260 million in North America, and although this was not the birth of the blockbuster, which had been around for many years, it was the first instance of the summer 'event' movie, which still obsesses Hollywood. The following year *King Kong* opened on 961 screens, and now big movies commonly open on over 5000 screens; *Harry Potter and the Philosopher's Stone* (aka *Harry Potter and the Sorcerer's Stone*, 2001) opened on over 8000 screens.

Two years after *Jaws*, *Star Wars* showed how important merchandising would become to Hollywood's profitability. This helped put another facet of the 'high concept' (see 3.11) into place – the tie-ins that would make more money than the movie.

3.10.1 The implications of saturation distribution

If a movie is distributed nationwide more prints are required, and the audience must be fully aware of the film before it opens. Because of this 'four-walling', a film's 'p and a' (prints and advertising) is very costly. Prints cost around £1,000 each to strike, and television advertising, absolutely essential for blanket coverage, is exceptionally expensive. This makes it a high-risk strategy, because if a film does not open 'big' the studio will lose a lot of money. The opening three days (Friday–Sunday) of a film's release then become absolutely crucial to a film's success, as next week, particularly in the summer, another studio will be releasing a would-be blockbuster and exhibitors will be removing under-performing films to accommodate it.

The new distribution pattern meant that the awareness built by a 'roll out' release was lost. The 'old' type of 'platform' release is still used occasionally, for example with the phenomenally successful *The Blair Witch Project* (1999), which opened on 27 screens, in North America. This was increased to 31 in week two. In week three it was showing in 1101 sites, and 2412 in week four, peaking at 2538 in week six. However 'platform' releases are only used for films that are not obviously big box office material: the British films *The Full Monty* (UK–USA, 1997) and *Elizabeth* (UK–France, 1998) both benefited from this distribution pattern in North America.

By the late 1990s a film's box office gross usually dropped around 30 per cent in the second weekend; more if it bombed. *The Wild, Wild West* (1999) dropped a then massive 54 per cent after its opening four-day weekend (it was the July 4 holiday) of $36.4 million. Because of its big opening, supported by an enormous publicity blitz, it had virtually reached 50 per cent of its final take, of just over $111 million, in its first six days. After that, poor 'word of mouth' kicked in and the film sank. By the early years of the twenty-first century, 50 per cent-plus drops in the second weekend were becoming common, reflecting how the marketing hype was successful in getting a greater proportion of the potential audience into the cinemas in the first week of release. On the downside, these films' 'legs' did not carry them for very long. *The Matrix Revolutions* (2003) opened in North America with a five-day gross of $82 million and dropped 56 per cent and 67 per cent on the following weekends. Eventually it totalled $139 million in 15 weeks.

Contrast this with 1999's late summer box office phenomenon, which dropped a miniscule 3 per cent on its second weekend and only a further 7 per cent on the third. *The Sixth Sense*, the film in question, is what is known as a 'sleeper' because it unexpectedly has 'legs' that carry it for weeks. In 1998 *There's Something About Mary* stayed in the top 30 for 23 weeks. 2002's sleeper hit, *My Big Fat Greek Wedding*, was the biggest independent box office success ever and spent 45 weeks in the top 30.

This distribution pattern virtually requires multiplex cinemas, as this allows the 'week's blockbuster' to be shown on more than one screen at any one cinema (hourly for the biggest hits). So it is not surprising that the rise of 'high concept' (see 3.11) cinema coincided with the growth of the multiplex. In Britain the multiplex probably saved cinema in that the 'turning point' in UK box office fortunes coincided with the opening of the first multiplex in 1985. While the opening of one cinema would not arrest the decline on its own, there is no doubt that the vast increases in audiences at the end of the twentieth century were significantly influenced by the growth of multiplexes – see Box 3.1.

Because of the need to build awareness rapidly, particularly during the summer months which are crammed with commercial projects, a film needs to be easily marketable. Enter the high concept.

3.11 Hollywood and the high concept

Justin Wyatt (1994) has argued that the dominance by the late 1980s of Paramount, Warner and Disney was due to the way these studios embraced the 'high concept'. Various executives have been credited with the invention of the term; one of its origins was ABC television in the early 1970s.

During the 1960s Hollywood had increased the price of its movies for broadcast, so programme executive Barry Diller introduced the made-for-TV movie which, because audiences had never had a chance to see it in the cinema, had to be easy to summarize in television trailers. Diller approved films that could be reduced to a single sentence. Michael Eisner has also been credited with inventing the term, and when the two came together at Paramount, in the mid-1970s, they took away whatever control 'movie brat' directors (see 3.8) had had, and put the producer back in the driving seat, with the emphasis upon a easily saleable narrative. Crucial to the formation of the high concept style were the films of Jerry Bruckheimer and Don Simpson, both Paramount producers.

Although Simpson was involved with *An Officer and a Gentleman* (1982), the full flowering of the high concept film did not occur until Simpson was sacked for allegedly excessive behaviour. He teamed up with Bruckheimer to make the low-budget, big box office, MTV-influenced *Flashdance* (1983). The follow-up was the even more successful *Beverly Hills Cop* (1984). These films were cheaply made as they did not use stars (although *Beverly Hills Cop* made Eddie Murphy one), were easy to market, and crucially tied the films to massive hit records: 'What a Feeling' by Irene Cara and Glen Frey's 'The Heat is On' respectively.

Their biggest hit was *Top Gun* (1986), which reduced the high concept to an image. Simpson's pitch for this film was:

> … two guys in leather jackets and sunglasses standing in front of the biggest, fastest fucking airplane you ever saw in your life.
>
> (Fleming, 1999: 64)

Box 3.1 Exhibition – the multiplex

Multiplexes are purpose-built multi-screen environments situated on an 'out of town' site, which are usually only easily accessible by car. So when the inner cities 'declined', leading to an increase in poverty and associated crime, the 'clean' multiplex offered a safe haven where parents were happy to leave their children for a couple of hours.

As auto ownership has increased, public transport has not only been cutback but has become increasingly associated with the poorest sections of the population. Out-of-town multiplex developments are, in part, seen as safe exactly because only certain sections of the population have the transport necessary to gain access to them.

Furthermore, as leisure and consumption have increasingly moved out to these developments, town centers have declined still further.... Unlike in America, where they were produced out of the processes of urban sprawl...

(Jancovich and Faire, 2003: 192)

By the late 1990s multiplex screens outweighed those of traditional cinemas. Although the number of sites has increased only slightly since the early 1980s, the number of screens has almost doubled. It is this increase in screens that has helped boost attendances. If the film you want to see is full, there is likely to either be another film you are happy to watch or, for new wide releases, the film will be showing again soon. In the pre-multiplex cinema a new release would only be shown at most four times in a day, whereas for example *American Pie: The Wedding* (2003) opened with 14 daily screenings at Cineworld in Bradford.

While multiplexes offer more choice than traditional cinemas, this choice tends to be narrow. In one particular week Cineworld was showing a solitary 'arthouse' film, *L'Homme du Train* (France, 2003), and that was only screened *once*. Four Bollywood movies were being screened, reflecting the large number of British Asians who lived in the area. Even when multiplexes offer 'arthouse' films they often fail to reach much of an audience, as audiences for this type of film prefer to see them in less commercial cinemas. For example, Bradford's two-screen arthouse cinema, Pictureville, was showing 14 films in the same week, all of which could have been described as 'arthouse'. Arthouse films do not appeal to a mass audience, so they have to cultivate a niche. In this the publicity generated by film festivals is exceptionally important (see 3.13).

As noted in Box 3.3, cinemas use films as a shop window to get people to buy the concessions and merchandise on offer. The location of multiplexes, often situated in a retail park, allows audiences to have a day out spending money in the cinema, restaurants and shops:

> design company FITCH, advised multiplex operators to increase the amount of 'experience' their customers got from going to the cinema, adding that 'instead of a product-based decision (going to a particular film) the consumer must be invited to make a lifestyle decision (going for an evening out)'.
>
> (Hark, 2002: 51)

This emphasis on lifestyle is also particularly evident in the UK Film Four cable/satellite channel, as its marketing attempts to make movies part of 'cool youth' culture.

Box 3.2 High concept cinema: *Charlie's Angels*
(USA-Germany, 2000)

The essence of the high concept movies is that they should be easy to sell to audiences (and, initially, the financial backers). Remakes are, by their nature, pre-sold. Hollywood has always cannibalized literature (novels and plays) however it was not until the 1990s that television came to be seen as a rich source of material.

In 1991 *The Addams Family* earned $113.5 million at the North American box office, and this led to a slew of adaptations of old TV programmes. While most of today's core cinema-going audience (16–25s) will not remember these programmes, they had cultural resonance and a proven appeal. Essentially, though, they needed to be adapted to the contemporary mode of making movies (with a reliance on computer-generated special effects, CGI) and changing modes of representation. The original TV *Charlie's Angels* executive producer, Leonard Goldberg, is quoted on the film's DVD notes: 'The feature version would include the most recent recruits, women who are representative of Angels in the year 2000.'

Contemporary blockbusters are invariably 'action' movies, facilitating scenarios for CGI pyrotechnics, with a male hero saving the world (and the girl). Apart from notable exceptions such as Ripley in the *Alien* series (plus Buffy and Xena on television), women in action movies have had subsidiary roles focusing on their looks: they are feisty but ultimately need the bloke to save them. *Charlie's Angels* self-consciously attempts to adapt the macho action hero in a feminine way. Cameron Diaz is quoted on DVD notes:

> Drew said, 'It's going to be a chick action movie. We get to be beautiful and tough, and we wear bad-ass clothes. We will not have guns, and we get to do kung fu. In this movie, it's the girls that are going to kick ass.'

The 'tongue-in-cheek' mode of address is a crucial component of contemporary action movies. Audiences are not expected to suspend their disbelief, but join in the fun of the absurd game being played out on the screen.

Drew Barrymore produced the film (with Goldberg and Nancy Juvonen, her partner in Flower Pictures); amongst the executive producers is Betty Thomas, one of the few women entrusted to direct big budget movies (*The Brady Bunch Movie*, 1994). The presence of a number of female 'players' in the production team highlights the gender politics being played out in the film.

The director, as in 90 per cent of Hollywood movies, is male (as are the scriptwriters). Typically for a high concept film, director McG's background is in music video and advertising. The visual sheen, and postmodern playfulness, nurtured by MTV, are seen as prerequisites for entertaining today's mass audience. However, the musical sequences in *Charlie's Angels* have more in common in the way they are shot with the MGM musical than MTV video.

As noted above, action films usually have male protagonists. The narrative hero resolves the problem created by the villain and in doing so often saves the 'princess'. Although the 'angels' are, literally, 'kick ass' characters they ultimately defer to Charlie. Indeed they relate to the patriarchal figure in a 'girly' fashion. In addition, they take their orders from Bosley. This may suggest that the 'angels' are only apparently the film's protagonists because they defer to men. However in *Charlie's Angels* the narrative 'princess' is Charlie, as it is he who needs saving from the villain.

Hollywood action movies often cast British actors in the role of the villain (a sign of cultural insecurity or stars' reluctance to tarnish their persona by playing the 'baddy'?). Gary Oldman, in *The Fifth Element*

(France-USA, 1997) satirized this tendency with his deep southern drawl. The casting of Tim Curry in *Charlie's Angels* is part playful, part narrative misdirection.

Although it is often assumed that high concept films are politically conservative, the 'efficiency scene' suggests that Karl Marx was correct. Of course its 'S & M' playfulness negates any seriousness in this potential subversive comment.

Richard Maltby (1998: 38) summarized the high concept as follows:

1. A style of 'post-generic' filmmaking based on the simplification of character and narrative.
2. Extended montages, which are in effect pop videos.
3. The physical design (look) frequently reflects the graphic design and layout of contemporary advertising.
4. Easily replicated in trailers, TV commercials or publicity stills.
5. Formal excess which simply 'looks good', be it in the lighting or in the acting of the star.
6. The music track interrupts the narrative.
7. Self-conscious allusion to films and TV.
8. Detached appearance of the stars.
9. Hyperbolic physiques of the protagonists and hyperbolic action.
10. Ironic distancing: a walking-talking brand.

For many observers high concept films exemplify all that is worst about commercial cinema. The aesthetic is subordinated to the commodification of films. However, films have always been commodities and the high concept simply exaggerates this fact – see also Box 3.2 and Section 3.14.

3.12 The independent sector in North America

In the 1990s the nature of the independents changed as they:

> differed from the failed mini-majors of the 1980s ... in several important ways: (1) the newcomers ran 'lean machines' with only skeletal staffs rather than emulating the structure of the large studios; (2) most concentrated exclusively on filmed entertainment

rather than branching into TV; (3) most produced only a few high-quality productions each year rather than large rosters aimed at different segments of the market; (4) most distributed domestically through the majors rather than organizing their own distribution arms; and (5) most raised their production financing by keeping their eyes on the burgeoning foreign market rather than on home video deals.

(Balio, 1998: 64–5)

Both Morgan Creek (formed 1989) and Imagine Entertainment (1986) were still in business as genuine independents in 2004. Possibly the most successful independents of the era, Miramax and New Line, were purchased by Disney in 1992 and Turner Broadcasting Corporation (which also swallowed the independent Castle Rock a year later), before Time Warner merged with Turner, in 1996. Despite being part of a major corporation, they still acted as independents.

New Line came to prominence on the back of the increase demand for films caused by the video boom of the 1980s. This helped generate finance for films by pre-selling them for video distribution and 'independent films increased from 193 in 1986 to ... 393 in 1988' (Wyatt, 1998: 74). However, as Wyatt points out, success on video was found to relate directly to success in cinema. So if independent films performed poorly at the box office, the video distributors were not going to 'get their money back'. New Line and Miramax survived the ensuing shake-out (because there were too many independents) because they created films that would cross over from the arthouse market (see 3.13), and the former was adept at developing franchises, such as those spawned by *A Nightmare on Elm Street* (1985) and *Teenage Mutant Ninja Turtles* (1990). Franchises are the delight of Hollywood accountants as, once established, they promise a large number of sequels. At the time of writing, *Nightmare's* Freddie was fighting it out with another 1980s franchise monster, Jason of the *Friday the 13th* series, in the surprisingly titled *Freddie vs. Jason* (2003).

While Miramax eschewed sequels, its 'genre' arm Dimension (at the end of 2004 there was talk that Disney was going to sell Miramax and retain Dimension) revelled in them, making its mark with the *Scream* (1996–2000) films. Miramax itself rose to prominence with Steven Soderbergh's *sex, lies and videotape* (1988) and the British film *The Crying Game* (1992), which grossed an astonishing $62.5 million in North America. They refined the arthouse crossover pattern by targeting Oscar nominations, and won Best Picture in 1996, 1998 and 2003.

The 2003 winner *Chicago* (2002) was released on the last possible day of the year to qualify for the following March's competition. It used the 'old-fashioned' platform release (see 3.10) by starting on 77 screens, building up to over 2000 screens seven weeks later, after the nominations had been announced. The weekend after it won, its box office revenue increased by 25 per cent, despite the fact it had been on release for nearly three months.

The types of films that win Oscars tend to be 'middlebrow', offering more intellectual thought than strictly entertainment movies, but not proving too taxing to put off a large portion of the audience. Building the release pattern slowly (which of course depends on how successful the film is) in the award season allows the film to benefit from the publicity generated by any victories it might have in, say, the Golden Globe awards. The key is the Oscar nomination, which invariably offers a big boost to the box office. By the time *Chicago* had won Best Picture it had grossed over $150 million in North America alone, excellent business for a musical, a genre that had been regarded as financially dead for years.

Some in the independent sector will take more risks with their films. USA Films, when run by ex-major studio executive Barry Diller, released the surreal *Being John Malkovich* (1999), one of the most interesting films of the decade, and Artisan Entertainment was responsible for *The Blair Witch Project* (1999). Both these films were a commercial success; however many independently released films barely register at the box office.

3.13 The arthouse sector

As we have seen, cinema's origins are commercial in nature, and the high cost of making movies means there is always pressure to find a reasonably sized audience to recoup at least some of the costs. Because most audiences seek entertainment from films, movies that attempt to offer primarily 'food for thought', rather than emphasizing entertainment, are inevitably addressing a niche audience.

Defining a film as 'arthouse' fare is not straightforward. For example, any foreign language film is likely to be treated as arthouse whether it is aimed at that niche or a mainstream audience in its country of origin. The exception is Hollywood films that are seen worldwide, although they are usually dubbed. Occasionally foreign language films can break out of their ghetto and be seen in multiplexes: for example *Crouching Tiger, Hidden Dragon* (*Wo Hu Cang Long*, USA-Hong Kong-China-Taiwan, 2000) was the first foreign language film to break $100 million in North America. *Amélie* (*Le Fableux Destin d'Amélie Poulain*, France, 2001) was also very successful. However, these films were aimed at a mainstream audience.

Films aimed solely at the arthouse audience can, of course, be in any language. The arthouse sector began in earnest during the 1950s, although before the Second World War film societies had played a major role in the exhibition of films deemed inappropriate by the mainstream distributors, such as Eisenstein's *Battleship Potemkin* (*Bronenosets Potyomkin*, USSR, 1926).

> Although art theatres date back to the 'little cinema' movement of the 1920s, it is in the 1950s that the popularity of art film theatres came to the mass public's attention in the United States.
>
> (Wilinsky, 2002: 67)

Wilinsky points out that there were a number of reasons why the arthouse exhibition circuit should have been established at this time, including the Paramount decrees (see 3.6), which led to less Hollywood production and greater imports:

> Less than 100 … art cinemas existed in 1950 [in North America]; 15 years later that number had increased … to over 600.
>
> (Allen, 2003: 31)

Although art cinema's increasing popularity was relative, and was always far below the mainstream's, there is little doubt that the presence of (female) nudity in *Summer With Monika* (*Sommeren med Monika*, Sweden, 1953) helped establish director Ingmar Bergman as a favourite. European arthouse films such as this helped break the censor's stranglehold. The nudity would not have raised many eyebrows in un-puritanical Scandinavia. As the nudity was not obviously sensational, and the film was received as art (putting it, in cultural terms, on a similar level as the nude of Renaissance painting) and consumed by a middle-class audience, it was difficult for the film to be censored.

While *Summer With Monika* is an entertaining teen pic, dealing with the vicissitudes of first love complicated by pregnancy, the portentousness of Bergman's films later in the decade meant they reeked of art. *Wild Strawberries* (*Smultronstället*, Sweden, 1957) focused on a repressed old man's journey in which he relives his youth and understands that his ascetic lifestyle has led to emotional atrophy. *The Seventh Seal* (*Det Sjunder Inseglet*, Sweden, 1957) casts death as a character who plays chess with a knight. Only a very few popular culture films offer bleak assessments of the world, *Se7en* (1995) being one (see Lacey, 2001).

The (relative) popularity of arthouse cinema grew during the 1960s, associated with the rise in the number of people attending universities, and the growing acceptance of 'film as art' (see 4.3). A growing number of filmmakers found it possible to sustain a career with films that offered an elliptical personal vision, as their profundity was celebrated in the middle-class press. Geoffrey Nowell-Smith summed up the time:

> New cinemas sprang up all over the world. In France there was the nouvelle vague, in Britain Free Cinema, in Germany the Young German Cinema, in Brazil Cinema Novo. The years 1959 and 1960 saw first features by Francois Truffaut … Jean-Luc Godard … Alain Resnais … Karel Reis …John Cassavetes …and Nagisa Oshima.… Within a couple of years these new directors were joined by Glauber Rocha … Pier Paolo Pasolini … Agnes Varda … and Roman Polanksi. This unparalleled explosion of new talent helped create conditions of greater freedom also for more established artists – for Ingmar Bergman in Sweden, Federico Fellini in Italy, Satyajit Ray in India, Stanley Kubrick in the United States.
>
> (Nowell-Smith, 1997: 10–11)

While these films would play in mainstream cinemas, possibly as late-night showings, they were far more likely to be found on the specialist arthouse circuit in university towns and large cities. Arthouse cinema also developed its own specialist distributors.

Box 3.3 Box office revenue

In 2002 *Harry Potter and the Chamber of Secrets* was top of the British box office, grossing over £50 million. This £50 million taken at the box office has to be split between the exhibitor, the distributor (in this case Warner Bros., the same company that produced the film) and the producer. In our example, we will assume one screen in a cinema took £10,000 box office revenue for *Harry Potter*.

According to the UK Competition Commission's report into the sector (www.competition-commission.org.uk/fulltext/357c4.pdf, published August 2002), the split can be calculated in several ways:

1. The 'nut' is a negotiated figure representing a cinema's over-head costs – for example, lighting and heating – (plus a profit margin). If the 'nut' was £5,000, this would leave a further £5,000 to be split between the parties.

2. The 'rental' is the amount paid by the exhibitor to the distributor, and this is the greater of 25 per cent or about 90 per cent of what is left after the 'nut' has been deducted. In our example 25 per cent would have been £2,500; the 90 per cent of the gross less 'nut' would be £4,500. The latter would be that week's 'rental' for the screen.

3. The sliding scale method increases the percentage paid in rentals as the box office increases above the 'nut'. These are normally limited to 50 per cent. However this can be breached, particularly in the first weekend of an expected blockbuster film.

4. The 'straight percentage' – a set percentage of the takings, and a guaranteed minimum to cover distribution costs, is agreed. This is often used in the arthouse circuit or second-run cinemas.

Whatever the film being shown, exhibitors tend to make very little, if anything, from their box office takings. They make money through their concessions: fizzy drinks, popcorn and so on.

Once the distributor has received its 'rentals', this must, in turn, be passed on to the producer. The Film Distributors' Association describe what happens:

> Out of the net share, the distributor usually recoups any minimum guarantee plus the p&a costs incurred in releasing the film. Any outstanding balance is shared with the producers, according to a pre-agreed formula, as set out in the distribution contract. Alternatively, the distributor may simply retain a distribution fee, with all net proceeds being paid to the producer.
>
> (www.launchingfilms.com/uk_film_distribution_guide/
> box_office_takings accessed June, 2003)

The p and a (print and advertising) costs can be substantial, as prints are about £1,000 to strike, and blockbuster movies require a lot of promotion. In 2002:

> UK film distributors spent more than $403.2m (£255m) on prints and advertising in 2002, around one-third of the total value of UK cinema ticket sales during the year.
>
> Of the total p&a spend, around $219.3m was spent on advertising according to the FDA [Film Distributors' Association]...

The lion's share of this went on TV ads ($87.3m) with some $75.3m on outdoor. $41.7m was spent on press ads, $14.2m on radio, $637,172 on in-cinema advertising, and $177,758 on direct mail. Advertising spend was spread relatively evenly across the year.

(Forde, 2003)

It's not surprising that very little, or nothing, is left to the producer. For example, producer James Schamus reckoned that a $1 million independent film that took $10 million at the box office would leave a $333,000 loss (Schamus, 1998).

How do producers stay in business? The majors distribute their own films and hit pay dirt with spin-offs such as video and television sales. It is exceptionally difficult for a producer that is not a major studio to make any money.

3.14 Selling cinema

Films are manufactured as products, and the exhibitors are retailers who offer a shop window for sales of films in ancillary markets (such as video), and use films as a lure into their shop so punters purchase popcorn and fizzy drinks and other comestibles – see Box 3.3.

Hollywood realized belatedly, in the 1980s, that video offered a massive additional marketplace to go alongside that of television in its various platforms (pay TV, subscription TV and terrestrial TV), and merchandising. Home video helped stimulate demand for films, and production went up in USA from 350 in 1983, when videocassette recorders were not yet ubiquitous, to nearly 600 in 1988 (Balio, 1998: 58).

Even as recently as 20 years ago movie theaters supplied more than three-fourths of the revenue for an average Hollywood feature film. Today, theaters provide less than one-fourth because of the extraordinary cable TV and home-video markets. In 1980, the Hollywood majors collected about $20 million from world-wide sales of videocassettes. By 1997 the figure was well in excess of $16 billion.

(Gomery, 1998a: 144)

A film such as *Space Jam* (1996) was conceived of wholly in 'shop window' terms, and it mattered not at all that the film barely covered its cost – around $90 million – at the North American box office. The film accrued billions of dollars through merchandise, and aided the introduction of the Looney Tunes characters to a new generation. This helped give Warners' back catalogue new life, which can be seen on its Cartoon Network television station.

Merchandising also helps in the promotion of the film. *South Park – The Movie* (1999) was probably a big success, in the UK at least, outside its core audience partly because numerous products had been available months before its release.

Hollywood has always flogged successful properties in the form of sequels. These are ideal commodities as they are pre-sold – audiences already know what to expect. The high concept allows properties to be sequels in themselves: sold as soundtrack albums, novelisations, videos, TV broadcasts and spin-offs. Spin-offs do not even have to be of successful films. For example *Buffy the Vampire Slayer*, which grossed a modest $16.6 million in 1992, became a very successful TV series by the late 1990s. Another way of conceiving cinemas is as a voting booth which helps determine how the property will be dealt with, as the film is rolled out in other formats.

Production was also stimulated by the growth of multiplexes. During the 1980s, the prevailing 'free market' philosophy led to a liberalization of many markets in western Europe, further encouraging Hollywood's penetration of indigenous film cultures. Overseas box office can turn home market flops, like *Striptease* (1995), into profitable films. The increasing reliance upon the global market is not restricted to Hollywood. Indian cinema relies heavily on a diasporic audience for 'around 65 percent of a film's total earnings' (Banker, 2001: 8 quoted in Willis, 2003: 255).

The high concept allows the benefits of synergy to be fully utilized. Cross-promotion becomes cross-fertilization, and the same property can be churned out in numerous formats and spin-offs. Once the 'development costs' (actually creating a successful film) have been met, what follows can be enormous profits. Media corporations can cross-promote their product and recycle properties. Sony's *Spider-Man* (2002) would, in addition to the film, appear as a soundtrack album on Columbia records, feature 'Sony' artist Macy Gray in a cameo and be turned into a video game, particularly for Play Stations. Plus, Sony licensed the concept for the manufacture of merchandise. However, *Spider-Man* was originally a Marvel Comics creation, and in 2003 the companies were locked in legal dispute about what proportion of monies should be shared between them.

It is worth noting the importance of product placement within the films themselves, although this is not limited to high concept films. Again, this has been a factor in Hollywood since its early days. However, in the 1990s 'product placement' occurred on a large and organized scale; there are numerous companies whose sole purpose is to find suitable films for the placement of their clients' products. The cost of placement will be determined by the product's profile within the film: a character naming a product would be more expensive to the manufacturer than if he or she simply used it.

By the end of the twentieth century it seemed the Internet would be a crucial medium for selling cinema. The ill-starred merger between AOL and Time-Warner was meant to herald a new era for media corporations. AOL could advertise its broadband services as offering film trailers and music downloads, supplied by the Time-Warner side of the company. However the only thing the merger prefaced was the bursting of the dot.com boom, and in 2003 the AOL was dropped from the company's title.

The Internet was also influential in the trend towards worldwide releases, as audiences around the world knew what was opening in America. The international market for Hollywood films grew during the last decades of the twentieth century, and was often responsible for roughly 50 per cent of a film's box office, or even more.

One of the most 'shameless' types of movie, in terms of selling themselves, is the exploitation film. These do little to disguise their intent to make money by being tasteless, and exist almost underground in mainstream cinema. While some exploitation films, such as those by Russ Meyer and John Walters, become cult hits, the fate of most is 'straight to video' distribution – see Box 3.4).

A crucial element to the selling of film, in all countries, is genre.

3.15 Genre and industry

The film industry uses genre in three ways:

➤ as a way of determining what elements to include in a film (which may draw upon the 'repertoire of elements' – see 2.3)
➤ as a marker for what type of films are currently popular – genre cycles – see 2.6:9)
➤ to market the film to particular audience(s).

In recent years Hollywood's emphasis on spin-offs, such as merchandise, has encouraged the development of the 'family film'. The 'family film', however, is not a genre in itself but is the way Hollywood reaches an important demographic. It has become:

> the discursive marker for a set of narrative, representational and institutional practices designed to maximise marketability and profitability across theatrical, video, licensing and merchandising markets by means of what we might call cross-generational appeal.
>
> (Allen, 1999: 114)

It is interesting that Allen does not include 'genre' among the practices listed, suggesting that audiences, of the family film at least, cue into narrative and character (representation) more than the film's use of iconography and setting. However, genre will be used in these films, as can be readily seen in Table 3.3.

Table 3.3	
Finding Nemo	37.0
Matrix Reloaded	33.3
Pirates of the Caribbean: Legend of the Black Pearl	28.2
Lord of the Rings: The Return of the King	27.9*
Bruce Almighty	23.6
Lord of the Rings: The Two Towers	21.9
Love Actually (UK-USA)	21.1*
X-2: X-Men United	20.6
Calendar Girls (UK)	20.2
Johnny English (UK)	19.6

* Still on release at the year's end.

UK top box office films in 2003 (£)

The *Lord of the Rings* films were event movies: that is, 'everybody' had to see them. Only *The Matrix Reloaded* and *Love Actually* were certified above a 12, and *Calendar Girls* was aimed more towards women. With the possible exceptions of *X2* and *Bruce Almighty*, the other five films fit comfortably within the 'family film' category, emphasizing their importance to the industry. The cross-generational appeal is apparent in the dual address (such as the risqué Robin Hood of *Shrek* (2001)).

Box 3.4 Exploitation movies – *Hemoglobin*
(Canada-USA, 1997)

Exploitation cinema may be understood as any (usually cheaply made) film that seeks to exploit a current trend or phenomenon for ostensibly commercial rather than artistic imperatives. This is achieved by including titillatory and often taboo elements such as gratuitous nudity, sexual acts, graphic depictions of violence, and 'anti-social' or 'gross activities'...

(Wells, 2000: 64)

Hence titles such as *Chopper Chicks in Zombietown* (1989), and 'rip-offs' such as the short *Saving Ryan's Privates* (1998); the former suggests sex and horror and – I'll leave the latter to your imagination.

Exploitation films usually appeal to young and predominantly male audiences. Youth culture is often defined in opposition to that of their parents, and this opposition is most obvious in the realm of 'bad taste'. The horror film was obviously perfect for this, and the exploitation horror movie thrived in the late 1950s with the newly created youth market. Roger Corman's American International Pictures supplied youngsters with films that displayed their obvious debt to Universal studio's 1930s horror and their target audience in their titles: *I Was a Teenage Werewolf* (1957) and *I Was a Teenage Frankenstein* (1958). These films circumvented Hollywood's self-censorship by not playing at respectable theatres: their audience could be reached at drive-in cinemas.

Hemoglobin was known as *Bleeders* in most countries (it was renamed for the British market presumably because it is also a slang word, as in 'you dirty ...'). On the face of it the film has a decent pedigree, as the marketing announces, 'From the Creators of *Aliens* and *Total Recall*'. This refers to two of the film's writers, Dan O'Bannon and Ron Shusett, though they in fact scripted *Alien* and not *Aliens*. The lead is taken by Rutger Hauer, whose best known role was as Roy Batty in *Blade Runner* (1982); however he has appeared in many 'straight to video' films since.

'Straight to video', as the sobriquet suggests, means the film bypasses a theatrical release; this is often, although not always, because the distributors do not believe the film will benefit from exposure to critics who write about films in cinemas. Going straight to video avoids both bad reviews and the costs associated with a theatrical release. These non-theatrical films are usually low-budget, and so can more readily cover investment and go into profit on the basis of video distribution and TV rights alone.

Hemoglobin has relatively high production standards, evident from the helicopter shot that opens the film and the impressive make-up of the monsters. It concerns the remains of an incestuous Dutch family who ended up on the New England coast (although it was filmed in Canada). The central character, John Strauss (Roy Dupuis) is a long-lost relative of the family, which disappeared 75 years ago, who returns to find a cure for his mysteriously diseased blood. Hauer plays the doctor, the man of science who rationalizes the events and explains that Strauss will only live if he eats a foetus that had been pickled in formaldehyde. His family, it transpires, have devolved and become vampire-like creatures that feed on corpses.

As this brief plot summary suggests, the 'gross out' quotient is an important factor in attracting its audience. However *Hemoglobin* under-plays some of these elements. Strauss enjoys his meal mostly off camera, although the dissection of one mutant is quite 'gross'. Another 'exploitation' ingredient is soft-core sex, filmed as a distinct interlude with soft-focus lighting and emphasis on female nudity. In *Hemoglobin* this is 'spiced up' as the participants are brother and sister.

The link between soft-core pornography and horror is evident in an advertisement for SeductionCinema releases in *Fangoria*, January 2001. The titles include *Mistress Frankenstein* and *Vampire's Seduction*. *Vamps: Deadly Dreamgirls* is graced by the tagline 'Tonight … Heather will be Lap Dancing for her Soul'.

Pornography is a branch of exploitation film, and it too is usually straight-to-video. In Britain most pornographic films (that is, those designed to sexually arouse the viewer) are rated R-18 and so can only be purchased from licensed sex shops. Arthouse porn (also known as erotica) usually has higher production values – see Tinto Brass' work such as *The Key* (*La Chiave*, Italy, 1983).

3.15.1 Trade genres

In the 2001 American Film Market (where films are sold to distributors) edition of the trade paper *Screen International,* only one of six companies advertising their films used genre to describe its product. While all the advertisements featured the stars and director, only the In-Motion AF group of companies named the genres of the eight films it was touting. These were two 'dark comedies' (presumably a version of 'black comedy'); two comedies; two thrillers; drama (a particularly nebulous category); suspense.

This lack of highlighting of genre shows how Hollywood tries to avoid using restrictive categories because that may limit the prospective audience. The films themselves, however, will use generic conventions to engage the audience.

These categories can be very different from what audiences understand; for example Gledhill (2000a) cites the example of the trade paper *Variety* using melodrama to describe action movies. The perception that this fluidity has increased during the last few decades has led postmodern theorists to suggest that contemporary genre is characterized by pastiche and hybridity rather than a solid set of elements. However, Hollywood has always stretched a film into as many genres as possible in order to market it – see 2.8.

3.16 How new is contemporary Hollywood?

Much critical effort has been put into precisely defining the classical period of Hollywood (1917–60, see Bordwell et al. 1985), and quantifying how post-1960 (or post-1948 or post-1970, depending on which account) Hollywood differs. One of the prevalent ideas is that classical Hollywood is characterized by 'Fordism' while post-classical, interestingly, is 'post-Fordist'. Fordism is related to the vertically integrated major studios of the Golden Age (see 3.3), while post-Fordism is characterized by a differentiated product brought about by the 'package' system (see 3.8). However, it is likely that Hollywood is too complex a beast to be neatly categorized, as Smith says of Bordwell et al.'s mammoth tome:

> For all the wealth of historical detail contained in their work, the description of the classical Hollywood mode becomes an ahistorical one. The classical system they posit becomes so abstract, generalized and encompassing that anything can be assimilated and nothing can make a difference.
>
> (Smith, 1998: 15)

Although Wyatt's conception of the high concept (3.11) is a convincing description of contemporary Hollywood, it would be wrong to suggest that it is vastly different from what went before. While the early 1970s did see a brief flowering of 'art', rather than primarily commercial, cinema in Hollywood, this was a response to the social conditions of the time and an attempt to make money. Post-*Jaws* Hollywood knows how to make money. Geoff King, in his investigation into the uniqueness of New Hollywood, concludes that although there are differences there are also 'substantial continuities' (King, 2002: 223). Yvonne Tasker suggests:

> New Hollywood may be defined not so much in terms of stylistic and thematic changes in filmmaking... but in terms of a post-modern multi-media world which undermines the very notion of film as a distinct medium.
>
> (Tasker, 1996: 226)

In other words it is no longer satisfactory – if it ever was – to look at film in isolation. The postmodern landscape (see 4.10) demands we understand films intertextually. Certainly, as we have seen with the development of the high concept, Hollywood looks to other media both for the source material of its films and for spin-offs from its films.

3.17 Stars

Since before the Golden Age, Hollywood had used stars to sell films. Probably the greatest impact was producer Carl Leammle's planting of the story that the Biograph Girl (Florence Lawrence) had died in an accident. A week later he placed an advertisement in the *St Louis Post-Dispatch* suggesting that enemies of his production company had 'foisted [the story] on the public of St. Louis ...' (quoted in Barbas, 2002: 19). 'Coincidentally' Lawrence appeared, the following month, in St. Louis to promote her film (sorry, to prove she was still alive). This mendacious showmanship struck the template for much of the promotion of stars that followed and is still used today.

The early film studios were not in the habit of promoting their actors as stars, arguably in order to keep the cost of the actors down, and also because of some actors' reluctance to be associated with 'disreputable cinema'. Early cinema, however, was not concerned particularly with narrative or the development of character. However, as the nascent studios attempted to widen their audience to include the affluent middle classes (see Box 2.6), it became necessary to develop a more complex film language for the literary and theatrical adaptations. As a result:

> Many moviegoers experienced strong feelings of intimacy with actors. Since narrative films, through point-of-view shots, often allowed viewers access to characters' thoughts and perspectives,

audiences were able to identify and sympathize with the men and women they saw on screen. Acting had also become increasingly realistic ...

(Barbas, 2002: 16–17)

As a result, in the years 1908–10, the studios were inundated with requests for information about the anonymous actors. Barbas suggests that these requests were motivated by a desire, apparent from the very early days of cinema, to prove that what audiences were seeing was real. The verisimilitude of cinema was such that audiences were anxious about being able to distinguish between reality and cinema, and Barbas reports that many magazines and newspapers included articles telling their readers how to tell the difference. This may seem ridiculous to audiences now. However the DVD extras that explain how the special effects were created is simply another way of showing audiences how the 'unreal' was really created.

Once cinema started being narrative-based it became much more like traditional theatre, which already had its own star system. The cult of the celebrity is not a new phenomenon: theatrical stars of the nineteenth century could build a very large following. In addition, the birth of cinema coincided in the West with the rise of consumer culture, and so by the 1920s:

Many fans found themselves using their knowledge of stars' lifestyle as a guide for their own personal behavior. Fans wanted to dress, shop and look like stars, and magazines showed them the way.

(Barbas, 2002: 29)

From a Marxist perspective this split between the public (stars' lifestyles) and private (the audience's private life) spheres, encapsulated in bourgeois ideology's emphasis on the individual, has led to:

a massive preoccupation with identifying the truth [about] ourselves [so] it is possible to understand that stars fascinate because their performances make the private self into a public spectacle.

(McDonald, 1995: 84)

Consumer culture relied upon the development of mass communications which allowed, in the first instance, national dissemination of brands and products; at the beginning of the twenty-first century the speed and quantity of communications had increased to a level where an electronic 'global village' was coming into existence. Cinema was the first *global* mass medium. Although the cult of the celebrity was in place in the nineteenth century, film stars could utilize the mass communications of the twentieth century to far outstrip the fame experienced by celebrities of the nineteenth century:

> Stardom and consumerism both share an element of fantasy and desire. Consumerism is escapist, promoting the fantasy of living beyond basic necessities. The market suggests consumers are free to choose what they want rather than what they need. Through the exercise of choice, consumption takes on the appearance of an act of individual self-expression.... Images of wealth, freedom and individualism are therefore fundamental to consumerism and since the start of the star system, popular film performers have played a significant role in promoting those values.
>
> (McDonald, 1995: 32)

As noted in Section 1.10, the study of stars can be approached in different ways. There we focused on 'stars as a text', while here we consider the economics of stardom, which can be broken down into three parts:

a) *capital*. Stars represented as a form of capital possessed by the studios ...

b) *investment*. Stars were a guarantee ... against loss on investment and even a profit on it.

c) *outlay*. Stars were a major portion of a film's budget – hence their handling, in filmic terms, had to be careful and correct.

(Dyer, 1979: 11)

During the Golden Age of Hollywood stars were contracted to one studio and so were an asset; the biggest stars being worth the most, and costing the most. These stars were occasionally loaned to other studios. Despite their apparent power, the stars had little or no choice in what films they were to appear in. The battle between stars and the studios had begun in 1919 when four of the biggest stars – Charlie Chaplin, Douglas Fairbanks, Mary Pickford, and producer/director D.W. Griffith – formed United Artists.

Despite this, most stars remained under contract, and by the 1930s some began to chafe under the constrictions imposed upon them by the studios; that is, they had to appear in bad films. Bette Davis took a stand against her studio Warner Bros. by refusing to appear in *God's Country and the Woman* (1936) despite being promised, if she had taken the role, Scarlett O'Hara in *Gone With the Wind* (1939). She was suspended and went to Britain to make two films. However Warner Bros. served an injunction preventing her from doing so, Davis counter-sued but lost.

It was not until the break-up of the studio system (see 3.6) that most A-list – that is, 'big' – stars could wield the power that the 'Big Four' had done in 1919. Since then stars have not been part of a studio's capital assets.

As noted in 3.8, stars are a very important part of the 'package' system. It is virtually impossible to imagine *Terminator 4* being made without Arnold Schwarzenegger, which obviously gives his agent a very good bargaining position. Possibly the biggest price extracted by a star for appearing in a picture was Jack Nicholson, who received a percentage of the box office receipts of both *Batman* (1989) and the sequel *Batman Forever* (1992), in which he did not appear. He also received a percentage of the merchandise revenue. Stars are normally paid a flat fee, around $20 million for the A list, and a percentage of the gross. For example:

> On the sleeper hit *The Sixth Sense*, Willis netted $50 million from the $600 million-grossing film (the studio made about $300 million) with a combination of his $20 million salary, 17 percent of the gross and his share of video revenues – and the movie's still playing in some cities around the country.
>
> (www.eonline.com/Features/Features/Salaries/index2.html, accessed January 2004)

After the success of *The Lord of the Rings* trilogy it was announced that Peter Jackson would be paid $20 million to direct *King Kong* (2005), the first director to receive such a 'star'-like advance.

Because stars are such a large proportion of the outlay, films tend to be built around maximizing the use of their talents. Often this is in the form of star vehicles, where the narrative is created to exploit a star's commercial appeal, such as Jim Carrey in *Bruce Almighty* (2003). However not all stars demand an 'extortionate amount of money'/ 'reasonable share of the studio's takings': for example, Brad Pitt and Julia Roberts did not get their usual fees for *The Mexican* (2001).

Stars are also crucial components of the publicity circus.

3.18 The publicity circus

Marketing is crucial for any film, and prints and advertising costs are, on average, over 50 per cent of Hollywood production costs. The lack of

For _The Mexican_ (2001) neither Julia Roberts nor Brad Pitt took their usual fee

finance that afflicts the British film industry (see 6.5) is apparent in the paltry marketing budgets most productions have; it is virtually impossible to compete with American distributors. When a British film does well it invariably has an American distributor behind it: for example, 20th Century Fox spent £600,000 on a television campaign five weeks before _28 Days Later_ (2002) was released, and £137,000 on outdoor posters. In addition _The Times_ newspaper carried a CD-ROM of the film's opening scene. The fact that _The Times_ and the distributors were both owned by News Corporation meant the cost of distributing that 'promo' was effectively nothing to the holding company; an example of synergy.

Not all publicity relies upon advertising. The film medium's popularity ensures that newspapers and magazines will devote editorial to new releases. The distributors have to make sure that their film gets attention in the media that addresses their target audience. For example, the February 2003 issue of the British film magazine *Empire* featured the 'King of the World' (Leonardo DiCaprio) on its front cover. Both *Gangs of New York* and *Catch Me if You Can* were being released during this edition's shelf life (that was January). There are also feature articles on both films.

Movie fans, the target audience of *Empire*, are likely to be interested in these films. This is also true of the coverage given to *8 Mile*, *Star Trek: Nemesis* and *Spider*. Laudably the edition also features foreign language films released in that month, *City of God* (*Cicade de Deus*, Brazil–France–USA) and *Irreversible* (France) (all films 2002). Everything – reviews apart – is given 'positive copy'; and the whole magazine is linked to products. The 'New Talent' section features Adrien Brody of *The Pianist* (UK–France–Germany–Netherlands–Poland, 2002) and at the back of the magazine the Remote Control section is full of reviews of recently released DVDs, videos, books and soundtrack CDs.

Empire, and similar magazines, offer an 'airbrushed' view of films, so their editorial is little different from the ads that pepper the publication. Publications, and broadcasters, only get access to the stars and pictures with the tacit understanding that nothing bad is written or said. If DiCaprio had been criticized in the issue as a one-movie wonder, the next time the 'King of the World' was releasing a movie *Empire* would probably not get access to him. Occasionally stars do get 'negative copy'. A *Premiere* magazine article suggesting that Schwarzenegger was a 'has been' in 2001 created a stir: he went on to be Governor of California.

Other elements of the publicity include the film's premiere where the stars, who will be contractually obliged to attend, generate news stories which in turn create coverage. The stars will also spend a day in a hotel giving journalists a very short interview where no awkward questions will be answered; and if they are asked, that journalist may not be invited again. The publicity circus is symbiotic to businesses: the magazine gets a big star on its cover helping to sell issues; the star and associated film get free publicity (disguised as information).

Distributors recognize that it is not always necessary to generate blanket coverage in order to open a film. For example for *X2 – X-Men United* (2003):

> Fox seems to be taking a more restrained, strategic approach reminiscent of how they've handled the *Star Wars* prequels instead of the 'throw-a-ton-of-ads-at-the-wall-and-hope-some-stick' method that is common for tent pole releases... Much of *X2*'s awareness has been built on promotional tie-ins, such as Dr. Pepper, Baskin

Robbins and Mazda, which is using the movie to help launch its rotary-powered sports car, the RX-8.

(Gray, 2003)

Poor marketing can destroy a film's box office potential. For example, it was quite clear 20th Century Fox's marketing department did not have a clue how to sell David Fincher's *Fight Club* (1999). The tagline 'Mischief. Mayhem. Soap', coupled with an image of a bloodied Brad Pitt in a boxing pose obviously did not appeal to a significant number of the cinema audience, who later flocked to the DVD, as word of mouth spread that this satire was a comic tour de force.

3.19 The DVD revolution

After the false start of laser discs, the digital revolution of home entertainment happened when DVD was taken up by consumers faster than any previous system. DVD's main advantage over its predecessor, video home system (VHS), was a vastly improved quality of image and sound. In addition, the aspect ratio of films was usually much more closely adhered to.

VHS won the format battle with Betamax in the 1970s, despite being an inferior system:

> Matsushita's VHS format prevailed for several reasons: VHS was less expensive … and more flexible and efficient in off-the-air recording, and Matsushita was more savvy and aggressive in acquiring 'software' (i.e. the rights to movie titles) as a means of pushing its hardware.

(Schatz, 2003: 28)

It was probably this that led Sony to purchase Columbia, and so avoid lacking the software for any future new home entertainment technology. In Britain, the manufacturers of videocassette recorders (VCRs) struck a deal with the biggest rental company, and this also encouraged the take up of the inferior format.

DVD's use of 'value added' extras has also changed the way films are consumed. The add-ons can offer fascinating information into the filmmaking process: for example M. Night Shyamalan's description of storyboarding on *The Sixth Sense* (1999) DVD. These extras frequently include 'making of …' documentaries which often appear on network television as a marketing device.

Unlike VHS, the manufacturers of DVD players agreed on a format, and this undoubtedly persuaded consumers to embrace the product. However, not all players would play all DVDs. This was Hollywood's attempt to combat piracy. Because of the staggered worldwide release patterns, it could be many months before a blockbuster reached some overseas markets; indeed, the film might already be available on DVD in North America before it had opened in the cinemas of a particular country. As the Internet had made it easy to purchase from other countries, the world was split into four DVD regions, and North American region 1 DVDs would not play on European region 2 machines. This did not prove to be a very effective deterrent, as many players were easily hacked to play all regions.

Another problem Hollywood faced was piracy; according to a report the 'theft' reached $3–3.5 billion per year (Frater, 2003). Films, from shakily held recordings made by camcorders in a cinema, with dreadful sound, to pristine copies made off original prints, found their way into the hands of pirates who would sell them with no regard to Hollywood's distribution patterns. The Internet, particularly as broadband became readily available, was also used to illegally distribute movies. One response to this was to release films simultaneously worldwide. *X2 – X-Men United* (2003) opened at number one in 92 of the 93 territories it blitzed in May 2003; only one pirate copy was reported (Kay, 2003). If audiences did not have to wait to see the hyped blockbuster, pirates were less likely to make sales.

Obviously the logistics of opening in nearly 80 different countries ('territories' are not the same as countries) simultaneously are difficult. However, this pattern was likely to continue, emphasizing globalization.

3.20 Film festivals

On the face of it film festivals, such as Cannes, appear to be celebrations of the art of cinema; indeed that is their primary purpose. However, in a capitalist global economy, art cinema, like popular films, is a commodity that needs selling. So, festivals are in effect shop windows for arthouse distribution. Winning Cannes' Palme d'Or is not necessarily a ticket to relative box office success but it inevitably raises the profile of the successful film.

Robert Redford took over the operation of the Utah/United States Film Festival in 1981, renamed the Sundance Film Festival in 1985, as a showcase for independently produced films. Although Redford's perspective was not particularly commercial – he was looking to

nurture talent – the festival has become an important part of distributors' calendars as they look to buy small movies in the hope of a
breakout hit. The satire *Series 7: the Contenders* (2001) originated in a
Sundance writers' workshop.

It would be wrong to suggest that film festivals are wholly about
bolstering the arthouse market; the London Film Festival, for example,
is not competitive. Festivals also have a role in celebrating 'film as art',
and have helped filmmakers working under repressive governments. For
example Spanish producer Elias Querejeta would circumvent the fascist
censor of Franco's Spain:

> by getting his finished films to foreign festivals before they were
> submitted to the censor, whereby jurors, critics and audiences in
> Cannes, Berlin, New York and Venice became an essential support
> mechanism for dissident film-makers.
>
> (Stone, 2002: 7)

During the 1980s the 'Fifth Generation' of Chinese filmmakers found
similar support from festivals throughout the world – see 5.12.

3.21 Conclusion: the shadow of Hollywood

In terms of box office Hollywood dominates the world of film. However,
the first country to achieve 'world domination' was Italy before the First
World War. For example:

> In 1914, Argentina imported $44,775 worth of European films and
> only $4,970 from North America.... From 1916 ... US cinema had
> almost entirely replaced its European competitors.
>
> (King, 2000: 10)

The war had been a watershed, and Hollywood has consolidated its grip
ever since. The prime reason for Hollywood's hegemony is economic. A
large home market makes it possible to recoup production and marketing costs in North America; any export revenue is the icing on this cake,
hence Hollywood films can be competitively priced against local fare.
Hollywood's apparently universal appeal may also be due to the fact that,
during its formative years, it learned how to address a diverse audience.
The large immigrant population consisted of many different cultures.

The large home market, of over 300 million bodies including
Canada, allows Hollywood to use high production values against which

other cinemas find it hard to compete. In addition, the well-developed star system, and genre-based narratives, facilitated a wide appeal. In a way Hollywood was more of a 'melting pot' than American society as a whole, because most successful stars and directors find their road leads to Los Angeles. Their talent was not necessarily absorbed by Hollywood, but it did adapt to commercial constraints. This is one way in which Hollywood reinvigorates its product, seen most obviously in recent years in the influx of East Asian talent.

Hollywood's trade association, the Motion Picture Association of America (MPAA), continually lobbies against protectionist measures. For example, GATT 1993 trade talks almost floundered upon France's insistence upon restrictions on distribution of Hollywood films; France maintains a quota system that requires a limit of 40 per cent of non-European films shown in cinemas or on television.

California's export of $100 billion in trade is, in a large part, due to the film and television industries:

'The distribution of American movies and TV programmes in foreign markets is important to the health of our industry and our nation's economy,' Jack Valenti, MPAA president and chief executive officer, said. 'Therefore it is vital that any trade agreements with our trading partners include commitments to protect our products from theft and to allow our products to move freely in the marketplace.'

(Kay, 2003)

The MPAA has always maintained that the North American market is open to competition. However as has already been noted, the oligopoly of the major studios makes the barriers of entry too high for foreign companies (unless they buy the studio), and so in effect the trade agreements are one-way to the benefit of Hollywood.

This is not to say that foreign films do not occasionally have hits in North America. However, such foreign language movies that pulled in the dollars as *Crouching Tiger, Hidden Dragon* (*Wo Hu Cang Long*, USA-Hong Kong-China-Japan, 2000) and *Life is Beautiful* (*Le Vita è Bella*, Italy, 1997), were both distributed by Hollywood companies – Sony and Miramax – (although it should be noted that Sony is a Japanese company). In 2001, foreign language films took a massive, compared with previous years (but in actual terms miniscule), 2.3 per cent of the market:

when the top non-English film *Amelie* grossed $18 million (excluding 2001 box office), the sector still accounted for 1.3% of business and such films as *Y Tu Mamá Tambien*, *Brotherhood of the Wolf* and *Mostly Martha* were potent performers. Fifty-four French-language films played commercially in North America during 2002, seven from Spanish-language countries, 33 from India (the sole remaining active ethnic circuit) and six to 10 from Germany, Italy, Scandinavia, Asia and the Middle East. Adding in a smattering of selections from other countries, the overall total was more than 150 titles.

(Klady, 2003)

The MPAA argues that Hollywood is the most popular cinema in the world because of the quality of the films. A snapshot consideration of nine territories, for the week ending 8 June 2003, found that 57 per cent of the movies in the top ten were distributed by Hollywood companies. This ranged from one out of ten in France to eight out of ten in Australia, Spain and Argentina. While there is no doubt that Hollywood films are popular, it is also certain that Hollywood distributors will favour Hollywood films, and they have a stranglehold on many markets.

All films are a product of industry. The most obvious constraint that this creates is the need to make money. However, film is a cultural product and so cannot simply be reduced to money. All films, in some way, articulate ideas about the society that produced them, but there is little point in analysing this without remembering the conditions in which the films were made.

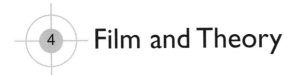

4 Film and Theory

4.1 Introduction

Although film theory has existed since the early days of cinema (for example Hugo Munsterberg – see Langdale, 2002, in 1916), post May '68 (see 5.10) theorists' ambitions were fired by structuralism, Marxism, psychoanalysis and feminism. While feminism used psychoanalysis, it also heralded the new direction of 'identity politics' which drew upon already existing 'third world' theory and developed new areas, such as Queer and post-colonial theory. By the end of the twentieth century, postmodernism had decreed that no theory could explain everything. The fecundity of film studies theories, particularly from the 1970s, was no doubt facilitated by the expansion of academia.

This chapter will first consider issues of realism and film, a debate that dominated film theory up until 1968. Using a chronological structure, the development of the *auteur* theory, in the early 1960s, will be followed by an examination of post May '68 ideas. Finally we shall look at an often-neglected aspect of film, the audience.

4.2 Film and realism

The technological basis of film as a medium, and cinema's origins as disreputable sideshows, meant it had to struggle to be considered as art. As the title of Erich Auerbach's history of Western literature, *Mimesis* (1953), suggests, mimicry of the 'real world' has preoccupied aesthetics. The attempt to 'reflect' reality seemed attainable with the invention of photography in the early nineteenth century, not simply because the images looked like what they were referring to (in fact early photography looks more like the 'smudges' of Impressionist painting) but because the intervention of technology was deemed to make the representation objective by avoiding the subjectivity of an individual artist. While technology is always required in art, the painter's paint and brush for example, photography was the first machine that could render reality. Although the camera obscura had been in use since the sixteenth century, films had the advantage that they could 'mechanically *reproduce*' reality in the same way a printing press could reproduce a book.

Walter Benjamin suggested that 'mechanical reproduction' fundamentally altered the status of the artefact. Instead of having one original, which guaranteed authenticity, there could be many copies, thereby denying the uniqueness of art and dispensing with the original's 'aura' and the whole artistic tradition:

> [Film's] social significance ... is inconceivable without its destructive, cathartic aspect, that is, the liquidation of the traditional value of the cultural heritage.
>
> (Benjamin, 1979: 79)

This 'liquidation' heralded the modern age of capitalism, where an audience's relationship to art was through its status as a commodity. This is certainly true of mainstream cinema, where value is measured by box office figures and the audience's prime requirement is entertainment (see 4.10). However Benjamin, a Marxist, did not celebrate film for its money-making potential. He was hoping that by denying the 'aura' of tradition, the art form could by appropriated for the masses.

Realism is one of the most slippery concepts in film studies. Even Sergei Eisenstein, with his emphasis on fragmenting montage (see 5.4), believed that by shattering our conventional conception of the world he was revealing the truth beneath. Documentary (see Box 4.1) maker, and theorist, John Grierson believed that cinema should be about the *interpretation* of life. Cesare Zavattini, who inspired the Italian neo-realists of the 1940s and 1950s, wanted to involve the spectator in *questioning* what was shown in film. All three writers were concerned with the depiction of 'ordinary people', an idea derived from naturalism, an artistic form that thrived in the latter years of the nineteenth century.

Box 4.1 Documentary

John Grierson apparently coined the term 'documentary' (see 5.5), and film's ability to represent reality in an iconic fashion (that is, its representations look like the original) made it ideal for factual cinema. However, film obviously cannot show reality, it can only re-present it using a particular set of conventions.

Bill Nichols suggested that there are four modes of documentary: expository; observational; interactive; reflexive:

> The expository text addresses the viewer directly, with titles or voices that advance an argument about the historical world.
>
> (Nichols, 1991: 34)

This is the most common mode, and is regularly found on television. Classically, in film, the Grierson-produced *Night Mail* (UK, 1936) falls into this category, with its use of a voice-over to anchor the meaning of the images. This anchorage is important in creating the documentary's argument. In *Night Mail*, the skill and social function of the overnight mail train is the theme of the film. It was not simply *showing* what happened, it was *telling* the audience.

> The observational mode stresses the nonintervention of the film-maker. Such films cede 'control' over events that occur in front of the camera …
>
> (Nichols, 1991: 38)

This mode, characterized by long takes and handheld camera that seems simply to follow the action, suggests that the camera is offering a 'window on the world'. This allows us to simply see what's happening and make our mind up about the events (there is no voice-over). This mode was pioneered by the 'direct cinema' of Richard Leacock and Frederick Wiseman, among others, in the early 1960s. It became possible with lightweight cameras and the ability to synchronously record sound.

Direct cinema is occasionally confused with *cinéma vérité*, which while using similar techniques had a different agenda, exemplified in the work of Jean Rouch (see *Chronicle of a Summer*, *Chronique d'un Été*, France, 1961):

> The direct cinema documentarist took his camera to a situation of tension and waited hopefully for a crisis; the Rouch version of cinema verite tried to precipitate one.
>
> (Barnouw, 1993: 254–5)

Few observational documentaries are shown in the cinema (they are not very popular and tend to be very long), although *Être et Avoir* (France, 2002) bucked this trend with its short running time and attractive portrayal of a rural school's dedicated teacher. Occasionally the film 'lapses', compared with the strict tenets of direct cinema, when children look into the camera and the editing eschews long takes and so, to an extent, draws attention to itself. To an extent this breaks the 'window on the world' effect.

Interactive documentary:

> stresses images of testimony or verbal exchange and images of demonstration (images that demonstrate the validity, or possibly, the doubtfulness, of what witnesses state). Textual authority shifts toward the social actors recruited: their comments and responses provide a central part of the film's argument.
>
> (Barnouw, 1993: 44)

Michael Moore's Oscar winning documentary *Bowling for Columbine* (Canada-USA-Germany, 2002) sought to find out why the United States had more gun-related deaths than any other country in the world (that is not at war). Moore's argument, that America is more violent because it is a society that is afraid of others, is clearly explained, but unlike the expository mode, it is apparently arrived at through discussion and investigation.

The reflexive mode draws attention to the act of making the documentary:

> We ... see or hear the filmmaker ... engage in metacommentary, speaking to us less about the historical world itself ... than about the processes of representation itself.
>
> (Barnouw, 1993: 56)

Man with a Movie Camera (*Chelovek s Kinoapparatom*, USSR, 1929) is a tour de force that shows the eponymous hero seeking out subjects for his documentary in the 'modern city'. Numerous devices, such as seeing the film being readied for projection, remind the audience that we are seeing a constructed text.

Nichols (1994) later added the 'performative' mode, although defining this is less straightforward than defining the other four. Stella Bruzzi suggests:

> A prerequisite of the performative documentary ... is the inclusion of a notable performance component ... performativity is based on the idea of disavowal, that simultaneously signals a desire to make a conventional documentary (that is, to give an accurate

account of a series of factual events) ... whilst also indicating ... the impossibility of [doing so].

(Bruzzi, 2000: 155)

Nick Broomfield's documentaries usually follow him attempting to make a documentary, in a similar style to that used by Michael Moore. He differs from Moore, however, in that he also, apparently, does the sound recording. In addition he talks, in voice-over and on camera, about the difficulty he is having in making the film. For example, in *Kurt & Courtney* (UK, 1997) we hear him fielding a call where he loses his financial backing, and we also see him negotiating with a detective's lawyer for an interview.

These modes are not mutually exclusive and documentaries can use more than one.

Finally we should consider docudrama and dramadocs, terms that are sometimes used interchangeably. The former are films made in the style of a documentary but are fiction, such as *Cathy Come Home* (UK television, 1967), while dramadocs are made in the style of a drama but are based on fact, such as *In the Name of the Father* (Ireland-UK, 1993). In addition films can reconstruct actual events and film them in a documentary style, such as *Bloody Sunday* (UK-Ireland, 2002).

Probably the most influential film theorist is Andre Bazin, for both his writings and his formation of *Cahiers du Cinéma*, a magazine that not only led to the acceptance of Hollywood filmmakers as artists but also nurtured the French *nouvelle vague* (New Wave). Bazin was less interested in the technological basis for cinema's claim to realism than in its ability to show what is going on in front of the camera, hence his preference for the long take, or shot, over editing:

around 1938 films were edited ... according to the same principle. The story was unfolded in a series of set-ups numbering as a rule about 600. The characteristic procedure was by shot-reverse-shot.... Thanks to the depth of field, whole scenes are covered in one take.... Dramatic effects ... were created out of the movements of the actors ...

(Bazin, 1967: 33)

Bazin celebrated directors, such as Jean Renoir (see Box 4.2) and Orson Welles, who favoured the long take and depth of field over editing, as he believed that 'direction in depth' allowed spectators to relate to film in a similar way to that in which they relate to reality.

Rudolf Arnheim, whose *Film* was originally published in German in 1933, asserted that, although film as art was based upon the mechanical reproduction of reality, it went beyond this re-presentation. He suggested that aesthetic devices, such as lighting, editing and special effects, allowed film to offer an artistic view of the world and not simply show it. While, for Bazin, these 'interventions' got in the way of the representation of reality, Arnheim thought they were crucial to film as art. Arnheim was a formalist, with his emphasis upon the *medium* of film, against Bazin's realist position, which is based upon the 'impassive lens, stripping its object of all those [preconceived] ways of seeing' (Bazin, 1967b: 15). They both shared an assumption that the photographic process was fundamental to film as art.

Eventually this focus upon the iconic qualities of film was transformed into an investigation into the idea of mimetic reproduction. The idea that films could simply reflect reality was regarded as naïve, and so the target of critical investigation became how film would transform what it was representing. Before we explain this shift we shall consider an extremely influential 'theory' in the acceptance of film as art that is still much used, and abused, today.

Further reading

Arnheim, R. (1997) *Film Essays and Criticism,* Madison: University of Wisconsin Press.

Kracauer, S. (1995) *Theory of Film: The Redemption of Physical Reality,* Princeton: Princeton University Press.

Langdale, A. (2002) *Hugo Munsterberg on Film: The Photoplay – A Psychological Study and Other Writings,* London and New York: Routledge.

Box 4.2 *The Rules of the Game (La Règle du Jeu, France, 1939)*

The Rules of the Game has featured in the top ten of every *Sight and Sound* magazine 'greatest movies ever made' ten-yearly poll, and has been in the top three for the last 40 years. Putting aside the question whether 'the greatest film ever made' is a valid question, it does suggest that Renoir's movie has succeeded in 'speaking' to successive generations.

In 1939 Renoir's stock in the film business was at its height, his previous film *La Bête Humaine* (1938) had played 'to full houses for months at the Madeleine [in Paris]' (Sesonske, 1980: 379), and his critical reputation was irreproachable.

The Rules of the Game was filmed between Chamberlain's grasp of a piece of paper at Munich (a vain hope for peace with Hitler's Germany) and the start of the Second World War. Renoir was consciously attempting to capture that historical moment: not the joy of many who believed war had been averted but their delusion in doing so:

> it seemed to me that a way of interpreting this state of mind ... was not to talk of that situation but tell a frivolous story. I looked for inspiration to Beaumarchais, to Marivaux, to the classical authors of comedy.
>
> (Renoir quoted in Sesonke, 1980: 378)

Compared with the optimism of *Le Crime de Monsieur Lange* (1935) and *La Marseillaise* (1938), *The Rules of the Game* — despite the fact it is a comedy — is strikingly pessimistic. Renoir used eighteenth-century classics, which satirized the divisions of social class, to comment upon the contemporary bourgeoisie. Like his predecessors, the satire did not go unnoticed on its premiere in July 1939:

> [it was] preceded by an interminable documentary consecrated to the glories of the French Empire.... The audience cheered. But as *La Regle du Jeu* unrolled, the applause turned to expressions of fury.
>
> (Sesonke, 1980: 384)

Attempts were made to burn down the cinema, and Renoir left shocked by the reaction. Later he realized that although he had taken care to present the bourgeoisie as sympathetic characters, driven by their weaknesses rather than malice, he had held up to the audience a mirror showing their inability to deal with the impending war: 'People who commit suicide do not care to do it in front of witnesses' (Sesonke, 1980: 384).

Renoir had dealt with the theme in *La Grand Illusion* (1937), where the officer class of the First World War stuck to a code of honour that had no relevance to the realities of the war. Despite his sympathetic portrayal of the officers (played by Erich von Stroheim and Pierre Fresnay), Renoir's sympathies lay with the Left (although he never joined the Communist Party, the only political group to vote against the Munich pact).

It is interesting to compare *The Rules of the Game* with *Gosford Park* (UK-USA-Germany-Italy, 2001) a film that also satirizes the bourgeoisie, of the inter-war period, and explicitly references the earlier film in the hunting scene. While the later film's view is retrospective, Renoir's was contemporary even though his characters seem – at the mansion – to be locked in the past. However, the anachronistic existence of the characters in *The Rules of the Game* is counterpointed by André Jurieux, whose arrival emphasizes modernity, with the technology of the aeroplane and radio.

Renoir's technique in the film is 'realist' in its use of relatively long takes and deep focus. Characters move into, and through, the scene as if we are observing them without needing to have the camera (through editing) pick out significant points. It is worth noting that this was not particularly a 'Renoir technique' as:

> long and mobile takes were quite common in 30s French cinema and many directors used longer takes than Renoir.... This was a style developed partly in response to the theatrical tradition ...
>
> (Vincendeau, 1992: 36c)

Each scene is carefully choreographed, and the spatial relationship of the characters to one another (and the camera) is crucial to the film's meaning. For example when Jurieux arrives at the mansion, characters sweep into the still frame, each movement changing the power relations between them, while the scene's protagonist – Christine – tries to take control of the situation:

> The sense of Christine's performance as one governed by strict rules, where a wrong move threatens disaster, emerges from another visual parallel that the décor permits: the camera sees the floor, with Christine and Andre moving across its black-and-white marble tiles, as a chess board.
>
> (Perkins, 1981: 1143)

Although the camera appears to be merely an observer, the tight choreography of characters by Renoir shows the scene to be highly manipulated. The film's conclusion, where the bourgeoisie re-enter the mansion having glossed over Jurieux's murder, is highly symbolic, as we see only their shadows. Renoir was suggesting that the old order was about to be shattered by war.

Further reading

O'Shaughnessy, M. (2000) *Jean Renoir,* Manchester: Manchester University Press.

Renoir, J. (2000) *My Life and My Films,* Cambridge and New York: Da Capo Press.

Sesonske, A. (1980) *Jean Renoir – the French Films 1924–1939,* Cambridge and London: Harvard Film Studies.

4.3 The *auteur* theory

One of the first films to attain artistic status was *The Cabinet of Dr. Caligari* (*Das Kabinett des Doktor Caligari*, Germany, 1920):

> The wonder film of 1920 indicated new aesthetic ambitions for the cinema; new relationships between film and the graphic arts, between actor and setting, between image and narrative.
>
> (Robinson, 1997: 7)

As cinema matured during the 1920s, directors such as F. W. Murnau, Fritz Lang, Sergei Eisenstein, Victor Sjostrom and Abel Gance (and later Jean Renoir) were lauded as artists. Films produced by Hollywood (with occasional exceptions such as Charlie Chaplin and Buster Keaton), however, were considered to be tarred by a commercial brush.

While Hollywood is still automatically maligned by many as incapable of producing anything other than films designed to appeal to either a lowest common denominator or, at best, a middlebrow audience, the academic consensus is happy to accept Hollywood products as art that can be both venal and fascinating. The roots of this acceptance lie in Alexandre Astruc's 1948 'The Birth of a New Avant-Garde: Le Camera-Stylo' and François Truffaut's *la politique des auteurs* of 1954.

Writing in *Cahiers du Cinéma,* Truffaut excoriated what he called French cinema's 'tradition of quality', films that were tasteful and bound by their scripts. He dubbed the directors of such films as *metteurs en scène,* those who merely filmed the script, and contrasted them negatively with *auteurs,* directors who brought a personal vision to the film.

Truffaut's attack was intended as a critical policy and not a theory; however Andrew Sarris' wrote in 1962:

> Henceforth, I will abbreviate *la politique des auteurs* as the *auteur* theory to avoid confusion.
>
> (Sarris, 1979: 653)

It could be argued that *auteurism* has been confused and confusing ever since. However, the view that certain directors can be seen as the author of their films continues to be held. Sarris believed that:

> The strong director imposes his own personality on a film, the weak director allows the personalities of others to run rampant.
>
> (Sarris, 1976: 246)

In Britain Victor Perkins, and his co-editors of *Movie* magazine, took up the *auteur* baton and, like their Gallic colleagues, used the 'theory' to eulogize Hollywood directors such as John Ford and Nicholas Ray (see Box 1.5). They believed the personal vision of such men (it was by necessity men, as women rarely directed during Hollywood's Golden Age) transcended the commercial context in which they worked. Hollywood became, for the first time, a respectable area of study. B (low-budget) pictures, by directors such as Sam Fuller, and the 'women's pictures' of Douglas Sirk, were seen to be offering subversive takes on the American dream from within the heart of capitalist Hollywood. *Auteurism* was particularly useful in allowing the revaluation of the American films of European directors, such as Fritz Lang and Alfred Hitchcock.

The approach was particularly in chime with the British academic tradition, exemplified in F. R. Leavis's work on literature, with its emphasis on close reading of canonical texts. So although it was radical in the way it treated the mass culture of Hollywood as art, it was simultaneously reactionary because it used the traditional discourse of Romanticism in eulogizing 'great men'. This conservatism did not coalesce with the zeitgeist of May '68 (see 5.10), and so *auteur* structuralism was conceived.

4.4 Structuralism and *auteurism*

Structuralism, and the science of signs (semiotics or semiology) derived from it, was one of the most important intellectual movements of the twentieth century. It enabled film theorists to conceptualize the view that film represented reality in a *particular* way and did not simply *reflect* the pro-filmic event. Foremost among early structuralists was Christian Metz, who attempted to define 'the Grande Syntagmatique', that is, the unseen structure (the *langue*) of film language, of which a film is simply the performance, or the 'tip of the iceberg' (the *parole*). While Metz's intervention was important in moving film theory away from a simplistic 'reflectionist' view of the medium, his attempts to pin film language down were fraught with 'exceptions that prove the rule'. Film form proved too malleable to be reduced to a series of 'linguistic' rules. However his analysis was rigorous, and he recognized the limitations of his conclusions; in *Language and Cinema* (1974) he proposed that his:

> Grande Syntagmatique [was] merely a subcode of editing within a historically delimited body of films, i.e. the mainstream narrative tradition from the consolidation of sound film in the 1930s through the crisis of the studio aesthetic and the emergence of the diverse New Waves in the 1960s.
>
> (Stam, 2000: 118)

Anthropologist Claude Levi-Strauss articulated another intellectual current inspired by Saussure's structuralism. He suggested that 'hidden' binary oppositions structured the way in which humans understood the world. Although part of the 'old school' (pre-structuralist) criticism, *auteurists* were given new hope by Levi-Strauss. In *auteurist* terms these binary oppositions could be seen as the themes that cropped up in a director's work regardless of which genre he was working in. Wollen used Howard Hawks as a test case, as he made many movies in different genres:

> For Hawks the highest human emotion is the camaraderie of the exclusive, self-sufficient, all-male group. Hawks' heroes are cattle-men, marlin-fishermen, racing-drivers, pilots, big-game hunters, habituated to danger and living apart from society, actually cut off from it physically.... The *elite* group strictly preserves its exclusivity. It is necessary to pass a test of ability and courage to win admittance. The group's only internal tensions come when one member lets the others down ... and must redeem himself by some act of exceptional bravery ...
>
> (Wollen, 1972: 82)

Wollen argued that this pattern was present in films as diverse as the Western *Rio Bravo* (1959), the musical *Gentlemen Prefer Blondes* (1953) and the screwball comedy *Bringing Up Baby* (1938). However Wollen was careful to point out that:

> Structuralist criticism cannot rest at the perception of resemblances or repetitions ... but must also comprehend a system of differences and oppositions. In this way, texts can be studied not only in their universality (what they all have in common) but also in their singularity (what differentiates them from each other).
>
> (Wollen, 1972: 93)

In a comparison between Hawks and John Ford's oppositions, or antinomies, Wollen (1972: 102) concluded that Ford's work was the richer:

> it is the richness of the shifting relations between antinomies in Ford's work that makes him a great artist ...

Wollen here is echoing the earlier *auteur* approach in using the 'theory' to create a hierarchy of great directors. By isolating the 'master antinomy' (opposition) in a director's work it was possible to see how each film articulated this defining feature differently, rather than simply look for commonality. For example in Ford:

> the element 'Indian' in the opposition European/Indian may be aligned with the element 'savage' in one film and with the element 'civilised' in another. Its meaning alters with context ...
>
> (Lapsley and Westlake, 1988: 110)

The structuralist would not consider Ford to be the conscious author of his films, but an 'unconscious catalyst' that articulated society's myths and so is investigating (inverted commas) 'Ford', the pattern found in films directed by John Ford. This pattern therefore was not intended by the director, but is unearthed by the critic, or reader of the film. And it is in this that:

> the historical importance of auteur-structuralism resides ... as a first step towards distinguishing the empirical author from the author constructed by ... the reader ...
>
> (Lapsley and Westlake, 1988: 111)

The influence of Levi-Strauss was also evident, in the use of antinomies, in genre criticism of the time (particularly the work of Jim Kitses – see 2.6.8). While genre criticism legitimized academic readings of non-*auteurist* directors, its approach was similar in that it privileged theme over visual style, and genre was often used as a template against which to measure a director's decisive input.

Today the industry would have us believe that all directors are *auteurs,* as most films are prefixed by 'A (name of director) film'. However, the industry has also recognized that certain directors, whether they be the arthouse favourites such as Atom Egoyan and Pedro Almodóvar, or cult genre directors, such as John Carpenter and Wes Craven, can be used effectively as a marketing device.

By the end of the 1960s Truffaut's polemic was viewed as a reactionary embrace of bourgeois values and not as a radical break with the past. *Auteurism* was always at its most useful in pinpointing directorial input in commercial cinema. Of current directors working in Hollywood, David Fincher, Martin Scorsese, Ridley Scott, Steven Soderbergh and Steven Spielberg have claims to be *auteurs.* For example Soderbergh followed the crowd-pleasing caper *Ocean's Eleven* (2001) with the box-office flop *Solaris* (2002), both starring George Clooney. On the face of it these movies were completely different. However:

> His *Solaris* is almost if not quite a rerun of *Ocean's Eleven* (out-of-towner invades hi-tech labyrinth in order to win his back wife), *The Underneath* (out-of-towner pursues former wife for second chance), *Traffic* (stranger-in-town searches for lost daughter to reunite family), or *The Limey* (troubleshooter from another continent arrives in town to avenge lost daughter).
>
> (Strick, 2003: 54d–55a)

Looking for this pattern in Soderbergh's films might cast light on individual films. However, it should be noted that simply mining films for *auteurist* features is, in itself, a sterile occupation. In practice, *auteur* criticism founders on the collaborative (and industrial) nature of film production. While it is possible to look at a few directors' oeuvres and see common themes and visual styles, it is a rather narrow way of considering film. While the director has potentially the most important creative input into a film, the scriptwriters, actors, cinematographers and producers can be even more influential.

Some critics still strive to place films into an *auteurist* framework. In her review of *Master and Commander: The Far Side of the World* (2003), Leslie Felperin performs the following linguistic acrobatics to suggest that the movie is a Peter Weir film:

> *if* there's a common theme running through his work then one *could* say it's a fascination with isolated communities and detached,

by choice or fate, solipsists.… Weir smuggles in serious ruminations on how civility survives in an untamed wilderness and the nature of leadership (*admittedly a key theme in Patrick O'Brian's original novels*).

(Felperin, 2004: 54a, emphasis added)

The fact that Weir is deemed to have to 'smuggle' 'serious' ideas into a Hollywood film shows that the assumptions of the original *auteurists* are still with us. However, as evidenced by book publishers' series such as the British Film Institute's 'World Directors', there is clearly a market for the *auteurist* perspective, although contemporary writers are more likely to acknowledge that there is more to film analysis than decoding the director's intentions.

Structural-*auteurism* is an uneasy mix of pre and post–May '68 theory, and heralded an explosion of ideas during the 1970s, which coalesced in *Screen* magazine.

Further reading

Classic *auteurist* writings including the work of Truffaut, Sarris, and Perkins' work are all represented in:

Caughie, J. (ed.) (1981) *Theories of Authorship,* London and New York: Routledge.

Mast, G. and Cohen, M. (eds.) (1985, 3rd edn.) *Film Theory and Criticism: Introductory Readings,* Oxford: Oxford University Press.

Nichols, B. (ed.) (1976) *Movies and Methods Vol. 1,* Berkeley: University of California Press.

Other books

Allen, R and Ishii Gonzales, S. (eds.) (1999) *Alfred Hitchcock: Centenary Essays,* London: British Film Institute.

Fawal, I. (2001) *Youssef Chahine,* London: British Film Institute.

Grant, M. (ed.) (2000) *The Modern Fantastic: The Films of David Cronenberg,* Trowbridge: Flicks Books.

Hillier, J. and Wollen, P. (eds.) (1996) *Howard Hawks: American Artist,* London: British Film Institute.

Jermyn, D. and Redmond, S. (eds.) (2003) *The Cinema of Kathryn Bigelow: Hollywood Transgressor,* London: Wallflower Press.

Nowell-Smith, G. (2003) *Luchino Visconti,* London: British Film Institute.

Polan, D. (2001) *Jane Campion,* London: British Film Institute.

Stevenson, J. (2002) *Lars von Trier,* London: British Film Institute.

Swallow, J. (2003) *Dark Eye: The Films of David Fincher,* Richmond: Reynolds and Hearn.

4.5 Screen theory – ideology

May '68, a time of intellectual revolution (and, virtually, political revolution in Paris – see 5.10) represented a break with the past for film theory, which was evident in *Screen* magazine's attempt to move away from an impressionist mode of criticism to one that had a firm theoretical basis. This basis drew primarily upon the French intellectuals Louis Althusser's and Jacques Lacan's updating of Marx's economic theory and Freud's psychoanalysis respectively. In attempting to break with the past they consciously used language and concepts that were far from straightforward.

While Marx had suggested that ideology created false consciousness, Althusser conceived it as 'the imaginary relationships of individual to their real conditions of existence' (Althusser, 1971a: 162). The key break with Marx's conception was that Althusser suggested that ideology created a new reality and did not simply *distort* existing reality. Drawing upon Gramsci's theory of hegemony, he suggested that individuals were subject to the dominant ideology, which interpellated them into a given subject position:

> So constituted, the individual perceives the perspectives of ideology as self-evident truths and experiences a world where ideology is constantly affirmed and confirmed.
>
> (Lapsley and Westlake, 1988: 8)

Marx suggested that the bourgeois ideology of capitalism had created a worldview that naturalized hierarchical society; communism, however, would restore the true way of seeing the world where everyone was born equal. Althusser, on the other hand, offered the view that communism, though more desirable than capitalism, could not offer a natural view of the world as it too was simply an ideology. He attempted to explain how individuals came to accept their subordinate status in the world, and 'interpellation' became a key concept in this. It was picked up by writers for *Screen* magazine, the British publication that was at the forefront of developing a new way of understanding film.

Interpellation explains how individuals are placed in a position from where they will see the world with, in a capitalist society, bourgeois eyes.

The spectator is interpellated into a fixed position, from which he or she is constructed as an obedient subject, by RSAs (repressive state apparatuses), such as the law, and ISAs (ideological state apparatuses), which include cinema. The law tries to force us to behave in certain ways, while film 'tells us' what is important in society (like heterosexual love and money). In this formulation Althusser was drawing upon Saussure's structural linguistics, which suggested that language creates us as subjects, and Lacan's psychoanalysis (see 4.6), where the subject is forever divorced from itself and requires language to become part of (interpellated into) society.

From this perspective mainstream cinema was complicit in creating bourgeois reality. Hence we find, in conventional films, an emphasis on individual (as opposed to communal), male (not female) endeavour, and the valorization of the nuclear (not the extended) family. In addition, gender roles are defined by patriarchal values so men remain the 'bread-winners' and women the 'nurturers'. As noted in 2.9, conventional narratives are structured to resolve in a 'happy ever after' ending, and so suggest that 'all is well with the world'.

One of the most well-known attempts to apply Althusser's notion of ideology to film was Colin McCabe's theory of the 'classic realist text'. McCabe suggested, taking his cue from the nineteenth-century realist novel exemplified by Flaubert, that films have a hidden narrator that tells the story from the viewpoint of bourgeois ideology. This narrator is hidden and so events appear to be described simply 'as they happened'. This is typical of the bourgeois realist aesthetic which effaces the means of its own production; for example, continuity editing is designed not to be noticed. The effect is that audiences of 'classic realist texts' 'forget' the contrivance of reading a book or watching a film, and therefore are less likely to think about what is being said to them.

A major stumbling block for this approach was that the process by which spectators are 'interpellated' into the (film's) desired ideological position was unexplained. In fact it required extremely docile spectators who actually forgot who they were while watching a film; in fact, in *Screen* theory, the spectators became a function of the film to such an extent that everyone would read the film in the same way. As we shall see in our consideration of Laura Mulvey's *Screen* work (see 4.6), the spectators of Hollywood films were seen to be male regardless of the individual's actual gender.

Another problem with McCabe's approach was that, in focusing on the formal aspects of film, it ignored the content. For McCabe the films of Ken Loach are no different from those of Steven Spielberg, because they both use conventional film style, despite the fact that Loach constantly criticizes the political status quo while Spielberg's films invariably conform to the tenets of bourgeois society. In addition, McCabe had a rather static view of realism, a concept that is better described as having constantly evolving formal conventions.

This contradiction probably had its source in *Screen's* valorization of avant-garde cinema above the mainstream, which in turn reflected the position of radical post-'68 film journals that:

> were ... in agreement in calling for a revolutionary cinema that would break with the dominant ideology in respect of both form and content.... For *Cinethique* virtually the whole of commercial cinema did no more than offer mere pseudo-pleasures as compensation for the alienation engendered by capitalism.... *Cahiers*, on the other hand, was inclined to take a more qualified view, which it supported with a ... classification of films ...
>
> (Lapsley and Westlake, 1988: 9)

It was believed that the formalism of avant-garde cinema (see 5.3) could break the bourgeois way of seeing, while anything using conventional film form could not (with the exceptions noted by Comolli and Narboni – see below).

The idea of a 'dominant' ideology, which structured the way the world was seen, had a wide currency in film studies during the 1970s. However it has been recognized that power relationships in society are more variegated than this monolithic conception could articulate. Although Althusser's conception of ideology proved to be limited, repudiated by many including himself, it was influential in the realization that films were not simply codifications of the world, but were *active* in creating *particular* representations of reality:

> Analysis would then call into question the reality so constructed, showing that its representations were historically contingent and that the mode of representation had effects of domination and subjection through its implication in power relations.
>
> (Lapsley and Westlake, 1988: 20)

Structuralism has taught us that film did not reflect reality. Althusser, and his followers, showed that films could represent reality from a particular political perspective. The task of post May '68 film studies (see 5.10), for those who saw themselves at the cutting edge of theory, became the ideological deconstruction of films. In an influential editorial published in *Cahiers du Cinéma* in 1969, and translated into English in *Screen* in

1971, Jean-Luc Comolli and Jean Narboni suggested there were five ideological categories of film:

a)   The vast majority of films, whose form and content both carry and endorse the dominant ideology unthinkingly.

b)   A small number of films which attempt to subvert the dominant ideology through both their content and formal strategies that breach the conventions of 'realist' cinema.

c)   Movies whose content is not explicitly political, but whose formal radicalism renders them subversive.

d)   The reverse of category c): movies whose explicitly political content is contained within the realm of dominant ideology by their conventional form.

e)   Films which seem at first sight to belong firmly within the ideological and to be completely under its sway, but which turn out to be so only in an ambiguous manner.... (Films which) throw up obstacles in the way of the ideology, causing it to swerve and get off course.

(Maltby, 1995: 397)

Most films fit into category (a), which encompasses western mainstream and arthouse cinema which tends to use conventional forms of representation, such as continuity editing, and the content of these films are bourgeois in nature – see Box 4.3.

Categories (b) and (c) were favoured by *Screen* theorists because they attempted to break the mould. Jean-Luc Godard's films, particularly of the late 1960s and early 1970s, were political in both form and content, and so belong in category (b). Category (c) films are not necessarily political in their content, but subvert conventional modes of representation: for example avant-garde films (see 5.3).

Comolli and Narboni were demonstrating the preference for a Brechtian cinema. Brecht's theory of 'epic' theatre was adapted to cinema; he believed that rather than offer Aristotelian catharsis, theatre should make the audience question society, and rouse them to action rather than purge them of their emotions. One way of doing this was to draw attention to the contrivance of theatre through direct address of the audience and mixing together different forms, such as bringing 'street' theatre into the 'respectable' auditorium. The title of McCabe's essay on the classic realist text, discussed above, emphasized Brecht's influence ('Realism and the cinema: notes on some Brechtian theses'); and Peter Wollen (1972) was clearly following Brecht with his conception of counter cinema.

Table 4.1

Old cinema	Counter cinema
Narrative transitivity	Narrative intransitivity
Identification	Estrangement
Transparency	Foregrounding
Single diegesis	Multiple diegesis
Closure	Aperture
Pleasure	Un-pleasure
Fiction	Reality

Old cinema versus counter cinema

Counter cinema worked in opposition to the mainstream by not using a clear narrative structure and by 'pushing' audiences away from the characters. The film's form was foregrounded by the lack of conventional techniques, and the film's world was subject to being punctured by other worlds (such as the 'real' one). Narratives ended without resolution, and the films demanded intellectual engagement by refusing to entertain audiences. Finally, because it acknowledged its own existence, counter cinema engages with the real world and not the fictional world of bourgeois cinema – see Box 4.4 and section 4.11 in Lacey (1998).

Category (d) films may criticize the dominant bourgeois ideology in their narrative; however their normal formal conventions drain any radicalism the film may possess – see Box 4.5.

Category (e) probably became the most influential, as it allowed the investigation of films that had previously been considered as simply articulating the dominant ideology but, with the 'right' sort of (symptomatic) reading, were found to actually critique that ideology. *Cahiers du Cinéma*'s editors were responsible for the prototypical symptomatic reading in their article 'John Ford's *Young Mr Lincoln*' (anthologized in Nichols, 1976) published in 1970. On the face of it Ford's 1939 film celebrated the American Dream; however by mining the 'silences', gaps and repressions of the film, the *Cahiers* editors concluded that the film 'contributes considerably to the subversion of the deceptively calm surface of the text' (editors of *Cahiers du Cinéma*, 1976: 529). Feminist film theory mobilized films in this category to great effect – see 4.7 and Box 4.6.

The processes by which spectators were interpellated into a bourgeois view by conventional film form were investigated by Jean-Louis Baudry, using ideas from psychoanalysis.

Box 4.3 Reading Hollywood

All films articulate ideas about society. This may be done quite specifically, as in *Boys Don't Cry* (1999), where 'redneck' intolerance is attacked,
or implicitly, such as *Cruel Intentions*' (1999) celebration of the *virginal*
Reese Witherspoon compared with Sarah Michelle Gellar's sexually
active vamp. As Hollywood produces films as commodities, it is no
surprise that, ideologically, the majority of its productions should be
conservative. As studios are capitalist institutions it is logical that,
on the whole, they should produce films reflecting, and reproducing,
bourgeois ideology. However, it should be noted that many (ultra)-
conservative commentators, such as Michael Medved (1993), believe
that Hollywood is a hotbed of radical (left-wing) values.

While most mainstream Hollywood productions do not directly deal
with politics, they usually offer a celebration of the American Dream:
the belief in the importance of the individual in the context of the free
market economy (anyone can succeed if they work hard enough). That
is, they are category (a) films. For many years this would find expression
in opposition to the 'communist' Eastern bloc who were the Cold War
villains. During the 1990s, the collapse of the 'Old World order'
necessitated a redefinition of the 'American Other': sometimes Arab
terrorists (*True Lies*, 1994) and less contentiously, alien species
(*Independence Day*, 1996).

However, although *Independence Day* celebrated (North) American
cussedness, the way audiences read the film was open to a variety of
positions. For example, right-wing redneck-survivalist types could
cheer the destruction of the White House, which they felt to be the
repository of the insidious liberal values.

In *Mercury Rising* (1998) Bruce Willis is pitted against a self-seeking,
high-ranking secret service official (Alec Baldwin). At a climactic point
the American flag is looked down upon from an extreme high angle
shot, suggesting we are seeing a very negative portrayal of America.
Similarly in *Enemy of the State* (1998), the narrative resolution, the death
of the 'bad apple', seems to suggest that there is nothing fundamentally
wrong with America. However, it is arguable that this is not sufficient to
alleviate the possibility that the state is acting in its own interests rather
than those of its people. Larry King, speaking the last words of the film,
states 'You've no right to come into my home.' While this is critical of
increasingly governmental surveillance of our lives, it offers its criticism
in bourgeois terms through emphasizing *individual* privacy.

The critique of the state in *Mercury Rising* is couched in left-of-centre terms (and so it is a category (d) film); that is, the government intervenes too much into people's lives. However right-wing groups in America share this view, so *Mercury Rising* establishes a distance between militia 'survivalist' groups and itself in the opening sequence, where one such group is represented as being demented (the father) and misguided (the son). The Bruce Willis character's humanity is emphasized in this scene, and he carries the moral weight of the film.

Even one of the meatiest meathead movie stars, Steven Seagal, has in *On Deadly Ground* (1994) made a political statement. After he has wrought mayhem, and saved the day, the film's coda is a quite astonishing pro-green and anti-industrial documentary.

Other category (d) films, of recent years, which offer subversive representations wrapped up as entertainment include *Gattaca* (1997), *The Truman Show* (1998), *Pleasantville* and *Fight Club* (both 1999), and *Donnie Darko* (2001).

One of the more explicitly left-wing filmmakers in Hollywood is Warren Beatty: see *Reds* (1981) and *Bulworth* (1998). Beatty obviously still has clout in Hollywood, in that he is able to make films that excoriate American democracy. *Bulworth* even includes a scene that mocks the studio bosses: no punches are pulled. *Bulworth* is a rarity in that it deals with political issues head on; Soderbergh's *Erin Brockovich* (2000) showed the culpability of a large corporation without investigating how or why such abuses occur.

Box 4.4 Brechtian cinema: *Tout Va Bien* (France-Italy, 1972)

The trajectory of the first two decades of Jean-Luc Godard's career – he directed and wrote *Tout Va Bien* (*All is Fine*) with Jean-Pierre Gorin – exemplify the political left's engagement with cinema. First by embracing the popular culture of Hollywood as art (see *Breathless*, *A Bout de Souffle*, France, 1960), then having doubts about American influence (*Pierrot le Fou*, *Pierrot the Fool*, France-Italy, 1965), then taking a Marxist, post-1968 position (*Le Gai Savoir*, *Joy of Learning*, France-West Germany, 1968) before moving onto a Maoist collective, the Dziga Vertov group (*Wind from the East*, *Vent d'Est*, France-Italy-West Germany, 1970). *Tout Va Bien*, as the film states at the beginning and the end, is a reflection on the aftermath of May '68.

**The Brechtian nature of Godard's and Gorin's *mise en scène* is
emphasised by the film showing the factory is a set (*Tout Va
Bien*, 1972)**

The film resists spectator emotional engagement by drawing attention to itself, in a Brechtian fashion, as a construct, and emphasizes
that the characters are fabrications (Wollen's counter cinema 'fore-
grounding' and 'estrangement'). It does this in the opening sequence by
showing the cheques being written for the film, and through a voice-
over conversation which discusses what the film should be about and
what characters should appear. During the film the camera rarely
moves, and the characters move in and out of frame in a 'frustrating'
fashion, as we expect the camera to follow the action.

Throughout the film several of the characters have long speeches
given direct to camera. This is not a film that aims to involve audiences
with a gripping narrative (Wollen's 'intransitivity' and 'unpleasure');
rather it posits the problem of what radicals should do after the
disappointment of the failure of May '68's revolutionary impulse to
change society. It has a sequence where the leads, who were big stars
of the time, Jane Fonda and Yves Montand, work in a factory ('multiple
diegesis'), questioning the idea that acting is work. (The workers in the
film were played by out-of-work actors – work that one out.)

The workers move in a group, and their scuffle with the shop steward owes more to the Marx Brothers (so much for 'unpleasure' there) than Eisensteinean revolutionary struggle – see 5.4. The exceptions are tracking shots of the factory (which is filmed as an obvious studio set: see photograph) and in the climactic supermarket scene. In the latter, which features 10 minutes of a slow tracking shot, a group of young people shout 'Help yourself, it's free!', a Maoist technique of the time, and consumers scuffle to exit with full trolleys.

As James Monaco states, if it was a bourgeois film it would be called 'tour de force'. Instead it is a radical film that deals with all:

> Levels of social practice – economic, political, and ideological. And all this in a movie, with stars and color and music and money and Jerry Lewis sets!
>
> (Monaco, 1977: 244)

The film is firmly rooted in 1972 ('reality') and has an open ending that questions how the public (work) and private (life) can be kept apart. Susan de Witt (Fonda) complains that their work and sexual lives are routine – typical bourgeois complaints – and Jacques (Montand) has 'sold out': once a would-be radical director, he now makes adverts.

Box 4.5 Comolli and Narboni's category (d): *Under Fire* (1983)

Under Fire (directed by Roger Spottiswoode) is set primarily in Nicaragua and chronicles the last days in power of a US-backed dictator, President Anastasio Somoza. Russell Price (Nick Nolte), a photojournalist, is the central character, as we follow his neutral disengagement from the conflicts he covers to 'falling in love' with the Sandinista Revolution. This leads him to fabricate a photograph showing Rafael, the dead rebel leader, as alive.

The film also deals with a 'love triangle' between Price, Alex (Gene Hackman) and Claire (Joanna Cassidy), who are both journalists. Early in the film Alex is heard telling his news organisation that 'we're [that is, the USA is] backing a fascist government again, I know that isn't exactly news'. In addition Somoza's troops are shown committing atrocities. When the film was released the revolutionary Sandinistas were in government, having toppled Somoza. However they were involved in a debilitating 'civil' war with the contras, who were backed by the American government. Hence the film was being critical of US foreign policy at the time.

The film's production company, Lions Gate, was created by maverick director Robert Altman, and this may explain why the film is so overtly critical of US involvement in the Central American country. When Alex's death is shown on television, Claire's crying is noticed by a Nicaraguan nurse, who states that 50,000 other people have died, but the death of one American is enough to get reported on television. 'Maybe we should have killed an American 50 years ago,' she states.

Despite its critical stance, the film is shot conventionally with stars in the lead. The film reduces the Nicaraguan civil war to the personal relationships of Price, Claire and Alex. At the end, Price and Claire leave the celebrating revolutionaries, smiling at the 'happy end'. The fact that the revolution was later stymied by further US interference is not mentioned. The key moment for Price's and Claire's conversion to the Sandanista cause is when a young lad (who dreams of being a baseball star) is gratuitously shot by the mercenary Oates (Ed Harris). Price's conversion – he realizes that he'd picked up a gun, rather than his camera, to chase after Oates – is shown as a compassionate rather than a political act.

This focus on individuals, in a conventionally structured narrative, is typical of bourgeois cinema. The narrative problem is twofold: the 'love triangle' (bourgeois ideology requires a heterosexual *couple*) and the faltering revolution. The 'triangle' is resolved both by Price and Claire's experiences and, redundantly, through Alex's death. The conventions of bourgeois cinema, with its focus particularly upon *male* action (Claire also has no surname), reduce the revolution to background colour.

The blatantly critical statements made also serve to legitimize the 'myth' of democracy; that is, democracies are built upon 'freedom of speech', and so in allowing such a critical film to be made, the bourgeois system shows its tolerance toward criticism. The absence of any formal distancing devices means audiences are swept along by the narrative, particularly in the journey to meet Rafael, which shows an astonishingly picturesque river accompanied by a Jerry Goldsmith pastiche score, mixing 'ethnic' panpipes and the western classical orchestra.

However, there can be no doubt that how a film is read, ranging from its being a startling critique of American foreign policy to an enter-taining (or not) thriller, depends upon the audience. A spectator who feels antipathy to what America does beyond its shores is likely to find the film interesting, as it reaffirms his or her view (a rare event for a Hollywood film). On the other hand, a 'patriotic American' might be dismayed by what he or she sees as one-sided propaganda.

Box 4.6 Melodrama and subversive readings

For many the characterization of anything out of Hollywood as subversive is surprising because it is, essentially, a collection of capitalist institutions whose bottom line is the creation of profit out of movie product. This usually necessitates conservatism in its films, consisting of, among other things, conventional gender roles and a narrative structure in which the hero (usually male) overcomes the villain to re-establish the status quo at the conclusion. However, during the 1970s, amalgamating *auteurism* and genre criticism, symptomatic readings of films suggested that great directors could use the excess of melodramatic *mise en scène* to create a 'secondary text' which subverted the apparently conventional ideological message of their films. For example, films that, on the face of it, offered a conventional narrative conclusion in fact undermined their conservatism by demonstrating how fragile the normality presented really was.

Writing about the 'women's picture', a precursor of 1950s melodrama, Jeanine Basinger suggested that contemporary audiences did see the contradictions inherent in the melodramatic films. The stock narrative of the 'women's picture' of the 1930s and 1940s shows the central character thrown out of, or leaving, a secure family situation, which leads her to forge a successful career for herself. A woman, as the narrative's hero, is shown as being able to act decisively, and through her actions is capable of motivating narrative development. However, as mentioned above, the sexist (patriarchal) ideology that informs much of Hollywood could not allow this success to be the narrative resolution. The woman had to be recouped for the family where she 'belonged'. So the successful woman's life is represented as essentially empty, and she usually returns to her family and her 'appropriate' role as mother and wife. Basinger suggests that, like the gangster movie before it where crime pays spectacularly until the last frame, the women's picture offered a narrative of subversion:

> seeds of unrest, even rebellion, were planted in some female minds by the evidence they saw on-screen, despite the conventional endings that turn a story into a cautionary tale. When morality has to dramatize its own opposite to make its point, the opposite takes on a life of its own. The film becomes accidentally ambivalent, contradictory. It sends two messages, though they're allegedly resolved by a hokey finale.
>
> (Basinger, 1994: 11–12)

Some melodramas had men as their central characters. In Nicholas Ray's *Bigger Than Life* (1956), a small-town schoolteacher, Ed Avery (James Mason), inadvertently becomes addicted to cortisone, and starts behaving tyrannically and spouting fascist views. In the end, although order is restored through Ed's cure:

> our confidence in the future is undermined by various factors. For one thing it is made clear that Ed's life depends on the continuance of the cortisone treatment. [His wife] is told that the doses must be carefully regulated, that Ed's disturbance was due to abuse of the drug: but the film has made it unambiguously clear that Ed's behavior changed significantly *before* he began abusing it.
>
> (Wood, 1972: 61)

Bigger Than Life focuses on Ed's family, their economic insecurity and the repressive nature of the patriarchal ('male as boss') role given to the father in the traditional family. The nuclear family is the prime social unit of western bourgeois culture, and melodramas often offer their subversive critique by showing how destructive families can be, and that they are therefore not the ideal social structure.

Douglas Sirk's *Imitation of Life* (1958) features two families, one black and the other white, with absent fathers. In addition, the white mother, Lora Meredith (Lana Turner), is a career woman who desires to be a great actress. The black mother, Annie Johnson (Juanita Moore), on the other hand, is totally domesticated and acts as Lora's maid. To add to the tension, Annie's daughter passes for white. *Imitation of Life* manages to combine a critique of gender roles (Lora's boyfriend constantly wants to possess her, which means she must give up her career) as well an excoriating attack on racism.

Although melodrama can offer a critique of society, it also supports society's dominant ideology: while the (ideological) function of most mainstream art is to vindicate the status quo, melodrama offers the dominant ideology on outlet:

> No ideology can even pretend to totality: it must provide an outlet for its own inconsistencies. This is the function of 50s melodrama. It works by touching on sensitive areas of sexual repression and frustration; its excitement comes from conflict not between enemies, but between people tied by blood or love.
>
> (Mulvey, 1987: 75)

Throughout *Imitation of Life*, Lora is accused of *acting* in order to get her own way; while she professes to love her daughter she spends a lot of time away because of her career. Annie's daughter is desperate to be taken for white, which she was 'mistaken for', while Annie believes that no one should hide the truth:

> The underlying disquiet of the movie – which renders its impact so pessimistic – is the collapse of matriarchy at the heart of the middle-American family. Both Annie and Lora fail their daughters: Annie from the moment she visits Sarah Jane at school to give her an umbrella, and Lora throughout the movie but especially in the scene where she makes a shallow promise to Susie to give up her boyfriend Steve rather than allow him to come between them.
>
> (Auty, 1980: 1037)

Through its representation of family strife, *Imitation of Life* possibly helped audiences to make sense of conflict within their own lives, and the happy ending may have given them a sense that 'everything would be all right'. Melodrama thrived in the 1950s as it was a time of social turmoil: traditional roles were challenged and new ones evolved. However patriarchy remained dominant; the genre helped to articulate this evolution. The era was a fertile ground for melodrama because many women, who had been forced back into the home after working during the Second World War, began to miss the independence they had experienced. They were a ready audience for films that were critical of the traditional gender roles, particularly their own roles as mothers and wives.

In addition, technological developments in the 1950s helped switch the emphasis from dialogue to *mise en scène*, from the word to the image – the 'proper' arena of melodramatic expression. The developments of colour, deep focus, crane and dolly-shots made a more complex *mise en scène* possible.

> The formal devices of Hollywood melodrama ...contribute a transcendent, wordless commentary, giving abstract emotion spectacular form, contributing a narrative level that provides the action with a specific coherence. *Mise en scene*, rather than undercutting the actions and words of the story level, provides a central point of orientation for the spectator.
>
> (Mulvey, 1987: 77)

In *Bigger Than Life*, the scene where Ed insists his son complete his sums before he is allowed to eat is transformed into an expressionist nightmare by the father's/teacher's shadow, which threatens violence on both his son and wife. Sirk's *All That Heaven Allows* (1955) has a climactic scene where the daughter, who is trying to persuade her widowed mother not to marry the man she loves, is 'painted' in lurid and grotesque colours that emphasize the insanity of the daughter's demands and the mother's self-sacrificial stance. Conventionally mother's were/are supposed to devote themselves completely to their children; that this is wrong is coded in the scene's colours. Elsaesser (1985) has also described how the growing influence of Freud's theories added to the essentially inward-looking focus of the genre.

In the 1950s the development of widescreen cinema created another tool for the melodramatist's armoury. Nicholas Ray, director of *Rebel Without a Cause* (1955), was one of the first directors who used widescreen cinema for melodramatic effect. For example, take the scene in *Rebel* where Jim's (James Dean's) family argues on the stairs: the camera's tilt, signifying domestic disruption, is made almost vertiginous by the width of the screen.

Further reading

Editorial collective (1992) *The Sexual Subject: A 'Screen' Reader in Sexuality,* London and New York: Routledge.
Kuhn, A. and Stacey, J. (eds.) (1999) *Screen Histories: A Screen Reader,* Oxford: Clarendon Press.

4.6 Screen theory – psychoanalysis

Psychoanalysis was born at about the same time as cinema. Although the discipline's 'father', Sigmund Freud, was dismissive of cinema – rejecting a $100,000 consultancy fee offered by Sam Goldwyn – his ideas have been among the most fruitful in understanding how spectators relate to film. In this the relationship between the spectator and the cinema screen was very important.

Jean-Louis Baudry, in 'Ideological Effects of the Basic Cinematographic Apparatus' (published in *Film Quarterly*, Winter 1974–75, Vol. 28 No. 2), showed how the use of the Renaissance perspective, for instance, helped create a transcendental subject (or spectator):

the camera lens was designed to produce the same ideological effects as the system on perspective in Renaissance painting. It organizes the world in relation to the spectator's vision, and so established the spectator as the centre of the world.

(Jancovich, 1995: 133)

If you stand in front of a Renaissance painting the contents of the image are placed so you can see everything clearly; contrast this with a cubist painting where your eye is likely to wander across the canvas trying to work out what the text is about. Baudry argued that by adapting this perspective, and often the frame ratio (although the widescreen format breaks this link, a point satirized when Newland Archer (Daniel Day Lewis) looks at paintings in Scorsese's *The Age of Innocence*, 1993), conventional cinema was apparently giving the viewer an omniscient view. In this way it 'interpellated' the spectator into the position desired by the dominant, bourgeois, ideology.

Baudry likens watching film in a cinema to Jacque Lacan's description of the 'mirror phase' of an infant's development. Up to this point, between six and 18 months, babies cannot speak and have no sense of themselves as distinct from their environment. They are, Lacan suggests, 'hommelettes' (similar to the broken egg that makes an omelette), a 'little man' whose self spreads out into the environment. However, at the 'mirror stage', the child suddenly realizes that he or she is distinct from the environment through seeing his/her mirror image, which appears coherent and complete compared with the lack of control felt by the child. Adults, usually the mother, can also offer an image of being all-powerful, an ego-ideal to which the infant can aspire.

The ego, or subject, of the child is therefore defined by its relationship with this image of 'the Other' (or imaginary realm). The Other is a powerful conception which can be applied in many different ways in film studies. For example the monster of horror movies (and alien in SF) is constituted as the 'Other' – see Creed (1993). However, the subject is forever split from the Other and hence is unstable. The individual subject is inherently paranoid. At the 'mirror stage' the child enters the symbolic realm of language, which enables him or her to become a member of society. However even here the conception of the self is slippery, as evidenced by shifting pronouns ('I' or 'me').

The combination of the darkened auditorium (although this begs the question how film works in the home: Baudry was dealing with the *cinematic* apparatus) and the all-seeing position engendered by the Renaissance perspective 'reconstructs the situation necessary to the release of the "mirror state"' (Baudry, 1985: 539). Thus:

> At the beginning of each shot, the spectator enjoys a secure imaginary relationship to the film, a feeling bound up with the illusion of privileged control over and unmediated access to its fictional world.
>
> (Johnston, 1999: 335a–336b)

Although as soon as an edit occurs this 'privileged control' is undermined, it is soon restored by the next shot:

> the various cinematic devices of framing, movement and editing are perceived by the spectator as acts of synthesis and constitution, and hence serve as evidence for the existence of a synthesising, constitutive, that is, transcendental, subject.
>
> (Lapsley and Westlake, 1988: 80)

Drawing on the work of Jean-Pierre Oudart, Daniel Dayan suggests that the shot/reverse-shot pattern, where we first see something or someone, is potentially disruptive as we do not know, at the start of the pattern, who is doing the looking. However, the reverse shot, when we see *who* is doing the looking, alleviates the possibility of disrupting the spectator's viewpoint. Eyeline matches work in the same way. This is how the spectator is sutured, stitched into, the film's point of view. Dayan argued that classical cinema is dominated by point-of-view shots; that is the spectator sees approximately (not actually, as this would be a subjective shot), what a character is seeing. In this way bourgeois film form strives, as do all bourgeois art forms, to be transparent, and so the spectator is far more likely to accept whatever (bourgeois) message is being conveyed. The cinematic apparatus is thus seen to be ideological in nature.

Dayan, like much of *Screen* theory, has his critics. For example, Barry Salt attacked the contention that the shot/reverse-shot pattern (or reverse-angle cuts) was dominant in classical cinema:

> The bulk of films [from the 1940s] continue to have between 30 and 40% reverse-angle cuts, as they have had since the nineteen-thirties.
>
> (Salt, 1992: 238b)

While Salt's observation may disallow a conclusion that the shot/reverse-shot pattern is solely responsible for how spectators understand classical cinema, it does not mean that it makes no contribution to an audience's engagement with film. In addition, Dayan's conception of the 'tutor-code' does draw attention to the way in which the 'continuity project' is ideological in nature:

> We know that ideology … must hide its operations, 'naturalizing' its functioning and its messages in some way. Specifically, the cinematographic system for producing ideology must be hidden. As with classical painting, the code must be hidden by the message. The message must appear to be complete in itself, coherent and readable entirely on its own terms.
>
> (Dayan, 1976: 447)

It should be noted that Dayan was referring to the *bourgeois* ideology. Eisenstein's attempt to create a Marxist ideological film style (see 5.4) was based upon drawing attention to the film language that was conveying the message and not disguising it. Stephen Heath (1981a) developed Dayan's concept of suture, in response to criticism by Rothman (1976) and Salt, by suggesting that editing, in general, was part of the suture process and by linking it to narrative:

> Suture is … a way of denying lack or absence, and it is in this sense that Heath connects suture with narrative. For Heath, narrative is concerned with the subject's sense of lack and is an attempt to compensate for this absence.
>
> (Jancovich, 1995: 139)

Hence the system of suture creates an *illusory* control on behalf of the spectator.

The fact that the performers in the film are absent in the cinema suggested, to Christian Metz (1986), that voyeurism is integral to cinema spectatorship. This concept was important in the feminist attempt to appropriate Lacanian film theory.

4.7 Screen theory – feminist analysis

Few articles have had the impact of Laura Mulvey's 'Visual Pleasure and Narrative Cinema', which first appeared in *Screen* (Autumn 1975), and has been regularly anthologized since. Mulvey's piece entirely chimed with film studies' intellectual currents – psychoanalysis and *Screen* theory – and social currents of the time – the continuing rise of feminism. And although many of Mulvey's ideas have been revised, not least by herself in 1981, 'Visual Pleasure' is still worth engaging with because it stimulated an enormous amount of theoretical work.

Mulvey concluded that narrative cinema (her focus was on Hollywood) was inscribed with patriarchal discourse, which was most obvious in the way males – within the film and as spectators – were given a privileged, active gaze that reduced women to passive images. Women's primary roles were to be looked at and to 'look good', and the scopophilic (the pleasure derived from looking at others as erotic objects) aspect of voyeurism was served up for men. Female characters could readily take on Propp's 'narrative function' of the 'princess' (see 2.13) as this was essentially passive. However, simply having a character whose primary function is to look good works against the economy of Hollywood cinema, as it freezes 'the flow of action in moments of erotic contemplation' (Mulvey, 1985: 309).

The character of a showgirl was an ideal combination, for show-girls, by their 'nature', are spectacles. So at the first appearance of Marilyn Monroe, in Otto Preminger's *River of No Return* (1954), she is singing in a bar; this allows Matt Calder (Robert Mitchum) to look at her as he searches for someone else. Hence the narrative motivates the display of Monroe's body. Although the spectator is put in the position of a voyeur, the 'showgirl' status validates 'his' gaze. 'His' because the spectator is seeing Monroe from Calder's viewpoint, via eyeline match editing; hence the audience is seeing Monroe from a male position.

Annette Kuhn demonstrated how men and women are filmed differently in her analysis of the first appearance of Sugar (Monroe again) in Billy Wilder's *Some Like It Hot* (1959). Kuhn contrasts the way in which Monroe is filmed compared with the male characters – who are also dressed as women. At first glance they appear to be shot in the same way, as the sequence of shots starts with a focus on both Monroe's and Jack Lemmon's and Tony Curtis' bums. However we see the men from a third-person viewpoint and Monroe – through an eyeline match – from the males' perspective (Kuhn, 1992: 64–73). So although there is equivalence in the way the sequences are shown, only Monroe is featured from a male viewpoint.

Mulvey shows that the way women are filmed also works against the 'harmony' of the Renaissance perspective (see 4.6). The use of close-ups, which serve to fetishize parts of women's bodies (Monroe's breasts, Greta Garbo's face, Marlene Dietrich's legs, Julia Roberts' lips), also works against the conventional film style that prioritizes narrative progression. (Orson Welles took this fragmentation to an extreme in his short *The Immortal Story, Histoire Immortelle*, France, 1968.)

While 'women as sex objects' has been a common trope in western visual arts (see Berger, 1990), male film stars too have always possessed erotic qualities; although Rudolph Valentino, from the 1920s, is probably the only male star to be wholly defined by his sex appeal. Mulvey suggests there are important differences because male protagonists – in the Proppian hero function – ultimately control the narrative:

> A male movie star's glamorous characteristics are thus not those of the erotic object of the gaze, but those of the more perfect, more complete, more powerful ideal ego conceived in the original moment of recognition in front of the mirror.
>
> (Mulvey, 1985: 310)

The 'mirror' refers to the 'mirror stage' of an infant's development when, psychoanalysts suggest, for the only time, we feel complete as human beings – see 4.6. In addition, male characters are spared the fragmentation thrust upon women, as they are usually filmed whole and often, particularly in the Western, in the context of the landscape.

Meanwhile the narrative trajectory subjugates the woman to the man:

> she falls in love with the main male protagonist and becomes his property, losing her outward glamorous characteristics … her eroticism is subjected to the male star alone.
>
> (Mulvey, 1985: 310)

Steve Neale suggested that men could be filmed for glamour, thus feminizing them, in melodrama, and have their bodies put on display in the musical. However, in action films men can also be subjected to the voyeuristic gaze albeit in a distinct fashion:

> War films, Westerns, and gangster movies, for instance, are all marked by 'action,' by 'making something happen.' Battles, fights, and duels of all kinds are concerned with struggles of 'will and strength,' 'victory and defeat,' between individual men and/or groups of men. All of which implies that male figures on the screen are subject to voyeuristic looking, both on the part of the spectator and on the part of other male characters.
>
> (Neale, 1993: 16)

It is a trope of action films that the hero should be severely beaten at some point. Drawing on Peter Willeman, Neale suggests that:

> In a heterosexual and patriarchal society, the male body cannot be marked explicitly as the erotic object of another male look: that look must be motivated in some other way, its erotic component repressed. The mutilation and sadism … are marks both of the repression involved and of a means by which the male body may be disqualified … as an object of erotic contemplation and desire.
>
> (Neale, 1993: 14)

As Neale points out, the eroticism of the male body (for the male spectator) makes the voyeur's gaze homosexual. This, like the potentially castrating effect of a strong female character (that is, she is more powerful than men), has to be disavowed by mainstream cinema.

Massively influential as Mulvey's ideas have been, they remain rooted in the *Screen* insistence that the film creates spectators. That is, we have no choice in how we are going to understand the film: we are either interpellated, or sutured (probably both), into the desired ideological position. There is little point, therefore, for a feminist to view mainstream films, as she will be either subjugated to the male viewpoint or forever disappointed by the patriarchal values offered. However, as we saw in 4.5, it is possible to read 'against the grain' and find progressive values in apparently reactionary films.

By the 1980s Roland Barthes (1977) and Michel Foucault (1991) had both declared the 'death of the author', and this intellectually allowed the reader to be reborn.

4.8 Spectatorship

Robert Stam (2000: 231) sums up the variables in play in spectatorship:

1. The work of the film itself: for example use of *mise en scène*, genre and narrative (see Chapters 1 and 2).
2. The role of technical apparatuses: for example DVD, IMAX.
3. The influence of institutional context: for example, cinema-going and analysing films in the classroom.
4. The ideological nature of society: for example, different societies are likely to understand films from their own perspective.
5. The actual spectator: his or her gender, class, ethnicity and historical context.

In this section we are mainly concerned with Stam's fifth point. However it is worth noting that an audience's experiences of the same film can change radically in different institutional contexts (point 3). For example, watching any film in the cinema is a different experience from watching it at home. Apart from the obvious improvement in the quality of the cinema's image, watching films with other people can alter our understanding. For example, comedies often appear to be funnier in the cinema because laughter is infectious. (The same might be said of screaming at horror films.)

The home environment, where most films are seen, can be full of distractions (telephones ringing, babies crying, mum and dad's presence being embarrassing during sex scenes). Films can often be paused, or rewound, in the home setting. This ability to watch films in ways not designed by the filmmakers has worried the censors, as it will allow audiences to watch, for example, particularly violent or sexually explicit scenes out of context. The fear is that watching such a 'strong' sequence divorced of its place in the narrative may change the meaning of what is being shown.

It often appears implicit in the work of censors that watching films is a passive activity, in the sense that audiences simply accept what a film is saying to them. However, as the first two chapters of this book have made clear, we *read* films, and so audiences have a vital input into the creation of meaning. Stuart Hall (1992) suggested that we could make three readings of films: preferred, negotiated and oppositional. The preferred reading accepts the meaning suggested by the film; the negotiated reading accepts the preferred meaning but alters it to the spectator's circumstance; the oppositional reading rejects the preferred meaning.

Box 4.7 Reading *Falling Down* (1993)

Social problem pictures usually set out to deal with a contemporary issue in an entertaining fashion. Its contemporary flavour helps sell the film, and appeals to those who like thought-provoking cinema without alienating the core cinema-going audience. On the one hand we might view films like *Falling Down* (directed by Joel Schumacher) as opportunistic in focusing on a contemporary problem in order to make money; or we can consider it as a 'state of the nation' statement. We can also do both.

One of the film's taglines stated the film's premise: 'The adventures of an ordinary man at war with the everyday world'. William Foster/ D-FENS (Michael Douglas) is unemployed, but he maintains the façade of work by commuting in traffic jams each morning. As the film starts he 'snaps' and starts walking (walking in LA is weird) across the city, determined to see his estranged family on his daughter's birthday. As it is a 'tale of urban reality' (another tagline), he encounters everyday problems that are symptomatic of a sick society.

What is the film's preferred reading? That America is a sick society because white patriarchy is in terminal decline, and this must be stopped? Or that both black and white men have been marginalized by the growth of feminism, and America's economic dominance has been badly affected by the Pacific Rim countries?

The above suggests a reactionary film, promoting a backlash against feminist gains. Sharon Willis suggests the film is misogynist:

> Prendergast's wife ... figures as the hideous subtext of his reluc-
> tant retirement and his ruined reputation.... D-FEN's ... parallel
> problem ... is his timid, paranoid, deranged mother, locked up in
> her house with her 'glass menagerie.'
>
> (Willis, 1997: 18)

However, the misogyny is not straightforward, as the macho atmosphere of the police station is mocked, and the Hispanic, Sandra (Rachel Ticotin), is positively represented. Jude Davies sees the film as offering a vision of American where white Anglo-Saxon Protestants are no longer at home:

> Cinematic signifiers of Vietnam abound.... As D-FENS walks past
> the pictures of Vietnam on the outside of the store, the sound of
> helicopters is heard ... [he] is dressed in black combat uniform
> [which] makes him look more like a Viet Cong soldier.... When he
> finally arrives at Venice Beach ... buildings are flimsy, the atmos-
> phere is hot. The place is swarming with colour and noise, with
> exotically dressed, tanned people.... D-FENS has arrived in Saigon.
>
> (Davis, 1995: 221–2)

But D-FENS is consciously identified with the black protester outside the bank, and clearly delineated from the fascist Nick (Frederic Forrest). On the other hand, we can consider the positive representation of ethnic minorities (including Sandra) to be a rhetorical device that aims to convince that this is not a reactionary film, and so makes it easier for us to share D-FENS' bewilderment when Prendergast (Robert Duvall) attempts to arrest him for being the 'bad guy'. By gaining the audience's sympathy, we are more likely to accept the film's message that the 'rot' of white patriarchy must be stopped. So while D-FENS is destroyed, the other representative of the white male, Prendergast, regains his manhood and demands his wife have his dinner ready for him when he gets home.

Falling Down, along with *Rising Sun* (1993) and *Disclosure* (1994), portrayed white, male anxieties about the economic decline of America, in comparison with Japan, and the rise of the women in business. However by the end of the decade the Far East was in a financial mess, and the threat of women no longer seemed so potent.

Although a film conveys these meanings, the spectator must do the actual reading. For some films, such as *Spider-Man* (2002), there is little debate about the message: the importance of acting morally by taking responsibility for one's actions. Although it is certainly possible that some may read the film differently, the great majority are likely to agree with the film's preferred reading, so clearly is it stated. While it is possible to offer divergent readings of mainstream Hollywood 'product' – see Box 4.7 – arthouse films are far more likely to be ambiguous; see 2.11 on Barthes' 'readerly' and 'writerly' texts. Rather than assume that spectators have to make one type of reading, it might be best to see the categories as possible ways of reading a film. This emphasizes that meaning is 'in play': not only is it likely to be different for different members of an audience, but individual spectators may change their understanding. This change can be achieved through the passing of time: a film thought of as being profound during teenage years can be seen as trite after more years of experience. Similarly, the view of a film can alter after discussion. This process is possibly most apparent in the classroom, where a teacher may show a film that students have difficulty understanding until it is discussed by the class.

More important variables, however, are likely to be the community in which the spectator is both situated, and the one from which he or she originates. The variables that go to make up community are many, and their inter-relationships complex. In the widest sense individuals can think of themselves as members of a nation (see 6.4). More locally, issues of regional identity are significant. Individuals may be part of subcultural groups. More importantly however, their gender, social class, religious orientation and ethnicity are likely to have a significant influence on how they understand films.

Finally, the conditions of reception can influence the reading of a film. As noted above, watching a film in isolation is very different from viewing in a group where, for example, friends might have the opportunity to discuss afterwards, and this might alter an individual's understanding of what he or she has seen.

Picking up on the ideas of Laura Mulvey (see 4.7), feminist theorists attempted to negotiate the negativity of Mulvey's position (that is, that female spectators were doomed to take the male's viewpoint). Most potent was the idea of masquerade. This dispensed with the spectator's passivity and allowed women to engage with female characters in an active fashion. Doane argues that while men are locked into a gender position in their spectatorship, women can readily switch between male and female viewpoints.

> The hypothesis could be supported by Freud's own later writings on women, which propose that, because femininity is gained through repressing the masculine tendencies.... Hollywood offers the female spectator ... a socially sanctioned access route to her repressed masculinity.
>
> (Lapsley and Westlake, 1988: 99)

So although a film might be insisting upon the male position, women can readily switch between characters, and also identify with the females in the film. In addition, Doane suggests, women can be represented in such an exaggerated way that there is no suggestion that spectators should identify with them. This was exemplified in *Stella Dallas* (1937), when the eponymous character (played by Barbara Stanwyck), the 'self-sacrificing mother' of maternal melodrama, exaggerates her uncouthness in order to convince her daughter to reject her for an upper-class family (see Doane, 1987: 181). This self-conscious masquerade, or 'double mimesis', is a process that female spectators can invoke, maybe subconsciously, when watching film:

> When Stella effectively parodies herself ... she demonstrates her recognition of herself as a stereotype ... while making the excessiveness of her role visible and strange, depriving the initial mimesis of its currency.
>
> (Wojick, 1999: 369a)

In other words, the obvious play-acting draws attention to the way the film is representing women, so spectators are as likely to think about what they are viewing as to uncritically accept the message.

It should be noted that there is no uniformity of readings of films from a feminist position. Patricia White quotes Linda Williams' argument that women recognize contradictory points of view: that they engage their 'multiple identificatory power', while Ann Kaplan says the film ends with 'an extravagant scene of female abjection' (White, 1998: 122b).

Although women are usually represented as objects of desire in film (the passive 'virgin' or the less passive 'whore' archetypes), or given the role of the (archetypal) 'mother', the very excessiveness of these roles allows female spectators to 'see through' them as male-produced:

> The masquerade, in flaunting femininity, holds it at a distance. Womanliness is a mask which can be worn or removed. The masquerade's resistance to patriarchal positioning would therefore lie in its denial of the production of femininity as closeness, as presence-to-itself, as, precisely, imagistic.
>
> (Doane, 1982: 81–2)

The attempt to liberate the spectator from Mulvey's monolithic view of a person's relationship with mainstream film led to an investigation of other gazes, especially those of gays and lesbians.

Further reading

Erens, P. (ed.) (1990) *Issues in Feminist Film Criticism,* Bloomington: Indiana University Press.

Johnston, C. (1973) 'Women's cinema as counter cinema' in Nichols (1976).

Modleski, T. (1988) *The Women who Knew too Much,* London and New York: Routledge.

4.8.1 Queer theory

Once spectators had been liberated from the (dominant ideology's) preferred reading, they (often film theorists) were at liberty to recoup films for their own perspectives. So, for example, the lesbian appeal of Marlene Dietrich (try *Blonde Venus,* 1932), Greta Garbo (*Queen Christina,* 1933), Katharine Hepburn (*Sylvia Scarlett,* 1935) and Mae West (*She Done Him Wrong,* 1933) and the homoerotic appeal of James Dean (*Rebel Without a Cause,* 1955) and Marlon Brando (*The Wild One,* 1954) were more widely recognized.

Queer theory, as it became to be known (using the appropriated term of 'deviance', in the same way as Hip-Hop artists appropriated the racist term 'nigger'), theorized gender as a performance, rather than a biological or social condition, and though not restricted to homosexual readings of cinema, has been most evident in this sphere. Judith Butler (1999), drawing on Michel Foucault's work, suggested that gender should be conceived outside of the female–male binary opposition. In addition, through necessity the theory had to work outside the film studies theoretical orthodoxy:

> Psychoanalysis had been blind to class, Marx had been blind to race and gender, but both psychoanalysis and Marxism had been blind to sexuality.
>
> (Stam, 2000: 262–3)

The term 'Queer cinema' is used in many different ways; Alexander Doty (1998) suggested a number of approaches. For example, Queer encapsulates three non-straight positions, bisexual, gay and lesbian, and so is distinct from gay and lesbian (and bisexual?) readings of films. It moves beyond considering gender (and sexuality) as binary oppositions and deals with:

> those films and popular culture texts, spectator positions, pleasures, and readings that articulate spaces outside gender binaries and sexuality …
>
> (Doty, 1998: 150b)

Hence androgyny is particularly interesting to Queer theory. In *The Crying Game* (UK-Japan, 1992) Dil's gender was both a crucial narrative conceit and a central selling point of the film.

On the other hand, B. Ruby Rich has suggested that Queer cinema is better used to describe a cinematic moment created by events of the early 1990s:

> The proliferation of small-format video as a medium for both production and distribution [and] the new alliances forged between lesbians and gay men in the wake of Aids organising, along with an exponential growth in gay and lesbian film festivals …
>
> (Rich, 2000: 23a)

Similarly Doty (1998) cites the Sundance Film Festival of 1991 and the Toronto Film Festival of 1992 as watersheds when they showed the films *My Own Private Idaho* (1991), *Young Soul Rebels* (UK-France-Germany-Spain, 1991) and *Edward II* (UK, 1991).

It was not surprising that Queer theory should start informing film-making. Instead of appropriating mainstream films for Gay subculture,

Queer films would address their audience directly. Derek Jarman managed to produce a distinct body of films which:

> Reread the past according to a gay, or 'queer' sensibility. This has included the reinterpretation of 'gay' artists as in *Caravaggio* (1986) [and] the 'rereading' of English literature from a gay perspective as in *The Angelic Conversation* (1985). ...
>
> (Hill, 1999: 155)

Queer cinema has continued to flirt with the mainstream; the independently produced *Boys Don't Cry* (1999) received wide attention when Hilary Swank won the Best Actress Oscar.

4.8.2 Reception studies

Theorizing the gaze of minority groups helped give diversity to an understanding of audience response. It was understood that it was no longer viable to consider individuals as taking one position and that any:

> categories repress the heteroglossia within spectators themselves. Spectators are involved in multiple identities (and identifications) having to do with gender, race, sexual preference, region, religion, ideology, class, and generation.
>
> (Stam, 2000: 233)

In this way minority groups can readily read against the grain of a text. Marsha Prescod highlighted this ability in a review of *Bringing Down the House* (2003):

> *Bringing Down the House* is so full of racial stereotypes, it could have been written by a reformed Klan member.... I laughed like a drain. So did the audience. ... even as our jaws dropped at some of the racist comments coming out of characters' mouths. And the black people laughed as hard as the white people.
>
> (Prescod, 2003: 8)

That said, we should not assume that audiences have total control over how they understand films. In order to make sense of other cultures, groups need access to information about those cultures. If a minority culture is rarely represented, the few representations that exist are burdened with carrying comprehensive information about the culture.

For example, Muslim fathers are rarely seen in British cinema, and so when *East is East* (UK, 1999) became a box office hit, the representation of the Muslim dad, George (Om Puri), was widely disseminated. The fact that he was portrayed as something of a monster would not matter if there were alternative representations of Muslim dads available. As there are not, the representation in *East is East* took on the burden of 'all' possible representations of this group, and there is a danger that those in the audience who have no experience of Muslim dads might assume that George is typical.

During the 1990s more research was conducted into how 'flesh and blood' audiences understood films. This is extremely difficult (human beings are complex variables) and expensive research to undertake. For example, an investigation into the processes by which audiences identify with characters found:

> There is evidence participants utilize a number of factors in building character relationships: consumer choice, personal experience and preferences, imaginative hypothesizing a character expansion. These factors combine to create complex and varied interpretations of this scene.
>
> (Hill, 1997: 39)

As the tentative beginning of the above quote suggests, it is very difficult to draw definitive conclusions. However, Hill's research did find that the term identification was problematic:

> Many participants did not consider the phrase 'identification' adequate to describe the variety of response they experienced when viewing this scene [from *Henry, Portrait of a Serial Killer*, 1986]; terms such as 'sympathy', 'empathy', 'relate', 'feel for', 'understand', were used to qualify what 'identification' meant to individual participants.
>
> (Hill, 1997: 40–1)

At the very least this suggests that we cannot assume that audiences relate to characters in a straightforward fashion. This is evident in many films directed by Alfred Hitchcock, as he was adept at suggesting that audiences should be 'rooting' for the bad guy. For example, in *Strangers on a Train* (1951), when Bruno Anthony (Robert Walker) drops down a grid a lighter with which he is intending to incriminate the hero Guy Haines (Farley Granger), he must retrieve it in order for the narrative to progress. Unless he succeeds, the film will end in anti-climax. Hill's research was using a film (*Henry, Portrait of a Serial Killer*) that was heavily censored in Britain, and the effects of extreme imagery on spectators has long bothered the censors — see 6.5.8.

4.9 Third cinema and post-colonialism

This chapter jumped on the *Screen* bandwagon in Section 4.5, but we need to skip backwards, chronologically, to consider theories of non-western cinema. The concept of a 'third' cinema was developed between 1969 and 1971 by Argentinean filmmakers Fernando Solanas and Octavio Gettino in an article first published in *Afterimage* No. 3, in 1971. They wanted to reject the dominant, first world, cinema defined by Hollywood by encouraging alternative cinemas. They defined two alternatives: the 'second cinema' of arthouse, including the French New Wave and the Latin American Cinema Novo (see 5.7 and 5.9). However, although 'second cinema' was at liberty to break the rules of 'first' cinema, it could only go so far. What was needed, they concluded, was:

> films that the System cannot assimilate and which are foreign to its needs, or making films that directly and explicitly set out to fight the System.... they can be found in the revolutionary opening towards a cinema outside and against the System, in a cinema of liberation: the third cinema.
>
> (Solanas and Gettino, 1976: 52, emphasis original)

There are more than echoes here of Comolli and Narboni's favoured categories (see 4.5). Western cinema was seen, from the perspective of the 'third (developing) world', to be inherently colonial and hence corrupt. The writers had already contributed to this new cinema with their *The Hour of the Furnaces* (*La Hora de los Hornos: Notas y Testimonios Sobre el Neocolonialismo, la Violencia y la Liberación*, Argentina, 1968). Inspired by a mixture of Peronist 'third way' politics and Franz Fanon's anti-colonial writing, the four-hour-plus film documents the imperialist legacy in Argentina and suggests the best way of forging a nation state in neo-colonial times. The film experimented with engaging audiences actively:

> The film demands the activity and involvement of the spectator, in screenings which were political acts and exceptional moments of communication. At the end of Part II a voice declares 'Now the

film is pausing, it opens up to you for you to continue it. Now you have the floor.'

(King, 2000: 86)

Solanas and Gettino's use of the term 'third' is distinct from the way in which the term 'Third World' was used for many years in the second part of the twentieth century. The 'Third World' referred to non-industrial nations that were not aligned to either the West or the Eastern bloc. Since the demise of the Cold War, the term has been replaced by 'developing world', suggesting that the non-industrial, and poor, nations are moving toward being prosperous. However the terms are entangled, as most filmmakers in the Third World were confronted with problems caused by colonialism whether they were trying to make commercial cinema in the style of Hollywood, or revolutionary cinema in the style of Solanas and Gettino.

Roy Armes, in his classic tome, described the factors that have defined Third World filmmaking:

➤ The nature of social structures shaped by the force of tradition and the impact of colonialism
➤ the emergence of Western-educated elites as ruling groups and as the prime movers in cultural production
➤ the problems of defining both a 'nation' and a 'national culture'
➤ the issue of language and the insights afforded by literature and theatre that bridge the gulf between Western and non-Western worlds.
➤ the nature of cinema as a product of Western capitalism.
➤ the role of U.S.-dominated film distribution as an examplar (sic) of the working of the capitalist world system.

(Armes, 1987: 7)

One glance at the map of Africa, or even the border between the USA and Canada, is enough to suggest that national borders can be artificial in nature. Geographical borders are normally created by barriers to movement, across seas, rivers or mountain ranges. However the colonial partitioning of Africa was based on treaties that used map coordinates, and so nation states were created regardless of whether the line went through the middle of a village or not. The idea of the nation state is western in origin:

the West invented nationalism, initially in the form of imperialism as nation-states extended their domination over others, creating at one and the same time the hegemonic sense of the 'national culture' and the 'problem' of national identity for the colonised territories.

(Willeman, 1989: 18)

Once a nation that only owes its existence to imperialism is decolonized, it no longer has a *raison d'être*. One way of dealing with this vacuum is to resurrect traditions that existed before colonization, on the assumption that they offer an authentic cultural voice. However:

the result is mostly a nostalgia for a pre-colonial society which in fact never existed, full of idyllic villages and communities peopled by 'authentic' (read folkloric) innocents in touch with the 'real' values perverted by imperialism ...

(Willeman, 1989: 18)

This coincides with what Fanon called the 'second phase' of how a native writer attempts to articulate her or his native culture. In the first phase the writer attempts to mimic the forms of the colonizer:

In the second phase we find the native is disturbed; he decides to remember what he is.... Past happenings of the bygone days of his childhood will be brought up ... old legends will be interpreted in the light of a borrowed aestheticism ...

(Fanon, 1967: 179)

As a way of counteracting the difficulties of finding a post-colonial voice, an internationalist perspective was developed in the 1960s among many countries that were being freed from the colonialist's yoke. Teshome H. Gabriel applied Fanon's idea to cinema, and suggested that the third 'combative' phase filmmaker:

is one who is perceptive of and knowledgeable about the pulse of the Third World masses. Such a film-maker is truly in search of a Third World cinema – a cinema that has respect for the Third World peoples.

(Gabriel, 1989: 34)

The internationalist idea struck a chord, among many filmmakers at least, as it chimed with the zeitgeist of the 1960s and early 1970s:

Aesthetically, the [Third Cinema] movement drew on currents as diverse as Soviet montage, Surrealism, Italian neo-realisms,

Brechtian epic theatre, *cinema verite*, and the French New Wave.

(Stam, 2000: 99)

Ironically one of the few exemplary Fanonist films was made by western filmmakers, *The Battle of Algiers* (1965), is about the liberation from the French of Algeria – see Box 4.8. However, non-western nations also used cinema as an anti-colonial device.

Regarding African cinema, Olivier Barlet argues that it is worth considering cinema to be a modern *griot*, a storyteller who is 'a messenger of his times, a visionary and the creator of the future' (Barlet, 2000: 164). As we have seen, colonized nations have an almost schizophrenic relationship with their culture, which holds back development. So in their cinema:

> In giving life to the word, they reject not only the domination of a fixed past but also the dictates of cultural neo-colonialism, to contribute to the invention of a future for the people to whom they feel committed.
>
> (Barlet, 2000: 165)

It is of no surprise that a culture should influence film language and so belie the myth that western film style is natural and therefore universal. For example, the shot/reverse-shot pattern that is conventionally used for conversations in western cinema is inappropriate in African cinema, which 'prefers' to use long and medium shots. Barlet quotes Burkina Faso filmmaker Maurice Kabore:

> 'In the Mossi region … it is not proper for a woman to look a man in the eye. When a young couple converse, the woman will be attentive, but her head will be lowered.' If such a scene is filmed in the shot/reverse-shot style, the woman will almost seem blind and the scene will assume another meaning.
>
> (Barlet, 2000: 161)

Ironically by the time (the 1980s and 1990s) academia had embraced Third Cinema the practitioners were, by contrast, disenchanted. The revolutionary spirit was spent and it was realized that not all of the 'oppressed' were politically bothered about their subservient situation. Fanon's 'wretched of the earth' may be too busy keeping 'body and soul' together to organize a revolution. As globalization became established, on very unequal terms, ideas of Third Cinema were developed in relation to post-colonial theory. See Box 4.9.

Box 4.8 *The Battle of Algiers*
(*La Battaglia di Algeri*, Italy-Algeria, 1967)

The Battle of Algiers is one of the few western films to offer a view of the colonized Third World from the perspective of the oppressed. The National Liberation Front (FLN) are shown to be the heroes of the film in overcoming French colonialism. Although one of the FLN's leaders, Ali La Pointe, bookends the film with his defiant last stand (most of the film is in flashback), it is the people of the Kasbah who are the true heroes of the fight for liberation (which cost 1.5 million Algerian and 20,000 French lives between 1954 and 1962).

A crucial innovation of *The Battle of Algiers* was to invert the Eurocentric focalizations typical of the western imperial adventure film. Instead director Gillo Pontecorvo 'deploys identificatory mechanisms on behalf of the colonized, presenting the Algerian struggle as an inspirational exemplum for other colonized peoples' (Shohat and Stam, 1994: 251–2).

Shohat and Stam suggest how the opposing forces are visually coded:

Algeria	*French colonists*
native medina	French city
civilian dress	uniformed (soldiers and police)
Kasbah as home	Kasbah as frontier
Arabic language	French language

(Shohat and Stam, 1994: 252)

Drawing upon the iconography of the war film, the Kasbah is encircled by barbed wire and checkpoints, reminiscent of Nazi Germany. The Algerians are not, as most of the colonized were (and are) in western film, 'local colour', but active participants in their emancipation.

One of the film's strengths is its refusal to caricature the colonizers as evil, so it is able to show the 'logic of empire' in all its cruelty. For example, the head of the paratroopers Colonel Mathieu (Jean Martin) mixes charm with ruthlessness. As he says to the assembled press when challenged on the torturing of Algerians, 'If we are here to stay then it must be done'. Mathieu is merely doing his duty, protecting French interests, and if violence is necessary for that, then 'So be it'. Mathieu's 'if' is important, for there can be no colonies without violence against indigenous populations.

The film has a grainy texture, giving it the look of news footage. This is particularly effective in the bombing of the French part of the city, as chaos is brought to civilian life. The film does not glorify the Algerian terrorists. We see, from a bomber's point of view, people socializing in a café just before she sets off a bomb. These victims are ordinary people and are innocent, except for the fact they are colonizers. I disagree with Shohat and Stam's (1994: 253) contention that:

> spectatorial identification is so complete that the audience is not shocked even by a series of close shots of one of the bombers' potential victims.

Our sympathy with the victims, while understanding the bombers' actions, breaks down the knee-jerk definition of terrorists as necessarily evil; the film is suggesting that, sometimes, terrorism is a necessary evil.

4.9.1 Post-colonial cinema

The shift from 'Third Cinema' to post-colonial cinema is not easy to place either in time or in theory. Arif Dirlik stated that post-colonialism began 'when Third World intellectuals have arrived in First World academe' (Dirlik, 1997: 294). This suggests that while it may represent an advance on the preceding intellectual framework (because it was being 'curated' by the peoples of the (old) Third World), it was nevertheless being formed in western academia. At the very least we may consider this to be an advance (at least non-westerners got a say in how to conceptualize non-western cinema); however it has to be considered as a concept that remains in flux.

The key text for post-colonialists is Edward Said's *Orientalism* (1979), where he showed that the west, through European culture, viewed the non-west (this is a cultural, not a geographical, divide) as the Other. For example, the exoticism of the Orient:

> Orientalism is a Eurocentric/Occidental view that dominates the Orient through its exercise of knowledge over and about the Orient. It interprets the Orient through its Western applied sciences of anthropology and philology/linguistics and in so doing it achieves 'knowledge' of the other which endows it with authority over the other.
>
> (Hayward, 2000: 269)

In film this could consist of, for example, western stereotypes of Arabs. Box 4.8 on *The Battle of Algiers* showed how the film offered a representation of the Kasbah as a place of community and resistance. This contrasts with the representation in Julien Duvivier's *Pépé le Moko* (1937), a classic French film, where the Kasbah is introduced with a:

> montage [that] establishes straight away the colonialist notion of the Casbah as starkly alien to the Parisian inspectors and, by extension, to the viewers... The sequence ends with another major colonialist theme, the identity of the Casbah as feminine and sexual …
>
> (Vincendeau, 1998: 13)

Post-colonial discourse found space for minorities other than the oppressed. The Third World cinema's focus on Marxist, and male, notions of revolution marginalized women among others. One of the shifts evident in post-colonial cinema can be seen in films made by women:

> Films like Mona Hatoum's *Measures of Distance* (1988), Tracey Moffatt's *Nice Coloured Girls* (1987), and Gurinder Chadha's *Bhaji on the Beach* (1993), use the camera less as revolutionary weapon than as monitor of the gendered and sexualised realism of the personal and the domestic, seen as integral but repressed aspects of collective history.
>
> (Stam, 1999: 123c)

Box 4.9 *Borom Sarret* (Senegal, 1963)

The influence of Italian neo-realism was felt, particularly in Latin America, where the 'low-tech' documentary style was a viable aesthetic. Neo-realism is also evident in what is reputed to be the first black African film, *Borom Sarret* (1963), directed by Ousmane Sembene. However it does not simply use its antecedents as a model:

> A crucial difference … is that *Borom Sarret* has none of the sentimentality found in *Bicycle Thieves*. Sembene is critical of his characters. The better-off refuse payment for services they accept while their victims are so servile and acquiescent that they make no protest. Sembene, unlike de Sica, is concerned with issues of race and postcolonial culture as well as issues of class.
>
> (Dahlberg, 2003)

In trying to define a nation against imperialist oppressors and, in filmic terms, define a cinema against Hollywood, the writings of Frantz Fanon have been particularly influential. He stated:

> Let us not pay tribute to Europe by creating states, institutions and societies in its mould. Humanity expects more from us than this caricatured and generally obscene imitation.
>
> (Fanon quoted in Stam, 2000: 99)

The problem for the filmmaker was whether to hark back to an – often imagined – pre-colonial idyll, or to try to reinvent the idea of the nation, bypassing the post-colonial power structures. The question of language is often crucial in this: some prints of *Borom Sarret* have the dialogue in French, while others are in the local Wolof. The latter offers more authenticity; however it is also likely to further limit the film's potential audience.

Sembene both shows what life is like for the poor in Senegal in 1963, and demonstrates how their acquiescence to the status quo is, at least in part, responsible for their subservient position. The Borom Sarret, a cart driver who taxis people to their destinations, is shown giving money to the *griot* (traditional storyteller) but not being paid by his passengers (who seem to regard him as a charity). Eventually he loses his cart after taking a rich man (signified by a suit) to the Heights (the bourgeois nature of which is shown by the switch from indigenous music to classical), a place he is forbidden to be. The film concludes with the Sarret's wife having to prostitute herself in order to feed their child.

The opening shot shows rush hour in a modern-looking city, imme-diately overturning many people's expectations of Africa (particularly in the early 1960s). This is contrasted with the hovel where the 'hero' resides. The Heights reeks both of modernity and soullessness, as the high-rise buildings appear to be deserted, except for the arresting policeman.

The fact that Sembene himself does the voice-over, narrating events (there is no synchronous dialogue) further draws attention to the didactic nature of the film.

Postcolonial theory allows an investigation into diaspora (see 6.5.1) as well as the hybrid cultures that spring up in the 'melting pot' of migra-tion and global communication systems. Shifting identities of peoples, such as Jess's (Parminder Nagra's) desire to be a footballer clashing with her parents' traditional Sikh expectations in *Bend it Like Beckham* (UK–Germany, 2002), are the subject of numerous films. *La Haine* (*Hate*, France, 1995), an example of *cinema beur*, has three protagonists who, while all French, are also Arab, Afro-Caribbean and Jewish. *Dirty Pretty Things* (UK–USA, 2002) shows the conflicting roles taken on by asylum seekers as they try to survive in a hostile London. *Monsoon Wedding* (India–USA–France–Italy, 2001) looks at the stresses created by partition when Muslims were 'driven' to Pakistan.

This conception of identity as fluid is one of the defining characteristics of postmodern theory, which is influential in contemporary film studies.

4.10 Postmodernism and poststructuralism

It is a cliché to start writing about postmodernism with the warning that it is extremely difficult to pin down. Its project is:

> the interpretation and re-evaluation of topics such as subjectivity, culture, meaning, gender, power, discourse, pleasure, language (to name but a few) …
>
> (Fuery, 2000: 2)

In addition, postmodernism is not simply content to analyse films, it is also an aesthetic style, exemplified in Baz Luhrmann's *Moulin Rouge* (USA–Australia, 2001), where characters mouth words obviously written many years after the film is set (for example, 'The hills are alive …'). This breaking down of chronological borders is symptomatic of postmodern aesthetics; spatial borders are eradicated as well, as is seen in the same director's *Romeo + Juliet* (1996). We have already seen how postmodernism has affected genre (see 2.6 and Box 3.2) and narratives (2.13), and the way in which Hollywood makes movies (see 3.11 and 3.16).

Frederic Jameson (1991) identified postmodern films that elicit a 'nostalgia for the present':

> It seems to me exceedingly symptomatic to find the very style of nostalgia films invading and colonizing even those movies today which have contemporary settings, as though … we were unable today to focus on our present, as though we had become incapable of achieving aesthetic representations of our own current experience.
>
> (Jameson, 1998a: 9)

So films such as *Body Heat* (1981) sidestep contemporary issues by using iconography that suggests the past; the small Florida town where the film is set has none of the accoutrements of modernity, such as skyscrapers. In addition, the *Indiana Jones* films repackaged the 1930s action serial in a manner that allowed audiences to enjoy the naïve simplicity of the gung-ho narrative without feeling patronized; for example when 'Indy' (Harrison Ford) shoots a sword-wielding dervish in *Raiders of the Lost Ark* (1981). This reinvention of the Saturday morning serial is:

> In the form of a pastiche; there is no point to a parody of such serials, they are long extinct. Far from being a pointless satire of such dead forms, *Star Wars* satisfies a deep … longing to experience them again …
>
> (Jameson, 1998a: 8)

Postmodernism also suggests that post-capitalist society (where the economy is driven by consumerism rather than manufacturing) has reduced everything to surfaces, including human beings. Our sense of ourselves, it is argued, is often derived from the media (for example 'lifestyle' magazines) and our understanding of the world is (virtually) wholly constructed by the media (for example through news and documentaries). There is no depth, only image. Similarly, we have become posthuman: the split and parallel identities of characters in *Sex and Lucía* (*Lucía y El Sexo*, France-Spain – see Box 2.8) offers this 'schizophrenic' representation of human beings. Jonathan Eig suggests that the 'mind fuck' movies of the late twentieth/early twenty-first century represent a new way of considering identity in Hollywood:

> all five of these movies seem to suggest that self-imposed delusion may be a valid alternative to reality. Even in *Fight Club*, which ends with the destruction of the illusory character at the hands of the real character, we must recognize the tremendous service that illusory Tyler Durden has provided for the real Tyler.
>
> (Eig, 2003)

As noted in 2.13, although postmodern films can be meaningful, in Hollywood's hands the concept is most likely to be apparent in the surface gloss of high concept narratives.

Jacques Derrida, one of the most influential poststructuralists, suggests that:

meaning is something that is not fixed and finite, but rather an action of continual deferral and difference. Meanings, he argues, are never really arrived at, but are premised on a multiplicity of possible meanings (the act of difference) and non-arrival (the act of deferral). As we watch a film, *différance* [in French] operates at a number of levels. We continually propose possibilities of actions, sequences, and meanings, abandoning some and creating others as the narrative progresses.

(Fuery, 2000: 36)

Genre works through *différance* (a neologism created by Derrida to convey this idea). For example, the way in which films may play with generic conventions alters the meaning of the generic trope. Fuery offers the gangster movie as an example where audiences expect the gangster(s) to die at the end; this, however, can be done in a number of ways. While in *Little Caesar* (1931) Rico's death is ignominious ('Is this the end of Rico?' he asks disbelievingly), in *White Heat* (1949) 'Cody's death is framed triumphantly' (Fuery, 2000: 37). In *Bonnie and Clyde* (1967) 'the portrayal of death of the two characters is more graphic in terms of violence, yet more sympathetic … than Cody' (ibid.). In *The Godfather* (1971) 'Don Corleone actually dies in the idyllic surrounds of a sunlit garden … there is no shower of bullets … ' (ibid.). For Derrida these only gain meaning through intertextual reference and not from any other knowledge. He conceived of meaning as created through supplements, which have no origin.

However, meaning is not something that is 'up for grabs' in an anarchic fashion; possible meanings remain socially conditioned. So the understanding of the different ways in which the gangsters die was inevitably structured by the social conditions of when the films were produced and when they are read.

> After Derrida there can be no question of specifying the text's effectivity independently of the context of reception: readings differ …
>
> (Lapsley and Westlake, 1988: 65)

By the 1980s film studies was established in western academia, and while many new theorists tried to build upon the *Screen*-inspired work of the 1970s, others rejected much of it, particularly the role of psychoanalysis. Indeed, some suggested that the emphasis on unifying theories was a result of seeking academic respectability (see Carroll, 1996). While some of the original *Screen writers*, such as Christian Metz (1991), have developed their ideas further, other theorists, such Teresa de Lauretis (see 1985) and Kaja Silverman (see 1988), have taken up the baton and continued to fruitfully use the discourse of psychoanalysis to make sense of cinema.

Amongst the most prolific of writers, from a psychoanalytic perspective, is Slavoj Žižek, who has specifically developed Jacques Lacan's ideas further in relation to cinema. On the other hand, French philosopher Gilles Deleuze (1986, 1989) has attacked the foundations of much of *Screen* theory, particularly Saussure and Lacan, and drawn on Henri Bergson to focus on movement and its relationship to time. While Žižek and Deleuze are intellectually in opposition, both use films as evidence for their respective positions as much as they use their theoretical approaches to elucidate films.

Neither writer is particularly approachable. Deleuze tended to focus on classical Hollywood (he died in 1995) while Žižek is happy to engage in analysis of contemporary commercial product (see his work on *The Matrix* – 2001). Their position in contemporary film studies is ambiguous. In his survey *New Developments in Film Theory* (2000), Patrick Fuery does not cite Žižek at all; Deleuze does feature in comparison with Michel Foucault. Barbara Kennedy sees Deleuze's ideas as an ideal way of engaging with film as an experiential, rather than simply a representational, experience:

> Like post-feminism, Deleuzian ideas are concerned to redefine and refigure theoretical practice. Deleuze moves beyond dualistic and binary thinking processes.
>
> (Kennedy, 2002: 24)

Žižek, on the other hand, interestingly adds a psychoanalytical perspective to auteurism. For example, he suggests that recurring motifs in Hitchcock's films are examples of a 'sinthom' that:

> gives body, in its repetitive pattern, to some elementary matrix of jouissance, of excessive enjoyment.
>
> (Žižek, 2001: 198)

The anthology *Reinventing Film Studies* (2000), edited by Christine Gledhill and Linda Williams, does mention Žižek but not Deleuze; and Bordwell and Carroll's (1996) critique of the psychoanalytical approach to cinema mentions Deleuze only in passing, while Žižek is not engaged with at all. Elsaesser and Buckland (2002) make an interesting case for both writers, but even their committed analysis is peppered with tentative assertions, such is the difficulty in applying these writers to film.

Box 4.10 Postmodernism and horror

Scream (1996) one of the few truly postmodern genre films?

The most recent teen horror cycle was launched by the massive box office success of *Scream* in 1996. The Kevin Williamson scripted, Wes Craven directed film reinvigorated the subgenre with its postmodern playfulness. Such postmodernism in horror was evident in *Wes Craven's New Nightmare* (1994), where the director appeared as himself, creating a new 'Freddie' movie for the *Elm Street* franchise (1984–94). The original actress, Heather Langenkamp, also played herself as an actress who was considering appearing in this new film (which of course she already was). Such self-referential playfulness is not limited to late twentieth-century postmodernist aesthetics; *Bride of Frankenstein* (1935) pokes more fun at itself than horror at the audience.

Scream foregrounded the conventions of the horror movie and then broke the rules. For example, the character who loses her virginity *does* survive. By drawing attention to the conventions of horror movies *Scream* was parodying them. Parody is often used to comic effect. Mel Brooks successfully mined many genres for his film parodies, including the Western in *Blazing Saddles* and horror in *Young Frankenstein* (both 1974). Humour in horror films usually dissipates fear, although in *Scream* the character of Sydney (Neve Campbell) is sufficiently well drawn for audiences to identify with her plight. The film manages to be an effective deconstruction of the horror movie (starting with the only name actor, Drew Barrymore, being killed off 'early', like Janet Leigh in *Psycho*, 1960) by being both funny and scary.

While parodies draw attention to a genre's conventions, a parody of a parody can only exaggerate this further, as it cannot draw attention to generic conventions in the way a parody can. Because of this *Scary Movie* (2000) could say nothing about the horror genre; it was a pastiche. As *Scream* had already parodied the repertoire of elements, *Scary Movie* could only repeat scenes from the earlier movies in an absurd way. Indeed, some scenes – such as Buffy's fatal encounter with the killer in the garage – are funnier in the original. *Scary Movie* emphasized the 'gross out' elements that appeal to young audiences: the penis inserted into a character's ear and the jet of semen that plastered Sindy to the ceiling.

Not all agree that the *Scream* series has postmodern sensibilities. Andrew Tudor has argued what sets the series apart from the teen horror cycle of the late 1990s and early 2000s is their self-reflexivity. That is, it is 'no more than a delayed application of modernist precepts in the hitherto largely traditional world of popular culture' (Tudor, 2002: 114).

However, postmodern self-reflexivity is not about drawing attention to the conventions of the text in order to distance the audience. Its intention is playful, revelling in the (postmodern) fact that we are adrift in a sea of signifiers:

> postmodernism's preoccupation [is] with the signifier rather than the signified, with participation, performance, and happening rather than with an authoritative and finished art object, with surface appearances rather than roots.
>
> (Harvey, 1990: 53)

Tudor is right, however, when he points out that few – if any – of the late 1990s–early twenty-first century horror-cycle films embrace self-reflexivity so readily as the *Scream* series. The other films are postmodern in the sense that other genre films are, in that they appeal to audience's 'insider' knowledge. *Cherry Falls* (2000), for example, is built on the conceit that the characters will only live if they lose their virginity.

4.11 Audience pleasures

While academics were trying to get their head around how, and why, audiences experienced film, in mainstream society the medium was getting embroiled in moral panics – see 6.5.8. The 'effects model' of audience suggests that susceptible members of the audience will act out extreme scenarios shown in a film in a copycat fashion. *A Clockwork Orange* (UK, 1971) supposedly set off a number of violent attacks when it was originally released (but failed to do so when re-released in 2000). As an antidote to the crassness of the 'effects model', a more active model of audience was proposed.

Jay Blumler, Denis McQuail and J. R. Brown posed four major categories of need that the media serve to gratify: diversion, personal relationships, personal identity and surveillance. While this model 'belongs' to cultural and media studies, it is useful to apply it to films. In brief, the 'uses and gratifications' model suggests that audience use films for entertainment, as a source of social interaction, to get a sense of their identity and to gain information. For example, in watching *Lara Croft: Tomb Raider* (USA-UK-Germany-Japan, 2001), members of the audience may be:

➤ entertained:
  – by the action sequences
  – (male heterosexuals) by Angelina Jolie's body
➤ discuss:
  – whether it was very entertaining
  – whether the Lara Croft is a feminist icon or a 'het male's' 'wet dream'
➤ consider:
  – whether they would like to be a strong woman like Lara Croft
  – whether they would like a strong woman like Lara Croft
➤ learn:
  – …

I am not sure what one could learn from *Tomb Raider*, although many blockbusters do attempt to offer information, such as the careful portrayal of the social class composition of the passengers in *Titanic* (1997). Issues of personal identity will be discussed further below. Here I will concentrate on the reason most of us view films – for entertainment.

Despite its ubiquity, entertainment tended to get short shrift within film studies, possibly a hangover from the time when the discipline had to fight to be taken seriously in academia. However, Richard Dyer investigated the notion of escapism in entertainment, and suggested that films offer audiences the possibility of experiencing 'utopian' feelings. These feelings are contrasted with the 'place' we are escaping from – reality.

To summarize Dyer's categories:

Reality

Exhaustion
'work as a grind, alienated labour, pressures of urban life'

Scarcity
'actual poverty in the society; poverty observable in the surrounding societies, material unequal distribution of wealth'

Dreariness
'monotony, predictability, instrumentality of the daily round'

Manipulation
'advertising, bourgeois democracy, sex roles'

Fragmentation
'job mobility, rehousing and development, high-rise flats, legislation against action'

Utopia

Energy
'capacity to act vigorously; human power, activity, potential to counteract this exhaustion'

Abundance
'conquest of scarcity; having enough to spare without sense of poverty of others; enjoyment of sensuous reality'

Intensity
'experiencing of emotion directly, fully, unambiguously, 'authentically', without holding back'

Transparency
'a quality of relationships – between represented characters (e.g. true love), between performer and audience ('sincerity')'

Community
'togetherness, sense of belonging, network of phatic collective relationships'

(summarized from Dyer, 1992: 20–1)

As Dyer noted, entertainment also has an institutional aspect as a:

> type of performance produced for profit, performed before a generalized audience (the 'public'), by a trained, paid group who do nothing else but produce performances which have the sole (conscious) aim of providing pleasure.

(Dyer, 1992: 17)

Dyer's conceptualization of entertainment was useful as it explained why audiences flocked to the 'fairy tales' of mainstream cinema. While audiences know they are watching a fantasy, and 'happy ever after' is impossible:

> the medium constitutes itself as a projected fulfilment of what is desired and absent within the status quo.... Through an artistic 'change of signs' the negatives of social existence are turned into the positives of artistic transmutation.
>
> (Stam, 2000: 310)

This 'artistic transmutation' gives audiences the 'idea of utopia'. Dyer applied his concept to musicals. However it works for most (all?) genre films. For example *Armaggedon* (1998) concludes with a montage showing the 'world *community*' celebrating the destruction of the asteroid. Harry Stamper's (Bruce Willis's) love for his daughter is palpably genuine (*transparent*). The other three aspects are all evident in the action sequences; the abundant 'sensual reality' is evident in the special effects – see 7.8.

Different genres can offer particular audiences specific pleasures – see Box 4.11. In addition, the pleasures offered by film can extend beyond the films themselves into the realms of fandom. Writing of the classical era, Samantha Barbas found:

> movie fandom was actually a serious attempt by fans to understand and to come to terms with the motion picture... [enabling] fans to fulfil three important objectives: to connect personally with the movies, to influence the filmmaking process, and to verify the authenticity of cinematic images.
>
> (Barbas, 2001: 185–6)

While Hollywood has always retained the 'final say' in filmmaking, there have been famous instances of studios buckling under fan pressure. For example, Clark Gable was cast as Rhett Butler in *Gone With the Wind* (1939) after fan pressure, even though it meant producer David O. Selznick would have to share the profits with MGM, to whom Gable was contracted.

While audiences may consume stars in the way the studios desire – Rock Hudson was the heterosexual 'hunk' of 1950s cinema despite being gay – subcultural groups can appropriate stars for their own use. Richard Dyer suggests Judy Garland's appeal to male gay culture was facilitated after she was sacked by MGM, in 1950, and attempted suicide:

This event, because it constituted for the public a sudden break with Garland's uncomplicated and ordinary MGM image, made possible a reading of Garland as having a special relationship to suffering, ordinariness, normality, and it is this relationship that structures much of the gay reading of Garland.

(Dyer, 1986: 142–3)

Box 4.11 Horror: subcultural and gendered pleasures

Some genres can form part, or indeed be the main constituent of, subcultural groups. Science fiction, for example, has its own fan base, many of whom attend SF conventions. Horror also has a subcultural group associated with it. The aficionados' expertise is a 'cultural competence' that allows them to read genre texts more densely than the mainstream audience. In other words, they understand more of the generic references.

While horror films have moved into the mainstream, and appeal to both genders as well as young and old, there is a subculture of horror fans who, while they may enjoy mainstream horror, relish the bad taste of horror that remains beyond the pale of bourgeois respectability. Horror aficionados understand the genre with the enthusiasm of zealots, and often like to share their knowledge by reading, creating or contributing to fanzines:

> Only available by mail and unpredictable in their publication, the fanzines are suffused with that juvenile fascination with grue (sic) and gore, most evident in their frequent inclusion of illustrations appealing to the lowest kind of prurient interest and guaranteed to offend.
>
> (Sanjek, 2000: 315)

Since Sanjek's piece was originally published, in 1990, the Internet has become the medium of choice of the fanzine, although there are publications, such as *Fangoria*, that straddle the border between the mainstream and the fanzine. Fanzines are characterized by an obsession with the minutiae about film production and a devotion to authenticity, whether it be in seeing uncut versions of films, or in the framing of the film. DVD has been a godsend to the horror aficionado. For example:

> thanks to the lengths VCI has gone to do right by these films. Finding new sources for their material, they've worked with

---

[Mario] Bava and historian (and *Video Watchdog* editor) Tim Lucas, to make sure the films have been given the best treatment possible. BLOOD in particular is jaw-droppingly beautiful, making all other home versions obsolete.

(Matthew Kiernan, www.fangoria.com, accessed May 2002)

Fanzines properly work outside conventional critical discourse. For example, in North America they have occasionally championed the work of European filmmakers, such as Dario Argento, who rarely if ever receive coverage from mainstream publications. They also treat Hollywood with suspicion, suspecting that films produced by the major studios are likely to be compromised by the need to make money.

There is a 'common sense' assumption that horror texts appeal more to males than females. Indeed so strong has the assumption been that many academics have tried to rationalize why some women will watch horror films. Their explanations include: it is part of a couple's role-playing (that is, male unafraid: female afraid) and the female spectator must be male-identified and so colluding with her own oppression.

Brigid Cherry challenged these presuppositions when investigating the pleasures of horror texts which females had reported to her. She found them to be a variant on the pleasures offered by romance:

female horror fans judge the quality of films on the basis of the relationships which develop between the characters. This explains the particular liking for vampire films among this group of viewers, since many seemed to read them in a similar way to romance fiction ...

(Cherry, 1999: 194–5)

Gothic romance, which includes such films as the 1992 *Bram Stoker's Dracula* (tagline: 'Love Never Dies') and *Interview with a Vampire* (1994), and novels such as *Wuthering Heights*, seems to have a particular appeal to women. This conclusion, however, may simply reinforce the idea that women are not really interested in horror.

It is unsurprising that it should be a subcultural group that *negotiates* its reading of stars as mainstream culture is likely to accept the *preferred* reading of the star persona.

Film theories, like the films themselves, are socially constructed, and so will continue to evolve as society changes; unless postmodernism's dictum that we are at the 'end of history' is true.

5 Film and History

5.1 Introduction

E. H. Carr (1964) used the apt metaphor that historical facts are sacks; that is, they have no shape until you put something in it. All history is a *re*-presentation of past events; it is obviously impossible to experience the events as they happened, so we are left with versions of events that we understand in a particular fashion. The evidence available to the historian is inevitably limited, and will be shaped (putting something in the sack) with her or his perspective.

The first shape given to the film studies 'sack' was of histories created on national lines. As noted in the Preface, categorizing film is both useful, in that it allows us to consider cinema(s) as a whole, and an impediment: differences are necessarily glossed over to allow films to fit in their category. However, in an introductory text we must follow the conventional approach while bearing in mind that, in reality, films do not fit so readily into such boxes.

Ginette Vincendeau suggested that a canon of European film movements, or waves, consists of:

> Soviet cinema, Weimar and German Expressionism, the British documentary movement, French poetic realism, Italian Neo-Realism ... the French New Wave ... New German Cinema.... Other movements that have gained coverage are: Early Scandinavian cinema, the British and Czech New Waves, and the Polish Cinema of Moral Concern ... pre-Soviet Russian cinema, Nazi cinema, French cinema of the occupation, post-Franco Spanish cinema, French cinema beur ...
>
> (Vincendeau, 1998: 441b)

We can add to this various world cinema (and in using this term I am being Eurocentric as, for other parts of the world, European cinema is part of world cinema) movements, such as Latin America's cinema novo (King, 2000), fifth and sixth generation Chinese cinema (Cornelius with Smith, 2002), new Iranian cinema (Tapper, 2002), Hong Kong new wave (Yau, 2001) and Japanese new wave (Schilling, 1999), not to mention developments in Danish, Korean, South Asian and African cinema.

What follows, then, is a brief introduction to a selection of movements or new waves, as well as a consideration of the events in Paris in May 1968, which had a profound impact on film studies. In each section there are suggested 'further viewings' of films not mentioned, and 'further readings' (usually of books not already referenced in the section), as this chapter is meant to signpost the interested reader where to look next. In addition there are five appendices at the end of the chapter on Australian and New Zealand, Balkan, Canadian, Hong Kong and Mexican cinema, which are an attempt to broaden the book's coverage of areas that do not readily fit into conventional categories.

5.2 German Expressionism

Since I have already cast doubt on the efficacy of looking at 'movements' and 'waves', it might seem ridiculous to further question this approach. However, when considering Expressionism we must acknowledge that:

> 'Expressionism' is a descriptive term which has to cover so many disparate cultural manifestations as to be virtually meaningless.
>
> (Furness, 1973: 1)

Like most (all?) artistic movements, Expressionism came about, and was consciously formulated, as a reaction against the status quo. The history of art can be written in terms of how this reaction against convention led to new artistic forms. Expressionism was initially an art movement, which started in the first decade of the twentieth century. It was reacting against impressionist painting and naturalism. Expressionists were also revolted by the older literary movement of romanticism, and the new social science of psychology, which promised to explain the mind. However, although Expressionism broke convention, it is not surprising that there were precursors to the new form, as it is impossible for a new artistic movement to spring from nothing. (It would be alien if it did so.) Furness (1973:1) mentions the influences of Dostoevsky, Nietzsche and Strindberg among others.

While impressionism and naturalism attempted to represent surface reality, the Expressionists focused on the interior world of the mind, and so emphasized subjectivity and extreme psychological states. In doing this, Expressionists externalized the state of mind of the artist onto the environment. Before the First World War this mental state was invariably optimistic and, like the contemporaneous futurists, the movement celebrated the modern world. However after the futile violence of the war, the 'second generation' Expressionists were more likely to offer the visions of tortured minds.

The period immediately following the First World War was one of most ferment in the arts. The rise of modernism, with its fractured forms, was possibly an expression of the social alienation experienced by many. In addition, the 'rationality' of science was challenged when Einstein published his *General Theory of Relativity* in 1915 (although serious testing of his ideas was not possible until after the war).

Edvard Munch's painting *The Scream* (*Shrik*), although it dates from 1895, epitomises the Expressionist aesthetic: an individual on a bridge with a skull-like face screams, with hands over ears. There is no apparent reason for the scream, suggesting it emanates from existential terror, a fear of the meaninglessness of life. Expressionism represented reality in a distorted manner, as if the world is being perceived by an unbalanced mind. Lotte Eisner suggested that Expressionism was ideally suited to Germans because of:

> Mysticism and magic, the dark forces to which Germans have always been more than willing to commit themselves.
>
> (Eisner, 1969: 9)

While this is unlikely, it was Germany that produced some extraordinary films, influenced by the movement, in the 1920s. *The Cabinet of Dr. Caligari* (*Das Kabinett des Doktor Caligari*, 1920 – see Box 5.1) was the first Expressionist film, and possibly the only truly Expressionist film. Its Expressionist sets represented the state of an insane mind.

> If no subsequent film was to commit itself so fully to the formal character of the style, the essence of expressionism as distinct from Expressionism – the use of setting, design, lighting and chiaroscuro to reflect and express the psychology of the characters – was to persist in German cinema of the 1920s.
>
> (Robinson, 1997: 54)

Nosferatu (1922, remade 1979), the first filmed version of Bram Stoker's Dracula, is generally regarded as a classic film (and was itself the subject of a film, *Shadow of the Vampire*, UK–USA–Luxembourg, 2000). The influence of Expressionism is visible, particularly in the grotesque shadow cast by Nosferatu (Max Schreck) as he approaches his virginal, and sacrificial, victim. In addition a chair in Knock's office looks as if it had come straight off the set of *Caligari,* and the house Nosferatu purchases is also Expressionist in design.

Although not particularly successful at the box office, the visuals of Expressionism were widely influential; in Britain Alfred Hitchcock's serial killer thriller *The Lodger* (1926) shows an obvious debt to German lighting techniques (Hitch had worked at Ufa, Germany's premiere studios). More importantly, Hollywood too took up the Expressionist influence. *The Man Who Laughs* (1925) and *The Cat and the Canary* (1927) were early Hollywood attempts at horror, both directed by the German Paul Leni.

Director Danny Boyle obviously had Expressionism in mind for the look of his zombie-SF film *28 Days Later* (2002, UK–USA). While the survivors are desperately trying to change a tyre, stuck in a tunnel under the Thames, rats swarm past them pursued by zombies, shown primarily through their grotesque shadows cast on the walls.

As a footnote (although Nazi cinema could fill a book-length study such as Rentschler, 1996), the Nazis' Minster of Propaganda, Goebbels, recognized cinema's potential to persuade a mass audience. He noted that straight propaganda documentaries, such as Leni Riefenstahl's *Triumph of the Will* (*Triumph des Willens*, 1934), would not find a mass audience, unlike entertainment films. Nazi entertainment, however, was anything but frivolous:

> The qualities that German feature films did promote during the remainder [of the 1930s] were unconditional submission to the absolute authority of an infallible leader, love of the Fatherland, comradeship and self-sacrifice.
>
> (Richards, 1980: 173b)

This did not, however, represent a big shift from films of the 1920s, where nascent fascist ideology can be found in the 'mountain films' (which featured Riefenstahl). Julian Petley (1979) argues that the Nazis had no great influence on the economics of the industry, as many of the studio operators, like numerous other companies, believed that the Nazis would be 'good for business'.

Box 5.1 *The Cabinet of Dr. Caligari*
(*Das Cabinet des Doktor Caligari*, Germany, 1920)

By the time Expressionism reached film, with *The Cabinet of Dr. Caligari*, the movement was no longer part of the avant-garde (see 5.3). Its influence on the medium, however, was to be immense. Written by Hans Janowitz and Carl Meyer, the film's intention was a make a pacifist statement:

The Cabinet of Dr. Caligari **(1920) was one of the few genuinely**
Expressionist films using a painted set to express the narrator's
mental world

> They had created Cesare with the dim design of portraying the
> common man, who, under the pressure of compulsory military
> service, is drilled to kill and be killed.
>
> (Kracauer, 1947: 65)

Dr Caligari was to have been portrayed as a sinister figure of authority. However Janowitz and Meyer's script was compromised by the
addition of a framing device that shows the story to have been told
by a madman, so the original critique of authority was seen to be
ravings of a madman. The film was produced by Erich Pommer, who
recognized that although the script was not obviously commercial, it
would gain critical acclaim as art cinema, and this would be a good
way to gain foreign sales.

The most startling aspect of the film, and it is saying something that
a film can still startle over 80 years after its release, is the fact that all
the settings are painted *including* the shadows (see the photograph
above). The design of the setting is Expressionist:

There are no verticals or horizontals, perspectives have been wilfully distorted, and the tortuous alleyways force a path between the twisted housefronts leaning toward each other.

(Barsacq, 1976: 25–7)

Although not the intention of the writers, the change in the narrative to be one *told* by a madman makes the Expressionist sets part of the diegesis, as they become a projection of an unbalanced mind. However, the framing device also has an Expressionist set, which suggests that the 'real' world is as demented as that told by the madman. *Caligari* is possibly the only 'purely' Expressionist film. The director, Robert Weine, went onto make *Raskolnikoff* (*Raskolnikow*, Germany, 1923), which has a similar visual style. However in this film the sets are all three-dimensional.

Expressionist theatre had an important influence on *Caligari* (Robinson, 1997), and theatre director Max Reinhardt helped shaped Fritz Lang's technique. In his *Destiny* (*Der Müde Tod*, Germany, 1921) the use of lighting, rather than painting, became the most important aesthetic device:

As a result of lighting effects employed in *Destiny*, it became general practice to light sets from below in order to emphasize architecture and ring our relief surfaces.

(Barsacq, 1976: 31)

Unsurprisingly, with its emphasis upon the distortion of everyday objects, Expressionist visual style had a great influence upon horror films, particularly those produced by Universal Studios in the 1930s, as well as being crucial in the development of *film noir*.

Siegfried Kracauer's 'classic' film history, *From Caligari to Hitler* (1947), suggested that the figure of Caligari was a premonition of Hitler. He argued that the doctor's hypnotic power, which bent Cesare to his will, was similar to that wielded by the dictator in the 1930s, and that Germans were predisposed toward kowtowing to tyranny. However Kracauer's work shows the falsity of a deterministic approach to history; that is, that what happened was an inevitable outcome of events that preceded it. Life is, fortunately, more complex, and so Kracauer's tome, which has much interesting material, is marred by his insistence that Hitler cast a shadow over German film from 1920 onwards.

Further reading

David Robinson (1997) *Das Cabinet des Dr. Caligari*, London: British Film Institute.

Further viewing

The Last Laugh (1924)
Metropolis (1927)
Die Nibelungen: Siegfried (1924)

Further reading

Lotte Eisner (1973) *The Haunted Screen: Expressionism in the German Cinema and the Influence of Max Reinhardt*, London: Secker & Warburg. Siegfried Kracauer (1947) *From Caligari to Hitler: A Psychological History of the German Film*, Princeton, N.J.: Princeton University Press.

5.3 Avant-garde

As we saw in Chapter 2, cinema is a narrative form. However, as noted in Chapter 3, it only became primarily a narrative form when it developed into an industry in the late 1900s. Films do not have to be narrative-based, or if they are, the narrative does not have to conform to the bourgeois cause–effect pattern described by Todorov and Propp among others (see 2.9).

The avant-garde ('advance guard'), in artistic terms, are artists who reject conventions both formal and political. Their aims are to challenge and subvert conventional ways of seeing and understanding the world. As such the label 'avant-garde' is used to cover many different types of filmmaking, including Expressionism described above.

Peter Wollen (1982) developed the idea that there were two avant-gardes:

> First, there is the apolitical avant-garde, concerned more with developing a purist film aesthetic, running from Leger and others in France in the 1920s through the co-operative movements in post-war Europe and the United States. Second, there is a political avant-garde, running from the Soviet montage directors in the 1920s through to the work of such directors as Jean-Luc Godard and Miklos Jansco from the 1960s onwards.
>
> (Smith, 1998a: 398ab)

Léger straddled Dadaism and surrealism, and made *Ballet Mechanique* (France, 1924), a formalist experiment consisting of over 300 shots, although it is only 15 minutes in length. Quintessential surrealists Luis

Bunuel and Salvador Dali, collaborated on _Un Chien Andalou_ (_The Andalucian Dog_, France, 1929), which launched the former's career as a director. Although surrealism was primarily a literary movement, greatly influenced by Freud's readings of dream symbolism, it leant itself readily to film. The 'logic' of the dream world could be represented, as in _The Andalucian Dog_, by a lack of continuity in the editing. For example, the 'young woman' (Simone Mareuil) opens the door of her first floor flat, in an urban area, and steps out onto a beach; this does not seem strange to her. Through special effects, such as the ants that appear to be coming out of the man's (Pierre Batcheff's) hand, the elasticity of 'dream reality' can be shown: the unreal appears real. Because _The Andalucian Dog_ resists offering meaning, it is an avant-garde film through both its formal attributes and content.

> Although [the founder of surrealism] Andre Breton [decreed] in 1927 that all members should join the French Communist Party as the only political group whose ideas corresponded even slightly with those of the movement, its real roots were in anarchism.
>
> (Baxter, 1994: 37)

This anarchist stance meant the surrealists could not readily offer a political manifesto, unlike Jean-Luc Godard, for example, whose avant-garde political tendencies are most clearly seen in the films he made as part of the Dziga Vertov group in the late 1960s and early 1970s. For example the documentary _British Sounds_ (UK, 1969), made for a British television company though never screened, juxtaposed a tracking shot of a production line of red cars with a Marxist–Leninist analysis of capitalism. A following segment focuses on a naked woman walking around a house:

> The struggle between images and sounds which composes the films starts here. If the image of the factory has a sound to go with it … there is no sound for these images of silence, of women.
>
> (MacCabe, 1980: 86)

As MacCabe goes on to point out, the naked woman is such a potent image of sexism, even when unerotically filmed as here, that it cannot be used without complicity with the patriarchal order of bourgeois society. However Godard, and his comrades, were attempting to decentre the dominance of the film image in favour of questioning the image. They did this by providing a didactic and political soundtrack that 'clashed' with what was being shown.

Almost by definition, avant-garde work will not be commercially popular, and so the support given by state subsidy can be important in nurturing alternative modes of expression. The National Film Board of Canada was very important in supporting filmmakers such as Norman McLaren (see Box 5.2 and Appendix 5.3). However the fate of many avant-garde movements (the ones that gain a degree of popularity at least) is to be assimilated into the mainstream; partly this is necessary in order to create 'space' for the next avant-garde. It may take years for this recuperation to take place, and it is possible that a movement may never be assimilated. There is also a 'halfway house': artists like David Lynch adapt avant-garde techniques and present them to the 'not quite mainstream' arthouse audiences.

Hollywood does not necessarily eschew avant-garde techniques. Choreographer Busby Berkeley's astonishing dance sequences owe much to European experiments in the 1930s; see *42nd Street* and *Footlight Parade* (both 1933). Title sequences (often non-narrative) offer a space for experimentation, as evidenced in the work of Saul Bass. The title sequence to *Se7en* (1995), designed by Kyle Cooper, used avant-garde materialist techniques when the film appears to be jumping in the projector. Music videos, and even advertising, have been unlikely (because they are promotional vehicles) havens for the avant-garde in the twenty-first century. For example see director Chris Cunningham's use of surrealism in Madonna's 'Frozen', Leftfield's 'Afrika Shox' and the Playstation 'Mental Wealth' advertisement. His video for Autechre's 'Second Bad Vibel', with its use of colour and loops, is reminiscent of *Berlin Horse* – see Box 5.2.

With the advent of video the lines between filmmaking and the art world became blurred in the hybrid 'installation'. For example, Douglas Gordan's installation *24 Hour Psycho* (1993) slowed Hitchcock's original down to two frames a second, defamiliarizing the images.

Further viewing

Blow Job (Andy Warhol, 1963)
Crossroads (Bruce Connor, 1974)
Diagonal Symphony (Viking Eggeling, Germany, 1924)
Epiphany (Cerith Wyn Evans, UK, 1984)
Flaming Creatures (Jeff Smith, 1963)
Introduction to Arnold Schoenberg's Accompaniment to a Cinematic Scene (*Einleitung zu Arnold Schoenbergs Begleitmusik zu einer Lichtspielscene*, Danièle Huillet and Jean-Marie Straub, West Germany, 1973)

London (Patrick Keiller, UK, 1994)

Meshes of an Afternoon (Maya Deren, 1943)

Moment (Steve Dwoskin, 1970)

Return to Reason (*Le Retour de la Raison*, Man Ray, France, 1923)

The Riddle of Lumen (Stan Brakhage, 1972)

Scorpio Rising (Kenneth Anger, 1964)

Trade Tattoo (Len Lye, UK, 1937)

The Work of Director Chris Cunningham (Director's Label, 2003)

Further reading

Rees, A. L. (1999) *A History of Experimental Film and Video,* London: British Film Institute.

O'Pray, Michael (2003) *Avant-Garde Film: Forms, Themes and Passions.* London: Wallflower.

Sitney, P. Adams (2002) *Visionary Film: the American Avant-Garde, 1943–2000.* (Oxford University Press).

Sitney, P. Adams (ed.) (2000) *Film Culture Reader,* New York: Cooper Square Press.

Box 5.2 Avant-garde films: *Berlin Horse* (1970)
and *Wavelength* (1967)

Berlin Horse (1970)

According to Michael O'Pray (2003), Malcolm Le Grice's short *Berlin Horse* is one of the few European avant-garde classics. Le Grice combines a film he made, of a horse being led in a circle, with early newsreel of a horse being rescued from a fire:

> The two film fragments are submitted to a series of printing operations...and then further transformed through colour filters. The films are also printed to run backwards. The end result is a complex rhythmic weaving of images assisted by the natural rhythms of the subject matter ...
>
> (O'Pray, 2003: 102)

The hypnotic, and fascinating, effect is heightened by Brian Eno's music (looped as the horse footage is looped). The superposition of positive and negative images of the horse draws attention to the representational nature of film, and the play with colour – at one point the horse

---

takes on the colour of the smoke from the fire – offers beautiful images that require close attention because, despite their sameness, they are constantly different.

The film was shot on 8 mm, the cheapest way to make moving image texts before the advent of video, and can be shown in one, two or four-screen versions. The 'extra' screens serve to defamiliarize the viewing process and help draw attention to the fact of spectatorship. Mike Figgis used a similar device, although it was based on one screen split into four rather than four screens, for his digital video 'real time' narrative *Timecode* (2000).

Wavelength *(USA-Canada, 1967)*

Wavelength (directed by Michael Snow) is a riveting 45-minute film that appears to be one zoom across a room to a picture of the sea on the wall. During the film a wardrobe is moved into the room; two women listen to the Beatles' 'Strawberry Fields Forever' and leave; a window is shut; a man walks in and collapses; a woman returns to find the man, and she phones to tell someone the man is dead. The diegetic sound is accompanied by a high-pitched whine (a sine wave).

As with many avant-garde films, spectators are 'given' time to consider what they are seeing; we are not 'swept away' by narrative. It is a 'structural' film in that it emphasizes film form and process on a number of levels. The zoom traverses the same space as the light that is 'imprinting' the film; through the zoom itself we literally see the narrative development; the setting of the apartment is transformed from a long shot to an extreme close-up.

O'Pray points out that *Wavelength* is both avant-garde and experimental (a term he suggests can also be used to describe conservative film traditions, while avant-garde must be radical), and exemplifies the romantic tradition of the American avant-garde:

> The structure is a shaping of a form of consciousness ... the film is a journey from a fairly straightforward realist shot which is then gradually transformed in an impossible way given that it mimics a single zoom.
>
> (O'Pray, 2003: 95)

It has accrued its own tagline: 'one room, one zoom'.

5.4 Soviet cinema in the 1920s

Karl Marx suggested, in the nineteenth century, that the movement from feudalism to capitalism, and then to communism, structured history. The 1917 Revolution, 'that had been talked over and fought for during the best part of a century' (Kochan, 1963: 243–4), began its decisive stage in March of that year with the abdication of the (feudal) Tsar. By November, the Bolsheviks (Communists), members of the working-class proletariat, were in power, and the seeds were set for the Cold War that raged throughout much of the twentieth century between the capitalist west and the 'communist' eastern bloc.

Having been devastated by both the Revolution and the First World War, the Soviet film industry did not start making films in any great number until the mid-1920s. By then writers such as Lev Kuleshov, Dziga Vertov and, most significantly, Sergei Eisenstein had theorized about cinema from a communist perspective. Vertov's 'Kino-Eye', for example, was premised on focusing on ordinary people instead of the elite:

> Down with the immortal kings and queens of the screen! Long live ordinary, mortal people, captured in the midst of life going about their daily tasks …
>
> (Vertov, quoted in Williams, 1980: 25)

Vertov's 'Kino-Eye' manifesto was an attempt to wipe away bourgeois mystification by jettisoning narrative, script and actors and film reality as it was (see *Man With A Movie Camera* (*Chelovek s kinoapparatom*, USSR, 1929)). However, in keeping with other Soviet theorists, the key to Vertov's filmmaking was in his use of montage.

It was Kuleshov who suggested that montage was crucial to filmic meaning. He conducted a much-cited experiment where he demonstrated that audiences, when shown a shot of an actor (with a neutral facial expression) followed by a shot of food, decided the character was hungry. However, if the same shot of the actor was followed by a shot of an old woman in a coffin, then he was thought to be grieving. This demonstrated that, in the absence of an establishing shot, audience would assume a link between images. Kuleshov's experiment, which has not survived, has its critics:

> it remains annoying specious to claim that shot one, 'man's face', plus shot two, 'woman in coffin', creates a *new* idea, 'man in grief'.

We could expect the same idea to be communicable in a single shot of both man and corpse.

(Perkins, 1972: 106)

Sergei Eisenstein also based his aesthetic on montage. His 'montage of attractions' was concerned with the:

> free montage of arbitrarily selected, independent (within the given composition and the subject links that hold the influencing actions together) attractions – all with the aim of establishing certain final thematic effects.

(Barna, 1973: 63)

The meaning of an individual shot, Eisenstein (and others) argued, is without intrinsic meaning and so requires a context. This context, the montage, creates meaning by clashing shots together to create a dialectically formed meaning in the spectator's mind. This 'clash' is often graphical in nature (that is, the look of one image clashes with the next) but can also serve to undermine the cause–effect chain associated with conventional narrative. For example in *October* (*Oktyabr*, USSR, 1927) Eisenstein breaks the narrative logic of the diegesis by juxtaposing shots of a peacock with the vain Prime Minister Kerensky.

Eisenstein believed that montage could create a dialectic where the first shot is the thesis, followed by a shot that is the antithesis, from

Sergei Eisenstein's revolutionary technique was based on montage

which the audience will create meaning: the synthesis. In *October* there is a sequence of religious icons that starts with an image of a Baroque Christ. Other icons, including pagan religious artefacts, follow. The audience is invited to 'synthesize' the sequence with the conclusion that Christianity is no more valid than any other religion.

Eisenstein was not always so indirect in his use of montage. For example in *Strike* (*Stachka*, USSR, 1925) the murder of the workers on strike is cross-cut with the slaughter of a bull at an abattoir which, Eisenstein argued, 'made for a powerful emotional intensification of the scene' (Eisenstein, 1979: 113). (*Apocalypse Now*, 1979, used the same device when Kurtz was killed.) The workers are treated like animals.

By the early 1930s, the montage theorists had been superseded by the doctrine of socialist realism, as set out by Zhdanov. Socialist realism was formulated in response to the economic difficulties experienced by the Soviet Union, which suffered economic blockades from western countries nervous that their own proletariats might overthrow their ruling classes. Instead of showing the world as it is, socialist realism portrayed the world as it should be under socialism. This appears to have produced very few films of lasting interest, although *Chapayev* (USSR, 1934) works well in its portrayal of a hero of the Civil War. In many ways this film reasserted bourgeois film style, as its eponymous hero is elevated above the collective mass.

Further viewing

Alexander Nevsky (*Aleksandr Nevsky*, 1938)
Battleship Potemkin (*Bronenosets Potyomkin*, 1925)
The End of St Petersburg (*Konyets Sankt-Peterburga*, 1927)
The Extraordinary Adventures of Mr West in the Land of the Bolsheviks (*Neobychainye Priklyucheniya Mistera Vesta v Strane Bolshevikov*, 1924)
Ivan the Terrible: Parts 1 and 2 (*Ivan Groznyj I and II*, 1945 and 1958)
Mother (*Mat*, 1926)

Further reading

Taylor, Richard (ed.) (1988) *S. M. Eisenstein: Selected Works: Writings 1922–1934*, London: British Film Institute.
Taylor, Richard (1998) *Film Propaganda: Soviet Russia and Nazi German*, I. B. Tauris.
Taylor, Richard and Glenny, Michael (eds) (1994) *S. M. Eisenstein: Selected Writings: Towards a Theory of Montage*, London: British Film Institute.

5.5 The British documentary movement

Although John Grierson coined the term 'documentary' in the 1930s, he was not the first documentary filmmaker; Robert Flaherty's *Nanook of the North* (1922) had already made its mark at the box office. Flaherty's innovation was to understand that even films that took the real world for its 'pro-filmic event', rather than manufacturing it as in fiction, needed to use film language:

> Flaherty had apparently mastered … the 'grammar' of film as it had evolved in the fiction film. This evolution had not merely changed techniques; it had transformed the sensibilities of the audiences. The ability to witness an episode from many angles and distances, seen in quick succession... Thus drama … was wedded to something more real – people being themselves.
>
> (Barnouw, 1993: 39)

Unlike Flaherty, Grierson committed his ideas to print, and was responsible for a whole school of documentary filmmakers who made a lasting impact on world cinema. He believed that documentary could alleviate the problems of widespread disengagement from the democratic process experienced by many people in the 1920s. While he admired Flaherty's films, which focused on the exotic and 'primitive', Grierson believed documentaries should focus on the lives of ordinary local people, and by 'dramatizing issues and their implications in a meaningful way, could lead the citizen through the wilderness. This became the Grierson mission' (Barnouw, 1993: 85).

His first film, *Drifters* (UK, 1929), like Eisenstein's *Battleship Potemkin,* which Grierson had been involved in getting screened in the west, represented the working class as heroes. Its success led him to create a team for the Empire Marketing Board, essentially a propaganda mouthpiece designed to justify the existence of the British Empire. As most of Grierson's team, including Harry Watt and Basil Wright who created the classic *Night Mail* (UK, 1936), were left-wing, this imperialist project could have led to tension. However Grierson's skill as a producer was to reconcile the potential conflict of interest (left wingers tend to be anti-colonial) and supervise the creation of films that satisfied both paymasters and artists. For example, *Song of Ceylon* (UK, 1935), made by Basil Wright, showed happy Ceylonese (Ceylon was renamed Sri Lanka after the end of Empire) harvesting tea for the British-owned company. However, the early part of the film spoke of how the Ceylonese were too proud to work for others, so while on the surface the workers seem to be content, it is clear that Empire has irrevocably changed the country's culture.

Night Mail celebrated the efficiency of the Post Office and the railways, by focusing on the hard work of 'ordinary' people. *Housing Problems* (UK, 1935) was effective in showing the appalling conditions of the slums. The team took exceptionally bulky 35 mm equipment into rat-infested homes, and allowed the occupants to speak directly to camera. In making this film Edgar Anstey and Arthur Elton helped kick-start the programme of slum clearance; this also had the effect of benefiting the Gas Light and Coke Company, which sponsored the film, as it could supply heating to the new housing.

While the received pronunciation (posh voices) of the voice-overs is jarring for modern audiences, and makes the films seem patronising, there is no doubt about the filmmakers' commitment to social justice. The British documentary movement is the only lasting contribution Britain has made to World cinema.

Further viewing

Coal Face (1935)
Spare Time (1939)

Further reading

Aitken, Ian (1992) *Film and Reform: John Grierson and the Documentary Film Movement,* London: Routledge.

5.6 Italian neo-realism

In fiction film, the Italian neo-realists of the 1940s and 1950s have probably been most influential on the development of the realist aesthetic. Devastated economically and politically by the war, Italian filmmakers made a virtue of their lack of equipment, studio facilities and actors.

Stylistically, Italian neo-realism was characterized by:

1. an avoidance of neatly plotted stories in favor of loose, episodic structures that evolve organically
2. a documentary visual style
3. the use of actual locations – usually exteriors – rather than studio sites
4. the use of nonprofessional actors, even for principal roles

5. use of conversational speech, not literary dialogue
6. avoidance of artifice in editing, camerawork, and lighting in favor of a simple 'styless' (*sic*) style.

(www.gpc.edu/~jriggs/film1301/notes10.htm,
accessed April 2003)

Like the films made in the Soviet Union and Grierson's documentaries (see above), neo-realism focused on 'ordinary people', people whom mainstream cinema usually only treats as extras. Cesare Zavattini, scriptwriter of the classic *Bicycle Thieves* (*Ladri di Biciclette*, Italy, 1948) stated:

> if I use living, real characters with which to sound reality, people in whose. life I can directly participate, my emotion becomes more effective, morally stronger, more useful.
>
> (quoted in Williams, 1980: 30)

He described making a two-hour film derived from an incident, lasting two minutes, where a woman buys shoes:

> The woman is buying the shoes. What is her son doing at the same moment? What are people doing in India that could have some relation to this fact of the shoes? The shoes cost 7,000 lire. How did the woman happen to have 7,000 lire? How hard did she work of them, what do they represent to her?
>
> (quoted in Williams, 1980: 30)

In *Bicycle Thieves*, Antonio (Lamberto Maggiorani) is lucky, at a time of massive unemployment, to get a job as a billsticker; this is the moment Zavattini uses to investigate Antonio's life. However, he needs his bicycle to do the job, and it is in hock. His wife pawns their best sheets to get it back – the camera lingers on the thousands of sheets already pawned in the shop – and he starts his job, only to have his bike stolen. The film charts his heartbreaking attempts, with the assistance of his young son, to find his bike. The 'documentary style', alluded to in point 2 above, is present through the *mise en scène*, with its location shooting of a bombed-out city, rather than in the actual camera style.

While *Bicycle Thieves* is undoubtedly a powerful film, it draws upon melodramatic coincidence to emphasize its message and so arguably compromises its realist intentions. As the title suggests, the narrative disruption is the theft; without this we might simply see Antonio happily sticking bills. In addition, during his search he stumbles across the thieves;

Antonio and his son search desperately for his bicycle (*Bicycle Thieves*, 1948)

a rather fortuitous coincidence, necessary to give the narrative dramatic force.

Ideologically, the characteristics of Italian neo-realism were:

1. a new democratic spirit, with emphasis on the value of ordinary people
2. a compassionate point of view and a refusal to make facile (easy) moral judgements
3. a preoccupation with Italy's Fascist past and its aftermath of wartime devastation
4. a blending of Christian and Marxist humanism
5. an emphasis on emotions rather than abstract ideas.

(www.gpc.edu/~jriggs/film1301/notes10.htm,

accessed April 2003)

Neo-realism was particularly important to post-war Italy as it formed part of the attempt to create a national identity in opposition to the 'fascist Italy' that had prevailed in the years from 1922 to 1945. It was, however, typically a far from unified 'movement', and according to Monticelli (1998), it was responsible for only about 10 per cent of films made during the period. (Monticelli also details the critical debates that raged around the term.)

Neo-realism has been particularly influential because its manifesto is appropriate to any society where films are being made about 'ordinary people', and its 'stripped down' style, with an emphasis on a documentary style (which emphasized the use of handheld camera once equipment was light enough), and use of whatever props and locations that were available, are perfect for any low-budget film-making.

From a formalist's perspective (where the focus is on the form and not the content of the film), neo-realism appeared to be realistic because it used a new set of conventions to represent reality. The neo-realists proved very influential on the development of the Indian cinema (particularly the films of Satyajit Ray), Egyptian film, the French *nouvelle vague* and British New Wave of the early 1960s. Ken Loach and Mike Leigh have continued this tradition in British cinema, and a number of Chinese directors have embraced the 'neo-realist' style.

Further viewing

Ossessione (1943)
Roberto Rossellini's war trilogy *Rome Open City* (*Roma, Città Aperta,* 1945) – not as strictly neo-realist as the following two films; many of the scenes were shot in a studio and well-known actors were used.
Paisà (1946)
Germany, Year Zero (*Germain, Anno Zero*, 1947)
La Terra trema: Episodio del mare (*The Earth Will Tremble*, 1948)

Further reading

Bondanella, Peter (2001) *Italian Cinema: From Neorealism to the Present,* London: Continuum.
Forgacs, David (2000) *Rome Open City,* London: British Film Institute.
Sorlin, Pierre (1996) *Italian National Cinema: 1896–1996,* London: Routledge.

5.7 The French New Wave (*nouvelle vague*)

The wave started with critics writing for *Cahiers du Cinéma*, under the aegis of Andre Bazin (see 4.2), where they railed against French cinema's 'tradition of quality' (see 4.3), which they identified as 'cinéma du papa'. In its place they celebrated Hollywood. The critics then made movies and broke the mould of cinematic form.

Taking Alexandre Astruc's idea that the camera was the equivalent of a pen, the New Wave filmmakers emphasized that films were not merely a medium for script and performance, but a personal (to the director) cinema which used the camera as an active participant:

> Apparent improvisations in camera technique (the long take, the freeze-frame), editing (the jump cut), dialogue, plot and perform-ance were all deployed because cinema was seen for the first time not as a neutral form through which something else (literature or 'reality') could be transmitted, but as a specific aesthetic system, a language in itself.
>
> (Kuhn, 1999: 83a)

Producers were receptive to this new way of making films, and the suc-cess of the low-budget *And Woman ... Was Created* (*Et Dieu Créa la Femme*, 1956) allowed François Truffaut to make *The 400 Blows* (1959), a literal translation of *Les Quatre Cents Coups* (see Box 5.3), which means 'to live a wild life'. Although this film is regularly cited as the first New Wave film, it was preceded by other films that can also be catego-rized as part of the New Wave, such as *Hiroshima, Mon Amour* (directed by Alain Resnais, 1958) and Agnès Varda's *La Pointe Courte* (1954).

As noted at the beginning of this chapter, forcing history into cate-gories is a contentious business. It is no surprise that there should be several films challenging the status quo at the same time. Usually artistic innovation is facilitated by the 'spirit of the times' (zeitgeist), and so no one individual breaks the mould. For example, French intellectual life of the time was in upheaval with the work of Roland Barthes and Claude Levi-Strauss. These theorists had an immense influence upon film theory and on Jean-Luc Godard's films in particular. Another important innovation at the time of the New Wave was the development of light-weight cameras, which helped in making the films low-budget because they are quicker to work with, and fast filmstocks, allowing greater use of natural light. These facilitated the improvisatory nature of many New Wave films. The ethnographic documentaries of Jean Rouch, which had also utilized the new technology, were also influential, particularly in

Godard's *A Bout de Souffle* (1960) changed the way films were made and seen

their use of location shooting. Godard, in particular, used editing to disorientate the viewer by showing the same event twice: for example, getting out of a car in *A Bande à part* (*The Outsiders*, France, 1964).

Cahiers' New Wave critics had celebrated American cinema and this is evident in their films:

> *Nouvelle vague* directors offered an affectionate pastiche of genre movies, for instance Godard's first feature *A Bout de Souffle* [*Breathless*] (1960) was dedicated to Monogram Pictures (a small studio which churned out 'B' pictures during Hollywood's Golden Age) and featured Jean-Paul Belmondo as a small-time Humphrey Bogart-type character.
>
> Truffaut's second feature, *Tirez sur le pianiste* [*Shoot the Pianist*] (1960), was based on a novel by American pulp writer David Goodis and mixed the conventions of several genres such as gangster films, romance, melodrama and thriller (with a film noir style opening thrown in). Although both these films featured a conventional narrative structure the form was used much more flexibly than characteristic Hollywood cinema.
>
> (Lacey, 1996: 33a)

It must be remembered that not all French cinema of the time was New Wave.

The New Wave, which lasted until about 1964, had an immense influence on film conventions (see 3.8), and it also inspired other new waves that created their own variations on film form, including Brazil's Cinema Novo (see 5.9.2) and West Germany's New Cinema (5.11). It also had a self-acknowledged influence on one of the most fashionable filmmakers of the 1990s, Quentin Tarantino. Naming his production company, A Band Apart, after Godard's movie, Tarantino foregrounded cine-literacy in his films with his self-conscious take on Hollywood tropes. This was similar to what New Wave directors were doing, as Godard said in a 1962 interview:

> We were the first directors to know that Griffith exists. Even Carne, Delluc and Rene Clair, when they made their first films, had no real critical or historical background.
>
> (quoted in Milne, 1981: 1163b)

By the 1990s knowledge of past cinema was even more intense, with access to videos and the dedicated film channels of cable and satellite television. What seemed new in Tarantino, such as the hitmen's irrelevant conversation about fries in Amsterdam (in *Pulp Fiction*, 1994), had already appeared over 30 years earlier, when the criminals in Truffaut's *Shoot the Pianist* have a sexist discussion when they kidnap the protagonist.

Box 5.3 *The 400 Blows (Les Quatre Cents Coups*, France, 1959)

If *The 400 Blows* was not the first New Wave film, it certainly was the one that put the incipient movement on the map. The director, and co-writer, François Truffaut, had been barred from 1958's Cannes Film Festival because of his diatribes against French cinema. Truffaut, however, triumphed a year later when his film won the Best Direction prize; at least the Cannes jury did not hold grudges.

The film is typical of the New Wave in its use of handheld camera, episodic narrative and 'no star' approach. One contemporary reviewer aptly summed up the film:

> It is a sad, bitter story of a child's gradual disaffection from society. The child is tough, imaginative, exuberant; the society is dull, timid, corrupt. And the film's viewpoint isn't sentimental.
>
> (Croce, 1978: 722)

Also arguably typical is the misogyny apparent in the film, with Antoine's mother represented as a self-centred woman who is happy to have her son taken off her hands. Forbes (1998) suggests that misogyny also runs through the films of Godard and Chabrol. The film does not, however, share the love of Hollywood that characterized the movement's early years. The narrative is occasionally allowed to wander, in a very non-Hollywood fashion, such as the overhead shot of the gym teacher taking children on a run. In one take we see them run off bit by bit, leaving the teacher to carry on oblivious to what is happening behind him.

One thing the New Wave had in common with the 'cinéma du papa' was in its emphasis on Paris. Truffaut in the main avoids the travelogue approach, although the title sequence focuses on the Eiffel Tower and there is a scene at the Pigalle. When the child, Antoine Doinel (Jean-Pierre Léaud), is being ferried in a police van, the scene is filmed with a long take from his point of view of Paris by night. The accompanying music gives the scene a poetic feel, until the camera cuts back to the boy and we see he is crying.

Truffaut gets a marvellously unaffected performance from Léaud, and the ending, when the boy reaches the sea, is ambiguous. Do we read the freeze frame as offering hope for the future, a moment of epiphany, or has Doinel simply reached the 'end of the road' and there is no hope for him?

The 400 Blows is a semi-autobiographical film missing one key figure in Truffaut's life, the father figure of Andre Bazin. He went on to make three more films in what became the Doinel cycle, all employing Jean-Pierre Léaud: the short Antoine et Colette (a segment of the anthology film Love at Twenty, L'Amour à Vingt Ans, 1962), Stolen Kisses (Baisers Volés, 1968) and Bed and Board (Domicile Conjugal, France-Italy, 1970).

Truffaut's maxim was that every film should be a reaction to the previous one. So he followed The 400 Blows with a genre film, based on a novel by American 'pulp' writer David Goodis, Shoot the Pianist (Tirez sur le Pianiste, 1960). His third film, Jules et Jim (1962) was a period bittersweet romance.

Further viewing (listed under the director)

Claude Chabrol:
  Le Beau Serge (Bitter Reunion, 1959)
Jacques Demy:
  Lola (France-Italy, 1963)

The Umbrellas of Cherbourg (Les Parapluies de Cherbourg, France-West Germany, 1964)

Jean-Luc Godard:

A Bout de Souffle (Breathless, 1960)

The Little Soldier (Le Petit Soldat, 1961)

A Woman is a Woman (Une Femme est une Femme, France-Italy, 1961)

Vivre sa Vie (It's My Life, 1962)

Le Mépris (Contempt, France-Italy, 1963)

A Bande à part (The Outsiders, 1964)

A Married Woman (Une Femme Mariée, 1964)

Jacques Rivette:

Paris is Ours (Paris Nous Appartient, 1960)

Eric Rohmer:

The Sign of Leo (Le Signe du Lion, 1959)

Agnes Varda:

Cléo from 5 to 7 (Cléo de 5 à 7, 1962)

Further reading

Hayward, Susan (1993) *French National Cinema,* London: Routledge.

Monaco, James (1977) *The New Wave: Truffaut, Godard, Chabrol, Rohmer, Rivette,* Oxford: Oxford University Press.

Wiegand, Chris (2001) *French New Wave,* Pocket Essentials.

5.8 The British New Wave (1959–63) and the 'Swinging Sixties'

The British New Wave's reputation for realism was one it possessed, to an extent, at the time. It was reinforced during the 1980s by such books as John Hill's *Sex, Class and Realism* (1986). Hill suggests that the break with conventions (which is what signifies realism most powerfully) of New Wave cinema was characterized by:

> an 'injection of new content': new characters (the working-class, juvenile delinquents), new settings (the factory, the housing estate) and new problems (race, homosexuality). Although this was accompanied by a certain degree of stylistic novelty (location shooting for example), it did not, in any major sense, entail the 'invention of new dramatic forms'.
>
> (Hill, 1986: 59)

Room at the Top (1959), credited as being the first New Wave film, certainly does not look 'realist' now, particularly with its use of melodrama, Laurence Harvey's acting style and the habit of the period of casting a foreign actress in the role of a 'loose' woman (Simone Signoret). However, its focus on a working class 'go-getter', and its use of location shooting (Bradford), did offer new subject matter and setting for British cinema. It has been described as an 'old-fashioned morality story' (Hutchings, 2001: 147b) directed by an established practitioner, Jack Clayton, who did not contribute further to the 'wave'.

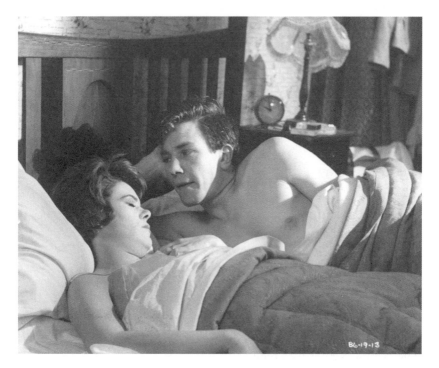

New Wave films introduced a new level of risqué representation to British cinema (*Saturday Night and Sunday Morning*, 1960)

Part of the freshness of the New Wave was the films' use of relatively unknown actors such as Albert Finney (*Saturday Night and Sunday Morning*, 1960) and Rita Tushingham (*A Taste of Honey*, 1961 – see Box 5.4). Similarly most of the directors were new, and a number, Lindsay Anderson, Karel Reisz and Tony Richardson, had gained their film making experience making Free Cinema documentaries. Free Cinema distinguished itself by focusing on the working-class life, such as in Anderson's Covent Garden market film, *Every Day Except Christmas* (1957), and Reisz's youth culture movie, *We Are the Lambeth Boys*

(1959). Richardson had been involved with the 'Angry Young Men' of the Royal Court theatre in London, and his first film was an adaptation of John Osborne's 'kitchen sink' play *Look Back in Anger* (1958). These texts followed Anderson's dictum, stated in his role as a critic, that films should engage with contemporary society (Anderson, 1957). While this dictum harked back to the 'Grierson school' of the 1930s (see 5.5), it avoided Grierson's educational mission. While Free Cinema did not deem it trivial to portray the lower classes, the middle class's patronising attitude could still be detected in Anderson's O *Dreamland* (1953) as it:

> attacked the leisure habits of the masses at 'Dreamland', an amusement park at Margate.
>
> (Hedling, 2001: 241b)

The commercial failure of Anderson's first feature, *This Sporting Life* (1963), heralded the end of the New Wave, although its melodramatic visual style puts it at odds with the realism of earlier films of the movement. Anderson himself emphasized that he was focusing upon the subjectivity of the characters (Milne, 1962). Audiences preferred the more whimsical *Billy Liar* (directed by John Schlesinger, 1963), which mixed an 'it's grim up North' attitude with comedic fantasy. *Billy Liar* also-introduced a symbolic moment when Liz (Julie Christie) departs from Bradford for London leaving Billy (Tom Courtenay) behind. One year later the Beatles arrived in London, at the beginning of *A Hard Day's Night* (1964), and with them the seeds of the 'Swinging Sixties'.

Revisionist historians have suggested that the critical emphasis on 'serious' films of the time had led to the neglect of genre films that also offered a 'realist' perspective. For example:

> in crime films such as *Hell is a City* (Val Guest, 1960), *The Criminal* (Joseph Losey, 1960) and *The Frightened City* (John Lemont, 1961) one finds location shooting coupled with a relatively explicitly representation of violence and sexuality …
>
> (Hutchings, 2001: 150b)

However the 'Swinging London' films (such as *Darling*, directed by John Schlesinger, 1965, and *Blow-Up*, 1966) came into fashion by emphasizing hedonism and sexual 'liberation' rather than the supposedly dead-end lives of Northerners. These films portrayed a growing consumer culture where female pleasures were not necessarily subordinated to those of men. The wider availability of the contraceptive pill was important, as was the burgeoning women's movement. However, if anyone was having 'promiscuous sex' they were probably within shouting distance of Carnaby Street in London:

> A survey carried out in 1970 found that only 19 per cent of married couples under forty-five used the pill, and the idea that most single girls were sexually promiscuous had little foundation in fact.
>
> (Murphy, 1992: 142)

London was the 'happening' place in the western world, as evidenced by *Time* magazine, April 1966, which dubbed London as 'swinging'. Unsurprisingly Hollywood had noticed this and hoped that a fashionable London would solve their problems created by falling audiences. The Beatles had conquered America and the distinctly 'un-New Wave' *Tom Jones* (1963) had won the Best Picture Oscar, with Tony Richardson picking up the Best Director, suggesting all things British were a sound investment.

The MGM-backed *Blow-Up*, directed by Michelangelo Antonioni (an Italian with arthouse success), featured the first glimpse of (female) pubic hair in British cinema, and *Repulsion* (1965), a horror film directed by Roman Polanski, offered the first sound of a (female) orgasm. Both these films looked at the underside of Swinging London. No film prised open the murky underworld of London, which was saturated by police corruption and gang warfare (epitomized by the Kray twins), more than *Performance* (1970), which was so hated by Warner Bros. that it only released it with reluctance.

Box 5.4 Sixties British cinema: *A Taste of Honey* (1961) and *Blow-Up* (UK-Italy, 1966)

For a brief moment in the 1960s British cinema rode the fashionable wave stimulated by the media creation that was 'Swinging London'. The New Wave, the first self-consciously art cinema in Britain since Grierson, manifested itself; this tendency was soon swamped by the commercial products of the mid-1960s, often funded by Hollywood.

A Taste of Honey, in common with a number of other New Wave films, had theatrical origins: Shelagh Delaney's play was premiered at the Liverpool Playhouse in 1958. Its focus on a white teenager, Jo (Rita Tushingham), whose sexual liaison with a black man leads to single motherhood, was atypical of theatrical subjects of the time, and so in

---

breaking conventions signified itself as 'realist'. In addition, the sympathetic portrayal of Jo's homosexual best friend (Murray Melvin), when this sexual orientation was illegal in Britain, further emphasized the unconventional representations. The focus on working-class characters, drawing upon naturalism, was enhanced by location shooting that dwelled on the still 'un-renovated' bombsites of the post-war years.

The frank portrayal of sexuality and the scene showing Jo's mum (Dora Bryan) in the bath offered sights never seen before in British cinema. As noted in 3.13, the growth of European arthouse cinema had encouraged less puritanical representations, and the French *nouvelle vague* (see 5.7) had pioneered the use of handheld camera on location. While Italian neo-realism (see 5.6) had used location shooting, the cameras and sound equipment were too bulky to offer much in the form of mobility. By the late 1950s, the lighter technology led to greater flexibility, which readily allowed filming next to the bleak canal of Salford, the dancehall and the Blackpool beachfront.

However, despite the 'artistic' intent of Richardson and his fellow New Wave directors, they failed to find favour with the burgeoning '*Movie* school' of criticism, which distrusted the lack of a coherent vision that was deemed necessary to qualify as an auteur (see 4.3).

In the same way that Raoul Coutard had made an indelible impression upon the *nouvelle vague*, Richardson's cinematographer Walter Lassally was also influential. He had worked in Free Cinema and also shot Richardson's follow-up, *The Loneliness of the Long Distance Runner* (1962). The independence of Woodfall, the production company that produced many of the New Wave films, was also important as it allowed a more flexible approach to film-making that the conventional studio-based work of the established companies would not allow.

A *Taste of Honey* was a commercial success and its star, the 'unknown' Rita Tushingham, went on to appear in a number of 'Swinging Sixties' movies such as *The Knack* (1965) and *Smashing Time* (1967).

The MGM-backed *Blow-Up* also used an 'unknown' lead, David Hemmings, who played a thinly disguised version of fashion photographer David Bailey. The introduction of the protagonist, Thomas, sees him exiting from a doss house where he has apparently stayed the night in order to get photographs of the homeless for his forthcoming book. While Bailey had not come from such a destitute background, Thomas's working-class origins are emphasized when an old proprietor of an antiques shop refuses to sell to 'the likes of him'. He drives a Rolls-Royce, a powerful image of how the nouveaux riches were appropriating the symbols of 'old money'.

The director Michelangelo Antonioni cast fashion icons of the decade, particularly the model Verushka, to lend verisimilitude to his critique of the swinging scene. When Thomas states, to Verushka, that he 'thought she was were supposed to be in Paris,' she, stoned, replies 'I am in Paris.' This palpable lack of grip on reality (the whole film is set in London) is further emphasized by the central thrust of the film's narrative: Thomas's attempts to discover whether he photographed a murder victim, by blowing up his photographs to such an extent they look like the dots of abstract art.

While most of the few truly Swinging Sixties films celebrated youth, fashion and the working class, and emphasized a freer attitude toward sex, *Blow-Up* critiqued the phenomenon as being superficial. Although *Blow-Up* was a commercial success, most of the Hollywood-backed films failed to recoup their costs, and the Americans disappeared as quickly as they had arrived, leaving the British film industry lurching into another of its periodic crises.

The 1960s saw a slight democratization of class in Britain; indeed to have a working-class background was virtually a benefit, and the 'lower' classes no longer had to disguise their origins by adopting a 'posh' accent. This breaking down of class barriers coincided with the growth of youth culture, which was primarily defined in terms of consumerism.

The James Bond series, beginning with *Dr No* (1962), was very successful and was still running during the early years of the twenty-first century. The Bond co-producer Harry Saltzman also had success with Michael Caine's portrayal of Harry Palmer (see for example *The Ipcress File*, 1965), an anti-Bond figure in a world where glamour is replaced by mundane routine. Caine went on to be one of the few enduring stars produced by the post-war British film industry, although he felt his working-class background was always held against him in Britain and he only could achieve full recognition in America.

The 1960s was a watershed decade, separating the deprivations of pre- and post-war Britain from the consumer society that seems entrenched in the early years of the twenty-first century.

Further viewing

Catch Us If You Can (1965)
Georgy Girl (1966)
A Kind of Loving (1962)

The Knack (1966)
The Leather Boys (1963)
The Loneliness of the Long Distance Runner (1962)
The L-Shaped Room (1962)
Poor Cow (1967)
Smashing Time (1967)

Further reading

Hill, John (1986) *Sex, Class and Realism: British Cinema 1956–1963*, London: British Film Institute.
Murphy, Robert (1992) *Sixties British Cinema*, London: British Film Institute.

5.9 Other 1960s new waves

It is not simply the necessarily compact nature of an introductory book that demands that both Cinema Novo of Brazil, and the 'new cinemas' of Poland, Czechoslovakia (and other Eastern European countries) are collapsed into one short section. The main problem is access to these films. At the time of writing, in Britain there is no opportunity to see these films in the cinema or on DVD, with the exceptions of *Knife in the Water* (*Noz w Wodzie*, Poland, 1962) and *The Tragedy of the Switchboard Operator* (*Ljubavni Slucaj ili Tragedija Sluzbenice P.T.T.*, Yugoslavia, 1967). Even the astonishing 'war trilogy' directed by Poland's Andrzej Wadja: *A Generation* (*Pokolenie*, 1955), *Canal* (*Kanal*, 1957) and *Ashes and Diamonds* (*Popiól i Diament*, 1958) is not available. Brazilian films from the 1960s cannot be seen.

5.9.1 Eastern Europe

Neither Czechoslovakia nor Yugoslavia currently exists, and the political geography of the 1960s (from after the Second World War until the late 1980s) was dominated by the Cold War. The 'iron curtain' separated east from west; its border split Germany in two and ran between Austria and Czechoslovakia. The east was dominated by the policy of the Soviet Union, while the west was united militarily by NATO and economically by capitalism. When after the death of Stalin in 1956 the Soviet grip on the Eastern bloc (comprising Bulgaria, Czechoslovakia, East Germany, Hungary, Poland and Romania) loosened, more freedom of expression was allowed and film received much government support:

An attempt was made to forge national cinemas predicated upon and guided by Marxist-inspired aesthetic, ideological, and political doctrines promulgated and enforced by the state… [the governments] made a deep and unprecedented commitment in their respective countries to building up the material infrastructure of film production, exhibition, and distribution and in subsidizing the development of film education and film culture.

(Goulding, 1997: 471a)

Foremost amongst Hungarian directors was Miklos Jancsó:

His films are among the most distinctive in modern cinema with their highly stylised use of camera – circling and tracking the action – and minimal editing…. Jancsó's films were inspired by key periods in the development of Hungarian socialism but the re-examination of history was also the preoccupation of many other directors.

(Hames, 1981: 1303a)

The greater opportunity for self-expression resulted in many filmmakers investigating the new freedoms, just as those in the west were. In *The Tragedy of the Switchboard Operator,* director Dusan Makavejev reflected the turbulence and confusion of 1960s Yugoslavia with its mix of politics, sex and murder. Makavejev mixed the narrative, of the switchboard operator seeking 'romance', with a murder investigation and real-life academics telling the audience about sex and forensic investigation.

It was not necessary, however, for films to try to engage directly with the turbulent politics of the times. For example, *Knife in the Water* put a couple with a young male hitchhiker together on a yacht. Sexual tensions manifest themselves as both men attempt to prove their virility in front of the woman. The director, Roman Polanski, soon moved west to make his mark in Britain, then went on to Hollywood (followed by exile in Europe after skipping bail in the USA). Milos Forman, another Czech who became an exile, directed *The Firemen's Ball* (*Horí, má Panenko*, 1967, Czechoslovakia), an allegory about bureaucratic influence on society.

Such a critical film could only have been made in Czechoslovakia during the 'Prague Spring' of the 1960s. Alexander Dubcek, Czechoslovakia's leader, attempted to modify Soviet influence with 'socialism with a human face'. The greater freedoms were eventually crushed by Soviet tanks (memorably recreated in *The Unbearable Lightness of Being*, 1988).

Western criticism tended to read and value these films because of their perceived criticism of the 'communist' governments. However there was much more to them than that. This criticism also ignored the fact that many in the west were also calling for a revolution from the tyranny of their own governments (see 5.10).

Further viewing

Closely Observed Trains (*Ostre Siedované Vlaky*, Czechoslovakia, 1966)
Daisies (*Sedmikrasky*, Czechoslovakia, 1966)

Further reading

Goulding, Daniel J. (ed.) (1989) *Post New Wave Cinema in the Soviet Union and Eastern Europe,* Indiana University Press.

5.9.2 Cinema Novo and Latin American cinema

Brazil experienced massive economic expansion in the late 1950s and early 1960s. However, this was followed by an International Monetary Fund intervention to recoup foreign investment, leading to social instability and a military coup in 1964. Against this background of social change and turmoil, filmmakers were attempting to articulate a cinema for the 'new' ('novo') times.

In 1962 Glauber Rocha filmed *Barravento* (*The Turning Wind*), the first feature-length Cinema Novo film. It has a very clear message that religion prevents a fishing community from understanding the real conditions in which they live (King, 2000: 108).

Inspired by both Italian neo-realism and the French New Wave, Cinema Novo attempted to fuse the 'low-tech' post-war Italian approach with the *auteurist* emphasis of the French. Rocha quoted Truffaut's contention that the *auteur* was a revolutionary (King, 2000: 107). By mixing documentary techniques with social concern for the working people, Rocha and his fellow filmmakers used popular culture and myth:

> Proposing these as the essential source for a renewed and authentic Brazilian culture, but simultaneously defining them as insufficient to confront the realities of mid-twentieth-century exploitation and hunger.
>
> (Coad, 1981: 1395b)

239

In many ways the filmmakers found themselves caught between reactionary tradition and the iniquitous policies of modern capitalism. They had to find a way to convince the people that they should take responsibility for change through not resisting 'progress' but shaping it to their needs.

In Bolivia, *Blood of the Condor* (*Yawar Mallku*, 1969) investigated how the US Peace Corps sterilized Quechua Indian women under the pretence of general medical treatment. The director Jorge Sanjines attempted to change the way films were made by involving whole communities in each stage of planning, financing, production and exhibition. The film was shown in villages, miles from any cinema, as a communal event as a focus of discussion. The political agenda was to free Bolivia of American influence.

In Cuba, with which America has been at loggerheads since the 'communist revolution' of the late 1950s, *Memories of Underdevelopment* (*Memorias del Subdessarrollo*, 1968) followed the wanderings of bored bourgeois Sergio (Sergio Corrieri) who, as Elena (Daisy Granados) puts it, is 'neither revolutionary nor counter revolutionary ... you're nothing'. The film starts in 1961, when many of the bourgeoisie were leaving Havana for Miami, and ends during the Cuban missile crisis of the following year. Sergio is an alienated observer who spends his time fantasizing about and seducing women. Director Tomas Gutierrez Alea mixed documentary style, including a photomontage of starving Latin American children, with French New Wave techniques.

While Latin American 'new wave' cinema embraced politics, it was not until May '68 that political issues engulfed European 'cutting edge' cinema.

Further viewing

Antonio das Mortes (*O Dragão da Maldade contra o Santo Guerreiro*, 1969)
Barren Lives (*Vidas Secas*, 1963)
Black God, White Devil (*Deus e o Diabo na Terra do Sol*, Brazil, 1964)
Ganga Zumba (1963)

Further reading

Elena, Alberto and Diaz Lopez, Marina (eds) (2004) *The Cinema of Latin America*, Wallflower Press.

5.10 May '68

The events in Paris of May 1968 sit slightly awkwardly in this chapter, as they were obviously not a film 'wave' or 'movement'. However, the events had a profound and lasting impact on film studies and, to a lesser extent, on filmmaking.

A student revolt at the Sorbonne escalated to include a total strike by the Film Technicians' union, and then to a general strike that united students and workers, but not the French Communist Party. The Gaullist government almost fell in the face of the popular uprising, which was mirrored elsewhere in the world:

> Students and intellectuals in Berkeley and Berlin, Rio de Janeiro and Tokyo, Bangkok and Mexico City, all participated in a global revolt against capitalism, colonialism, and imperialism, as well as authoritarian forms of communism.
>
> (Stam, 2000: 132)

These protests were mirrored in the early years of the twenty-first century, with demonstrations opposing globalization and the destruction of the earth's resources. What is significant for film studies was:

> one of the effects of May was to open up the sphere of cultural production to a class analysis and to encourage the asking of the question: which classes were served by which forms of cultural production?
>
> (Harvey, 1980: 28)

In other words, after May '68 it was realized that films are created ideologically. The fact that certain types of films were made in certain ways was no longer thought of as being an 'accident' or 'just the way it is': it was seen to be a product of a society's underlying values. If it is an over-exaggeration to say that pre-'68 was an 'age of innocence' – Godard's *La Chinoise* (France) dealt with many of the 'May '68' issues the year before – afterwards to make non-political films became, in itself, a political statement in favour of the status quo.

Although many filmmakers throughout the world began to try to articulate the new voices and so find new ways of making films, it was far easier to write about films in a new way, and many journals sprang into existence and some venerable ones, such as *Cahiers du Cinéma*, were reborn with a radical agenda. As the *Cahiers* editorial of the June-July issue of that year stated:

> There is one supreme desire: to transform the 'system', the state of affairs in which the cinema in France has been so self-enclosed, so cut off from any social or political reality.
>
> (Hillier, 1986: 309)

This principle had a major impact upon film theory. During the 1970s *Screen* magazine was in the forefront of trying to articulate Marxist and psychoanalytical explanations of film – see 4.5.

5.11 New German cinema

New German cinema was, like Cinema Novo, inspired by the French New Wave. Filmmakers such as Alexander Kluge and Jean-Marie Straub worked in opposition to mainstream cinema, and produced the Oberhausen Manifesto ('The old cinema is dead. We believe in the new') as a rallying point for young German cinema. However it was not until the early 1970s, when directors such as Rainer Werner Fassbinder, Werner Herzog and Wim Wenders established themselves, that *West German* (Federal Republic of Germany) cinema directors attained international recognition as *auteurs*. The emphasis on the 'west' draws attention to the fact that Germany was split from 1945 until the collapse of the Berlin Wall in 1989: the capitalist west versus the 'communist' east, which was aligned with the Soviet Union. Television was instrumental in this renaissance as, through the state-owned public service broadcasting remit, investment in 'arthouse' films was encouraged.

Possibly uniquely, much of New German cinema presented itself as a national cinema (see 6.4). After the fall of the Nazis, German national identity became a topic of enormous debate. The Americans took over the German film industry after the Second World War as part of the process of 'denazification'. However:

> The Cold War ... brought the denazification process to a premature end, and subsequent American anti-communist policies led to the promotion of only the most conservative film personnel, who tended to be those with a Nazi past.
>
> (Sieglohr, 1998: 467a)

Many personnel who were tainted by associations with the National Socialists were still in positions of power in the film industry, and in many other industries. The remaining influence of the 'old order' inspired left-wing activism, making the 1970s a rich time for German culture, as politically committed left-wing artists tried to articulate West German identity in the shadow of the Nazi atrocities.

Germany was geographically split at the time (the 'iron curtain' ran through the country), further stimulating artistic debate about national identity. Add to the mixture the anti-Vietnam war movement of the late 1960s, which had politicized many students, and it is unsurprising that the 1970s were a decade of ferment for the country. The fact that there was an audience for films critiquing the German state obviously stimulated production of New German cinema.

The Baader-Meinhof gang was 'terrorizing' the nation in pursuit of the overthrow of capitalism and, partly in response, the state became more totalitarian as it 'cracked down on terrorists'. Films critiquing the state, however, were exempt from censorship as they:

> became a means … to prove its ability and readiness for self-criticism both at home and abroad. Internationally, this cinema became a kind of cultural ambassador (the Goethe Institut, a government-funded agency for promoting German culture abroad, exhibited the majority of these films …) that would bear witness to the liberalization brought about by the Social Democrats.
>
> (Sieglohr, 1998: 467b)

So films such as *The Lost Honour of Katharina Blum* (*Die Verlorene Ehre der Katharina Blum oder: Wie Gewalt entstehen und wohin sie führen kann*, West Germany, 1975) could readily question the role of the state in modern West Germany. *Katharina Blum* showed how human rights, even in a supposedly liberal society, could readily be trampled on by the state. The film was an adaptation of celebrated writer Heinrich Böll's novel by director Volker Schlondorff, and reserved particular vitriol for the role of the gutter press. New German cinema's critique of society left no 'liberal' hostages:

> [the] generation … of 1968 [blamed] the education system, authoritarian family values, Germany's lack of democratic institutions, the absence of civic responsibility for the aggressive notions of national identity which led to genocide and territorial expansionism.
>
> (Elsaesser, 1996: 14)

Like the French New Wave, the German filmmakers looked to Hollywood in part for inspiration – see Fassbinder's melodramas – and in part as an attempt to understand West Germany's relationship to America (for example, Wenders' *Alice in the Cities*, *Alice in den Städten*, 1974 and Herzog's *Stroszek*, 1977).

Although Fassbinder was eventually acknowledged to be the most important of New German filmmakers, he eschewed the self-consciously arthouse cinema of his contemporaries. Instead he reworked the tropes of American melodrama. This was particularly evident in *Fear Eats the Soul*

(*Angst essen Seele auf,* West Germany, 1974), a remake of the Douglas Sirk-directed *All That Heaven Allows* (1955). The original focused on the 'illicit' love affair between a middle-class widow (Jane Wyman) and her much younger gardener (Rock Hudson). Fassbinder throws together an old cleaning woman (Brigitte Mira) and Moroccan *Gastarbeiter* ('guest worker') (El Hedi ben Salem), so substituting race for class. (Sirk's film was given a postmodern remake as *Far From Heaven,* USA-France, in 2002, in which Fassbinder's focus on race was returned to 1950s America, with homosexuality thrown into the mix.)

Fassbinder's version of melodrama was the antithesis of Sirk's 'hysterical' *mise en scène*. He pares down the contents of the frame, and has little movement either in the scene or from the camera. The compositions are frequently striking, emphasizing the characters' entrapment. The focus on race – the characters are ostracized because of their inter-racial affair – means that 'Hitler's Germany' is present as a discourse, and this is emphasized when the characters dine at the dictator's favourite restaurant.

The demise of New German cinema, supported by television, also had its roots in the medium, although it was not helped by Fassbinder's early death (aged 37) in 1982, at the time the industry was deregulated:

> Rather that investing in home-grown 'author-directors', it filmed literary classics or heavy-duty national self-examinations, these new television co-productions ... relied on formula plots and character stereotypes ... drawing on American television.
>
> (Elsaesser, 1999: 6)

Although New German cinema did not succeed overall at the box office, it did open up debates about the nature of West German society.

Further viewing (listed under the director)

Rainer Werner Fassbinder:
  Lola (1981)
  The Marriage of Maria Braun (*Die Ehe der Maria Braun,* 1979)
  The Merchant of Four Seasons (*Der Händler der vier Jahreszeiten,* 1972)
  Veronika Voss (*Die Sennsucht der Veronica Voss,* 1982)
Werner Herzog:
  Aguirre Wrath of God (*Aguirre, der Zorn Gottes,* 1973)
  The Enigma of Kaspar Hauser (*Jeder für sich und Gott gegen alle – Kaspar Hauser,* 1974)
Helma Sanders-Brahms:

Germany Pale Mother (*Deutschland bleiche Mutter*, 1980)

Volker Schlöndorff:

The Tin Drum (*Die Blechtrommel*, 1979)

Hans-Jürgen Syberberg, 'German Trilogy':

Ludwig – Requiem for a Virgin King (*Ludwig – Requiem für einen jungfräulichen König*, 1972)

Karl May (1974)

Our Hitler (*Hitler – ein Film aus Deutschland*, W. Germany-UK-France 1978)

Margarethe von Trotta:

The Second Awakening of Christa Klages (*Das Zweite Erwachen der Christa Klages*, 1978)

Wim Wenders:

Kings of the Road (*Im Lauf der Zeit*, 1976)

The American Friend (*Der Amerikanische Freund*, W. Germany-France, 1977)

Further reading

Elsaesser, Thomas (1996) *Fassbinder's Germany: History, Identity, Subject,* Amsterdam: Amsterdam University Press.

Elsaesser, Thomas (ed.) (1999) *The BFI Companion to German Cinema,* London: British Film Institute.

5.12 Chinese cinema: fifth and sixth generation

The classic melodramas of 1930s Chinese cinema are hidden from western eyes through long unavailability. However, the flowering of Chinese cinema did grab the west's attention after the end of the Cultural Revolution. From 1966 to 1976 the state imposed extremely tight controls over all cultural production, and it was only at its end that the Beijing film school could reopen, allowing its 'fifth generation' into class. Given the thaw it was unsurprising that:

> Fifth Generation directors [should] focus their interest on the structure of a society which resists change.... Whether obsessively depicting the feudal past or narratives of life in remote rural areas, the central cultural dilemma addressed by these film-makers is that of being caught between the tyranny of this feudal past and an apparently spiritless commodity-orientated future.
>
> (Cornelius with Smith, 2002: 37)

Despite the thaw, tension remained between the government and film-makers, the former often being unhappy with the representation of China being shown to the 'outside world'. Both Zhang Yimou's *Ju Dou* (Japan-China, 1990) and *Raise the Red Lantern* (*Da hong deng long gao gao gua*, China-Hong Kong-Taiwan, 1991) were banned in China and feted in the west. Zhuangzhuang Tian so upset the authorities with his portrayal of Communist Chinese history in *The Blue Kite* (*Lan feng zheng*, China-Hong Kong, 1993) that he (reportedly) could not direct another film for nearly 10 years.

In these films the village is often seen as symbolic of China, and the role of women, suffering under the extremely patriarchal precepts of Confucius, was shown to be crucial to the modernization of feudal society. For example, *Yellow Earth* (*Huang Tudi*, 1984), the first fifth-generation film to be shown widely in the west, contrasts the extreme poverty and traditional life in a Shaanxi province in 1939 with a commu-nist soldier's optimism about change. The film focuses particularly on the plight of young girls sold into marriage, and ends with an extraordinary shot of the bride's brother fighting his way, in extreme slow motion (and sound), through the 'backward' peasants towards the returning soldier.

In Zang Yimou's *The Road Home* (*Wo de fu qin mu qin*, China, 1999), the film starts with a son's journey into the countryside where he was brought up. During the credit sequence the road starts to disappear under falling snow, emphasizing the location's isolation. Here he finds his mother determined to carry his recently deceased father home, in the traditional fashion, across hostile terrain. She appears to be a stubborn old woman clinging to the past, and her son tries to dissuade her. However, the flash-back that takes up most of the film shows his mother and father's courtship, and it becomes clear that tradition must be fulfilled.

The same director's *Not One Less* (*Yi ge dou bu neng shao*, 1999) also features the town–country opposition. This time a 13-year-old is dragooned into teaching a class of children with the admonition that she will only be paid if there is 'not one less' of the children present when the teacher returns. She 'loses' a child to the city and so goes to seek him there. As in *The Road Home* the country is seen as a place of community (despite its poverty), while the city in *Not One Less* is shown to be dehumanized and soulless (at least until the local TV station comes to the rescue).

While the Fifth Generation was going global, a Sixth Generation was waiting in the wings. Also graduates of the Beijing Film Academy, these filmmakers rebelled as much against the glossy historicism of their predecessors as against the Chinese authorities.

What the cultural revolution was to the Fifth Generation, the 1989 shootings in Tiananmen Square were to the Sixth. Their films were usually made illegally, cheaply and angrily, combining punk spirit with Italian neo-realism. They depicted modern Chinese cities as places of poverty, misery and hopelessness.

(Rose, 2002)

Although it was made officially, *Suzhou River* (*Suzhou he*, Germany-China, 2000) portrays 'slacker' youth who seek meaning for their lives with reference to conventional ideas of romance. They are more likely to be critiquing 'western' ideas of consumerism than China's politicians:

Under Mao the 'Four Musts' had been a bicycle, a radio, a watch and a sewing machine. In Deng Xiaoping's reforms they were replaced by the 'Eight Bigs' – a colour television, a refrigerator, a stereo, a camera, a motorcycle, a suite of furniture, a washing machine and an electric fan.

(Cornelius with Smith 2002: 93)

There is little doubt, regardless of the success of Chinese films, that China will become a crucial territory for films. Since it has the world's largest population, if China continues to open its markets to capitalist expansion it will attract the avaricious Hollywood. On the other hand, the international box office success of films such as *Hero* (*Ying xiong*, Hong Kong-China, 2002) and *House of Flying Daggers* (*Shi mian ma fu*, China-Hong Kong, 2004), both directed by Zhang Yimou, suggests that the traffic may not be simply one-way.

Further viewing

The Emperor and the Assassin (*Jing ke ci qin wang*, 1999, France-Japan-China)
Farewell My Concubine (*Ba wang bie ji*, China-Hong Kong, 1993)
Red Sorghum (*Hong gao liang*, 1987)
To Live (*Huozhe*, China-Hong Kong, 1994)
Shanghai Triad (*Yao a yao yao dao waipo qiao*, France-China, 1995)
Springtime in a Small Town (*Xiao cheng zhi chun*, China-Hong Kong-France, 2002)

Further reading

Yingjin Zhang (2004) *Chinese National Cinema*, London: Routledge.

5.13 Iranian cinema

Iranian cinema has been particularly interesting because the country is a nation in flux. In 1979 the western-backed Shah was deposed in an Islamic revolution. Cinemas, closely linked to the Shah's western ways, were destroyed. In its place the industry was supposed to make Islamic films; according to Richard Tapper, *The Runner* (*Davendeh*, 1985) was the only film of quality made at this time.

> What happened in the world of Iranian cinema parallels other developments in Iranian society: a gradual stretching of the limits imposed by the jurists, and … a further redefining and reinventing of culture.
>
> (Tapper, 2002: 7)

Unsurprisingly many films dealt with this tension between the autocratic mullahs and the secularists who wanted more freedom of expression. *Secret Ballot* (*Raye makhfi*, Italy-Canada-Switzerland-Iran, 2001) shows the difficulties in bringing democracy to the island of Kish. The election agent (Nassim Abdi) has to deal with vote rigging, the condescension of women and indifference as she attempts to convince locals that their vote will make a difference. In addition, the candidates are so remote from the inhabitants that the process appears to be meaningless. *The Day I Became a Woman* (*Roozi khe zan shodam*, 2000), also shot on Kish, shows three generations of women: the nine-year-old Hava (Fatemeh Cherag Akhar), who is told that now she's nine she can no longer play with boys; the married Ahoo (Shabnam Toloui), who defies her husband, family and tribe by joining a cycle race; the aged Hoora (Azizeh Sedighi), who fulfils a fantasy by purchasing all the consumer goods she had ever wanted – although there remains one item, she cannot remember what, that she still wants. Each story is left unfinished, emphasizing that the fate of each, like women in Iran in general, is hanging in the balance.

The Day I Became a Woman was directed by Marzieh Meshkini, wife of co-scenarist Mohsen Makhmalbaf, a prodigious family of filmmakers. Mohsen made *Kandahar* (*Safar e Ghandehar*, Iran-France, 2001), which followed an Afghan journalist Mafas (Nelofer Pazira) when she tried to return to the misogynistic Taliban-ruled Afghanistan to save her sister who had threatened to kill herself. In one astonishing scene amputees hobble after artificial limbs that have been parachuted to them. The surrealism of this scene, like the consumer goods on the beach in *The Day I Became a Woman*, seems typical of Iranian cinema.

Mohsen's daughter, Samira, made her first feature when aged 18. *The Apple* (*Sib*, Iran-France, 1997), features the first steps into the outside

The spirit of Italian neo-realism is present in *Time for Drunken Horses* (Iran, 2000), focusing on the plight of the Kurds using non-professional actors

world of twins who had been incarcerated in their home by their father. *Time for Drunken Horses* (*Zamani barayé masti asbha*, Iran, 2000), using non-professionals, has a narrative driven by a young Kurdish lad's (Ayoub Ahmadi) desire to raise money for his crippled brother to have an operation. However, this is obviously futile, making Ayoub's struggle an act of love in a world whose bleakness is emphasized by the treacherous weather and terrain.

At the time of writing, the 'battle' between the 'religious fundamentalists' and the 'progressive reformists' had yet to be resolved. What will Iranian cinema deal with once this conflict has ended?

Further viewing

At Five in the Afternoon (*Panj é asr*, 2003)
Silence Between Two Thoughts (*Sokoote beine do fekr*, 2003)
Ten (2002)

Further reading

Dabashi, Hamid (2001) *Close Up: Iranian Cinema, Past, Present and Future*, Verso.

5.14 Denmark's Dogme

One of the consequences of the growth of film education was a greater cine-literacy in both audiences and filmmakers. Lars von Trier, the 'inventor' of Dogme '95, made this plain when he explained this 'new wave':

> It is clear that during great periods, such as The New Wave in France, or new German film ... a lot of people can suddenly become incredibly inspired and a great amount of exciting films can get made.
>
> (quoted in Stevenson, 2002: 103)

Possibly the first postmodern 'new wave' (in that it was self-consciously created), Dogme '95's manifesto was constructed as a reaction against Hollywood. The first of 10 rules is:

> Shooting must be done on location. Props and sets must not be brought in (if a particular prop is necessary for the story, a location must be chosen where this prop is to be found).

The 'back to basics' philosophy runs through many of Dogme's precepts, including no post-production sound, an insistence on handheld camera, and no use of optical effects and filters. Von Trier and Thomas Vinterberg, who was also responsible for the manifesto, intended to liberate filmmakers from the 'trappings' of technology and so go 'back to basics' (the movement's neo-realist roots are obvious). There was also a determination not to make genre films, which suggests an arthouse bias.

The Idiots (*Idioterne*, Sweden-France-Netherlands-Italy, 1998) appears to non-Danish eyes to be a satire on bourgeois mores. It focuses on a group of middle-class dropouts who behave as if they are spastic. They spasm uncontrollably and behave inappropriately in social situations. In doing so they embarrass the diners of a posh restaurant and find bikers in a pub more caring. The film, however, does not simply mock the bourgeoisie, the 'idiots' themselves are shown to be unable to keep up their pretence, as the group fragments at the end. However, the last word is given to Karen (Bodil Jorgenson), who had accidentally joined the group at the beginning of the film, after her baby – we find out at the end – had died. She rejoins her family, only to find their 'proper' behaviour dysfunctional, so she 'spasses' and leaves them.

Stylistically, von Trier keeps to his manifesto by using a handheld camera and 'natural' lighting throughout. The most obvious devices he uses are jump cuts which draw attention to themselves as they do not appear to serve a particular purpose; indeed, they appeared to be examples of 'bad' filmmaking when Godard used them throughout *Breathless* (*A Bout de Souffle*, France, 1960). The use of handheld camera, which appears to follow the action, means that aesthetically framed shots are eschewed in favour of a *mise en scène* that offers little more than the action. In addition, restricting the film to using natural light also cuts off to a great degree an expressive use of cinematography.

This style of camerawork and editing has become familiar in recent years in what are usually termed in listing magazines as 'fly on the wall' documentaries. While 'direct cinema', the original 'fly on the wall' observational style, did use handheld camera, long takes were the norm. In addition, television's 'fly on the wall' usually includes a 'voice of god' anchoring the meaning of the image; a device that was anathema to Frederick Wiseman, Richard Leacock and others who pioneered 'direct cinema' (see Box 4.1). *The Idiots* reinforces the documentary feel by having characters talk about their experiences as idiots direct to camera, with a slightly hectoring, off screen, interviewer asking about what they felt (a precursor to the *Big Brother/The Weakest Link* 'debrief' interview).

It is worth noting that cultural differences between countries that are geographically close can also alter readings of films. While westerners may be ready to accept that they do not fully understand the cultural resonance of, say, African cinema, it is less likely that they would realize that *The Idiots* has specifically Danish meaning. Von Trier was exploring:

> the concept of 'The Group' which is instilled in Danes almost from birth and which stands as the cornerstone of modern Danish identity.... The Group ... is all-encompassing.... The outsiders, be they foreigners or Danes, are the ones who are identified, categorised, counselled debated over and dealt with.... But to Stoffer [a central character] ... it is more like a conspiracy.
>
> (Stevenson, 2002: 129)

This 'lo-fi' style of filmmaking has its critics, and with *Dogville* (Denmark-Sweden-France-Norway-Netherlands-Finland-Germany-Italy-Japan-USA-UK, 2003) von Trier ignores the manifesto with a totally stylized setting of a warehouse, where buildings are signified by chalk marks. He appears to be embracing the Brechtian alienation effect, where attention is drawn to the fact that we are watching a film.

In Sweden, though not directly following von Trier's lead, Lukas Moodyson used the realist aesthetic to great effect in *Show Me Love*

(*Fucking Åmål*, 1998) and *Together* (*Tillsammans*, Sweden-Denmark-Italy, 2000), films united by their febrile use of handheld camera.

Further viewing

Celebration (*Festen*, Denmark–Sweden, 1998)
Dancer in the Dark (Denmark–Germany–Netherlands–USA–UK–France–Sweden–Finland–Iceland–Norway, 2000)
Lila 4-ever (Sweden–Denmark, 2002)
Mifune (*Mifune Sidste Sang*, Denmark–Sweden, 1999)

There's little doubt that cinematic 'new waves' will continue, although with increasing globalization these may be less likely to be nation-based. At the time of writing Korean cinema was receiving a lot of attention with films such as *A Tale of Two Sisters* (*Janghwa, Hongryeon*, 2003) and *Oldboy* (2004) both being lined up for Hollywood remakes. Whether it consists of a distinctive new wave, however, will be determined by academia.

 Appendices

Australians' and New Zealanders' relationship with their heritage is different from Britain's (as is Americans'), as it is based on two backgrounds: the native (that is, those who were there before colonization) and the 'motherland' (seen as Britain). In Australian cinema this duality manifests in the way films represent the 'bush'. Nicolas Roeg's *Walkabout* (UK, 1971) a seminal Australian film, recounts two children's journey, after they have been abandoned in the outback, back to 'civilization' with the assistance of an aboriginal boy (David Gumpilil). The freedom of the 'savage' is contrasted favourably with the repression of white (English) 'civilization'. However the bush took on a more sinister role in Peter Weir's *Picnic at Hanging Rock* (1975); from the opening shot when the rock outcrop suddenly looms across the landscape, it is clear that the bush will remain a mystery to the white inhabitants. And the mystery of the missing schoolgirls, and their teacher, is never explained.

Walkabout was crucial to the Australian industry because it, along with *Wake in Fright* (Australia–USA, 1971), signalled:

> The transition between a feature industry marked by the 'almost totally foreign-made films being made in Australia' and an 'Australian cinema'.
>
> (O'Regan, 1996: 58)

The National Film School opened in 1973, and government financial support throughout the decade helped Australian cinema make an international impact. Direct government support (often through tax breaks), or state television, is crucial to the development of national cinemas, as only the American and Indian film industries produce the most popular films in their own nations. It is this sort of state subsidy that Hollywood campaigns against, saying it distorts the marketplace, although it ignores the fact that Hollywood also receives government support when it exports movies (presumably because it disseminates the 'American way of life' across the world).

Since the 1990s:

> there has been an increasing interest in conceptualising Australia as post-colonial. The relations between Aboriginal and non-Aboriginal Australia have naturally been a major force of this work.
>
> (Jacka, 1998: 519a)

In 2002, *Rabbit Proof Fence* confronted white treatment of mixed-race aboriginals (they were forcibly taken from their parents and put in 'orphanages' where they were taught to be servants). This film mostly avoids the 'noble/mystic savage' representation of the aboriginals, and lays bare the racism of the time. On the other hand the Maori film *Whale Rider* (New Zealand-Germany, 2002) shows the Maori community to be corrupted by 'western ways'. The film is reactionary, progressive gender politics aside, as it suggests that the future lies in the past. At the film's climax Pai (Keisha Castle-Hughes) unites the divided community by saving a whale:

> At the end of the film, Pai's voiceover asserts that 'our people will go forward – united.' But united around what? Fighting with bamboo sticks, apparently, carving decorative longboats and communicating with whales. It seems less forwards than backwards …
>
> (Kemp, 2003: 63c)

It is possible to read the film as suggesting that there is no place for Maoris in modern society. However this would work against the 'feel good' nature of the piece. This film can be contrasted with *Once Were Warriors* (New Zealand, 1994), whose first shot emphasizes the journey the Maori have taken to the city by showing a beautiful mountain landscape which turns out to be a poster next to a busy inner city road. In this film the plight of the Maoris is unremittingly bleak.

If collapsing Australian and New Zealand cinema together erases differences, it is an elision practised by filmmakers themselves. For example, Jane Campion:

> sometimes describes herself as an Australian; just as often she associates her work … with her Kiwi identity.
>
> (O'Regan, 1996: 72)

Her *The Piano* (Australia-New Zealand-France, 1993) was the first film directed by a woman to win the Palme d'Or at Cannes. Its feminist take on arranged marriages has stimulated much debate on the degree to

Is *The Piano* (1993) a progressive feminist film with racist representations of the aborigines?

which it is a progressive film, in terms of its gender politics, as well as whether its treatment of the aboriginals is racist (see *Screen* Vol. 36, No. 3, Autumn 1995).

A5.2 The Balkans – civil strife

The civil war in former Yugoslavia, culminating in NATO bombing the country in 1999, was ripe for cinematic treatment. The Serbian film *Cabaret Balkan* (*Bure baruta*, Yugoslavia-Macedonia-France-Greece-Turkey, 1998) has:

> interweaved stories [that] 'illustrate the Balkan spiral of madness,' according to press notes, 'in which they are all living. [The director] Paskaljevic focuses on the lives of ordinary people caught in the fray who are nonetheless still compelled to cope with day-to-day realities.'
>
> (Block, 1999)

The film's interesting narrative structure is linked loosely by a taxi driver (who has been made impotent after being beaten up by the police) observing the absurd events on one night in Belgrade. The civil war is only alluded to indirectly through news announcements on his radio, but the violence that erupts in every narrative segment suggests the war is never far away. However it is unclear whether the war is causing the violence, or whether the filmmakers are suggesting that the war is caused by this violent culture.

A more obvious allegory, from one of the other sides in the conflict, can be seen in the Bosnian *No Man's Land* (*Nicija zemlja*, Bosnia-Herzegovina-Slovenia-Italy-France-UK-Belgium, 2001) where a Serb and two Bosnians are trapped in a trench in 'no man's land' between the warring factions. The central protagonists' inability to find a common ground, and the United Nations' ineffectual intervention, are a micro-cosm of the civil war. Emir Kusturica's films also attempt to get to grips with the region's history; for example see *Underground* (*Bila Jednom Jedna Zemlja*, France-Yugoslavia-Germany-Hungary, 1995).

Ulysses' Gaze (*To Vlemma Tou Odyssea*, 1995, Greece-France-Italy), directed by Theo Angelopoulos, uses the civil war as a backdrop to film-maker A's (Harvey Keitel's) search for missing reels of early Balkan filmmakers. A, who meets many women on this journey (most played by Maia Morgenstern), moves from Greece through Albania to war-torn former Yugoslavia, and ends up in a shattered Sarajevo. The extremely slow pace of the film, coupled with many moments of stun-ning visual grandeur (including a massive statue of Lenin on a barge and the blue ship at the opening), and the obviously symbolic nature of the film (A as a cipher sharing an initial with the director, and the repeated appearance of Morgenstern as both lover to A and his mother) place this firmly in the arthouse sector.

Although the film revels in its ambiguity, there is no mistaking the meaning of the ending (stop reading now if you plan to see this amazing film), where A witnesses (aurally, not visually, as it is hidden by fog) the murder of his 'new family', and finds that the reels he was seeking were imageless. The film starts as one man's quest for meaning – he is appar-ently experiencing a mid-life crisis – but it becomes increasingly clear as he enters the war zone that his concerns are pathetic compared with the tragedy of those caught up in war.

A5.3 Canada – engulfed by America?

Issues of nationality are complicated for Canada, as it can be seen to consist of two countries if the French-speaking province of Quebec is taken to be a distinct nation. In addition, the 'suffocating' presence of the United States, a hair's breadth away (Hollywood considers Canada as part of its 'home market'), has made it very difficult for Canadian cinema to make much of an impact, the avant-garde work supported by the National Film Board of Canada excepted.

Following recommendations by John Grierson, the Board was set up to promote films in the 'national interest'. As Grierson concluded, Canada had no movies that offered an 'emotional presentation' of Canada:

> 'It is another nation's effort and pride we see on our screen, not our own. We are on the outside looking in.'
>
> (quoted in Gittings, 2002: 79)

Such is the dominance of the USA that some Canadian filmmakers, such as James Cameron, Jim Carrey and Mike Myers, are thought by many to be American, and *Ghostbusters* (1986) is creatively if not financially a Canadian production. In addition, there are the 'Native Canadians' to consider as well as Afro-Canadians (this group's first feature, *Rude*, was only released in 1995) and Eastern European Canadians. There are also the Inuit: *Atanarjuat: the Fast Runner* (2001) made an impact in arthouse cinema. It retells an ancient legend, and suggests that Christianity has destroyed the Inuit way of life.

David Cronenberg is probably the highest profile Canadian director. His films have appealed to the fans of exploitation cinema (*Scanners*, 1980), mainstream audiences (the Hollywood-produced *The Fly*, 1986) and the arthouse (*Spider*, 2002, France-Canada-UK). *Crash* (Canada-USA, 1996) used Toronto's roads and skyline to great effect. Atom Egoyan, though born in Egypt, has also had considerable arthouse success. While these filmmakers work in English, Denys Arcand has made a number of films consciously about the 'nation state' of Quebec.

Arcand's *Jesus of Montreal* (Canada-France, 1989) uses Christ's story as a parable of modern-day Canada. It critiques the banality, and exploitative tendencies, of the advertising industry in particular. However its targets are not particularly Canadian, and the film could have been transposed to any western country. His *The Decline of the American Empire* (*Le Déclin de l'Empire Américain*, Canada, 1986) is, though:

> A commentary on the failure of Quebec nationalists of Arcand's generation to see a mature, responsible nation into being.
>
> (Fricker, 2004: 18a)

The film starts with one of the characters being interviewed about a book she has written, suggesting that decadence in a nation can be measured by its obsession with personal happiness. The rest of the film consists of two sets of conversations between a group of men and women, who then meet for a meal. Their obsession with seeking sexual happiness is shown to be sterile, figuratively expressed in the final shot of the film showing their snowbound house.

The same characters reappeared in the Oscar-winning *The Barbarian Invasions* (*Les Invasions Barbares*, 2003, Canada-France). Remy (Remy Girard) is on his deathbed, an opportunity for him, his friends and son to reflect upon their lives post-September 11. Although ostensibly bleak, the film does offer the possibility of life affirmation through friendship.

A5.4 Hong Kong – (not) a national cinema?

Hong Kong's cinema has been split between two languages: its 'own', Cantonese, and mainland China's Mandarin. Bizarrely, for five years (1968–72) Cantonese cinema disappeared:

> It was as though the people of Hong Kong had lost their voice or the desire to speak in their own language.
>
> (Leung, 1998: 554b)

This was probably linked to the riots of 1967, where suppressed political activism (the island was a British colony at the time) erupted with the support of 'leftists whose loyalty lay with the Cultural Revolution in mainland China' (Kar, 2001: 32).

While for some filmmakers, notably Wong Kar-Wai, the handover of the colony to China in 1997 was of utmost importance, Esther Yau argues:

> Relatively free from obligations of national self-representation and having for many years now adopted an apparently apolitical stance with regard to the antagonisms between mainland China and Taiwan, Hong Kong movies do not lock themselves within the old impasses on issues of national culture.
>
> (Yau, 2001a: 2)

She emphasizes the postmodern elements of the island, with its cosmopolitan take on popular cultures and emphasis on speed in its films:

> as many of them follow a fast-paced rhythm in terms of shot length, dialogue duration, bodily movements, and use of multiple ellipses within scenes.
>
> (Yau, 2001a: p. 3)

After the impact in the west of 'kung fu' movies, particularly those of Bruce Lee, Hong Kong went on to gain an arthouse reputation, with filmmakers such as John Woo, who combined visceral generic elements with thoughtful reflection in films such as *A Better Tomorrow* (*Ying huang boon sik*, 1986), *Bullet in the Head* (*Die xue jie tou*, 1990) and *Hard Boiled* (*Lashou Shentan*, 1992). Woo's films often focus on the relationship between two men on either side of the good/bad divide. However, it is usually difficult to be certain of the differences between the morality of, for example, the cop Inspector Li (Danny Li) and triad member Ah Long (Chow Yun Fat) in *The Killer* (*Die xue shuang xiong*, 1989). The instability of identity is a common theme in Hong Kong cinema (also see *Infernal Affairs* (*Wu jian dau*, 2002)), and is probably related to its colonial status, until 1997, and 'special territory' status with mainland China since. Elaine Yee-lin Ho (2001) shows how director Ann Hui's films focus on women and issues of identity.

John Woo pursued the same themes in his Hollywood hit *Face/Off* (1997), and Hong Kong's affect on American action cinema has been immense. However, Woo in particular had been influenced by Hollywood. Stokes and Hoover (1999), for example, point out the links between his films and those of Sam Peckinpah, as well as the recycling of the generic trope of the older cop 'breaking in' the rookie, which is common in Hollywood.

While Hong Kong's action cinema has garnered a cult following in the west, fuelled more recently by DVD, Wong Kar-Wai's *Fallen Angels* (*Duo luo tian shi*, 1995) and *Chungking Express* (*Chong qing sen lin*, 1995) cemented his arthouse reputation with a visually stylish *mise en scène* and elliptical narratives. Identity is also a common theme in Wong's films. *Chungking Express* features two stories about unrequited love, offering parallels between the four characters, and *In the Mood for Love* (2001) and *2046* (2004) both deal elliptically with the 1997 handover of power to the Chinese.

A5.5 Mexican Cinema – renaissance on America's doorstep

The renaissance in Mexican cinema in the 1990s was due to an enlightened policy of encouraging new talent through state funding (via IMCINE) and the development of two film schools. During the 1990s Mexican cinema enjoyed a high international profile, which can – in part – be measured by film festival success. Another index is directors' migration to Hollywood. Guillermo del Toro has made *Mimic* (1997) and *Hellboy* (2004), while Alfonso Cuaron was responsible for the visually brilliant *Great Expectations* (1998) and *Harry Potter and the Prisoner of Azkaban* (2004). The migration to Hollywood was probably encouraged by the policy of supporting popular films:

> The government funded [films have] produced a string of local hits. These have most recently been crowd-pleasing comedies that could not be more different from … earnest art movies …
>
> (Smith, 2002: 16a)

And Your Mother Too (*Y Tu Mamá Tambien*, 2001), directed by Cuaron, broke box office records when in opened. Mixing staple North American genres, the road movie and youth pic, Cuaron manages to combine raucous comedy and pathos with social commentary. Using the omnipotent narrator, derived from Jean-Luc Godard's *Masculin Feminin* (France-Sweden, 1966), the boys' testosterone-fuelled hedonism is contrasted with class-ridden everyday life. However, the gently ironic commentary does not intrude upon the entertainment, hence its international success, offering lashings of sex for its target audience and intellectual satisfaction for the arthouse coterie (or is that the other way around?).

Smith (2002: 16b) quotes one critic as dismissing the film as 'south-of-the-border *Beavis & Butthead*', and there's no doubt that Mexico suffers culturally and economically because of its proximity to the world's most powerful nation. Generically it does draw upon Hollywood's teen pics and road movies; however there the resemblance ends. Stylistically the film is characterized by long handheld shots – see 1.8.

An omniscient narrator explains that a traffic jam, which the boys blame upon protestors, was caused by the death of a labourer who risked crossing the road in order to earn more money by arriving at work earlier. Tenoch's (an Aztec name) (Diego Luna) sister is seen protesting against the government, contrasting with her brother's vacuity, as his only concern is to 'get laid'. His mate Julio's (Gael Garcia Bernal) surname is Zapata, linking him to the Zapatistas, whose grassroots protest rocked the Mexican establishment at the end of the 1990s.

In an interview, when the director was questioned about his sympathy for the underclass, Cuaron replied:

> There are many different Mexicos that exist at the same time and sometimes in the same space, though they don't really co-exist. The

barriers between the classes are a big problem, though everyone tries to deny it.

(Smith, 2002: 19b)

Cuaron cites Godard as an influence, the omniscient narrator of *A Band à part* (France, 1964) and *Masculin Feminin* (1966), and the 'love triangle' is reminiscent of *Jules et Jim* (France), directed by François Truffaut in 1962. Presumably these 'high culture' influences would not have upset the establishment.

Virtually all world cinemas measure themselves in some way against Hollywood. Even Indian cinema, which produces more films than North America, has seen a transformation in its trademark musical numbers after the advent of MTV. *Amores Perros (Love's a Bitch,* 2000) is clearly influenced by Tarantino. However, like *Y Tu Mamá Tambien (And Your Mother Too)*, it is undoubtedly culturally Mexican, particularly in the middle story, which is Bunuelian in character.

The films mentioned above attained international success. However these represent only a very small portion of Mexican cinema. There are many other films that deserve wide distribution:

> Regional themes of Mexican society are found in *Danzón, Pueblo de Madera* and *El Jardín del Edén*, which is the only recent major production to focus upon the border and Chicano experience.
>
> Politics were well-represented by *Días Difíciles, El Bulto, Los Vuelcos del Corazón, Morir en el Golfo, Playa Azul* and *Rojo Amanecer*. Of these films, the most innovative and important was *Rojo Amanecer*, the first feature film to squarely focus on the student movement of 1968.
>
> The contemporary social crisis in all of its individual and societal dimensions was clearly reflected in such productions as *Angel de Fuego, El Costo de la Vida, Golpe de Suerte*, and *Lolo*. These films projected the critical nature of the current situation and the disintegration of values and institutions in Mexico.
>
> Adventure and science fiction was also a theme of preference by recent directors in such films as *Bandidos, Cronos* and *El Largo Camino a Tijuana*.
>
> Three outstanding films, thrillers with anti-heroes as protagonists are, *En Medio de la Nada, Hasta Morir*, and *Dos Crímenes*.
>
> AIDS awareness was dealt with in two excellent productions, *Solo Con Tu Pareja* and *Bienvenido/Welcome*.

(Maciel, 1995)

At the end of 2002 the State's support for cinema was thrown into doubt by a proposal to close the publicly owned studio and film school. This crisis was one of many the industry has faced since the Second World War. Bureaucrats of whatever nationality tend to suspect the cultural value of film, as they are often more concerned with the 'bottom line' and worried about their own position in power, and are more than unsympathetic to films that criticize society.

6 Film and Representation

6.1 Introduction

Chapter 1 investigated how films are put together: how formal conventions are used to represent the narrative world, or diegesis. The content of the film too must utilize conventions, often generic, for audiences to understand the narrative – see Chapter 2. This chapter considers what films say about individuals in society, through the use of types, and about society as a whole, by looking at the concept of national cinema with reference to Britain.

6.2 Representation and types

Archetypes, derived from the ideas of Carl Jung, are broad categories that are meant to be applicable to all cultures; for example, the 'mother' or 'wise old man'. Stereotypes, on the other hand, are more culturally specific.

> ➤ They involve both a categorising and an evaluation of the group being stereotyped.
> ➤ They usually emphasize some easily grasped feature(s) of the group's (usually negative) position …
> ➤ Stereotypes often try to insist on absolute difference where in fact the idea of a *spectrum* of difference is more appropriate, whether about the skin colours of human beings or about degrees of 'masculine' and 'feminine' attributes across the sexes.
>
> (Branston and Stafford, 2003: 91)

As Richard Dyer (1993) suggested, stereotypes are both an 'ordering process' and a 'short cut to meaning'. He quotes Tessa Perkins to demonstrate how a woman with blonde hair, voluptuous figure and pouting expression offers many connotations:

> It refers immediately to *her* sex, which refers to her status in society, her relationship to men, her inability to behave or think

rationally, and so on. In short, it implies knowledge of a complex social structure.

(Perkins, 1979: 139)

A small amount of information enables audiences to quickly (the 'short cut') categorize ('ordering process') a character. These categories have distinct boundaries and so there is little, or no, ambiguity. Clearly it is ridiculous to assess a person's intelligence from her hair colour, and this conception of blonde women illustrates how stereotypes articulate ideological values. The dumb blonde stereotype is a manifestation of patriarchy, a discourse that values women for their sexual attractiveness and subordinate status (the lack of intelligence).

Marilyn Monroe epitomized the dumb blonde during the 1950s in classic comedies such as *The Seven Year Itch* (1955) and *Some Like It Hot* (1959). Monroe was the first *Playboy* centrefold, in 1953, and in answering the question 'What did you have on when the photo was taken?' with 'I had the radio on,' she emphasized her 'dumbness'. However, it is possible to read Monroe's answer, and her performance in both films, as parodying the stereotype, as it is highly unlikely that she was dumb enough to misunderstand the question. So being conscious of, and able to exaggerate an aspect of, the type necessitated her not being dumb.

Following the 1960s feminist movements, audiences are more able to read the sexism of images, and although the 'dumb blonde' type has certainly not disappeared it is likely to be ameliorated. For example, Reese Witherspoon's character, Elle Woods, in *Legally Blonde* (2001) may embody the stereotype, but she miraculously overcomes her intellectual incapacity to succeed at Harvard Law School.

While the dumb blonde is a negative representation, stereotypes are not necessarily wholly negative. For example, the 'noble Native American Indian':

> He is courteous, hospitable, brave, simple and innocent. This romanticized image of the Indian was influenced by the writing of eighteenth-century European Romantics, who presented Indians as noble savages ...
>
> (Hoppenrath, 1997: 6)

However, while the first three adjectives are positive, the 'simple and innocent' gives a clue to the patronising nature of the type. In addition, whether a stereotype is understood to be positive or negative will depend upon who is reading the film – see 4.8. Much of the controversy, for example, surrounding films such as *Do the Right Thing* (1989), directed by Spike Lee, and *Boyz N the Hood* (1991) was generated by critics who suggested that the representations of the subordinate position of African-Americans was designed to stir up trouble. As Ed Guerrero says:

> When a commercial film depicting a social issue or perspective challenges Hollywood's strategies of ideological containment, that film usually comes under attack for inflaming and exacerbating the very problem that it seeks to expose, engage or change.
>
> (Guerrero, 2001: 18–19)

On the one hand these films were seen as true reflections of racist American society, while on the other they were seen to be a travesty of reality. In recent years the Hispanic population has become the biggest non-white group in America, but it is only recently that Hispanics have began to register in any great numbers on Hollywood's 'radar'. Carmen Miranda was one of the few who gained stardom in classical Hollywood, although Rita Hayworth was born Margarita Carmen Cansino.

The rise of the Hispanic population in America is likely to be complemented by the appearance of more stars like Jennifer Lopez (with Ralph Fiennes in *Maid in Manhattan*, 2002)

The next section focuses on the representation of African-Americans in Hollywood.

6.3 African-Americans and Hollywood

African-Americans' roles in films have been affected by their subordinate position in society, and they have been even more absent than women behind the camera (although all-black crews did make films solely for black audiences in the 1920s). From the racist representations of *The Birth of a Nation* (1915), through limiting the use of black actors to the roles of servants or performers, to the 'liberal' 1960s which saw, on the face of it, positive representations of blacks, Hollywood's racism has been consistent.

In the first Hollywood blockbuster, D. W. Griffith's *The Birth of a Nation*, the Ku Klux Klan ride to the rescue of the virginal Elsie (Lillian Gish), who is about to be forced to marry the 'mulatto' (someone who has black and white parents) Lynch (George Siegmann). To portray the KKK, a group of racists who regularly lynched black men in the southern states of America, as heroic, in a movie that was a box office hit, gives a good indication of the racism of the time; although as Thomas Cripps (1977) points out, the film was nowhere near as racist as its source material, the novel *The Clansman* written by Thomas Dixon. However, the film remains a landmark as it utilized many different techniques of film form to dramatic effect and drew millions to the movies.

In his seminal history of Blacks in American films, Donald Bogle used *The Birth of a Nation* to exemplify the 'brutal black *buck*' type:

> Bucks are always big   a niggers, over-sexed and savage, violent and frenzied as they lu for white flesh.
>
> (Bogle, 2002: 13–14)

The other types he describes are:

Tom: 'socially acceptable, Good Negro characters. Always as toms are chased, harassed, hounded, flogged, enslaved, and insulted, they keep the faith ...' (Bogle, 2002: 4)

Coon: 'the pickaninny ... a harmless, little screwball creation whose eyes popped, whose hair stood on end with the least excitement, and whose antics were pleasant and diverting' (ibid.: 7) and 'The pure coons ... no-account niggers, those unreliable, crazy, lazy, subhuman creatures good for noting more than eating watermelons, stealing chickens, shooting crap, or butchering the English language. A character named Rastus was just such a figure' (ibid.: 8).

Tragic mulatto: Born of black and white parents, the mulattoes' tragedy is seen to derive from their mixed-race parentage. *Imitation of Life* (1934 and 1959) focused on such a character who tries to pass for white. However, once it is discovered she has black blood in her she is rejected.

Mammy: 'is distinguished by her sex and her fierce independence. She is usually big, fat, and cantankerous.' (Ibid.: 9)

The five types serve to reinforce racist discourses about race: good black folk know their place while those who refuse to kowtow are deemed to be savage. In between, the 'coons' and 'mulattoes' serve to emphasize the superiority of the white race. Such stereotypes are still with us: *Charlie's Angels 2: Full Throttle* (2003) cast Bernie Mac as Bosley, whose 'comic' repertoire includes the 'eye-popping' and 'childlike enthusiasm and naivety' of the coon (even Eddie Murphy's donkey in the *Shrek* films (2001, 2004) draws on this type). His mother, played by Ja'net DuBois, is the epitome of the 'mammy'; her character's name is even Momma Bosley. Spike Lee satirized hypocritical American attitudes to race in *Bamboozled* (2000) – see Box 6.1.

Box 6.1 Spike Lee – African-American filmmaker:
Bamboozled (2000)

Spike Lee is the only African-American filmmaker who regularly makes films that speak about the African-American's (usually male) place in American society. Since the short-lived early 1990s boom in 'black' movies (*Boyz N the Hood* and *New Jack City*, both 1991) there have been a number of black-themed films (such as *Soul Food*, 1997). These have been more about addressing the 'black demographic' rather than reflecting upon contemporary society. However mainstream Hollywood has also been careful to address the black audience, with sidekick characters such as that played by Danny Glover (the *Lethal Weapon* series, 1987–98).

Although Samuel L. Jackson in *Die Hard With a Vengeance* (1995) is placed as Bruce Willis's sidekick, he does at least raise issues of race. When the Willis character (John McClane) tells him to 'chill', Jackson's character (Zeus) demands that McClane 'talk to me like a white man'. During the opening scene, where McClane is forced to walk around Harlem with a racist placard, Zeus explains he only helped him to avoid the police 'coming down' on Harlem. However, inevitably, the characters are united by the narrative conclusion, with the white man in the superior, heroic, position.

Spike Lee has dealt directly in most of his films with the issue of race in American society. Indeed, the (white) critical establishment have deemed Lee to be a 'native interpreter': that is, the voice of African-Americans. This is despite the fact that Lee's persona in the films themselves is as a:

> slippery, ambivalent, and slightly shady character, who is often the object of implicit critique ...
>
> (Willis, 1997: 165)

In *Mo' Better Blues* (1990) his character is addicted to gambling; in *Girl 6* (1996) his Jimmy is constantly broke because he has invested in memorabilia that he hopes will be worth something in 20 years. Lee does not set himself up as a commentator in his films, although there is no doubt he feels very strongly about racism.

While Lee has addressed the issues raised by the civil rights movement (*Malcolm X*, 1992), most of his films deal with the fall-out from the 1960s, when black people were invited into (their own) middle class. This meant that for the first time, many African-Americans had a vested financial interest in maintaining the status quo; those espousing a pro-black view might find their job prospects threatened.

During the 1990s Hip-Hop, which originated as a street protest against the white appropriation of black disco, became the most potent force in youth culture. It became influential because of its popularity. However it was 'white' corporations that were able to commercially exploit the subculture and so make money out of black culture. Lee satirized this in *Bamboozled*, where fashion designer Tommy Hilfiger is mocked in a character called Hilnigger; Dunwitty (Michael Rapaport) claims he is blacker than Delacroix (Damon Wayans). Dunwitty is a 'wigger', the 'white nigger' defined, in politer terms, by Norman Mailer in 1957:

> So there was a new breed of adventurers, an urban adventurer who drifted out at night looking for action with a black man's code to fit their facts. The hipster had absorbed the existentialist synopses of the Negro, and for practical purposes could be considered a white Negro.
>
> (Mailer, 1968: 274)

Significantly the 'wigger' of the twenty-first century is not a rebel but a corporate suit.

Hip-Hop managed to cross over into the mainstream without completely losing its underground credentials. However in *Bamboozled* the rap group, the Mau Maus, are an object of satire as much as the television and advertising industries. This contrasts with Lee's use of Hip-Hop in *Do the Right Thing* (1989); Public Enemy's 'Fight the Power' was written for the film. Lee has said that, while he remains a fan of Hip-Hop, the emphasis on violence and accumulated wealth in gangsta rap is not a form of black culture he admires:

> I like rap music, but I'm not a fan of a lot of gangsta rap. I think it's obsessed with the 'bling bling,' with the gold chains and diamonds and Bentleys and all other trappings – you know, the titties and the butts shaking and jigging into the camera. I don't think that's uplifting, not at all. It's all about massive amounts of consumption.
>
> (Crowdus and Georgakas, 2001: 5b)

The role of music is extremely important in most of Lee's movies, and this points to his use of melodrama (see Box 2.5). As in *Do the Right Thing* and *Mo' Better Blues*, music in *Bamboozled* is important in defining characters and cultural boundaries. The use of character types is also a melodramatic technique, and satire is associated with melodrama in terms of how it represents reality. As a form, satire exaggerates to such an extent that the narrative world becomes distorted and often grotesque.

Some of the criticism levelled at *Bamboozled* suggested that its central premise – that audiences would warm to the 'new minstrel' show – was ridiculous. However, it could be argued that only such ridiculousness can make modern audiences think again about issues that seem to have disappeared. In the postmodern world, where eclecticism and playfulness often take the place of serious discussion, Lee rams racism down our throats, and even if we dismiss his film as 'flawed' we are likely to enter into debate about where his exploration on the representation of race erred. *Bamboozled* concludes with extracts during its end credit sequence showing the extremely racist representations of African-Americans in classical Hollywood.

One of the problems facing African-American filmmakers is the expectation, in the liberal press at least, that they should necessarily make a statement in their films about 'being black'. It is arguable that *To Sleep with Anger* (1990), written and directed by Charles Burnett, is even more radical that Lee's films, as he dispenses with *black* types with a narrative about 'ordinary' people. The fact that the characters are black is irrelevant, just as it would be in a world that was not racist.

Tessa Perkins (1979) pointed out that stereotypes have their origins in the real world; so how can such a degrading set of types be attached to people whose skin happens to be black? One suggestion is that the 'fat mammy' derives from the fact that:

> women were often treated simply as breeding stock by the slave owners ... their bodies were perhaps enlarged by repeated pregnancies, they were often moved into the main house and used as nursemaids to the white children.
>
> (Branston and Stafford, 2003: 93)

Similarly the 'coon's' 'shuffling gait' derived from the plantation owners' practice of cutting the calf muscles of any slave who tried to run away.

K. Anthony Appiah (1993) has suggested the addition of the 'Saint' type exemplified by Simon (Danny Glover) in *Grand Canyon* (1991). This is an evolution of the 'Tom', but has an enhanced status because he represents the 'ethical principle' of the film. This, Appiah argues, allows liberal (as reactionaries do not feel this guilt) 'white guilt' about racism to be assuaged, as they view a positive representation of an African-American.

Even films that deal with the subject of slavery, or apartheid in South Africa, usually do it from a white perspective, for example in *Mississippi Burning*:

> The veterans of the 1960s civil rights struggle are surely in a position to critique *Mississippi Burning* (1988) for turning the movement's historical enemy – the racist FBI which harassed and sabotaged the movement, into the film's heroes, while turning the historical heroes – the thousands of African-Americans who marched and braved beatings and imprisonment and sometimes death – into the supporting cast, passive victim-observers waiting for official White rescue.
>
> (Shohat/Stam, 1994: 178-9)

Similarly *A World Apart* (UK–Zimbabwe, 1988) and *A Dry White Season* (1989) looked at South Africa's racist system through white protagonists. The focus on 'liberal white' experience in times of racial segregation is not necessarily the result of the ethnicity of the filmmakers; the white Oliver Schmitz directed *Mapantsula* (South Africa, 1988), which told of a petty black thief's growing political awareness. However, who is doing the representing can be a crucial component of what is said about the group being represented. Here the dearth of black filmmakers, especially female (Julie Dash's *Daughters of the Dust*, 1991, and Leslie Harris' *Another Girl on the I.R.T.*, 1992 are exceptions), is a particular impediment to reforming conventional modes of representation of black people.

Black male film directors have been fashionable twice in Hollywood: during the early 1970s, the era of 'blaxplotiation', and in the early 1990s. *Shaft* (1971, remade 2000) featured Richard Roundtree in the eponymous, and phallic, role of the hard-boiled detective. Although certainly not the first Hollywood black protagonist, Sidney Poitier had been the star of many films during the 1960s (his persona was of the 'non-threatening black man'); *Shaft* was different because he strutted the street afraid of no one. The film sparked a cycle that included two sequels, and was part of the wave of black cinema that included *Sweet Sweetback's Baadassss Song* (1971).

The early 1990s spate of black-themed movies attempted to recoup 'black history' from white historians. For example, *Boyz N the Hood* (1991), a teen pic, included a radical statement voiced by Furious Styles (Laurence Fishburn). The opening minutes of *Menace II Society* (1993) gives us a potted history of why the ghetto of south central Los Angeles has become, in films at least, a zone of gang warfare (a point satirized by Michael Moore in *Bowling for Columbine* (2002, Canada-USA-Germany), when he stands at a street corner in the ghetto and cannot find any trouble).

It should be noted that the term 'black' homogenises many different people:

> They are 'homogenizing' because of the assumption that black people were all really alike, which not only negated the impact of other politics (especially of gender, but also of class, age, sexual orientation and so on), but also tended to reproduce the binary oppositional logic of black/white, thereby pre-empting an understanding of how... 'Whiteness' is a politically constructed category parasitical on 'Blackness'.
>
> (Davies and Smith, 1997: 61)

One of the more interesting portrayals of race from Hollywood in recent years was Eminem's film debut *8 Mile* (2002). Probably because of the loosely autobiographical nature of the film, ethnicity was defined in terms of social class rather than race. So Rabbit (Eminem) could browbeat his black challenger by pointing out that, despite his looks, he did not come from the 'street', which was the domain of 'white trash' Rabbit (Eminem).

One of the central issues for African-Americans, as well as Afro-Caribbean Britons (or any diasporic groups), is a sense of belonging to a specific place – hence the 'back to Africa' movement of Marcus Garvey. It could be argued that one of the functions of national cinemas is to give society a sense of identity rooted in place.

6.4 National cinema

This central question of 'national cinema' is what role films take in formulating a nation's understanding of itself and other nations. During the 1920s the rise of nationalism, in Germany, Italy, the Soviet Union and Spain, saw cinema being utilized by the state for political purposes. While Nazi cinema was trying to convince the nation that Jews were degenerate, the Establishment in Britain and France was talking about the 'corrupting' influence of Hollywood, and of American culture in general. As Richard Maltby points out, the idea that Hollywood represents national culture is one that exists only outside America. As far as Hollywood is concerned, movie making is simply about entertainment (and so making money from its production). The need to defend indigenous industries from American product, Maltby argues, was not economic but cultural:

> American culture has appeared dangerous to elites because it is radically democratic; at a variety of levels, it challenges hierarchies of discrimination, taste and class.
>
> (Maltby, 1998a: 106)

Maltby goes on to argue that the many non-Americans who habitually consume American product see it as part of their 'second culture', rather than one that is seeking to usurp indigenous values. In addition, it does not take a film scholar to realize that foreign influences on Hollywood are many; for example, Hong Kong filmmakers have irrevocably altered American action cinema (see Feng, 2002).

Another complication when considering national cinemas is the fact that the popular indigenous films are different from those that are exported. In other words, popular cinema tends not to travel (unless it is made in America), so foreign films tend to be arthouse in nature (see 3.13). So the view an indigenous film gives of its nation to other countries may be very different from the views seen in films consumed at home.

Benedict Anderson's concept of 'imagined communities' has probably had most influence upon recent academic investigation into national identity. Anderson's insight was to conceive of nationalism as imagined:

> It is *imagined* because the members of even the smallest nation will never know most of their fellow-members, meet them, or even hear of them, yet in the minds of each lives the image of their communion.
>
> (Anderson, 1991: 6)

In the context of film studies this imagined community is reified by film, and Andrew Higson suggested the key questions of analysing the films of a national cinema are:

> what are these films about? Do they share a common style or world view? What sort of projections of the national character do they offer? To what extent are they engaged in exploring, questioning and constructing a notion of nationhood in the films themselves and in the consciousness of the viewer?
>
> (Higson, 1989: 36)

Higson points out that this is merely one way of considering national cinema, and Stephen Crofts (1998) refined Higson's work by suggesting the following approaches:

1. Production – examining the way films are made in a country.
2. Distribution and exhibition – what films are available for audiences to view?
3. Audiences – focusing on box office statistics; what national films are audiences viewing?
4. Discourses – the way in which academics/critics routinely approach national cinema, such as John Hill's (1986) focus on class and gender in British cinema.
5. Textuality – while in the past this has tended to focus upon a canon of a nation's 'great films', more recent work has considered filmic conventions and how genres articulate ideas of nation.
6. National-cultural specificity – acknowledges that some of a nation's films will work in opposition to mainstream representations of nation. For example, black British cinema could be seen to have worked against 'heritage' films.

Thus national cinema is a complex mesh of variables. So while it is possible to state that during the 1950s, Ealing comedy thrived by projecting 'the landscape and the mood of post-war Britain' (Barr, 1977: 5), this cannot be anything other than an over-simplification. Indeed there is often a healthy debate about what particular strands of film history actually mean. For example, the 'heritage' films (costume dramas such as *A Room with a View*, UK, 1985) that were relatively popular during the 1980s have provoked widely differing views:

> Some writers have dismissed [these] films as reactionary, finding them overly nostalgic and selective in their presentation of the past. Others have claimed that they provide a critique of social repression and sexual politics which can be seen as progressive.
>
> (Gibson, 2000: 113)

The next section considers British cinema as a national cinema. It offers a brief outline of its economic relationship with Hollywood, then applies the six points noted above to the country. The section concludes with a look at censorship, where the boundaries of what is permitted to be represented (and how) can be seen.

6.5 British cinema

The British film industry is not the only country to struggle to compete with Hollywood, and indeed it benefits financially more than many from the American use of British studios. Neil Watson (2000) suggests that it is financially viable for the major studios to use British crews and studio space if the exchange rate is below $1.70. However although *The Phantom Menace* (1999) was shot in Britain, competition for Hollywood money is strong, and *Star Wars Episode II: The Attack of the Clones* (2002) was filmed in Australia. Eastern Europe, particularly Czechoslovakia, was also putting up severe competition at the start of the decade.

With a market about a tenth of the size of North America – the UK has about one-fifth of the population and goes to the cinema half as often – it is much harder for films to break even in the indigenous market. Therefore the industry often looks to the American market, and it is possible to see the history of British cinema as one of continuing failed attempts to compete directly with Hollywood.

From Rank's star-studded *Caesar and Cleopatra* (1945) to ITC's *Raise the Titanic* (1980), Thorn-EMI's *Honky Tonk Freeway* (USA, 1981) and Goldcrest's *Revolution* (1985), British cinema has consistently failed in its attempts to break into the American market with big-budget films. The Rank box office disaster excepted, these films contributed greatly to the production companies' demise as makers of films. By reputation these are all bad films and deserved to flop. However, Britain is capable of making films that capture North American box office: *The Private Life Of Henry VIII* (1933), Best Picture Oscar winner *Chariots of Fire* (1981), *Four Weddings and a Funeral* (1994), *The Full Monty* (1998), *Bend it Like Beckham* (2002) and *Love Actually* (2003) all made an impact. All these films are culturally British; that is, they use forms of representation that are immediately recognizable, to the home audience, as being typically British. However it appears that when a producer tries to make a film that will appeal directly to the US market, and so internationalizes the forms of representation used, the attempt usually makes a splash only in the 'mid-Atlantic'; that is, it appeals neither to the Americans nor the British. (Working Title Films, however, seemed to avoid this problem – see below.) Because of the relatively small size of the British market, any film that seeks only to appeal to 'home' audiences must necessarily be low-budget.

British companies such as Goldcrest suffered like their American independent counterparts from under-capitalization; one big flop places enormous strains on their cash flow. One of the most vibrant production companies, Palace Pictures, eventually foundered just before the massive North American box office success of *The Crying Game* (1992) (see Lacey, 2000b).

Channel 4, the public service broadcaster launched in 1982, contributed greatly to the renaissance of British cinema during the 1980s. The first chief executive of C4, Jeremy Isaacs, was aware how television companies had made important contributions to indigenous cinemas – see 5.11. However the Cinematograph Exhibitors Association (CEA) barred films from appearing on television for three years after a theatrical release. It would be very difficult for a new company, without a catalogue of films to broadcast, to wait so long before showing its films:

> In 1986 ... the CEA [agreed] that the bar would not apply to films costing under £1.25 million (a figure subsequently increased to £4 million in 1988).
>
> (Hill, 1999: 55)

The theatrical release of C4 films meant they gained more critical attention and 'bigger' talents (who might have thought television beneath them) were more likely to appear. C4 also got involved in pre-purchasing: in other words, it would invest in a film before it was made in return for broadcasting rights.

David Rose, the commissioning editor, focused on British films that had a predilection for realism. However, both foreign and experimental filmmakers also received support. Among the most successful films were *My Beautiful Laundrette* and *Letter to Brezhnev* (both 1985).

FilmFour was created as a stand alone production and distribution company. However it was closed in 2002, and the channel's budget for films was cut from £30 million to £10 million a year. The closure probably had more to do with the advertising recession, and the company's costly investment in digital television, which put pressure on C4 itself. The box office failure of the relatively big-budget *Charlotte Gray* (UK–Australia–Germany, 2001) was widely blamed for the demise of FilmFour. However the costs to C4 of this film had been defrayed by pre-sales. Investment in the Hollywood flop *Death to Smoochy* (USA–UK–Germany, 2002) was far more likely to have led to the £7 million losses that FilmFour had reported. The film, a co-production, cost $50 million to make and took only $8 million at the US box office. Scriptwriter and director David Hare summarized the problem succinctly:

> It was … when a fresh generation of square-rimmed, crop-haired executives went whoring after Hollywood, crazed by the barren fantasy that the Brits might compete with everything that is uninteresting in American cinema that FilmFour suicided into the sea, making almost as resounding a splash as Goldcrest before it.
>
> (Hare, 2003)

The following applies Higson's six perspectives on national cinema, outlined in the previous section, to Britain.

6.5.1 Production

As noted above, Britain is an important place for the production of Hollywood films. It has the requisite large studios, such as Pinewood's 15-plus stages, which housed the production of *Die Another Day* (UK–USA, 2002), *Lara Croft: Tomb Raider* (USA–UK–Germany–Japan, 2001) and *The Hours* (USA, 2002). Britain also has a thriving post-production/special effects sector: technically, Britain can compete with any filmmaking nation in the world. The headaches for the country are a lack

A British film? *The Hours* **(2002) featured Australian and American leads, a British script based on an American novel, and was filmed in Britain by a British director**

of finance and a distribution sector dominated by American companies. So paltry is the financial markets' faith in the film industry (which is undoubtedly high risk) that even the 'sure fire' hit *Harry Potter* went to Hollywood for the money; although author J. K. Rowling ensured a high degree of 'Britishness' in the films by insisting upon a 'Brits only' policy in the casting.

PolyGram Filmed Entertainment (PFE) was the most successful 'British' (it was 80 per cent owned by Dutch electronics giant Polygram) company during the 1990s. However, the company was sold to drinks group Seagram, which sold it to Vivendi as part of Universal Studios. Vivendi, originally a French sewer company, closed PFE. Before this 'disaster' PFE 'cracked' the American and international market with films such as *Four Weddings and a Funeral* (UK, 1994) – in association with C4 – and *Notting Hill* (UK–USA, 1999). PFE worked with Working Title, and has also had international success with *Bridget Jones's Diary* (UK–France, 2001, and its 2004 sequel) and *Love Actually* (UK–USA, 2003).

Although these films were not their only successes, they do demonstrate a heavy reliance on Hugh Grant and scriptwriter Richard Curtis, who also directed *Love Actually*. Grant is one of the few British stars who has any profile in America, although there is no doubt that it was the presence of Julia Roberts that made *Notting Hill* the only British Film to exceed $100 million at the North American box office. (All of these films are romantic comedies, which might be a comment of how Americans view the British.)

In 2002, 369 films were released in Britain. Of these 104 could in some way be defined as British. The British Film Institute (Bfi) helpfully defines four types of British film:

➤ *Category A*: Feature films where the cultural and financial impetus is from the UK and where the majority of personnel are British.

➤ *Category B*: Majority UK co-productions. Films in which, although there are foreign partners, there is a UK cultural content and a significant amount of British finance and personnel.

➤ *Category C*: Minority UK co-productions. Foreign (non US) films in which there is a small UK involvement in finance or personnel.

➤ *Category D*: American financed or part-financed films made in the UK. Most titles have a British cultural content.

(Dyja, 2003: 26–9).

Table 6.1

Category	Example film	No. of films produced in 2002
A	*In This World*	18
B	*Girl with a Pearl Earring* (UK-Luxembourg)	44
C	*Underworld* (USA-Germany-Hungary-UK)	23
D	*Calendar Girls* (USA-UK)	19

Source: Dyja, 2003: 26–9.

Examples of the categories for films made in 2002

(It should be noted that the Film Council – see below – introduced a different way of defining 'Britishness' in film, but it was less precise than the Bfi's; see www.filmcouncil.org.uk.) As category D suggests, the origin of the finance matters little in determining whether a film is British or not. The key element is 'cultural content'. It does however matter to the industry. For example, *The Full Monty* (UK, 1997) was financed by 20th Century Fox, and as a result of that much of the profit of the most successful British film at the British box office went to Hollywood.

The key factor in determining the nationality of a film is the cultural content. However, this is a vague concept that is difficult to pin down. For example *In This World* is subtitled and focuses on the journey of a Pakistani migrant, and *Girl with a Pearl Earring* investigates the life of a Dutch painter.

The number of films produced in 2002 was the third highest since 1981 (the low point with 24), with a total production cost of £618.5 million (making the average cost around £6 million, although a few big budget films, such as *Die Another Day*, *Cold Mountain*, *Lara Croft Tomb Raider: The Cradle of Life* and *Shanghai Knights* accounted for £216 million alone! Stripping these out brings the average cost down to £4 million (Dyja, 2003: 26–9)).

At the time of writing, the UK film industry is assisted by tax concessions which allow investors to write off the cost of film production in its first year; in other words, money invested in a film can be written off against tax. This encouraged the development of a number of schemes that were more to do with tax avoidance than film investment:

> From an investor's point of view, most sale and leaseback schemes are very low risk. The benefit to the investor is not dependent on the film being commercially successful (or even being released) but is merely predicated on the film obtaining a certificate confirming that it has qualified as a British film in accordance with the legislation... The resultant tax break to the investor is effectively a 15 year loan at a rate of approximately 4% to 5% per annum.
>
> (Eagles, 2002)

Such tax breaks are hardly substantial foundations upon which to build an industry. In February 2004 the Inland Revenue closed a loophole because it thought that the concessions were being used for the distribution of American films. As a result a number of films about to go into production found their figures no longer added up.

The Film Council was set up, with a mixture of Government and lottery money, to:

stimulate a competitive, successful and vibrant UK film industry and culture, and to promote the widest possible enjoyment and understanding of cinema throughout the nations and regions of the UK.

(www.ukfilmcouncil.org.uk, accessed February 2004)

The Council was formed in 2000 to put the Government's film initiatives under one roof. Its highest profile activity was distributing lottery money to producers via three funds: Premiere (£8 million planned spend for 2004-5), New Cinema (£5 million) and Development (£4 million). The Premiere's prime interest is in commercial features, while the others are intended to help develop talent and non-mainstream fare.

In 2003 it was responsible for the spending of £31 million on the franchises set up in 1997. These franchises were meant to give stability to the industry through guaranteed funding for several years. They were a mixed success at best, with few commercial hits and the franchises being subject to the criticism that public money was being used to subsidize Hollywood productions.

Since the demise of the British Film Institute's production fund in 1998, getting finance for experimental, or arthouse, films has become increasingly difficult – see 6.5.6.

6.5.2 Distribution and exhibition

Cinema admissions in Britain peaked in 1948 at over 1.5 billion a year, then (as in North America) the long decline set in, reaching the depths of 54 million (3 per cent of the 1948 total) in 1984. Since then admissions have risen each year (with the exceptions of 1995, 1998 and 2003), to 167 million in 2003 (down from 2002's 176 million) (Screen Digest/CAA/Neilsen EDI/Screen Finance, quoted in Dyja, 2003: 39).

John Hill (2001) argues that a British national cinema, based upon theatrical exhibition, was possible up until the 1970s. By then the audience had declined so much that films rarely, if ever, recouped their cost in the domestic market alone. During this decade the enduring *Carry On* series fizzled out, and Hammer Horror met its demise as a film production company.

Such was the decline in audiences that the end of cinema was widely predicted in the early 1980s. Although videocassette recorders were getting established in British homes during the decade, the decline was probably primarily caused by the fact that many cinemas were in poor condition. Many cinemas, situated in the inner city, partitioned their buildings to turn one large screen into a theatre with two small and one medium-sized screen. This lessened the 'unique selling point' (the large screen) that cinema had over television. The sound also tended to 'leak' between theatres.

In a gesture of defiance 1985 was dubbed British Film Year, and the attendant publicity may have helped boost attendances to 72 million. However, the most significant event for the industry that year occurred in Milton Keynes: the opening of the first multiplex cinema – see Box 3.1.

By 2002 Britain appeared to have reached capacity in the number of screens, as this was the first year that the number of multiplexes had fallen. However, the British go to the cinema only five times a year on average, so there is still the potential for growth.

The healthiness, at least when compared with the disastrous 1970s, of the British exhibition sector needs to be compared with that of the British distribution sector. In 2002 the five major distributors – all American – were responsible for 148 of the 420 films distributed (35 per cent). The other 272 films were split between 51 independent distributors (a number of which were not British). Financially the majors were responsible for £595,589,197 in takings, representing 73 per cent of the total £812,193,118 (Nielsen EDI/bfi/RSU, quoted in Dyja, 2003: 48).

Having a distributor's support is crucial to a film's success, and the dominance of the 'big five' means that Hollywood films get preferential treatment (because they are likely to be the most successful financially). Hence the difficulty for British films to get distribution, although the majors would argue that they will distribute any film that is likely to be successful.

6.5.3 Audiences

In this section we are interested in who goes to see which films. In 2002 audiences hit a 30-year high with 176 million admissions. While middle-class people were slightly more likely to attend, the key cinema-going group were 14–35-year-olds.

As has been noted in Chapter 2, the films they were viewing were primarily products of Hollywood. In the top ten of that year only *Die Another Day* (UK-USA, 2002) was arguably culturally British. This ignores the claims of *Lord of the Rings: The Two Towers* (New Zealand-USA, 2002): although it is written by a Briton, and starred a number of British actors, it was very much an international production.

Although images of Britishness thrive on television, their absence on film is a problem. Some countries, like South Korea and France, have a quota system that demands a certain amount of homegrown product is shown in cinemas. Britain tried this in the late 1920s:

> 25 per cent of all screen time had to be, by law, devoted to British film... But our American friends were very, very clever. They all formed British companies. There was British Warner, there was British Fox ... British MGM ... And they financed these films. They gave a British producer five thousand pounds for a five-thousand-foot film. The producer would make the film for four thousand pounds in six days ['quota quickies'], and put the other thousand in his pocket. Now, obviously these films weren't good, but they did help us with our training.... They opened the theatre at eight o'clock in the morning (by the theatre I mean every-where in the country). The theatres opened at eight o'clock, and the British film was run from eight to nine thirty, to the cleaners. And then at around about nine thirty, they ran it again. And at eleven thirty, they put it in the back of the projection box and they didn't bring it out till the next morning; they showed their own film all day long.
>
> (Ronald Neame interviewed on www.bfi.org.uk/showing/ nft/interviews/neame/05.php accessed February 2004)

While audiences prefer Hollywood films to British, the 'market' will insist that local product be marginalized. One non-Hollywood growth area in recent years has been the success of Bollywood films, fuelled by British Asian audiences.

6.5.4 Discourses

Academically British cinema received scant attention before the 1970s, reflecting the elitist view that mainstream film was a commodity and therefore should not be considered as art. Only those British films that were obviously not made with the box office in mind, such as those produced under the auspices of John Grierson and the 'documentary movement', received 'serious' attention – see 5.5.

Another problem for British cinema was its apparent lack of *auteurs*, especially as Hitchcock had gone to America. *Movie* magazine, which espoused *auteurism*, seemed to concur with François Truffaut's view that 'British cinema' was an oxymoron.

When academics started taking British cinema seriously, it was of no surprise that issues of social class should be seen to be important; John Hill's *Sex, Class and Realism: British Cinema 1956–1963* (1986) is a particularly useful book. He suggests that the British New Wave films (see 5.8) of the era see class:

> primarily as an individual, rather than collective, experience, a moral, rather than socially and economically structured, condition.
> (Hill, 1986: 57)

He links this to the 'demands' of conventional narrative structure. While class remains important in his book *British Cinema in the 1980s* (1999), issues of gender and race are added. In addition, the shadow cast by the Thatcher administration (1979–90) on cultural production becomes important; the Thatcher years were a watershed in British society.

As British cinema increasingly gained ground, during the 1990s, in universities, Routledge published the British Popular Cinema series, which:

> Rediscovers and evaluates not only individual films but whole genres ... that have been ignored by a past generation of critics.
> (Chibnall and Hunter, 1999: series policy statement frontispiece)

These genres are mined for what they can tell us about contemporaneous attitudes toward subjects such as Britain's declining empire.

6.5.5 Textual

Textual analysis attempts to 'read' a nation through its films; while this can be individual texts, genre, as we shall see, is a useful tool. It is obviously easier to see in retrospect whether any particular genre has been predominant during a decade (itself an arbitrary division). For example, the 1980s were the decade of the heritage film, exemplified by Merchant–Ivory productions. While most cinemagoers would not recognize the term 'heritage' film – it being an academic construction – Andrew Higson argued that it does constitute a genre, as it:

> reinvents and reproduces, and in some cases simply invents, a national heritage for the screen.
> (Higson, 1997: 26)

Higson (1989: 27) characterizes the genre as:

> ➤ based on canonic literary texts

- ➤ having an iconography of antiques, period décor, furniture and ornaments
- ➤ focusing on the aristocracy, played by predominantly theatre actors
- ➤ set 'in the sorts of buildings and landscapes which are now conserved by bodies such as the National Trust and English Heritage'.

This more or less fulfils the genre paradigm, suggested in Chapter 2, of narrative, iconography, characters and setting.

In terms of the British film industry, the heritage film proved to be a money-spinner in America, starting in the 1980s with the Oscar-winning *Chariots of Fire* (1981). As Hill points out, these films were often more successful in America than Britain:

> Rather than attempting to compete with Hollywood directly by imitating its norms ... the [heritage film adopted] aesthetic strategies and cultural referents which distinguish it from Hollywood and so foreground its 'national' credentials ... just as heritage culture permits Britain to carve out a niche for itself within the global tourist economy so heritage films may be seen to provide the British cinema with a distinctive product in the international media market-place.
>
> (Hill, 1999: 79)

Locally these films were perceived as 'middle-brow' products: those that offer cultural kudos with the guarantee that they will not be too intellectually taxing. Their popularity cannot be divorced from BBC television's period dramas (institutionalized with the massive success of *The Forsyte Saga*, 1967) which were once a staple of Sunday evening viewing.

In Britain, maybe their popularity is due to nostalgia for the past 'glories' of the days of Empire. This may be too simplistic, as Hill notes, as the past is not necessarily portrayed through rose-tinted lenses (for example, the anti-Semitism in *Chariots of Fire*) and the nostalgia is for an era that, for most, is known only through media texts.

The emphasis on period effects in the heritage film often leads to a similar preoccupation with 'surface' simulation of the past rather than the encouragement of a historical sensibility (Hill, 1999: 83).

These films are still with us, as Gibson (2000) points out. The 1990s version offered a postmodern spin, as in *Shakespeare in Love* (USA–UK, 1998).

In addition to focusing on 'canonic' films, such as Powell and Pressburger's *A Matter of Life and Death* (1946), it is also possible to consider how the technology that is available in particular countries can affect the films. For example, in writing about Ealing studios of the 1940s, John Ellis stated:

> British studios, in contrast to most others, had no curved tracks. In short, to get a complicated camera movement 'right'... required several takes ... this tended to slow down shooting and to increase costs [so] directors ... tended to avoid such movements.
>
> (Ellis, 1975: 88)

Many movies made during the Second World War, which dealt directly with the war, had a particular ideological function at the time. The British films *Went the Day Well?* (directed by Alberto Cavalcanti, 1942) and Launder and Gilliat's *Millions Like Us* (1943) were designed to show the nation pulling together regardless of class differences or gender roles. They were, in effect, propaganda encouraging the British people to 'pull together' in adversity, which is what indeed happened (although not in such a 'consensus' way shown by the films).

6.5.6 National-cultural specificity

Outside the mainstream, the 1970s and 1980s were distinguished by oppositional filmmaking, such as the Black Audio Collective's *Handsworth Songs* (1986). However, funding from the British Film Institute dried up in the 1990s, leaving experimental filmmaking even further out on a limb. The institute was particularly important in funding films such as *The Riddle of the Sphinx* (1977) and *Amy!* (1979), made by film theorists Laura Mulvey and Peter Wollen.

Many of the radical films of the 1970s were made by collectives, such as the Berwick Street Collective's *Night Cleaners* (1975). These functioned as workshops which intended to democratically give participants a creative input into the film, in contrast to the hierarchical organization of conventional filmmaking.

Channel 4 in its early days helped support this alternative sector, but by the 1990s the funding, and possibly the ideas, dried up (for more details see Lacey, 2002: 125–7). Another lack on mainstream screens has been portrayals of Britain as a multicultural society:

> Although there is a renaissance in British Cinema – backed by millions of pounds of Lottery money – the Britain that is being

disseminated on cinema screens around the world is steeped in heritage, literary culture, and conventional ideas of class relations. It is also overwhelmingly white, in sharp contrast to our workplaces, high streets and bedrooms which tell a very different story.

(Alexander, 2000: 113)

As Alexander points out, while black characters were not absent in British films (they were important protagonists in films such as *Secrets and Lies,* France-UK, 1996), black *culture* is missing. Whether 'black' includes Afro-Caribbeans, British Asians and those of mixed race is open to debate. Horace Ove made a feature on the black experience in Britain in the 1970s, *Pressure* (1976), and one recent film that was indubitably about black culture was Julian Henriques' *Babymother* (1998). It focused on a young ('baby') mother of two, and her crew's attempt to break into the dance hall scene with their DJ-ing and 'outrageous' costumes and hairstyles.

6.5.7 British cinema now

British cinema is not monolithic. While Scottish, Welsh (and Irish) cinema is even more enfeebled than Britain's as a whole (which might, in fact, be English), it is possible to see distinctive views on nationality produced by these 'national' cinemas. *Trainspotting* (1996) was equally acerbic about Scottish and English culture, while *Twin Town* (1997) emphasized how the English marginalize Wales.

The only recent recognizable genre cycle in British cinema was the gangster films that attempted to follow the box office success of *Lock, Stock and Two Smoking Barrels* (1998). None did so, except the same director's (Guy Ritchie's) *Snatch* (2000), which included the star appeal of Brad Pitt. However there were many attempts, including the very poorly received *Rancid Aluminium* and *Essex Boys* (both 2000). Although neither were a commercial success locally, both *Sexy Beast* and *Gangster No. 1* (both 2000) were brilliant examinations of masculinity. In purely commercial terms the genre only had two hits, and it is unlikely that without 'public' money, so many gangster films would have been made.

This failure to produce indigenous genre cycles makes it very difficult for the industry to gauge what audiences want:

in British cinema we never know what to expect. The sheer diversity of our film product in the late 90s may be a sign of artistic strength, but it presents a big marketing difficulty.

(Brown, 2001: 32)

"**HILARIOUSLY**
FRESH & FUNNY. THIS IS THE
BEST BRITISH COMEDY
SINCE BRIDGET JONES'S DIARY."

BEND IT
LIKE BECKHAM.

Who wants to cook Aloo Gobi
when you can bend a ball like Beckham?

NAGRA KNIGHTLEY RHYS MEYERS KHER PANJABI LEWIS HARPER STEVENSON

**By the turn of the century British cinema, at last, was acknowledging
the existence of a multi-cultural society (*Bend it Like Beckham*, 2002)**

One of the biggest successes of 2002, *Bend it Like Beckham* (UK-Germany), focused on a Sikh girl who wanted to play football; the producers found it very difficult to get backing for such an 'uncommercial' product, which went on to gross over $20 million in North America. Although superficially similar to *East is East*, a domestic hit in 1999, the 'feel good' nature of the melodrama did not gloss over the racism suffered by both the Asian characters and the Irish coach. *East is East*, on the other hand, sanitized the racism of the 1970s (see www.watershed.co.uk/east 'Debates' section).

Bend it Like Beckham offers a multicultural view of British society. In focusing on a Sikh *girl* wanting to play football, writer-director Gurinder Chadha had issues of both ethnicity and gender to deal with. Chadha had also dealt successfully with the South Asian diaspora (see below) in her first feature *Bhaji on the Beach* (1993), and benefited from British Film Institute support with her short *I'm British But …*(1990).

Trying to decide what, if any, 'imagined community' is being offered by films is an incredibly complex process, possibly more so when we are considering indigenous cinema, as we are part of what is being represented, and so it is difficult to get an 'objective' perspective. It may be easier to get a sense of other nations from film, as we can view them more objectively. However the poor distribution of world cinema obviously restricts what we can see, and who is to say that a national cinema accurately represents a nation?

During the early years of the twenty-first century the notion of nation states is being threatened by economic and political migrations. This has consequently reinforced reactionary notions of nationhood, leading to certain members of the indigenous population seeking to keep foreigners out. While people have always migrated, the growth of mass communications during the twentieth century meant that it was far easier to remain in contact with 'back home'. This contact could be physical, flying long distances for visits, or electronic, via phone calls. Globalization manifested itself in film with the growth of overseas demand for domestic films; this has been particularly evident in the South Asian diaspora:

> Bombay (Bollywood) cinema which (as shown in cinema halls and viewed at home on videos and on cable TV such as ATN in Canada or Sahara TV in the United Arab Emirates) has been crucial in bringing the 'homeland' into the diaspora as well as creating a culture of imaginary solidarity across the heterogeneous linguistic and national groups that make up the South Asian (Indian) diaspora.
>
> (Mishra, 2002: 235)

Dil Se (India, 1998) proved popular with the South East Asian diaspora

In recent years, Bollywood films have regularly appeared in the UK box office top ten. The cultural influence, unsurprisingly, is not one-way. While the 'immigrant' culture may not become assimilated into the host nation (which may, as in the case of twentieth-century Britain, to a large extent reject its 'guests' culture), it is inevitable that the surrounding culture will influence that of the immigrants. In the case of Bollywood this manifested itself, in 2003, with a widening of the subject matter of popular Indian cinema:

> there are at least three new trends emerging in films being produced in Mumbai. First there are a spate of productions dealing with taboo subjects such as sex. Another group of Indian film-makers are announcing period epics or films on famous Indian historical personalities. And the third genre is the low cost youth-oriented Hinglish (Hindi-English) productions.
>
> (Lal, 2003)

Members of what Lal calls the 'second diaspora', a largely middle-class emigration 'into the metropolitan centers of the former empire as well as the New World and Australia' (Mishra, 2002: 235), key 'into the social imaginary of the larger nation' (ibid.: 236). So the Hanif Kureishi-scripted *My Beautiful Laundrette* (1985) and *My Son the Fanatic* (1997) attempted to articulate the hybrid culture that has arisen through the negotiation between the host and immigrant cultures.

Recently there have been a number of films that deal with the migration and identity. *In This World* (UK, 2002) follows the trail, and trials, of Jamal (played by himself, Jamal Udin Tarabi) to London; *Dirty Pretty Things* (UK, 2002) shows, in a thriller form, what happens when asylum seekers reach the capital, are forced to work incognito, and are sexually exploited and harassed by immigration officials. The use of the long take in *Code Unknown* (*Code Inconnu: Récit Incomplet de Divers Voyages*, France-Germany-Romania, 1999) (the only edits in the film, except for a sequence from a film within the film, are fade-ins and outs at the end of each scene) is integral to the film's investigation into migration, displacement and racism.

6.5.8 Censorship in Britain

Censorship is an index of where a society draws a line between permissible representations and those that are banned, either outright or for certain age groups. The 'effects' debate centres around the assumption that audiences are directly affected by whatever media text they consume. Indeed, widely reported cases of murder by spectators who had recently seen films such as *Reservoir Dogs* (1992) and *Natural Born Killers* (1994) go some way to contribute to the idea that our behaviour can be influenced directly by movies. Occasionally, these fears escalate into 'moral panics', where the popular press in particular seem to tap into issues that concern the nation:

> From the penny dreadfuls (Britain) and dime novels (US) of the late nineteenth century, through the street theatres and music hall of the turn of the century, early cinema, the 50s crime and horror comics, paperback novels, television, video nasties, to video games, the same litany of fears has endlessly been rehearsed.
>
> (Barker, 1993: 11a)

Over a decade later we can add the Internet to Barker's list of 'folk devils'. A common thread between all these media is that they were new at the time of the panic. The advent of new technology threatens the status quo by creating new forms of communication. Until this form is brought under institutional control, often through government legislation, it is deemed to be a threat by the Establishment (that is, those in positions of power). This legislation manifests itself as censorship.

In Britain the Board of Film Censors, as it was honestly known, was set up in 1912 as a self-regulatory body. The idea was to pre-empt local censorship of films, to enable the industry to maintain control over its product. What a society deems allowable tells us much about the mores of the time. For example in the Film Censor's report of 1913 it was stated that films had been censored because of:

> 'indecorous dancing', 'confinements', 'native customs in foreign lands abhorrent to British ideas' … 'scenes tending to disparage public characters and institutions'.
>
> (quoted in Mathews, 1994: 24)

While contemporary censorship is not as trenchant as that of 100 years ago (although it is not impossible that the above criteria would be used), one constant is that the Board's 'taste', unsurprisingly, will reflect the dominant bourgeois values of society. The British Board of Film Classification (BBFC), as it is now, cannot now be as blasé about its role as its Secretary, ATL Watkins, was in 1949:

> The effect of a good censorship should not be noticed ... the cinema public, which sees only the completed and apparently untouched film, is happily ignorant.
>
> (Watkins, 1949: 61)

Watkins explains the rationale for censorship in terms that suggest class prejudice, when he says that it would be fine for 'intelligent adults' to view an uncensored film:

> while an intelligent adult audience might be relied on to reject bad taste and to remain undisturbed by immoral influences, he would be an optimist who would expect such qualities of resistance in the average patrons of the local Odeon or Granada.
>
> (Watkins, 1949: 61–2)

For 'intelligent' read middle class and 'average' read working class. In addition, the undefined 'bad taste' would have been based upon middle-class values, and the emphasis on 'adult' suggests that children need special protection. Watkins' patrician character is obvious to us now. However, although the BBFC's tone has changed, its attitude toward the working class and children has not. In addition bourgeois taste, which automatically excludes certain types of film such as horror (horror used to have its own classification – H), is still evident.

The X certificate was introduced in 1951 as a widening of the H category, and stipulated that the films were for adults only. Despite the new category, the Board continued cutting: for example a one-second glimpse of 'Eva Dahlbeck's' left nipple had to be removed from Bergman's *Smiles of a Summer Night* (*Sommarnattens Leende*, Sweden, 1955) (Mathews, 1994). It was not simply nudity, or violence, that upset the Board:

> The Board was keen to discourage the normalisation of premarital or extra-marital sex, with cuts made to provocative or overtly sexual language, e.g. in Ingmar Bergman's *Smiles of a Summer Night*, 'lust' was changed to 'passion', 'lecherous fantasies' to 'unspeakable dreams', and the lines 'Nearly everything that's fun is a sin. Then I say three cheers for sin', were cut completely.
>
> (www.bbfc.org.uk, 'History of the BBFC', accessed July 2003)

Cutting was not the only option: *The Wild One* (1954) was banned out-right until 1967 when it was released with cuts. The 'problem' with the film, a social problem picture and nascent teen pic, was that the rebels were not ultimately punished for their 'crime' of rebellion. By 1988 whatever subversive force the film had possessed was dissipated, and its video release was given a PG (Parental Guidance) certificate.

In an attempt to differentiate itself from the new mass media, television, film companies began using the X certificate as a way of branding their product as risqué and/or violent.

> The number of films awarded an 'X' certificate by the British censor rise remorselessly from 1954 onward and especially at the end of the 1950s, when it quadrupled ...
>
> (Pirie, 1980: part 3)

Indeed Hammer used the X in its marketing for *The Quatermass Xperiment* (1955), and this film launched the production company on a successful series of Gothic horror movies including both 'Universal's' monsters *The Curse of Frankenstein* (1956) and *Dracula* (1957). Using lurid colour combined with the British theatrical tradition of acting (exemplified by Peter Cushing), Hammer's films were condemned by most critics and loved by audiences. Like the Victorian Gothic of its source material, Hammer movies sublimated the sexual into the violence of the monster. As censorship shackles lessened, the sex became less sublimated, and in the 1970s, when Hammer was struggling to survive economically, became exploitation fare in films such as *Lust for a Vampire* (1970).

In the early 1980s videotapes were the subject of a moral panic. Urged on by campaigners such as Mary Whitehouse:

> The Director of Public Prosecutions issued a list of titles that were potentially actionable under the Obscene Publications Act. Publicity focused initially on *The Evil Dead* (1982). It was eventually cleared of obscenity in the courts, but the case led directly to the Video Recordings Act (1984), which required all video recordings to be certified.
>
> (Richards, 2001: 161a)

While it was an anomaly that films should be certified, but videos not, the criteria used to classify videos differed from that of cinema. The easier access for children and the different viewing conditions that would allow instant, and slow motion, replay, so allowing scenes to be played out of context, meant that classification and censorship of scenes was more severe on video.

Class-based censorship is evident in the different way in which films for different audiences are censored. For example, by the early twenty-first century the 100-year old prohibition on the erect penis in films classified for mainstream consumption (rather than as pornography, which can receive an R18 and is only available through licensed sex shops) was dropped. In addition, hardcore sex (that is, where the actors are actually having sexual intercourse and not simulating it) was passed in the arthouse *The Idiots* (*Idioterne*, Denmark–Sweden–France–Netherlands–Italy, 1998), whereas the 'not hardcore but explicit' *Showgirls* (1995), aimed at the multiplex audience, had 13 seconds taken out.

6.6 State-of-the-nation films

There are always more than one way of reading a film, and simply 'reading a nation' off a film, like Kracauer and Eisner tried to do (see 5.2), is far too reductive. However, it is possible to glean a sense of the discourses that were important at any particular moment in a nation's history from films (indeed, this also shows what discourses are important now, for if they were not, it is unlikely that an investigation into particular discourses would become relatively widely disseminated):

> films take the raw material of social history and of social discourses and process them into products which are themselves historical events and social forces.
>
> (Kellner, 1998: 355b)

The films of Pedro Almodóvar can be seen to be symptomatic of the liberation felt by many Spaniards after the death of the fascist dictator, General Franco, in 1975. In *Matador* (Spain, 1986) the shifts in gender roles in post-Franco society are shown through three male characters: the bullfighter, the policemen and a youth:

> three archetypes of Spanish machismo are subverted by the story and also structurally subservient to their female counterparts in the film.
>
> (Arroyo, 1975: 492a)

Almodóvar's films were not only important to Spaniards, his arthouse status allowed this 'new Spain' to be better understood by foreigners, or at least those who watch arthouse cinema.

Taiwan used cinema in an attempt to create an identity for itself separate from mainline China. Taiwanese New Cinema (TNC) was put to political use:

> In its concern to join the United Nations ... the Taiwanese government recognized the value of TNC as registering the name of Taiwan in the American mind.
>
> (Chen, 1998: 560b)

If, in this case, films were being used with a specific international intention, how films are actually understood is less controllable:

> films intended for one kind of (national) audience ... undergo a sea change as they cross the Atlantic and on coming back find themselves bearing the stamp of yet another cultural currency.
>
> (Elsaesser, 1994: 25a)

So *The Chant of Jimmie Blacksmith* (Australia, 1978) was a commercial failure and critically reviled in Australia, but was embraced elsewhere, particularly by the 'New York critical establishment' (O'Regan, 1996: 59). It 'returned' to Australia, garlanded with plaudits, to be re-evaluated positively domestically.

Cinema is the one medium that can directly communicate about nations to other countries (distribution allowing, of course). What constitutes national cinema is becomingly increasingly difficult to pin down, as globalization further blurs already unclear borders, and mass communications mean that space and time are collapsed into instantaneous news and cultural exchange. However, studying one's own cinema and that of others cannot but help in creating a dialogue between self and others. John Hill's conclusion is one worth bearing in mind when studying this subject:

> National identities, as with all identities, are not fixed and static... but are subject to historical change and redefinition. Nor are they, in some way, 'pure' and 'authentic' but are also involved in on-going transcultural dynamics. They do not, moreover, provide an exclusive form of identification but one which is interwoven with other forms of identity ...
>
> (Hill, 1999: 243–4)

Film and Technology

7.1 Introduction

Film was the distinctive art form of the twentieth century. While its origins lay in the Industrial Revolution of the early nineteenth century, the medium blossomed from its sideshow status in the 1900s into a global art which was consumed in cinemas and in the home. Unlike most art forms, film requires sophisticated technology both to be made and to be shown. To suggest that the history of cinema can be viewed as a history of technological improvements, such as the 'coming of sound' then the 'coming of colour', is to simplify events with hindsight. What follows intends to suggest how technological developments can affect the aesthetics of cinema.

7.2 Precursors

Thompson and Bordwell (1994) suggest that there were five requirements for the invention of cinema:

➤ an understanding of visual perception
➤ the ability to project images
➤ the ability to photograph images quickly onto a clear surface
➤ the ability to print the images onto a flexible surface
➤ the invention of the 'intermittent' mechanism on cameras and projectors.

The Phenakistoscope and Zoetrope were both forerunners of cinema in that they relied upon the 'persistence of vision' to create the illusion of movement from still images. Both these were slightly more sophisticated versions of drawing a stick person, with slightly different positions each time, on the edge of a book's pages and then flicking through the pages rapidly.

During the seventeenth century 'magic lantern' shows were very popular, with images placed on glass lantern slides. Indeed, some lantern narratives were adapted as films during the early years of cinema, for example R. W. Paul's *Buy Your Own Cherries* (1904) (Salt, 1992).

Eadweard Muybridge in 1878 photographed a running horse to illustrate how the animal ran (and thereby showed the conventional painting of horses in motion as wrong), and this required light-sensitive film. The first photograph, by Niepce in 1826, had used glass and required eight minutes to make an impression.

The 'flexible surface' did not appear until George Eastman developed rolls of sensitized film in 1888; the 'intermittent mechanism' had already been 'invented' by the sewing industry.

7.3 Projecting frames

The technology of cinema, which covers both photography and projection, obviously requires the ability to place images on a medium, such as celluloid or videotape, and the possibility of showing these images via a projector or using a television.

The template for film is the frame. Originally filmstock (that is, unexposed film) was made out of nitrate, which is highly flammable and deteriorates relatively rapidly unless carefully stored; hence many films from the first half of the twentieth century no longer exist. Since the 1950s the more stable celluloid has been used.

The design of the frame was almost 'perfected' by W. K. L. Dickson in 1891:

> Dickson cut the Eastman film into 1-inch-wide strips (roughly 35millimeters) and punched four holes on either side of each frame so that toothed gears could pull the film through the camera and Kinetoscope.
>
> (Thompson and Bordwell, 1994: 7)

The width of the film, its gauge, varies according to format. 16 mm film will only have sprocket holes on one side, while 70 mm can offer a better picture quality; the most familiar is the 35 mm of commercial cinema. While 16 mm, which used to be regularly used for independent film but has now been usurped by video, has room for a soundtrack, 35 mm offers four times the picture quality and has room for up to four soundtracks. IMAX cameras use 70 mm but run it horizontally, rather than vertically, giving the extremely large and high-quality image.

The projector's 'grippers' pull the frame into position in the projector's gate, because if the film simply ran continuously it would be projected as a blur. So each frame pauses for 1/24th of a second in the gate. To prevent the line between frames being seen, as the next frame is dragged into position, the shutter moves across the light so we cannot see the frames' movement; this causes the flicker effect that gives cinema one of its nicknames, the 'flicks'.

The psychological effect of 'the persistence of vision', which is supposed to render this succession of still images into a seamless flow, is often used to explain the phenomenon that we perceive these stills as movement. However as Bill Nichols (1981, Appendix A) shows, there is no evidence that this effect actually exists. Even at 24 frames per second (fps) it is impossible to capture each stage of a rapid movement, such as a hand waving, and there will be gaps in between each hand position. However the *phi* phenomenon creates movement:

> The brain applies the real-world laws of cause and effect to this series of stills and deduces that the hand *must have moved* from one photographed position to another.
>
> (Kawin, 1992: 28)

24 fps was the speed required for sound film. The approximately 16 fps of silent cinema did not give enough space on the film to store the sound-track. There was a time when silent films were routinely projected at 24 fps, giving people's movements the jerky look associated with pre-sound film. At 16 fps, of course, the movements are normal. It's worth noting that different frame speeds can be used for aesthetic effect. For example, over-cranking (that is, faster than 24 fps) 'plays back' as slow motion.

7.4 Aspect ratio

The standard aspect ratio in Hollywood is currently 1:1.85 (in Europe it is 1:1.66); widescreen is 1:2.35 (which was the original CinemaScope dimensions), although there are other formats. Television mimicked the Academy ratio – established in the early days of cinema – of 1:1.33; although television's ratio is normally described as 4:3, it is the same. Widescreen televisions, however, are 16:9, which 'translates' to 1.78 (so a small amount of 1:1.85 is lost).

Although widescreen formats had been experimented with as early as the late 1920s (see Salt, 1992: 208–9) it was not until 20th Century Fox introduced CinemaScope with *The Robe* (1953) that there was a significant threat to the Academy ratio.

Showing a standard film on an ordinary television in the correct frame ratio requires a letterbox – a black band above and below the picture. Obviously the bands would have to be thicker to show widescreen films correctly. Even widescreen televisions require black bands for films over 1:1.85 ratio.

Letterboxing is far preferable to 'panning and scanning', a process of adapting films for television's 4:3 frame. A 4:3 frame can only show approximately 72 per cent of 1:1.85, which means over a quarter of the frame is missing. To try to avoid losing important plot information in the film, an optical printer moves across the frame, focusing on the important action. It has been estimated that up to half of the original image is lost in the transference of a 1:1.85 film to fullscreen television; part of this is caused by pan and scan technology, the rest is caused by the transference to television technology (see King, 2002: 233–4).

Widescreen had been introduced by Hollywood in the early 1950s to offer a unique selling point for cinema in competition with television. However, by the late 1950s the major studios realized that television could offer significant cash for their films, so there was a conflict between widescreen and the small-screen demands of television. During the early 1960s the American Society of Cinematographers dreamed up the 'safe action zone', an area roughly 1:1.33 of whatever aspect ratio was being used, where all the significant action should take place. Steve Neale argues that the design of *Blade Runner* (1982) demonstrates the ubiquity of the 'safe action zone':

> the edges of the widescreen film are frequently filled with images and objects related to the film's concern … these images and objects often disappear when the film is panned and scanned … though, the configurations in which the principal characters and their actions have been placed remain intact.
>
> (Neale, 1998: 135)

The use of this zone is varied. *The Graduate* (1967), for example, uses the 'Scope dimensions of 1:2.35. In some scenes the edges are not used and so 'panned and scanned' versions do not 'chop' characters out of the scene. However, particularly when director Mike Nichols wants to emphasize the characters' isolation from one another, the whole width is utilized and someone must be lost on a 'pan and scan' version.

Uncertainty as to whether a director is using a 'safe action zone' can lead to confusion in understanding. For example, the ending of *Great Expectations* (1998) shows the central characters (played by Ethan Hawke and Gwyneth Paltrow) holding hands in union. However, they barely fill half the cinemascope frame: is this to make sure they will be visible on a 4:3 television, or is an unbalanced composition meant to signify that their union is doomed?

The picture quality of television is obviously inferior to cinema; it offers only 625 lines of resolution in Europe, compared with cinema's equivalent of up to 4000 lines. Television, however, has not simply had a deleterious affect on film. For example, technical developments in the medium have benefited film:

> the use of 'non-classical' techniques such as rack-focus [where the focus is abruptly changed between objects in the frame], overlapping sound, and, particularly, the zoom which were adopted by television in the interests of speed and cost... became commonplace in filmmaking practice.
>
> (Hill, 1998: 608a)

Film aesthetics cannot be divorced from technology, and other major influences on what is seen when a film is shown are the lens and filmstock used – see also 1.4.

7.5 Lenses and filmstock

In order to shoot in very low light levels a small f-stop can be used, combined with fast (more light-sensitive) filmstock. Changing the f-stop will alter the depth of field; the lower it is, the shallower the depth. In order to get the characteristic deep-focus look of *Citizen Kane* (1941), cinematographer Gregg Toland:

> Used a wide-angle lens, set it at a narrow [that is, high f-stop] aperture, and had to increase the amount of light on the set in order to compensate for that aperture; his work was facilitated by the introduction of new, high-powered arc lights and more sensitive filmstock.
>
> (Kawin, 1992: 138)

Filters can be used to reduce the amount of light reaching the film. For example, 'day for night' shooting will use filters, as well as exposure times and printing techniques, to give the appearance of darkness when the scene was filmed during the day. These scenes are not convincingly 'night-time' (they look as if they were shot under an extremely bright moon) but they do serve to signify darkness, and are much cheaper to shoot than actual night scenes.

7.6 Sound and colour

As noted in Chapter 1, 'silent cinema' was not silent as it usually had at least musical accompaniment. It was not until the late 1920s when the first viable sound-on-disc system, Vitaphone, was used for the musical accompaniment (thereby saving the cost of the orchestra) in Warner Bros's *Don Juan* (1926). *The Jazz Singer* (1927) incorporated a short dialogue sequence, in addition to Al Jolson singing, and its success led Warner Bros. to transfer all its production to the 'talkies'.

Edward Buscombe has suggested that the arrival of sound was for both economic and aesthetic reasons. In a mature oligopoly (see 3.3), one way a film studio could gain advantage over their rivals was through technical innovation:

> Such an innovation was sound, a wholly new kind of product which would make all other kinds obsolete.... No new technology can be introduced unless the economic system requires it. But a new technology cannot be successful unless it fulfils some kind of need.
>
> (Buscombe, 1985: 86–7)

In cinema this 'need' was realism, and sound could instantly reinforce the realist aesthetic. Until the 1970s, apart from some experiments such as *Fantasia* (1940), the soundscape remained resolutely monophonic.

Although most films record sound synchronously, it invariably needs to be remixed and supplemented in post-production. For example, Walter Murch describes how the fateful conversation in Coppola's *The Conversation* (1974) was re-recorded three times in another location (DVD commentary, Chapter 2). The Foley artist is responsible for sound, and works on three different tracks for sounds made by actors alone:

> The *Moves* Track is a layer of sound that recreates the clothing rustle of actors as they walk, run and move.
>
> *Feet* Track – a Foley artist is sometimes called a 'Foley Walker' or 'Stepper' because one of the most important elements we provide is the sound of the footsteps. When the original dialogue is replaced, due to noise or bad performance, the sound of the actors walking also needs to be redone.
>
> *Specific* Track – anything an actor touches or effects is considered a Specific and recorded as a separate element often involving layers of sound.
>
> (Singer, 2002)

In recent years stereo, then surround sound, systems have been developed. Dolby was among the pioneers of more three-dimensional sound systems, with less background noise. The system now consists of 15 separate tracks that are later transferred onto film. Surround sound uses multiple speaker systems that allow audio to emanate from in front of, behind, and to the side of the spectator.

Unlike sound, colour did not offer an aesthetic justification for its development:

> Color would serve only to distract the audience from those elements in the film which carried forward the narrative: acting, facial expression, 'the action'. The unity of the diegesis and the primacy of the narrative are fundamental to realist cinema. If color was seen to threaten either one it could not be accommodated.
>
> (Buscombe, 1985: 88)

This may seem to be an eccentric position, since most of us see the world in colour. However realism is a convention, and nothing to do with the 'real world'. So the early use of colour was more or less limited to genres of spectacle, such as the musical and the Western, while newsreels, gangster movies and war films were far more likely to be shot in 'realist' monochrome. This is evident in *The Wizard of Oz* (1939), where the Kansas scenes are in black and white, and Dorothy's dream of the fantasy world of Oz is in lurid Technicolor. Colour has only been used with regularity since the 1960s.

7.7 Animation

Animated film refers to numerous techniques including:

> Drawing, paint, cels, clay, plasticine, puppets and marionettes, dolls, computers, sand, glass, film footage, paper cut-outs, special effects.
>
> (O'Pray, 1998: 434a)

This can be subdivided into how they are filmed: through 'stop motion' photography, filming animated objects (such as puppets), or created using computer-generated imagery (CGI). However, it should be noted that the conventions of the latter differ from the other two because it uses the same rules as 'live action' cinema. From *Toy Story* (1995) onwards, part of the 'wow' effect of CGI cartoons has been how 'life-like' they are. Similarly, things that can move, such as people, can be filmed in such a way as to appear animated; this is 'pixillation' and is used in Norman McLaren's *Neighbours* (Canada, 1952). In addition, it is possible to mix the different forms of animation, as well as integrating it with live action (see *King Kong*, 1933).

The popularity of CGI animation may see the demise of cel animation, which was made extremely popular by Walt Disney, whose first feature was *Snow White and the Seven Dwarfs* (1937). For cel animation the background is drawn on one transparency and the movement is placed on top of it, ensuring a consistent background. For many the height of cel animation can be seen in Hanna-Barbera's *Tom and Jerry* and Warner Bros's *Looney Tunes*, where Tex Avery – among others – offered an antidote to the saccharine of Disney with the acerbic wit of such characters as Bugs Bunny, Daffy Duck and Sylvester (all voiced by Mel Blanc). These short cartoons were shown as part of cinema programmes, which would often include two features as well as newsreels.

'Direct animation' refers to films made without a camera, where images are painted, or scratched, directly onto the frame. This technique has been exploited by avant-garde (see 5.3) filmmakers such as Stan Brakhage.

7.8 Special effects

Special effects have been a selling point for films since Georges Méliès' concoctions. Méliès could turn a bus into a horse by simply stopping the camera (that is, editing in camera). The use of matte photography allowed him greater sophistication. In brief, matte photography allows the filmmaker to combine two separately filmed images. For example footage of a big 'creepy-crawly' spider was combined with a shot of James Bond (Sean Connery) looking anxious at something crawling up his body in an assassination attempt in *Dr No* (UK, 1962).

Models are also an extremely effective special effect. For example, in *Blade Runner* (1982) the Los Angeles of the opening shot was only 13 feet by 18 feet wide. Forced perspective (used to give full-grown actors the stature of hobbits in *The Lord of the Rings* series, 2001–3), gave the sense of depth and the:

> Front-projection (an effects procedure in which an image or background is 'front projected' onto a highly reflective screen), was used to produce the sulphurous flames writing and spewing from the landscape's industrial towers.

> (Sammon, 1996: 231)

The growth of CGI (computer generated images) has been fuelled by the decrease in computing costs and the increase in power. Computers deal in digital data while film, where the image on the celluloid looks like what it is representing, is analogue:

> The difference between the two ... is that whereas the photographic record automatically assumes a referent, an original object whose image has been captured by light passing through a camera lens and altering the chemical make-up of a strip of celluloid, a digital image need have no such referent.
>
> (Allen, 2002: 110)

The rendering of the fabricated digital image has become more sophisticated: compare the leap in verisimilitude between the first two *Toy Story* films (1995/1999) and with *Monsters Inc.* (2001), all Pixar productions. In the latter movie the fur on Sulley is breathtakingly detailed, just as is the CGI Gollum who splashes through puddles alongside the live-action characters in *The Lord of the Rings: The Two Towers* (2002). Gollum is a visible special effect while the splashes he makes are invisible:

> Practitioners of the special effects industry distinguish between invisible and visible special effects. Invisible special effects, which constitute up to 90 per cent of the work of the special effects industry, stimulate events in the actual world that are too expensive or inconvenient to produce.... Visible special effects, on the other hand, simulate events that are impossible in the real world (but which are possible in an alternative world), such as the dinosaurs in *Jurassic Park* and *The Lost World*.
>
> (Elsaesser and Buckland, 2002: 210)

Elsaesser and Buckland focus on the 'visible' special effects, which work, like continuity editing, to render the construction of the effect *in*visible. Using Bazin's theory of realism, they demonstrate how important it is for the rendered dinosaurs to appear in the same shot as the undoubtedly existing actors. Realism is then signified by *mise en scène* rather than editing.

They also note the importance of camera movement in special effects shots. Whereas special effects in classical cinema were limited to the use of a static camera, for such things as matte shots, the ability to move the camera – implying three-dimensional space – 'creates both ontological realism and dramatic realism' (Elsaesser and Buckland, 2002: 214). In other words, the scene both looks real and does not limit the film's dramatic devices. They cite *Who Framed Roger Rabbit?* (1988) as the breakthrough movie for this technique; the effects were created by George Lucas's Industrial Light and Magic (ILM). Lucas's *Star Wars* (1977) also featured breakthrough special effects using a moving camera, although this film used models.

The other crucial breakthrough, seen in *Jurassic Park* (1993), is motion blur. Stop-motion animation, the staple technique for creating dinosaurs before the digital era, cannot show motion blur, which 'reinforces the impression that digital and analogue events take place in the same unified space and diegesis' (Elsaesser and Buckland, 2002: 210).

Elsaesser and Buckland's 'analogue event' refers to the pro-filmic existence of, for instance, actors; the digital effects are added in post-production. However, with digital cameras the pro-filmic event is immediately digitized. The creators of digital cameras have strived to make their instruments mimic analogue cameras; they have recently been able to show the apparently backward movement of a rapidly forward moving wheel's spokes.

Since the early days of cinema the tension between film as a realist medium and one that can make the fantastic appear real has been evident. The first public screenings by Louis Lumière took place in Paris 1895, and were images of real people leaving the factory or a train entering a station; a few years later Georges Méliès was producing *A Voyage to the Moon* (1902). Although to today's eyes the special effects of Méliès' work look risible we must bear in mind that – in one hundred years' time – *Hulk* (2003) is likely to look similarly pathetic. The point was that audiences at the time, suspending their disbelief, could see a journey to the moon, which was impossible. On the other hand, famously, the audiences ducked for cover as the Lumières' train entered the station in all too real a fashion.

Although not all special effects are concerned with showing the impossible, those that do (such as the dinosaurs of the *Jurassic Park* films) are likely to generate the 'wow' response from audiences. This was certainly the effect, one that Spielberg was obviously angling for, in the first of the series:

> In the first scene in which one of the much-anticipated computer-generated dinosaurs is finally unveiled – both to the characters in the film and the audience in the cinema – the narrative all but comes to [a] halt, the music gradually builds, and shots of character reacting to the appearance of the dinosaur with wonder and amazement are interspersed with long takes displaying the computer-generated brachiosaur centre-screen.
>
> (Pierson, 1999: 167)

This pause in narrative flow works against the conventions of classical narrative, where the progression of the plot is deemed paramount. In this sense films' special effects can be seen to be similar to the musical numbers in musicals, where the narrative is momentarily halted for the performance. However, the narrative is rarely brought to a complete standstill. In musicals the numbers usually help the narrative advance, albeit by using excessive techniques to do so.

There can be little doubt that special effects teams, and effects houses, will continue to have a major influence on Hollywood blockbuster production. The special effects supervisors will work on films at their inception to make sure that it is possible to render the effects required by the script properly.

7.9 Digital distribution

As noted in the above section, the digitization of the image has had a massive impact on special effects. However its influence is wider. Even films that use traditional celluloid are edited digitally, which is much faster than analogue (linear) editing. Digital cameras can now offer the same image quality as analogue: *Star Wars: The Attack of the Clones (2002)* was wholly filmed digitally. More importantly, digital cameras are lightweight compared with their analogue counterparts, and require fewer crew, so shooting can be done much more quickly. Director Michael Winterbottom's ability to make a film a year is due primarily to using digital technology.

There is no doubt that digitization will have a dramatic effect on the distribution of film, although when this will happen is uncertain. If a cinema has a digital projector (which, at the time of writing, is far more expensive than a 35 mm projection system), there is no need to distribute a print, as the film can be sent to the theatre via satellite or fibre-optic line. After the investment in equipment, this is far cheaper, and it also reduces the:

> Wear and tear that is common with film prints, with fewer scratches and less dust. In addition, multi-language audio tracks become possible, as well as simultaneous worldwide release dates. Distributors would be able to move poorly performing films more easily or possibly alter or re-edit films during their theatrical runs.
> (Wasko, 2002: 203)

The major studios, however, are reluctant to transfer to digital partly because of their fear of piracy, as digital films are easier to copy and can be distributed in a pristine form. Also they do not wish to pay for the conversion to digital projection. The exhibitors do not think they should foot the bill, hence the uncertainty as to when transferring extremely expensive prints around the world will end.

The studios' record at embracing new technology, with the possible exception of sound, is pretty miserable, so they will probably be forced into the change at some point. In Brazil there are very few cinemas (one per 100,000 people compared with one per 20,000 in the UK) and distribution is very expensive (because the country is large and it is priced in US dollars). However, the development of Mpeg4 (the motion picture expert group's fourth compression system) allowed, in 2003, a much cheaper form of distribution. Using Mpeg4, a 90-minute film in high definition can be compressed into about seven gigabytes. The quality is not as good as Mpeg2, but to the untrained eye is as good as 35 mm. The majors are resistant to Mpeg4 because since it is cheaper, uses smaller files and is easier to manipulate, the risk of piracy is seen as greater (Bellos, 2003: 21).

Film is a technological medium, although its meaning is determined by the social context of both the makers and the audience. Technology can set a limit to what films can do at any particular time, and it is important to be aware of such constraints. Looking to the future, a satisfactory 3D system has yet to be developed and advances in CGI will no doubt continue. However, the technology will always require the vision of filmmakers to weld script, performance and look together (although actors may be dispensed with in favour of cheaper and less irascible virtual thespians – see the film *SimOne*, 2002).

7.10 Conclusion

Films can entertain and help give us a sense of our, and others', place in this world. They can offer information, in both fiction and non-fiction form, and give us something to talk about with our friends, whether we are sharing pleasures or arguing about the relative merits of a movie. Such is the power of certain films that they can even unify a whole generation in a (sort of) collective memory. It is likely that there are now more people who remember the first time they saw the opening shot of *Star Wars* (1977) than those who remember where they where when they heard John F. Kennedy was assassinated! Indelible moments can, of course, also be personal: for me the memory of the alien's first appearance in *Alien* (1979) is as clear as yesterday (a patron nearby immediately walked out).

Although some critics (such as David Thomson) believe that contemporary cinema cannot reach the heights of the past, not a year passes without great films being released. Hence film studies have a constant flow of artefacts to integrate into the subject, and these films, in turn, can modify theoretical ideas. These new ways of seeing film can then be applied to 'canon', and so old films can be 'refreshed'. The pattern is potentially never-ending.

With its multimedia basis, consisting of sound, music and vision, film, particularly in the communal theatre, has the ability to create an indelible experience. Its ubiquity exceeds that of any other medium, and it can be experienced all around the world (unlike dramatic theatre, where every performance is unique). This is not to claim that film is the superior art form, but simply to stress that the richness of cinema, which this book only suggests at, is such that we could spend a lifetime indulging ourselves in its grasp.

# Bibliography

Alexander, K. (2000) 'Black British cinema in the '90s: going, going, gone', in R. Murphy (ed.), *British Cinema in the 90s*, London: British Film Institute.

Allen, M. (2002) 'The impact of digital technologies on film aesthetics', in D. Harries (ed.), *The New Media Book*, London: British Film Institute.

Allen, R. C. (1999) 'Home Alone together: Hollywood and the "family film"', in M. Stokes and R. Maltby (eds), *Identifying Hollywood's Audiences: Cultural Identity and the Movies*, London: British Film Institute.

Allen, M. (2003) *Contemporary US Cinema*, Harlow: Pearson Education.

Althusser, L. (1971) *Lenin and Philosophy and Other Essays*, New York and London: Monthly Review Press.

Althusser, L. (1971a) 'Ideology and ideological state apparatuses (notes towards an Investigation)', in Althusser (1971).

Altman, R. (ed.) (1992) *Sound Theory Sound Practice*, New York and London: Routledge.

Altman, R. (1992a) 'Sound space', in Altman (1992).

Altman, R. (1999) *Film/Genre*, London: British Film Institute.

Anderson, B. (1991) *Imagined Communities: Reflections on the Origin and Spread of Nationalism*, 2nd edn, London and New York: Verso.

Anderson, L. (1957) 'Get out and push!', in T. Maschler (ed.), *Declaration*, London: Macgibbon & Kee.

Appiah, K. A. (1993) 'No bad nigger', in M. Garber, J. Matlock and R. L. Walkovwitz (eds), *Media Spectacles*, London and New York: Routledge.

Arijon, D. (1976) *Grammar of the Film Language*, Los Angeles: Silman-James Press.

Armes, R. (1987) *Third World Film Making and the West*, Berkeley and Los Angeles: University of California Press.

Arroyo, J. (1998) 'Pedro Almodóvar', in J. Hill and P. C. Gibson (eds), *The Oxford Guide to Film Studies*, Oxford and New York: Oxford University Press.

Auerbach, E. (trans. Willard R. Trask) (1953) *Mimesis: The Representation of Reality in Western Literature*, Princeton, N.J.: Princeton University Press.

Auty, M. (1980) 'Imitation of Life', *The Movie*, No. 52.

Balazs, B. (1979) 'The close-up', in G. Mast and M. Cohen (eds), *Film Theory and Criticism: Introductory Readings*, 2nd edn, New York and Oxford: Oxford University Press.

Balio, T. (ed.) (1976) *The American Film Industry*, Madison: University of Wisconsin Press.

Balio, T. (1998) '"A major presence in all of the world's important markets": the globalization of Hollywood in the 1990s', in S. Neale and M. Smith (eds), (1998) *Contemporary Hollywood Cinema*, London and New York: Routledge.

Banker, A. (2001) *Bollywood*, Harpenden, Herts: Pocket Essentials.

Barbas, S. (2001) *Movie Crazy: Fans, Stars and the Cult of Celebrity*, New York and Basingstoke: Palgrave Macmillan.

Barber, M. (2002) *Miami Herald*, Friday, August 9, 2002 – www.rotten tomatoes.com/click/movie-1115429/reviews.php?critic=columns& sortby=default&page=1&rid=753034, accessed October 2003

Bardin, B. (2002) 'Who says comedy can't be pretty?', www.premiere.com/ premiere/features/diaz1 accessed October 2002

Barker, M. (1993) 'Sex, violence and videotape', *Sight and Sound*, Vol. 3, No. 5.

Barlet, O. (trans. C. Turner) (2000) *African Cinemas: Decolonizing the Gaze*, London and New York: Zed.

Barna, Y. (1973) *Eisenstein*, London: Secker and Warburg.

Barnouw, E. (1993) *Documentary: A History of the Non-Fiction Film*, 2nd rev. edn, New York and Oxford: Oxford University Press.

Barr, C. (1977) *Ealing Studios*, London: Cameron and Tayleur.

Barrett, M., Corrigan, P., Kuhn, A. and Wolff, J. (1979) *Ideology and Cultural Production*, London: Croom Helm.

Barsacq, L. (1976) *Caligari's Cabinet and Other Grand Illusions: A History of Film Design*, rev. and ed. E. Stein; trans. M. Bullock, New York and Scarborough, Ontario: New American Library.

Barthes, R. (1977) *Image-Music-Text*, Glasgow: Fontana.

Barthes, R. (1990) *S/Z*, London and New York: Blackwell.

Basinger, J. (1993) *A Woman's View: How Hollywood Spoke to Women 1930–1960*, London: Chatto & Windus.

Baudry, J.-L. (1985) 'Ideological effects of the basic cinematic apparatus', in B. Nichols, *Movies and Methods Volume 2*, Berkeley, Los Angeles and London: University of California Press.

Baxter, J. (1994) *Bunuel*, London: Fourth Estate.

Bazin, A. (1967) *What is Cinema? Volume 1*, sel. and trans. H. Gray, Berkeley and Los Angeles: University of California Press.

Bazin, A. (1967a) 'The evolution of film language', in Bazin (1967).

Bazin, A. (1967b) 'The ontology of the photographic image', in Bazin (1967).

Bellos, A. (2003) 'The main attraction', *Guardian* Online, 4 Dec.

Bellour, R. (2002) *The Analysis of Film*, Bloomington and Indianapolis: Indiana University Press.

Benjamin, W. (1979) 'The work of art in the age of mechanical reproduction', in G. Mast and M. Cohen (eds), *Film Theory and Criticism: Introductory Readings*, New York and Oxford: Oxford University Press.

Berger, A. A. (1992) *Popular Culture Texts: Theories and Texts*, Newbury Park, Calif., London and New Delhi: Sage.

Berger, A. A. (1997) *Narratives in Popular Culture, Media, and Everyday Life*, Newbury Park, Calif., London and New Delhi: Sage.

Berger, J. (1990) *Ways of Seeing*, London: Penguin.

Bhaba, H. (1994) *The Location of Culture*, London and New York: Routledge.

Biskind, P. (1998) *Easy Riders Raging Bulls: How the Sex 'n' Drugs Generation Saved Hollywood,* London: Bloomsbury.

Block, A. B. (1999) 'Come to the Balkan cabaret', www.ifmagazine. com/common/articleNonInlineImages.asp?articleID=311 accessed February 2004: *If*, issue 6, 8 June.

Blumler, J and Katz, E. (1974) *The Uses of Mass Communication*, Beverley Hills: Sage.

Bogle, D. (2002) *Toms, Coons, Mulattoes, Mannies, and Bucks: An Interpretive History of Blacks in American Films*, 4th edn, New York and London: Continuum.

Boorman, J. and Donohue, W. (eds) (1994) *Projections 3: Film-makers on Film-making*, London and Boston: Faber and Faber.

Bordwell, D. (1985) *Narration in the Fiction Film*, Madison: University of Wisconsin Press.

Bordwell, D. (2003) 'Technology and technique: Hollywood, Hong Kong, and the emergence of contemporary film style', www.info. gov.hk/sfaa/Form/sgl/Manuscripts/11%20-%20Bordwell.doc accessed December 2003.

Bordwell, D. and Thompson, K. (1979) *Film Art: An Introduction*, Reading, Menlo Park, London, Amsterdam, Don Mills and Sydney: Addison-Wesley.

Bordwell, D. and Carroll, N. (1996) *Post-Theory: Reconstructing Film Studies*, Madison and London: University of Wisconsin Press.

Bordwell, D., Staiger, J. and Thompson, K. (1985) *The Classical Hollywood Cinema*, New York: Columbia University Press.

Bordwell, D. and Thompson, K. (1993) *Film Art*, 4th edn, New York: McGraw-Hill.

Bosley, R. K. (2003) 'Native sons', American Cinematographer, January. http://www.theasc.com/magazine/jan03/native/index.html accessed May 2003.

Bourdieu, P. (1984) *Distinction: A Social Critique of the Judgement of Taste*, London and New York: Routledge.

Branigan, E. (1992) *Narrative Comprehension and Film*, London and New York: Routledge.

Branston, G. and Stafford, R. (2003) *The Media Student's Book*, 3rd edn, London and New York: Routledge.

Braudy, L. and Dickstein, M. (eds) (1978) *Great Film Directors: A Critical Anthology*, New York: Oxford University Press.

Brignell, J. (2003) *An Introduction to Television Studies*, London and New York: Routledge.

Brookner, W. (ed.) (2005) *The Blade Runner Experience*, London: Wallflower Press.

Brown, G. (2001) 'Something for everyone: British film culture in the 1990s', in R. Murphy (ed.), *The British Cinema Book*, London: British Film Institute.

Bruzzi, S. (2000) *New Documentary: A Critical Introduction*, London and New York: Routledge.

Buckland, W. (2003) 'The role of the auteur in the age of the blockbuster; Steven Spielberg and DreamWorks', in J. Stringer (ed.), *Movie Blockbusters*, London and New York: Routledge.

Buscombe, E. (1985) 'Sound and colour', in Nichols (ed.), *Movies and Methods Volume 2*, Berkeley, Los Angles and London: University of California Press.

Butler, J. (1999) *Gender Trouble*, London and New York: Routledge.

Byars, J. (1991) *All That Hollywood Allows: Re-Reading Gender in 1950s Melodrama*, London: Routledge.

Carney, R. (1994) *The Films of John Cassavetes: Pragmatism, Modernism, and the Movies*, New York and London: Cambridge University Press.

Carnicke, S. M. (1999) 'Lee Strasberg's paradox of the actor', in A. Lovell and P. Kramer (eds), *Screen Acting*, London and New York: Routledge.

Carr, E. H. (1964) *What is History?*, Harmondsworth: Penguin.

Carroll, N. (1996) 'Prospects for film theory: a personal assessment', in D. Bordwell and N. Carroll (eds), *Post-Theory: Reconstructing Film Studies*, Madison and London: University of Wisconsin Press.

Caughie, J. (ed.) (1981) *Theories of Authorship*, London and New York: Routledge.

Cawelti, J. G. (1976) *Adventure, Mystery, and Romance*, Chicago and London: University of Chicago Press.

Chen, K.-H., (1998) 'Taiwanese new cinema', in J. Hill and P. C. Gibson (eds), *The Oxford Guide to Film Studies*, Oxford and New York: Oxford University Press.

Cherry, B. (1999) Refusing to refuse to look: female viewers of the horror film', in M. Stokes and R. Maltby (eds), *Identifying Hollywood's Audiences: Cultural Identity and the Movies*, London: British Film Institute.

Chibnall, S. and Hunter, I. Q. (1999–2002) *British Popular Cinema Series*, London and New York: Routledge.

Clover, C. J. (1993) *Men, Women and Chainsaws: Gender in the Modern Horror Film,* London: British Film Institute.

Coad, M. (1981) 'Cinema novo', *The Movie*, No. 70.

Cohan, S. and Hark, I. R. (eds) (1993) *Screening the Male: Exploring Masculinities in Hollywood Cinema*, London and New York: Routledge.

Collins, J., Radners, H. and Collins, A. P. (1993) *Film Theory Goes to the Movies*, New York and London: Routledge.

Comolli, J.-L. and Narboni, P. (2000) 'Cinema/ideology/criticism', in J. Hollows, P. Hutchings and M. Jancovich (eds), *The Film Studies Reader*, London and New York: Arnold.

Conant, M. (1976) 'The impact of the Paramount decrees', in T. Balio, *The American Film Industry*, Madison: University of Wisconsin Press.

Cook, P. (ed.) (1985) *The Cinema Book*, London: British Film Institute.

Cook, P and Bernink, M. (eds) (1999) *The Cinema Book*, 2nd edn, London: British Film Institute.

Cornelius, S. with Smith, I. H. (2002) *New Chinese Cinema: Challenging Representations*, London: Wallflower Press.

Creed, B. (1993) *The Monstrous Feminine: Film, Feminism, Psychoanalysis*, London and New York: Routledge.

Cripps, T. (1977) *Slow Fade to Black: The Negro in American Film 1900–1942*, London, Oxford and New York: Oxford University Press.

Croce, A. (1978) '*The 400 Blows*: a review', in L. Braudy and M. Dickstein (eds), *Great Film Directors: A Critical Anthology*, New York: Oxford University Press.

Crofts, S. (1998) 'Concepts of national cinema', in J. Hill and P. C. Gibson (eds), *The Oxford Guide to Film Studies*, Oxford and New York: Oxford University Press.

Crowdus, G. and Georgakas, D. (2001) 'Thinking about the power of images: an interview with Spike Lee', *Cineaste*, Vol. 26, No. 2.

Cubitt, S. (1999) 'Introduction. Le reel, c'est l'impossible: the sublime time of special effects', *Screen*, Vol. 40, No. 2, Summer.

Curran, J., Morley, D. and Walkerdine, V. (eds) (1996) *Cultural Studies and Communications*, London: Arnold.

Dahlberg, A. (2003) 'Film as social catalyst: Ousmane Sembene's *Borom Sarret'*, www.brightlightsfilm.com/42/borom.htm accessed January 2004; *Bright Lights Film Journal*, Issue No. 42, November.

Davis, J. (1995) 'Gender, ethnicity and cultural crisis in *Falling Down* and *Groundhog Day'*, *Screen*, Vol. 36, No. 3 Autumn.

Davies, J. and Smith, C. R. (1997) *Gender, Ethnicity and Sexuality in Contemporary American Film*, Edinburgh: Keele University Press.

Davis, M. (1998) *City of Quartz: Excavating the Future in Los Angeles*, London, Sydney, Auckland and Parktown: Pimlico.

Dayan, D. (1976) 'The tutor-code of classical cinema', in B. Nichols (ed.), *Movies and Methods Volume 1*, Berkeley, Los Angeles and London; University of California Press.

de Lauretis, T. (1985) *Alice Doesn't: Feminism, Semiotics, Cinema*, Bloomington: Indiana University Press.

Deleuze, G. (1986) *Cinema 1: The Movement Image*, London: Athlone Press.

Deleuze, G. (1989) *Cinema 2: The Time Image*, London: Athlone Press.

Dirlik, A. (1997) 'The postcolonial aura: third world criticism in the age of global capitalism', in P. Mongia (ed.), *Contemporary Postcolonial Theory: A Reader*, London and New York: Arnold.

Dixon, W. W. (1997) *The Films of Jean-Luc Godard*, Albany: State University of New York Press.

Doane, M. A. (1982) 'Film and the masquerade: theorising the female spectator', *Screen*, Vol. 23, Nos. 3–4, Sept/Oct.

Doane, M. A. (1987) *The Desire to Desire: The Woman's Film of the 1940s*, Basingstoke and London: Macmillan Press.

Doty, A. (1998) 'Queer theory', in J. Hill and P. C. Gibson (eds), *The Oxford Guide to Film Studies*, Oxford and New York: Oxford University Press.

Dyer, R. (1979) *Stars*, London: British Film Institute.

Dyer, R. (1986) *Heavenly Bodies: Film Stars and Society*, Basingstoke and London: Macmillan Press.

Dyer, R. (1992) *Only Entertainment*, London and New York: Routledge.

Dyer, R. (1993) *A Matter of Images: Essays on Representation*, London and New York: Routledge.

Dyja, E. (ed.) (2003) *BFI Film and Television Handbook 2004*, London: British Film Institute.

Eagles, B. (2002) 'Taking the breaks off', www.hk.law.co.uk/articles/article10.html, accessed February 2004.

Eagleton, T. (1983) *Literary Theory: An Introduction*, Oxford and Cambridge: Blackwell.

Eaton, M. and Neale, S. (eds) (1981) *Screen Reader 2: Cinema and Semiotics*, London: Society for Education in Film and Television.

Editors of Cahiers du Cinema (1976) 'John Ford's Young Mr. Lincoln', in B. Nichols (ed.), *Movies and Methods Volume 1*, Berkeley, Los Angeles and London: University of California Press.

Eig, J. (2003) 'A beautiful mind(fuck): Hollywood structures of identity', www.ejumpcut.org/currentissue/eig.mindfilms/, accessed March 2004,

Eisenstein, S. (1979) 'A dialectical approach to film form', in G. Mast and M. Cohen (eds), *Film Theory and Criticism: Introductory Readings*, New York and Oxford: Oxford University Press.

Eisenstein, S. (1968) *The Battleship Potemkin*, Lorimar Publishing.

Eisner, L. (1969) *The Haunted Screen: Expressionism in the German Cinema and the Influence of Max Rheinhardt*, trans. R. Greaves, London: Thames and Hudson.

Elsaesser, T. (1985) ' Tales of sound and fury: observations on the family melodrama', in B. Nichols (ed.) (1985) *Movies and Methods Volume 2*, Berkeley, Los Angeles and London: University of California Press.

Elsaesser, T. (1987) 'Tales of sound and fury: observations on the family melodrama', in C. Gledhill (ed.), *Home is Where the Heart Is: Studies in Melodrama and the Woman's Film*, London: British Film Institute.

Elsaesser, T. (ed.) (1990) *Early Cinema: Space, Frame, Narrative,* London: British Film Institute.

Elsaesser, T. (1994) 'Putting on a show: the European art movie', *Sight and Sound*, Vol. 4, No. 4, April.

Elsaesser, T. (1996) *Fassbinder's Germany: History, Identity, Subject*, Amsterdam: Amsterdam University Press.

Elsaesser, T. (1999) *The BFI Companion to German Cinema*, London: British Film Institute.

Elsaesser, T. and Buckland, W. (2002) *Studying Contemporary American Film: A Guide to Movie Analysis*, London and New York: Arnold.

Eyles, A. (1979) 'Warner Brothers present…', *The Movie*, No. 1.

Fanon, F. (1967) *The Wretched of the Earth*, London, New York, Ringwood, Toronto, New Delhi, Albany and Rosebank: Penguin.

Felperin, L. (2003) '*Master and Commander: The Far Side of the World*', *Sight and Sound*, Vol. 14, No. 1, Jan.

Feng, P. X. (2002) 'False and double consciousness: race, virtual reality and the assimilation of Hong Kong action cinema in "The Matrix"' in Z. Sardar and S. Cubitt (eds), *Aliens R Us: The Other in Science Fiction Cinema*, London and Sterling: Pluto.

Film Action website (2003) 'The stars are making lots more than you think', www.filmaction.com/hollywood.

Fischer, P. (2001) 'Charlie's Angel heads to Tom's *Vanilla Sky*', www.darkhorizons.com/2001/VanillaSky.htm, accessed October 2002.

Fleming, C. (1999) *High Concept: Don Simpson and the Hollywood Culture of Excess*, London: Bloomsbury.

Fleming, M. (1999) 'Unwrapping "The Mummy"', *Movieline*, May.

Forbes, J. (1998) 'The French nouvelle vague', in J. Hill and P. C. Gibson (eds), *The Oxford Guide to Film Studies*, Oxford and New York: Oxford University Press.

Forde, L. (2003) 'UK p&a spend climbs to record levels', www.ScreenDaily.com, 17 March.

Forster, E. M. (2000) *Aspects of the Novel*, London: Penguin.

Foucault, M. (1991) 'What is an author?', in P. Rabinow (ed.), *The Foucault Reader: An Introduction to Foucault's Thought*, London: Penguin.

Frater, P. (2003) 'Global film industry losing up to $3.5bn from piracy', www.ScreenDaily.com, 6 June.

Fricker, K. (2004) 'Philistines all', *Guardian Review*, 14 Feb.

Fuery, P. (2000) *New Developments in Film Theory*, Basingstoke: Macmillan.

Furness, R. S. (1973) *Expressionism*, London: Methuen.

Gabriel, T. H. (1989) 'Towards a critical theory of third world films', in J. Pines and P. Willeman (eds), *Questions of Third Cinema*, London: British Film Institute.

Garber, M., Matlock, J. and Walkowitz, R. L. (eds), (1993) *Media Spectacles*, London and New York: Routledge.

Gibbs, J. (2002) *Mise en Scène: Film Style and Interpretation*, London and New York: Wallflower Press.

Gibson, P. C. (2000) 'Fewer weddings and more funerals: changes in the heritage film', in J. Hill and P. C. Gibson (eds), *The Oxford Guide to Film Studies*, Oxford and New York: Oxford University Press.

Gittings, C. E. (2002) *Canadian National Cinema*, London and New York: Routledge.

Gledhill, C. (1985) 'The western', in P. Cook, *The Cinema Book*, London: British Film Institute.

Gledhill, C. (ed.) (1987) *Home Is Where the Heart Is: Studies in Melodrama and the Woman's Film*, London: British Film Institute.

Gledhill, C. and Williams, L. (eds) (2000) *Reinventing Film Studies*, London and New York: Arnold.

Gledhill, C. (2000a) 'Rethinking genre', in C. Gledhill and L. Williams (eds), *Reinventing Film Studies*, London and New York: Arnold.

Gomery, D. (1992) *Shared Pleasures: A History of Movie Presentation in the United States*, Madison: University of Wisconsin Press.

Gomery, D. (1998) 'Hollywood corporate business practice and periodizing contemporary film history', in P. Neale and M. Smith (eds), *Contemporary Hollywood Cinema*, London and New York: Routledge.

Gomery, D. (1998a) *Media in America: The Wilson Quarterly Reader*, rev. edn, Washington D.C.: Woodrow Wilson Centre Press.

Gomery, D. (1998b) 'Hollywood's business today' in Gomery (1998a).

Gorbman, C. (1998) 'Film music', in J. Hill and P. C. Gibson (eds), *The Oxford Guide to Film Studies*, Oxford and New York: Oxford University Press.

Goulding, D. J. (1997) 'East Central European cinema: two defining moments', in J. Hill and P. C. Gibson (eds), *The Oxford Guide to Film Studies*, Oxford and New York: Oxford University Press.

Grant, B. K. (1995) *Film Genre Reader*, 2nd edn, Austin: University of Texas Press.

Gray, B. (2003) '"X2" unites 3,741 theaters in record bow', www.ScreenDaily.com, 1 May.

Greimas, A. J. (1970) *Du Sens*, Paris: Editions du Seuil.

Guerrero, E. (ed.) (2001) *Do The Right Thing*, London: British Film Institute.

Gunning, T. (1990a) 'Non-continuity, continuity, discontinuity: a theory of genres in early films', in T. Elsaesser (ed.), *Early Cinema: Space, Frame, Narrative*, London: British Film Institute.

Gunning, T. (1990b) 'The cinema of attractions: early film, its spectators and the avant-garde', in T. Elsaesser (ed.), *Early Cinema: Space, Frame, Narrative*, London: British Film Institute.

Gunning, T. (1990c) 'Weaving a narrative: style and economic background in Griffith's Biograph films', in T. Elsaesser (ed.), *Early Cinema: Space, Frame, Narrative*, London: British Film Institute.

Hall, S. (1992) 'Encoding/ecoding', in Hall, Hobson, Lowe and Willis (1992).

Hall, S., Hobson, D., Lowe, A. and Willis, P. (1992) *Culture, Media, Language*, London and New York: Routledge.

Hallam, J. with Marshment, M. (2000) *Realism and Popular Cinema*, Manchester and New York: Manchester University Press.

Hames, P. (1981) 'Clear skies... for a while', *The Movie*, No. 66.

Hare, D. (2003) 'Made in the UK', www.guardian.co.uk/arts/friday review/story/0,12102,880587,00.html, accessed Feb. 2004.

Hark, I. R. (ed.) (2002) *Exhibition: The Film Reader*, London and New York: Routledge.

Harries, D. (ed.) (2002) *The New Media Book*, London: British Film Institute.

Harvey, D. (1990) *The Condition of Postmodernity*, Cambridge and Oxford: Blackwell.

Harvey, S. (1980) *May '68 and Film Culture*, London: British Film Institute.

Hawkes, T. (1977) *Structuralism and Semiotics*, London and New York: Routledge.

Hayward, S. (2000) *Cinema Studies: The Key Concepts*, London and New York: Routledge.

Heath, S. (1981) *Questions of Cinema*, London and Basingstoke: Macmillan.

Heath, S. (1981a) 'On suture', in Heath (1981).

Hedling, E. (2001) 'Lindsay Anderson and the development of British art cinema', in R. Murphy (ed.), *The British Cinema Book*, London: British Film Institute.

Henderson, B. (1976) 'Toward a non-bourgeois camera style', in B. Nichols (ed.), *Movies and Methods Volume 1*, Berkeley, Los Angeles and London: University of California Press.

Higson, A. (1989) 'The concept of national cinema', *Screen*, Vol. 30, No. 4, Winter.

Higson, A. (1997) *Waving the Flag: Constructing a National Cinema in Britain*, Oxford and New York: Clarendon Press.

Hill, A. (1997) *Shocking Entertainment: Viewer Response to Violent Movies*, Luton: John Libbey Media.

Hill, J. (1986) *Sex, Class and Realism: British Cinema 1956–1963*, London: British Film Institute.

Hill, J. (1998) 'Film and Television', in Hill and Gibson (1998).

Hill, J. (1999) *British Cinema in the 1980s*, Oxford and New York: Clarendon Press.

Hill, J. (2001) 'British cinema as national cinema: production, audience and representation', in R. Murphy (ed.), *The British Cinema Book*, London: British Film Institute.

Hill, J. and Gibson, P. C. (1998) *The Oxford Guide to Film Studies*, Oxford and New York: Oxford University Press.

Hill, L. (1996) *Easy Rider*, London: British Film Institute.

Hillier, J. (ed.) (1985) *Cahiers du Cinema; 1950s: Neo-Realism, Hollywood, New Wave Volume 1*, (trans. D, Wilson), Cambridge, Mass.: Harvard University Press.

Ho, E. Yee-Lin (2001) 'Women on the edges of Hong Kong modernity: the films of Ann Hui', in C. M. Yau (ed.), *At Full Speed: Hong Kong Cinema in a Borderless World*, Minneapolis and London: University of Minnesota Press.

Hollows, J., Hutchings, P. and Jancovich, M. (eds) (2000) *The Film Studies Reader*, London and New York: Arnold.

Hollows, J. and Jancovich, M. (eds) (1995) *Approaches to Popular Film*, Manchester and New York: Manchester University Press.

Hoppenrath, J. (1997) 'Changing stereotypes in film', http://webrum.

uni-mannheim.de/phil/trevors/StuPapers/FilmStereo.pdf, accessed Aug. 2003.

Hunter, A. (2003) 'Arthouse films benefit from Edinburgh exposure', www.ScreenDaily.com, 22 August.

Hutchings, P. (2001) 'Beyond the new wave: realism in British cinema 1959–1963', in R. Murphy (ed.), *The British Cinema Book*, London: British Film Institute.

Irwin, W. (2002) *The Matrix and Philosophy: Welcome to the Desert of the Real*, Chicago and LaSalle: Open Court.

Jacka, E. (1998) 'Australian cinema', in J. Hill and P. C. Gibson (eds), *The Oxford Guide to Film Studies*, Oxford and New York: Oxford University Press.

Jameson, F. (1991) *Postmodernism or the Cultural Logic of Late Capitalism*, London and New York: Verso.

Jameson, F. (1998) *The Cultural Turn: Selected Writings on Postmodernism 1983-1998*, London and New York: Verso.

Jameson, F. (1998a) 'Postmodernism and consumer society', in Jameson (1998).

Jancovich, M. (1995) 'Screen theory', in J. Hollows and M. Jancovich (eds), *Approaches to Popular Film*, Manchester and New York: Manchester University Press.

Jancovich, M. and Faire, L. (2003) 'The best place to see a film: the blockbuster, the multiplex, and the contexts of consumption', in J. Stringer (ed.), *Movie Blockbusters*, London and New York: Routledge.

Johnston, S. (1999) 'Structuralism and its aftermaths', in P. Cook and M. Bernink (eds), (1999) *The Cinema Book*, 2nd edn, London: British Film Institute.

Kar, L. (2001) 'An overview of Hong Kong's new wave cinema', in C. M. Yau (ed.), *At Full Speed: Hong Kong Cinema in a Borderless World*, Minneapolis and London: University of Minneapolis Press.

Kartas, G., Fielding, S. and Moylan, C. (2003) 'Fallen angels', *Sight and Sound*, Vol. 13, No. 9, Sept.

Kavanaugh, J. (1980) '"Son of a Bitch": feminism, humanism, and science in "Alien"', *October*, No 13.

Kawin, B. (1992) *How Movies Work*, Berkeley, Los Angeles and London: University of California Press.

Kay, J. (2003) 'X2 global rampage keeps pirates at bay', www.ScreenDaily.com, 6 May.

Kellner, D. (1998) 'Hollywood Film and Society', in J. Hill and P. C. Gibson (eds), *The Oxford Guide to Film Studies*, Oxford and New York: Oxford University Press.

Kemp, P. (2003) 'Whale Rider', *Sight and Sound*, Vol.13, No. 8, Aug.

Kennedy, B. M. (2002) *Deleuze and Cinema: The Aesthetics of Sensation*, Edinburgh: Edinburgh University Press.

King, G. (2002) *New Hollywood Cinema: An Introduction*, New York: Columbia University Press.

King, J. (2000) *Magical Reels: A History of Cinema in Latin America*, new edn, London and New York: Verso.

Kitses, J (2004) *Horizons West: Directing the Western from John Ford to Clint Eastwood*, new edn, London: British Film Institute.

Klady, L. (2003) 'Kulture and kommerce … kunundrum or cynergy?', http://movies.yahoo.com/news/mc/, 17 April.

Kochan, L. (1963) *The Making of Modern Russia*, Harmondsworth, New York, Ringwood, Markham and Auckland: Pelican.

Kracauer, S. (1947) *From Caligari to Hitler: A Psychological History of the German Film*, Princeton, N.J.: Princeton University Press.

Krutnik, F. (1991) *In a Lonely Street: Film Noir, Genre, Masculinity*, London and New York: Routledge.

Krutnik, F. (2002) 'Conforming passions?: contemporary romantic comedy', in S. Neale (ed.), *Genre and Contemporary Hollywood*, London: British Film Institute.

Kuhn, A. (1992) *The Power of Image: Essays on Representation and Sexuality*, London and New York: Routledge.

Kuhn, A. (1999) 'The French "nouvelle vague"', in P. Cook and M. Bernink (eds), *The Cinema Book*, 2nd edn, London: British Film Institute.

Lacan, J. (1986) *The Four Fundamental Concepts of Psycho-Analysis*, Harmondsworth, New York, Ringwood, Markham and Auckland: Peregrine.

Lacey, N. (1996) 'Pulp Fiction – Back to the Future', *Film Reader 1*, Keighley, West Yorks: itp publications (36 Hospital Rd, Keighley, West Yorks, BD21 3ND).

Lacey, N. (1998) *Image and Representation: Key Concepts in Media Studies*, Basingstoke: Palgrave.

Lacey, N. (2000) *Blade Runner*, London: York Press.

Lacey, N. (2000a) *Film Notes: The Matrix*, Keighley, West Yorks: itp publications.

Lacey, N. (2000b) 'Palace Pictures and Neil Jordan: not British cinema?', in *Film Reader 2: British Cinema*, Keighley, West Yorks: itp publications.

Lacey, N. (2001) *Se7en*, London: York Press.

Lacey, N. (2002) *Media Institutions and Audiences*, Basingstoke and New York: Palgrave.

Lacey, N. and Stafford, R. (2003) 'The sound and fury of signifiers: analysing the action film part 2', *in the picture*, No. 46, April.

Lal, B. (2003) 'Sex, history and hinglish – Bollywood's new genres', www.ScreenDaily.com, 3 March.

Langdale, (2002) *Hugo Munsterberg on Film: 'The Photoplay': A Psychological Study and Other Writings*, London and New York: Routledge.

Lapsley, R. and Westlake, M. (1988) *Film Theory: An Introduction*, Manchester: Manchester University Press.

Leung, N. K. (1998) 'China and 1997', in J. Hill and P. C. Gibson (eds), *The Oxford Guide to Film Studies*, Oxford and New York: Oxford University Press.

Linson, A. (2002) *What Just Happened? Bitter Hollywood Tales from the Front Line*, New York and London: Bloomsbury.

Look of the Con, The (2002) *Ocean's Eleven DVD extra*, New Wave Entertainment Television.

Lovell, A. and Kramer, P. (1999) *Screen Acting*, London and New York: Routledge.

MacCabe, C. (1980) *Godard: Images, Sounds, Politics*, London and Basingstoke: Macmillan Press.

Maciel, D. (1995) 'Mexican cinema in the '90s', www.sdlatinofilm.com/trends8.html, accessed Aug. 2003.

Magid, R. (2003) 'On Gangs of New York, production designer Dante Ferretti and ILM team up to transport viewers back to Manhattan's tumultuous past', http://www.theasc.com/magazine/jan03/mean/index.html#: *American Cinematographer*, January.

Mailer, N. (1968) *Advertisements for Myself*, London: Panther.

Mailer, N. (1968a) 'The white negro: superficial reflections on the hipster', in Mailer (1968).

Maltby, R. (1998) 'Nobody knows everything: post-classical historiographies an consolidated entertainment', in M. Stokes and R. Maltby (eds), *Identifying Hollywood's Audiences: Cultural Identity and the Movies*, London: British Film Institute.

Maltby, R. (1998a) '"D" for disgusting: American culture and English criticism', in G. Nowell-Smith and S. Ricci (eds), *Hollywood and Europe: Economics, Culture, National Identity 1945–95*, London: British Film Institute.

Maltby, R. (1999) 'Sticks, hicks and flaps: classical Hollywood's generic conception of its audiences', in M. Stokes and R. Maltby (eds), *Identifying Hollywood's Audiences: Cultural Identity and the Movies*, London: British Film Institute.

Maltby, R. (2001) 'The spectacle of criminality', in J. D. Slocum, *Violence and the American Cinema*, New York and London: Routledge.

Martin, A. (1992) 'Mise en scène is dead, or the expressive, the excessive, the technical and the stylish', *Continuum*, No. 5.

Maschler, T. (ed.) (1957) *Declaration*, London: Macgibbon & Kee.

Mast, G. and Cohen, M. (eds) (1979) *Film Theory and Criticisms: Introductory Readings*, 2nd edn, New York and Oxford: Oxford University Press.

Mathews, T. D. (1994) *Censored: What They Didn't Allow You to See, and Why: The Story of Film Censorship in Britain*, London: Chatto and Windus.

Matthews, P. (2001) 'Before Night Falls', *Sight and Sound*, Vol. 11, No. 6.

Mayer, D. (1972) *Eisenstein's Potemkin, A Shot-by-Shot Presentation*, Cambridge, Mass.: Da-Capo.

McArthur, C. (1980) 'Douglas Sirk's magnificent obsessions', *The Movie*, No. 52.

McCabe, C. (1974) 'Realism and the cinema: notes of some Brechtian theses', *Screen*, Vol. 15, No. 2, Summer.

McDonald, P. (1995) 'Star studies', in J. Hollows and M. Jancovich (eds), *The Film Studies Reader*, London and New York: Arnold.

McDonald, P. (2000) *The Star System: Hollywood's Production of Popular Identities*, London: Wallflower Press.

Medved, M. (1993) *Hollywood Vs America: Popular Culture and the War on Traditional Values*, London: Harper Collins.

Mellen, J. (2002) *Seven Samurai*, London: British Film Institute.

Metz, C. (1974) *Language and Cinema*, The Hague: Mouton de Gruyter.

Metz, C. (1986) *The Imaginary Signifier: Psychoanalysis and the Cinema*, Bloomington and Indianapolis: Indiana University Press.

Metz, C. (1991) *La Narration or Impersonelle, ou le Site du Film*, Paris: Klincksieck.

Milne, T. (1962) 'This Sporting Life', *Sight and Sound*, Summer 1962.

Milne, T. (1981) 'The French "nouvelle vague"', *The Movie*, No. 59.

Mishra, V. (2002) *Bollywood Cinema: Temples of Desire*, New York and London: Routledge.

Monaco, J. (1977) *The New Wave: Truffaut, Godard, Chabrol, Rohmer, Rivette*, New York: Oxford University Press.

Monaco, J. (1979) *American Film Now: The People, The Power, The Money, The Movies*, New York, London and Scarborough, Ontario: New American Library.

Mongia, P. (ed.) (1997) *Contemporary Postcolonial Theory: A Reader*, London and New York: Arnold.

Monticelli, S. (1998) 'Italian post-war cinema and neo-realism', in J. Hill and P. C. Gibson (eds), *The Oxford Guide to Film Studies*, Oxford and New York: Oxford University Press.

Moore-Gilbert, B. (1999) 'Hanif Kureishi and the politics of cultural hybridity', in J. Stokes and A. Reading (eds), *The Media in Britain: Debates and Developments*, Basingstoke, Macmillan.

Mulvey, L. (1981) 'Afterthoughts on "visual pleasure and narrative cinema" inspired by King Vidor's *Duel in the Sun*', *Framework*, Nos. 15, 16, 17.

Mulvey, L. (1987) 'Notes on Sirk and melodrama', in C. Gledhill (ed.), *Home is Where the Heart Is: Studies in Melodrama and the Woman's Film*, London: British Film Institute.

Murphy, R. (2000) *British Cinema in the 90s*, London: British Film Institute.

Murphy, R. (2001) *The British Cinema Book,* 2nd edn, London: British Film Institute.

Murphy, R. (1992) *Sixties British Cinema*, London: British Film Institute.

Neale, S. (1993) 'Masculinity as spectacle: reflections on men and mainstream cinema', in S. Cohan and I. R. Hark (eds), *Screening the Male: Exploring Masculinities in Hollywood Cinema*, London and New York: Routledge.

Neale, S. (1998) 'Widescreen composition in the age of television', in Neale and Smith (1998).

Neale, S. (2000) *Genre and Hollywood*, London and New York: Routledge.

Neale, S. (2002) 'Westerns and gangster films since the 1970s', in Neale (2002a).

Neale, S. (ed.) (2002a) *Genre and Contemporary Hollywood*, London: British Film Institute.

Neale, S and Smith, M. (1998) *Contemporary Hollywood Cinema*, London and New York: Routledge.

Nichols, B. (1976) *Movies and Methods Volume 1*, Berkeley, Los Angeles and London: University of California Press.

Nichols, B. (1981) *Ideology and the Image: Social Representation in the Cinema and Other Media*, Bloomington: Indiana University Press.

Nichols, B. (ed.) (1985) *Movies and Methods Volume 2*, Berkeley, Los Angeles and London: University of California Press.

Nichols, B. (1991) *Representing Reality*, Bloomington and Indianapolis: University of Indiana Press.

Nichols, B. (1994) *Blurred Boundaries: Questions of Meaning in Contemporary Culture*, Bloomington and Indianapolis: University of Indiana Press.

Nowell-Smith, G. (1997) *L'Avventura*, London: British Film Institute.

Nowell-Smith, G. and Ricci, S. (1998) *Hollywood and Europe: Economics, Culture, National Identity 1945–95*, London: British Film Institute.

O'Pray, M. (1998) 'The animated film', in J. Hill and P. C. Gibson (eds), *The Oxford Guide to Film Studies*, Oxford and New York: Oxford University Press.

O'Pray, M. (2003) *Avant-Garde Film: Forms, Themes and Passions*, London: Wallflower Press.

Opren, V. (2003) *Film Editing: The Art of the Expressive*, London: Wallflower Press.

O'Regan, T. (1996) *Australian National Cinema*, London and New York: Routledge.

Parrinder, P. (1980) *Science Fiction: Its Criticism and Teaching*, London and New York: Methuen.

Pearson, R. E. (1992) *Eloquent Gestures: The Transformation of Performance Style in the Griffith Biograph Films,* Berkeley: University of California Press.

Pierson, M. (1997) 'Authorship and the films of David Lynch' – chapter 3: *Blue Velvet* post-modernism and authorship, http://www.british film.org.uk/lynch/blue_velvet.html, accessed Oct. 2003.

Perkins, T. E. (1979) 'Rethinking stereotypes', in M. Barrett, P. Corrigan, A. Kuhn and J. Wolff (eds), *Ideology and Cultural Production*, London: Croom Helm.

Perkins, V. (1972) *Film As Film: Understanding and Judging Movies*, Harmondsworth, New York, Ringwood, Markham, Auckland: Penguin.

Perkins, V. (1981) 'Moments of choice', *The Movie*, No. 58.

Perkins, V. (1993) *Film As Film: Understanding and Judging Movies*, new edn, Cambridge, Mass.: Da Capo Press.

Petley, J. (1979) *Capital and Culture: German Cinema 1933–45*, London: British Film Institute.

Pierson, M. (1997) 'CGI effects in Hollywood science-fiction cinema 1989–95: the wonder years', *Screen*, Vol. 40, No. 2, Summer.

Pines, J. and Willeman, P. (1989) *Questions of Third Cinema*, London: British Film Institute.

Pire, D. (1980) *Hammer: A Cinema Case Study*, London: British Film Institute.

Pirie, D. (1996) 'Wave theory', *Sight and Sound*, Vol. 6, No. 6.

Place, J. A. and Peterson, L. S. (1985) 'Some visual motifs of film noir', in B. Nichols (ed.), *Movies and Methods Volume 2*, Berkeley, Los Angeles and London: University of California Press.

Prescod, M. (2003) 'Bringing down the cash', *bfm: black film and TV*, Summer, Vol. 5, No. 20: bfm: black film and TV.

Rabinow, P. (ed.) (1991) *The Foucault Reader: An Introduction to Foucault's Thought*, London: Penguin.

Radner, H. (1993) 'Pretty is as pretty does: free enterprise and the marriage plot', in J. Collins, H. Radner and A. P. Collins (eds), *Film Theory Goes to the Movies*, New York and London: Routledge.

Ray, R. B. (1998) 'Impressionism, surrealism, and film theory: path dependence, or how a tradition in film theory gets lost', in J. Hill and

P. C. Gibson, *The Oxford Guide to Film Studies*, Oxford and New York: Oxford University Press.

Rentschler, E. (1996) *The Ministry of Illusion: Nazi Cinema and Its Afterlife*, Boston: Harvard University Press.

Rich, B. R. (2000) 'Queer and present danger', *Sight and Sound*, Vol.10, No. 3, March.

Richards, J. (1980) 'Propaganda for war', *The Movie*, No. 9.

Richards, J. (2001) 'British film censorship', in R. Murphy, *The British Cinema Book*, 2nd edn, London: British Film Institute.

Robinson, D. (1968) *Hollywood in the Twenties*, London and New York: Zwemmer and Barnes.

Robinson, D. (1997) *Das Cabinet des Dr. Caligari*, London: British Film Institute.

Romney, J and Wootton, A. (eds) (1995) *Celluloid Jukebox: Popular Music and the Movies Since the '50s*, London: British Film Institute.

Rose, S. (2002) 'The great fall of China', http://film.guardian.co.uk/features/featurepages/0,4120,767253,00.html, accessed Dec. 2003.

Rothman, W. (1976) 'Against "the system of suture"', in B. Nichols (ed.), *Movies and Methods Volume 1*, Berkeley, Los Angeles and London: University of California Press.

Ryall, T. 'Teaching through genre', *Screen Education*, No 17.

Ryan, M. and Kellner, D. *Camera Politica: The politics and Ideology of Contemporary Hollywood Film*, Bloomington and Indianapolis: Indiana University Press.

Said, E. (1979/1991) *Orientalism*, London: Penguin.

Salt, B. (2001) Commentary *'Early Cinema: Primitives and Pioneers' Volume 1*, London: British Film Institute.

Salt, B. (1992) *Film Style and Technology: History and Analysis*, 2nd edn, London: Starword.

Salt, B. (2004) 'In the cut', *Sight and Sound*, Vol.14, No. 2.

Sammon, P. M. (1996) *Future Noir: The Making of Blade Runner*, London: Orion Media.

Sardar, Z. and Cubitt, S. (eds) (2002) *Aliens R Us: The Other in Science Fiction Cinema*, London and Sterling: Pluto.

Sardar, Z. (2002a) 'Introduction', in Sardar and Cubitt (2002).

Sarris, A. (1976) 'Towards a theory of film history', in B. Nichols (ed.), *Movies and Methods Volume 1*, Berkeley, Los Angeles and London: University of California Press.

Sarris, A. (1979) 'Notes on the auteur theory in 1962', in G. Mast and M. Cohen (eds), *Film Theory and Criticisms: Introductory Readings*, 2nd edn, New York and Oxford: Oxford University Press.

Schamus, J. (1998) 'To the rear of the the back end: the economics of independent cinema', in S. Neale and M. Smith (eds), *Contemporary Hollywood Cinema*, London and New York: Routledge.

Schatz, T. (2003) 'The new Hollywood', in J. Stringer (ed.), *Movie Blockbusters*, London and New York, Routledge.

Schilling, M. (1999) *Contemporary Japanese Cinema*, New York and Tokyo: Weatherhill.

Schubart, R. (2001) 'Passion and acceleration: generic change in the action film', in J. D. Slocum (ed.), *Violence and American Cinema*, New York and London: Routledge.

Sesonske, A. (1980) *Jean Renoir – the French Films 1924–1939*, Cambridge and London: Harvard Film Studies.

Shipman, D (1982) *The Story of Cinema, Volume 1 – From the Beginnings of Cinema to 'Gone With The Wind'*, London, Sydney, Auckland, Toronto: Hodder and Stoughton.

Shohat, E and Stam, R. (1994) *Unthinking Eurocentrism: Multiculturalism and the Media*, London and New York: Routledge.

Sieglohr, U. (1998) 'New German cinema', in J. Hill and P. C. Gibson (eds), *The Oxford Guide to Film Studies*, Oxford and New York: Oxford University Press.

Silverman, K. (1988) *The Acoustic Mirror: The Female Voice in Psychoanalysis and Cinema*, New York: Oxford University Press.

Singer, P. R. (2002) 'Art of Foley', www.marblehead.net/foley/mvs.html, accessed Aug. 2002.

Slocum, J. D. (ed.) (1999/2001) *Violence and American Cinema*, New York and London: Routledge.

Smith, J. (1998) *The Sounds of Commerce: Marketing Popular Film Music*, New York: Columbia University Press.

Smith, M. (1998) 'Theses on the philosophy of Hollywood history', in M. Stokes and R. Maltby (eds), *Identifying Hollywood's Audiences; Cultural Identity and the Movies*, London: British Film Institute.

Smith, M. (1998a) 'Modernism and the avant-gardes', in J. Hill and P. C. Gibson (eds), *The Oxford Guide to Film Studies*, Oxford and New York: Oxford University Press.

Smith, P. J. (2002) 'Heaven's mouth', *Sight and Sound*, Vol. 12, No. 4.

Solanas, F. and Gettino, O. (1976) 'Toward a third cinema', in B. Nichols (ed.), *Movies and Methods Volume 1*, Berkeley, Los Angeles and London: University of California Press.

Stafford, R. (2002) 'Who's that girl? Japanese horror moves into the mainstream', *in the picture*, No. 24, Dec.

Stam, R. (1999) 'Third world and postcolonial cinema', in P. Cook and M. Mernick (eds), *The Cinema Book*, 2nd edn, London: British Film Institute.

Stam, R. (2000) *Film Theory: An Introduction*, Malden and Oxford: Blackwell.

Starski, A. (1994) 'Art direction: Wajda to Spielberg', in J. Boorman and W. Donohue (eds), *Projections 3: Film-makers on Film-making*, London and Boston: Faber and Faber.

Stevenson, J. (2002) *Lars von Trier*, London: British Film Institute.

Stokes, J. and Reading, A. (eds) (1999) *The Media in Britain: Current Debates and Developments*, Basingstoke: Macmillan.

Stokes, L. O. and Hoover, M. (1999) *City on Fire: Hong Kong Cinema*, London and New York: Verso.

Stokes, M. and Maltby, R. (1999) *Identifying Hollywood's Audiences: Cultural Identity and the Movies*, London: British Film Institute.

Stone, R. (2002) *Spanish Cinema*, Harlow: Pearson Education.

Strick, P. (2003) 'Solaris', *Sight and Sound*, Vol. 13, No. 3, March.

Stringer, J. (2003) *Movie Blockbusters*, London and New York: Routledge.

Tapper, R. (ed.) (2002) *The New Iranian Cinema: Politics, Representation and Identity*, London and New York: I. B. Tauris.

Tasker, Y. (1993) *Spectacular Bodies: Gender, Genre and the Action Cinema*, London and New York: Routledge.

Tasker, Y. (1996) 'Approaches to the new Hollywood', in J. Curran, D. Morley and V. Walkerdine (eds), *Cultural Studies and Communications*, London: Arnold.

Taubin, A. (1993) 'Girl N the Hood', *Sight and Sound*, Vol. 3, No. 8, August.

Thompson, K. and Bordwell, D. (1994) *Film History: An Introduction*, New York: McGraw-Hill.

Thompson, K. (1999) *Storytelling in the New Hollywood*, Cambridge and London: Harvard University Press.

Todorov, T. (1977) *The Poetics of Prose*, Oxford: Blackwell.

Tudor, A. (1995) 'Genre', in B. K. Grant (ed.), *Film Genre Reader*, 2nd edn, Austin: University of Texas Press.

Tudor, A. (2002) 'From paranoia to postmodernism? The horror movie in late modern society', in S. Neale (ed.), *Genre and Contemporary Hollywood*, London: British Film Institute.

Ukadike, N. F. (1998) 'African cinema', in J. Hill and P. C. Gibson (eds), *The Oxford Guide to Film Studies*, Oxford and New York: Oxford University Press.

Vincendeau, G. (1993) 'The exception and the rule', *Sight and Sound*, Vol. 2, No. 8, Dec.

Vincendeau, G. (1997) *Pépé le Moko*, London: British Film Institute.

Vincendeau, G. (1998) 'Issues in European cinema', in J. Hill P. C. Gibson (eds), *The Oxford Guide to Film Studies*, Oxford and New York: Oxford University Press.

Vogler, C. (1998) *A Winter's Journey: Mythic Structure for Storytellers and Screenwriters*, London: Michael Wiese Productions.

Walker, M. (1982) 'Melodrama and the American cinema', *Movie*, No. 29/30.

Warshow, R. (2002) *The Immediate Experience: Movies, Comics, Theatre, and Other Aspects of Popular Culture*, Boston: Harvard University Press.

Wasko, J. (1994) *Hollywood in the Information Age*, Cambridge: Polity Press.

Wasko, J. (2002) 'The future of film distribution and exhibition', in D. Harries (ed.), *The New Media Book*, London: British Film Institute.

Watkins, A. T. L. (1949) 'Censorship in Britain', *The Penguin Film Review*, No. 9, May.

Watson, N. (2000) 'Hollywood UK', in R. Murphy (ed.), *British Cinema in the 90s*, London: British Film Institute.

Watt, I. (2000) *The Rise of the Novel: Studies in Defoe, Richardson and Fielding*, London: Pimlico.

Wells, P. (2000) *The Horror Genre: From Beelzebub to Blair Witch*, London: Wallflower Press.

White, P. (1998) 'Feminism and film', in J. Hill and P. C. Gibson (eds), *The Oxford Guide to Film Studies*, Oxford and New York: Oxford University Press.

Wilinsky, B. (2002) 'Discourses on art houses in the 1950s', in I. R. Hark (ed.), *Exhibition: The Film Reader*, London and New York: Routledge.

Willeman, P. (1989) 'The third cinema question: notes and reflections', in J. Pines and P. Willeman (eds), *Questions of Third Cinema*, London: British Film Institute.

Williams, C. (1980) *Realism and the Cinema*, London and Henley-on-Thames: Routledge and Kegan Paul.

Willis, S. (1997) *High Contrast: Race and Gender in Contemporary Hollywood Film*, Durham (North Carolina) and London: Duke University Press.

Willis, A. (2003) 'Locating Bollywood: notes on the Hindi blockbuster 1975 to the present', in J. Stringer (ed.), *Movie Blockbusters*, London and New York: Routledge.

Withall, K. (2000) *The Battleship Potemkin*, London: York Press.

Wojick, P. R. (1999) 'Spectatorship and audience research', in P. Cook and M. Mernick (eds), *The Cinema Book*, (2nd edn.), London: British Film Institute.

Waldron-Mantgani, I. (No Date) www.rottentomatoes.com/click/movie-1115429/reviews.php?critic=columns&sortby=default&page=1&rid=318987, accessed October 2003.

Wollen, P. (1972) *Signs and Meaning in the Cinema*, 3rd edn, London: Secker and Warburg.

Wollen, P. (1972a) 'Counter-cinema: Vent d'est', *Afterimage*, No. 4.

Wollen, P. (1982) *Readings and Writings: Semiotic Counter-strategies*, London and New York: Verso.

Wood, R. (1972) 'Bigger Than Life', *Film Comment*, Sept.–Oct.

Wyatt, J. (1994) *High Concept: Movies and Marketing in Hollywood*, Austin: University of Texas Press.

Wyatt, J. (1998) 'The formation of the "major independent": Miramax, New Line and the New Hollywood', in S. Neale and M. Smith (eds), *Contemporary Hollywood Cinema*, London and New York: Routledge.

Yau, C. M. (2001) *At Full Speed: Hong Kong Cinema in a Borderless World*, Minneapolis and London: University of Minnesota Press.

Yau, C. M. (2001a) 'Introduction', in Yau (2001).

Žižek, S. (2001) *Enjoy Your Symptom! Jacques Lacan in Hollywood and Out*, 2nd edn, New York and London: Routledge.

Zucker, C. (1999) 'An interview with Ian Richardson: making friends with the camera', in A. Lovell and P. Kramer (eds), *Screen Acting*, London and New York: Routledge.

DVDs

Note: dates given are those of the DVD release, not of the original film release.

Conversation, The (2004) Miramax Home Entertainment.

Early Cinema (2004) British Film Institute.

Ocean's Eleven (2001) Warner Home Video.

Others, The (2002) Dimension Home Video.

Requiem for a Dream (2001) Momentum Pictures

Sixth Sense, The (2002) Hollywood Pictures Home Video.

Index

Subject index